MW01000924

CAMBRIDGE STUDIES IN LAW AND SOCIETY

Cambridge Studies in Law and Society aims to publish the best scholarly work on legal discourse and practice in its social and institutional contexts, combining theoretical insights and empirical research.

The fields that it covers are: studies of law in action; the sociology of law; the anthropology of law; cultural studies of law, including the role of legal discourses in social formations; law and economics; law and politics; and studies of governance. The books consider all forms of legal discourse across societies, rather than being limited to lawyers' discourses alone.

The series editors come from a range of disciplines: academic law; socio-legal studies; sociology; and anthropology. All have been actively involved in teaching and writing about law in context.

Series Editors

Chris Arup *Monash University, Victoria*

Sally Engle Merry *New York University*

Susan Silbey *Massachusetts Institute of Technology*

A list of books in the series can be found at the back of this book.

INCITEMENT ON TRIAL

Prosecuting International Speech Crimes

Richard Ashby Wilson
University of Connecticut School of Law

CAMBRIDGE
UNIVERSITY PRESS

University Printing House, Cambridge CB2 8BS, United Kingdom

One Liberty Plaza, 20th Floor, New York, NY 10006, USA

477 Williamstown Road, Port Melbourne, VIC 3207, Australia

4843/24, 2nd Floor, Ansari Road, Daryaganj, Delhi – 110002, India

79 Anson Road, #06–04/06, Singapore 079906

Cambridge University Press is part of the University of Cambridge.

It furthers the University's mission by disseminating knowledge in the pursuit of education, learning, and research at the highest international levels of excellence.

www.cambridge.org
Information on this title: www.cambridge.org/9781107103108
DOI: 10.1017/9781316212875

First published 2017

Printed in the United States of America by Sheridan Books, Inc.

A catalogue record for this publication is available from the British Library.

Library of Congress Cataloging-in-Publication Data
Names: Wilson, Richard, 1964–, author.
Title: Incitement on trial : prosecuting international speech crimes /
Richard Ashby Wilson, University of Connecticut School of Law.
Description: New York : Cambridge University Press, 2017. | Series: Cambridge
Studies in Law and Society | Includes bibliographical references and index.
Identifiers: LCCN 2017018573 | ISBN 9781107103108 (alk. paper)
Subjects: LCSH: Hate speech – Law and legislation. | Hate crimes – Law and
legislation. | International criminal courts.
Classification: LCC KZ7177.I53 W55 2017 | DDC 345/.025–dc23
LC record available at https://lccn.loc.gov/2017018573

ISBN 978-1-107-10310-8 Hardback
ISBN 978-1-107-50126-3 Paperback

There are no economic, sociological, or psychological problems, but just problems, and they are all mixed and composite. In research, the only permissible demarcation is between relevant and irrelevant conditions.
                        Gunnar Myrdal, "Institutional Economics"

CONTENTS

FIGURES

ACKNOWLEDGEMENTS

I gratefully acknowledge the support I received for this research project from the University of Connecticut School of Law and appreciate the willingness of Dean Timothy Fisher and Associate Dean Anne Dailey to allow me to take time away from teaching and administrative duties. Colleagues at the University of Connecticut provided invaluable advice that shaped this book in many ways. At the law school, special thanks are due to Paul Chill, Todd Fernow, Julia Simon-Kerr, Thomas Morawetz, Molly Land and Steven Wilf. At the Human Rights Institute, I benefited from the wise counsel of Kerry Bystrom, Eleni Coundouriotis, Kathryn Libal and Nishith Prakash. In philosophy, Paul Bloomfield, Suzy Killmister and Michael Lynch went beyond the call to inform me about causation and ordinary language philosophy.

Doctoral student Jordan Kiper was a constant co-researcher in this project and he undertook the fieldwork and statistical analysis on Serbia that is presented in Chapter 7. The survey in Serbia was conducted in conjunction with Aleksander ("Sasha") Bošković and Bojan Todosijević at the Institute of Social Sciences, Belgrade, and I thank them for their willingness to participate in this project. Christine Lillie and Lasana Harris co-designed the survey conducted with the US population leading to the article we co-authored in 2015, "This is the Hour of Revenge: The Law and Psychology of Propaganda and International Conflict." Doctoral students Catherine Buerger and Katharine Richards asked all the right questions and helped me to make connections I might not have seen on my own. Research assistants Bryce Casavant, Alex Logier, Rojia Afshar, Janie Crocco, Ellen Reid, Corinne Tagliarina, Ruth Vaughan, Ahmad Wais Wardak and Monia Zgarni provided vital support at various junctures.

I offer my sincere thanks to the defense attorneys, prosecutors and judges for being so generous with their time and for their willingness to entertain undeveloped and often naïve questions from a social researcher; and, in particular, Matthew Gillett, Gregor Guy-Smith,

Beth Lyons, Nicole Samson, Dan Saxon and Wolfgang Schomburg. Predrag Dojčinović deserves special mention as a linguist, intellectual and practitioner of international criminal law who encouraged my interest in the applicability of speech act theory to legal problems. I have also benefited from the thoughtful commentary of a global network of scholars who helped me to understand hate speech and propaganda in politics and international law, including: Nanci Adler, Sindre Bangstad, Saskia Baas, Thijs Bouwknegt, Kamari Clarke, Thomas Hylland Eriksen, Gregory Gordon, Sally Engle Merry, Wiktor Osiatynksi, Vladimir Petrović and Susan Slyomovics.

A significant portion of the book was written while I was a member of the School of Social Science of the Institute for Advanced Study, Princeton in 2014–15, and I gratefully acknowledge the funding provided by the Friends of the Institute for Advanced Study. At IAS, special thanks are due to Danielle Allen, Manduhai Buyandelger, Didier Fassin, Hugh Gusterson, Serguei Oushakine, Gideon Rosen, Kim Lane Scheppele and Valentin Siedler. The Vrei Universiteit Amsterdam School of Law hosted me graciously twice during the period of the research for this book, and Wouter Veraart deserves particular mention for his hospitality.

Parts of this book were published previously, and I thank those who provided permission to draw on material. An earlier version of Chapter 2 appeared as "Inciting Genocide with Words," *Michigan Journal of International Law*, 2015, Volume 36, Issue 2, Spring, pp. 278–320. An abridged version of Chapter 4 appeared was published in 2017 as "Prosecuting Instigators: The Case of Vojislav Šešelj at the International Criminal Tribunal for the Former Yugoslavia" in *Palaces of Hope: The Anthropology of the United Nations*, edited by Ronald Niezen and Maria Sapignoli, Cambridge University Press. Research material from Chapter 6 appeared in an abridged and revised form as "Experts on Trial: Social Science Evidence at International Criminal Tribunals," *American Ethnologist*, Issue 43(4), 2016, published by the American Anthropological Association.

Finally, I thank Helene Kvale for her remarkable patience and her thoughtful advice and companionship, and our sons Thomas and Kai for their curious minds that opened up my own paths of thought and inquiry.

CHAPTER ONE

INCITING SPEECH IN INTERNATIONAL LAW AND SOCIAL SCIENCE

1.1 CRIMINAL ACCOUNTABILITY FOR INCITING SPEECH

A media campaign, fomenting ethnic, national, racial or religious hatred, in which political leaders incite their followers to initiate, or at least tolerate, acts of violence, is often the harbinger of an international or internal armed conflict. Observers highlighted the role of the media in the 1994 Rwandan genocide, and especially Radio Télévision Libre des Milles Collines, in inciting attacks on members of the Tutsi minority group, with one claiming that the primary tools of genocide were "the radio and the machete."[1] As a steady stream of commentators[2] referred to "radio genocide" and "death by radio" and "the soundtrack to genocide," a widespread consensus emerged that key criminal responsibility for the genocide lay with the Rwandan media.[3] A nexus between media incitement and political violence has been identified in many other contexts. Susan Carruthers (2000:46), writing about the 1991–5 Balkans conflict, claimed that "Every person killed in this [Bosnian] war was killed first in the newsroom."

This book evaluates the efforts of international tribunals to hold media owners and broadcasters, politicians and other public figures

---

[1] Chrétien et al. (1995:191).

[2] Both Straus (2007:612–13) and Carver (2000:189) document numerous instances of the "genocide by radio" theory. Scholars who have reproduced this language include La Mort (2009: 50–1) and Li (2004:6–9).

[3] Mitchell (2004); Misser & Jaumain (1994:23, 72).

criminally responsible for inciting speech acts, from the International Military Tribunal at Nuremberg in the 1940s to the International Criminal Court of today. The judges in the "Media Trial" at the International Criminal Tribunal for Rwanda boldly announced the necessity of holding broadcasters and media owners accountable thus, "The power of the media to create and destroy fundamental human values comes with great responsibility. Those who control such media are accountable for its consequences."[4] The notion that inciters are responsible for the misdeeds of others is deeply engrained in western law, and can be traced back at least to Aristotle's (2004:26) *Rhetoric*, which chronicles the widely held view in Ancient Greece that "[T]he man who prompted the deed was more guilty than the doer, since it would not have been done if he had not planned it."

Even though modern criminal jurisdictions conventionally pena-lize threatening speech and the solicitation of a crime, there is little international consensus on the boundary of impermissible speech. The desire to protect freedom of expression and robust democratic discourse in the "marketplace of ideas" has often impeded efforts to regulate and sanction hate speech and incitement. Yet even free-speech stalwarts such as John Stuart Mill (1989:13) acknowledge that authority can be legitimately exercised to prevent harm to others, consistent with Mill's renowned "Harm Principle." In the context of speech acts, Mill accepted that publicly declaring that corn dealers starve the poor in front of a corn dealer's house at a moment when there is an angry mob assembled "may justly incur punishment" (1989:53).[5]

It is worth noting at the outset that the speech acts adjudicated at international criminal tribunals are generally far removed from the typical instances of threatening or denigrating speech found in national criminal courts. Speakers charged with international speech crimes have generally articulated the most extreme animus and con-scious intent to harm, and gone beyond mere insult, libel and slander to incite others to commit mass atrocities. Moreover, their utterances usually occur in a context of an armed conflict, genocide and a widespread or systematic attack on a civilian population. Inciting speech has been such a prominent feature of national and global conflicts over the last century, from ethno-nationalist civil wars to

---

[4] *Nahimana* TC §945. [5] See also Warburton (2009:30).

terrorism based on religious extremism, that the international clamor has grown ever more insistent to criminalize incitement and halt the spiral into collective bloodshed.

And yet, historically, the international legal mechanisms available to interdict or punish inciting speech have been either meager or highly equivocal. At the International Military Tribunal at Nuremberg in 1945–6, one Nazi propagandist (Julius Streicher) was found guilty of crimes against humanity and hanged, but another (Hans Fritzsche) was acquitted. After Nuremberg, the United Nations Convention on the Prevention and Punishment of the Crime of Genocide (1948) established the international crime of "direct and public incitement to commit genocide" in Article III(c), overcoming resistance from the United States delegation which harbored concerns about freedom of the press.[6] This was followed in short order in 1950 by the European Convention on Human Rights that enshrined the right of freedom of expression in Article 10 and simultaneously permitted restrictions "prescribed by law and [that] are necessary in a democratic society, in the interests of national security, territorial integrity or public safety, for the prevention of disorder or crime, for the protection of health or morals, for the protection of the reputation or rights of others."[7]

Subsequent international declarations contained strongly worded prohibitions against inciting racial hatred, and the 1965 International Convention on the Elimination of Discrimination of All Forms of Racial Discrimination proscribed at Article 4(a): "all dissemination of ideas based on racial superiority or hatred, incitement to racial discrimination, as well as all acts of violence or incitement to such acts against any race or group of persons of another colour or ethnic origin . . .," and indicated that States Parties "(c) Shall not permit public authorities or public institutions, national or local, to promote or incite racial discrimination."[8] The 1966 International Covenant on Civil and Political Rights (ICCPR), one of the most widely signed and ratified multilateral treaties, contains two (at times, contradictory) articles, one advancing freedom of speech and the other prohibiting propaganda for war and incitement to hatred. Article 19 upholds the right to unfettered opinion and freedom of expression, but also admits two restrictions when necessary and provided by law: "(3)(a) For respect of the rights or

---

[6] Davies (2009:257, fn. 60).

[7] Council of Europe, Convention for the Protection of Human Rights and Fundamental Freedoms, Rome, 4.XI.1950.

[8] See Schabas (2009:582–3) for a discussion of Article 4.

reputations of others; (b) For the protection of national security or of public order (*ordre public*), or of public health or morals." Article 20 only proscribes, as follows: "1. Any propaganda for war shall be prohibited by law. 2. Any advocacy of national, racial or religious hatred that constitutes incitement to discrimination, hostility or violence shall be prohibited by law."

Although well intentioned, these international conventions were paper tigers with respect to the suppression of hate speech and incitement. States signed on to them to project a veneer of diplomatic respectability, but regularly violated their provisions. While the European Court of Human Rights ensures a degree of regional compliance amongst European governments, until the 1990s no international justice institutions existed to pursue individual criminal responsibility for inciters of hatred and violence.[9] In the absence of international tribunals with jurisdiction, there were no convictions of individuals for the international crime of direct and public incitement to commit genocide for nearly five decades after it was first promulgated in the UN Genocide Convention. United Nations prohibitions against the advocacy of hatred and inciting speech were applied only intermittently, as in the case of *Faurisson v. France* when the United Nations' Human Rights Committee invoked Article 19(3)(a) of the ICCPR in reaffirming the conviction under France's Gayssot Act of 1990 of Robert Faurisson for publicly questioning whether the Nazi regime used gas chambers to exterminate Jews.[10] Until the 1990s, public international law served as an anemic "soft law" adjunct to national law in the criminal sanctioning of inciters and hatemongers.

An expansive and systematic framework of criminal accountability for international speech crimes only took shape with the establishing of two *ad hoc* international tribunals, the International Criminal Tribunal for the Former Yugoslavia (ICTY, 1993) and the International Criminal Tribunal for Rwanda (ICTR, 1994), and one permanent tribunal, the International Criminal Court (ICC, 2002). These international justice institutions have undertaken an organized effort to criminalize speech that incites human rights violations against a civilian population. For instance, the ICTR found that the public statements and radio broadcasts of prominent Hutu political leaders,

---

[9] See Hare and Weinstein (2010:62) on free speech at the level of nation-states. See Janis, Kay and Bradley (2008:282–90) on hate speech cases before the European Court of Human Rights.
[10] *Robert Faurisson v. France*, Communication No. 550/1993, UN Doc. CCPR/C/58/D/550/1993 (1996).

a radio owner and a pop star, constituted direct and public incitement to commit genocide against ethnic Tutsis.[11] At the ICTY, Bosnian Serb politician Radovan Karadžić was found guilty of participating in a joint criminal enterprise to commit crimes against humanity on the basis of his public speeches and broadcasts.[12] The ICTY also convicted politicians Dario Kordić and Radoslav Brđanin for instigating persecutions on political, racial or religious grounds (a crime against humanity) in public speeches.[13] The *Brđanin* Trial Chamber conferred an outsized role to media incitement in explaining widespread popular participation in the persecution of members of other ethnic groups:

> Prior to the outbreak of the armed conflict, the SDS [Serbian Democratic Party] started waging a propaganda war which had a disastrous impact on the people of all ethnicities, creating mutual fear and hatred and particularly inciting the Bosnian Serb population against the other ethnicities. Within a short period of time, citizens who had previously lived together peacefully became enemies and many of them, in the present case mainly Bosnian Serbs, became killers, influenced by a media, which by that time, was already under the control of the Bosnian Serb leadership.[14]

Over the last ten years, this trend has continued unabated, and international criminal courts have increasingly targeted public speech that incites intergroup violence.[15] The Chief Prosecutor at the International Criminal Court has taken a particular interest in suppressing inciting speech, and thus far has issued warrants of arrest against six individuals[16] charged with ordering, inducing or co-perpetrating war crimes and crimes against humanity, in part on the basis of their public speeches or radio broadcasts.[17] At the time of writing, Charles Blé Goudé, youth leader and supporter of former President of the Ivory Coast Laurent Gbagbo, is standing trial for co-perpetrating, ordering, inducing or soliciting, aiding and abetting and contributing in any

---

[11] See, for example, *Ngirabatware* TC §1366–9; *Bikindi* TC §422–6; *Nahimana* TC §966–9; *Niyitegeka* TC §430–37; *Kambanda* TC §39(v)–(vii), (x), 40(3); *Akaysesu* TC §673–5.

[12] *Brđanin* TC §80, 323–32. See also *Karadžić* TC §3470–1 and *Popović et al.* TC §1812–21.

[13] *Brđanin* AC §320 and *Kordić and Čerkez* AC §700.   [14] *Brđanin* TC §80.

[15] On the criminalization of propaganda in international law, see Kearney (2007); Benesch (2008; 2012); Gordon (2008; 2010; 2012); Timmerman (2005; 2006, 2015).

[16] The ICC cases, in order of their indictments, are Harun, Mbarushimana, Ntaganda, Ruto, Sang, and Blé Goudé.

[17] *Ruto, Kosgey & Sang*, "Decision on the Confirmation of Charges," §363–67; *Mbarushimana*, "Decision on the Confirmation of Charges," §304–315; *Harun & Al-Rahman*, "Warrant of Arrest."

Figure 1.1 Kenya's Deputy President William Ruto addressing a crowd during a break in his trial at the ICC, 2013
Credit: Miriam Gathigah/IPS

other way to the commission of crimes against humanity, in part as the result of his "violent rhetoric and hate speech."[18] In another ICC trial, Kenyan radio broadcaster Joshua Arap Sang, a supporter of co-accused Vice-President William Ruto, was indicted for having "contributed, within the meaning of Article 25(3)(d)(i) of the Statute, to the commission of the crimes against humanity of murder, deportation or forcible transfer of population and persecution" on the basis of his broadcasts during the 2007 Kenyan Presidential elections.[19]

As international tribunals target speech crimes with ever more alacrity, some scholars and practitioners propose extending the scope of international law to create new atrocity speech offenses. Former ICTR staff member Gregory Gordon (2012:301–7), for instance, advocates the criminalization of "incitement to commit war crimes" in order

---

[18] *Blé Goudé*, "Decision on the Confirmation of Charges," at §94. See also §49–50. Blé Goudé is charged under articles 25(3)(a), 25(3)(b), 25(3)(c) and 25(3)(d) of the Statute, see §158, §166, §171, §181.

[19] *Ruto, Kosgey & Sang*, "Decision on the Confirmation of Charges" at §§366–367(a)–(d).

to deal with those acts that fall short of direct and public incitement to genocide.[20] Similarly, Wibke Timmermann (2015:8) applauds criminal sanctions against incitement to hatred in a number of domestic criminal jurisdictions, notably s. 130 of the German Criminal Code, and she advocates strengthening the prohibitions on hate speech in international criminal law.

1.2   THE RIGORS OF PROSECUTING SPEECH CRIMES AT INTERNATIONAL TRIBUNALS

On the face of it, applying international criminal law to inciting speech uttered during genocide or a widespread program of deportation and murder of civilians might seem a relatively straightforward proposition, but understanding and adjudicating speech crimes has been challenging for international courts. The regulation of speech is a particularly unsettled area of international criminal law, and the legal outcomes are surprisingly unpredictable. This has been the case since the earliest expressions of international criminal law, and here it is worth recalling that Hans Fritzsche, head of the Radio Division in Joseph Goebbels' Ministry of Propaganda, was one of only three defendants acquitted at Nuremberg.

More recently at the ICTY, ICTR and ICC, speech crimes trials have not enjoyed a sterling track record, with a high failure rate for the prosecution. At the ICC, for example, the case against Callixte Mbarushimana, the spokesman for a Congolese rebel group, was dismissed at the pretrial stage. In April 2016, after the prosecution's case collapsed amid charges of witness intimidation and bribery, an ICC Trial Chamber terminated the case against Kenyan Vice-President William Ruto and radio broadcaster Joshua Arap Sang and ruled, without prejudice, that the defendants had no case to answer.[21] Only a few days earlier at the ICTY, the most significant "propaganda trial" in the recent history of international law ended ignominiously for the prosecution with the complete acquittal of Serb nationalist politician Vojislav Šešelj on nine counts of crimes against humanity. At the ICTR, the only international tribunal to have convicted persons for the crime of direct and public incitement to commit genocide, there

---

[20] Gordon (2012:301–7).
[21] *Ruto and Sang*, Decision on Defence Applications for Judgments of Acquittal, §135.

were still numerous acquittals of defendants on the charges of incite-ment to genocide and instigating genocide.[22]

Even when politicians and radio broadcasters were found guilty at the ICTR for inciting genocide, commentators were critical of the tribunal's reasoning for being inconsistent and imprecise.[23] At the heart of the matter is causation. International prosecutors have struggled to demonstrate that a speech act constituted the proximate cause that triggered acts of persecution and genocide. In terminating the case against William Ruto, the ICC Trial Chamber articulated the requirement for a causal nexus between speech act and criminal act thus:

> Even if it were accepted that Mr Ruto's speeches contained a sufficiently clear message that he wanted others to engage in conduct that would, in the ordinary course of events, constitute any of the crimes charged, it still has to be established that this message was actually heeded by the physical perpetrators or that his speeches had a direct effect on their behaviour.[24]

As Chapters 3, 4 and 5 explain in detail, prosecutors did not present sufficient evidence regarding the direct effects of speech in a number of cases where an individual was charged with instigating crimes.[25] In part, evidence is lacking for the direct and injurious effects of a speech act because inciting speech seldom has a directly causal relationship to crimes. Speech crimes trials also seem particularly prone to logistical impediments, and "insider" perpetrators testifying that they were prompted to commit crimes by the speaker frequently recant their testimony after receiving threats (or bribes) from associates of the accused. Finally, judges themselves have not unequivocally articulated the evidentiary threshold required to prove a causal link between a speech act and a widespread or systematic campaign against a civilian population, leaving prosecutors wondering what it takes to show direct cause and effect with respect to instigation.

---

[22] Including the four accused, Bicamumpaka, Bizimungu, Mugenzi and Mugiraneza. Ferdinand Nahimana, who was found guilty of inciting genocide, had his conviction for instigating genocide reversed on appeal.

[23] For example, Benesch (2012), Dojčinović (2012), Gordon (2010) and Orentlicher (2005).

[24] *Ruto and Sang*, Decision on Defence Applications for Judgments of Acquittal, §135.

[25] In *Ruto and Sang*, Decision on Defence Applications for Judgments of Acquittal, the judges note that "it is striking that not a single press report or recording of any of the alleged 'hate speeches' was entered into evidence (§130)" by the Office of the Prosecutor.

Chapters 2 and 5 observe that in conceptualizing causation, prose-cutors and judges at international tribunals have relied on outdated models of propaganda. In the 1946 judgment against Julius Streicher, the Nuremberg Tribunal used a "hypodermic needle" metaphor, stating that Streicher's writings "infected the German mind with the virus of anti-Semitism." ICTR decisions revived the hypodermic needle image and invoked new metaphors such as "spreading petrol" and wielding "a violent instrument," despite the fact that these models were discredited by social science studies in the 1960s. Chapter 5 argues that recourse to such metaphors represents a mistaken attempt on the part of judges to establish intentionality and resolve the problem of mental causation. The judges' use of speech metaphors glosses over the obstacles to proving that a specific speech act transferred the speaker's intention-ality to the listener, causing him or her to become a material perpetrator.

If causation is at the heart of adjudicating speech crimes, then the agency of the listener is at the heart of causation. Absent threats or coercion, the voluntary agency of the listener represents an *interveniens novus actus* (or "new intervening act") that restarts the chain of causa-tion and diminishes the responsibility of the speaker for the events that follow, no matter how persuasive he or she might have been. In addition to this causal stumbling block, there are prosaic hurdles to showing mental causation. The most compelling evidence of mental causation, namely insiders who can testify that the speaker's words prompted them to commit the offence, has been hard for prosecutors to obtain and retain during the course of the trial. Unfortunately, expert evidence on the effects of speech has not always filled in the evidentiary gaps.

More worryingly, as documented in Chapter 2, judges have demanded proof of causation even when it is not warranted, as when defendants are charged with inciting genocide, which is an "inchoate crime." In inchoate speech crimes, the conduct is the crime and there need be no further consequences. Since the nexus element is absent, inchoate speech crimes are primarily crimes of intention (*mens rea*), and where the accused makes explicit calls to genocide, then his intention is transparent. However, the speeches tendered in evidence are seldom dispositive in and of themselves, and internal subjective states are notoriously opaque. If, during a court case, the evidence for the accused's intention is highly circumstantial, then judges have taken to reverse-engineering intention by highlighting the events that followed a speech or broadcast. Determining the genocidal intentionality of the accused on the basis of the consequences of his or her speech has damaging implications for international law. Most importantly, requiring a causal nexus between inciting speech acts and material acts of genocide thwarts the preventive function of the crime. This book proposes an alternative approach that draws on the speech act theory of philosophers J. L. Austin (1962) and John Searle (2010) in order to highlight the inchoate character of the crime of incitement to genocide by emphasizing the content, meaning and illocutionary force of utterances. One of the main normative objectives of this work is to recall the original intent of the drafters of the UN Genocide Convention and to reinvigorate the preventive function of the crime of direct and public incitement to commit genocide.

A close examination of intentionality and causation with respect to adjudicating speech crimes exposes deeper uncertainties in international criminal law, particularly with respect to fundamental legal concepts such as the standard of "beyond a reasonable doubt." International criminal law has not addressed core notions such as causation or the reasonable doubt standard in a systematic and detailed fashion, either in the case law or the legal scholarship. Stewart (2012a:1194) is one of the few legal scholars to remark on the relative absence of judicial comment on the concept of causation in international criminal justice. As Chapter 3 sets out, causation has received scant attention in leading international criminal law textbooks such as Cassese and Gaeta (2013), Cryer et al. (2014) or Schabas (2009), and the reasonable doubt standard even less.

International criminal law textbooks generally contain little reference to grey areas of uncertainty or contention. Reading international law texts, it is as if the doctrine of international criminal law has emerged fully formed, like Pallas Athene from the head of Zeus. The presentation of regularity and order is even more pronounced than in domestic criminal law textbooks, which are more likely to disclose and recognize the internal inconsistencies of criminal law and the areas of disagreement. A standard textbook on US criminal law, for instance, provides over a dozen examples of the instructions on the meaning of "beyond reasonable doubt" given by judges to juries.[26] Even a cursory comparison of, say, Cassese's textbook on international

---

[26] Dressler and Garvey (2012:9–13).

criminal law with Dressler and Garvey's *Criminal Law* is instructive insofar as the US authors openly admit the limitations, doctrinal contortions and vulnerabilities of their domestic criminal law. This is, in part, a matter of the prudence and candor that comes with the maturity of a criminal justice system. International criminal law, apart from episodic and disconnected efforts in the late nineteenth and early mid-twentieth centuries, is in fact a little more than a few decades old. The first permanent international criminal court, the ICC, has been functioning for just over a decade. Laboring at a glacial pace, it has completed only a handful of cases at the time of writing and has been repeatedly stymied by recalcitrant regimes in the countries in which it is operating. We are therefore still in the early stages of the formulation of the legal procedures and coherent doctrine of international justice.

International tribunals themselves are structurally fragile institutions, lacking their own coercive apparatus and regularly buffeted by hostile nation-states. Their beleaguered supporters are understandably reticent to expose the lacunae in their judicial reasoning or the inevitable breakdowns in due process.[27] Many advocates of international criminal law therefore adhere to an "institutional formalism,"[28] projecting an idealized image of cogent and settled doctrine and overlooking the fluid, contingent and contested features of organizational structure and procedures, as well as the attitudes and strategies of the central actors. For instance, Gregory Gordon (2005, 2012), a leading scholar of hate speech, simply denies any confusion on the question of causation in the law of incitement to commit genocide, and elaborates new crimes without first acknowledging the complications in the existing jurisprudence. One of the few scholars to have commented on the dry formalism of international criminal law is historian Samuel Moyn (2013:474), who astutely observes that "It is illuminating that early casebooks in the construction of the field of 'international criminal law' seem dedicated to the isolation of law from politics, stating rules and accumulating doctrines ... in spite of the strongly improvisational character of the field." This book takes the strongly improvisational character of international criminal law as its starting point.

---

[27] Again, with some exceptions such as Combs (2010) and Stewart (2012a; 2012b).
[28] See Pildes (2014) who has coined the term "institutional formalism."

1.3   SOCIAL SCIENCE, PART I: UNDERSTANDING THE LEGAL PROCESS

International tribunals have experienced more difficulty in investigating, prosecuting and adjudicating speech crimes than other categories of international crimes, such as war crimes. A central objective of this book (especially in Chapters 4–6) is to comprehend why this has been the case, and it proceeds by examining the internal procedures and organizational culture of international criminal courts, and documenting how legal actors frame and conceptualize international speech crimes. While existing legal research on inciting speech has focused primarily on trial and appeals chambers judgments, we also need to pay attention to the invisible assumptions and procedures guiding pretrial investigations and trial chamber proceedings and analyze what prosecuting attorneys, investigators, judges and legal officers actually do before and during a trial.

In addition, there has been little effort to learn from the trials that are generally excluded from textbooks because they were dismissed by the pretrial chamber (e.g., *Mbarushimana*) or because the prosecution's case collapsed mid-trial (e.g., *Ruto and Sang*) or because the accused was acquitted of all charges (*Šešelj*). At present, we have no empirical information on how prosecutors and defense attorneys construct their case theory in a speech crimes trial, and how they manage a mosaic of evidence in the pretrial and trial phases. What criteria and assumptions are used to determine the intentionality of the accused, or that there is a causal connection between a speech act and a violent crime? What weight do judges give to social science expert witness testimony, and how does social research on inciting language inform the courts' thinking?

This empirical study is inspired by theoretical developments in legal anthropology[29] and "new legal realism" in law and society studies.[30] Legal realism accepts that law is an inherently untidy human enterprise, resulting less from the arid application of abstract doctrine than from a process of contestation between legal actors including judges,

---

[29] See Goodale (2017) and Pirie (2013) for general statements on the anthropology of law. See Anders (2011), Clarke (2009, 2010), Dembour and Kelly (2007), Eltringham (2012, 2013), Kelly (2011) and Merry et al. (2015) for excellent empirical work on international legal institutions.

[30] Three recent texts set out the project of new legal realism; Klug and Merry (2016), Mertz, Macaulay and Mitchell (2016) and Miles and Sunstein (2007). On the history of legal realism, see Green (2005), Tamanaha (2008) and Twining (1943).

prosecutors, defense attorneys and others, each with their own set of assumptions and interests, jostling within a framework of shifting procedures, conventions and practices. One aim of empirical research is to lay bare the assumptions and strategies of legal actors, so as to understand the process that led to the judgments, and, ultimately, how international law knows about the conflicts it adjudicates. The legal realist approach to the living law of international tribunals adopted here builds upon and extends recent law-and-society approaches to legal epistemology.[31] In this theoretical model, process matters as much as product. This is not to deny that doctrine has its place, and without formal reasoning and predictability, there can be no claim to rule of law. Yet international criminal law of speech crimes could benefit from a strong dose of legal realism and a moment of pause and reflection on the nature of international fact-finding as it unfolds in the courtroom.

The empirical component of this study has drawn upon a variety of research methods, including qualitative interviews, focus group discussions with legal personnel, the statistical analysis of a new database of experts, a close study of the documents and transcripts of paradigmatic "propaganda trials," and historical research in the archives of Thomas Dodd, Executive Counsel at Nuremberg. This heterogeneous methodological mix emerged as a response to the specific needs of the research. In combining various methods and approaches in law and social and historical research, I have taken a leaf from Gunnar Myrdals' (1978:772) charter for institutional economics expressed in the epigraph at the beginning of this book. The problems raised by prosecuting incitement in international law are inherently mixed and composite, and understanding them cannot be achieved by one discipline alone, and necessitates delving into the methods and theories of, *inter alia*, social anthropology, economics, history, law, the philosophy of language, political science and social psychology.

More specifically, this study involved 35 interviews with judges, prosecutors, defense attorneys and expert witnesses at three international criminal tribunals. I convened two focus groups with three defense attorneys and prosecutors in each group, presented them with a fact pattern of an imaginary speech crimes case, and then asked them to reflect on how they might as international judges apply the law to the

---

[31] Douglas (2001), La Tour (2010), Mertz (2008), Sarat, Douglas and Umphrey (2007). On the "discursive battles" at international tribunals, see Meijers and Glashuis (2013).

facts provided. Additionally, I created a statistical database of over 470 defense and prosecution experts at the ICTY and analyzed their impact on trial chamber judgments. In collaboration with two psychologists and an anthropologist, I conducted original research on the effects of hate speech, using the speeches admitted in evidence against one of the accused at the ICTY, Vojislav Šešelj, who was at the time being tried for instigating crimes against humanity during the Balkans conflict.

A close study of the trial process at international criminal tribunals throws light on the failure to convict defendants in many speech crimes cases at international tribunals. Chapter 4 provides an account of the trial of Serb nationalist Vojislav Šešelj at the ICTY, and examines in detail the prosecutors' claim that the public speeches of the accused in three municipalities in 1992 triggered an attack on the non-Serb civilian population. The majority of high-level defendants who are charged at international criminal tribunals with instigating crimes against humanity are not accused of participating directly in physical acts of violence. Prosecuting political leaders for their speech acts conventionally requires proof of a causal link between a speech act and subsequent felonies. The analysis looks closely at what demonstrating such a nexus involved in the trial of Vojislav Šešelj and examines the direct model of cause and effect used by prosecutors and judges at the ICTY. To qualify as instigation, international criminal law requires that speech acts directly cause the crimes in question, and this necessitates a paring down of multiple factors into a single chain of causation that can be determined beyond a reasonable doubt.

In practice, prosecutors often lack reliable testimony from insiders who can confirm that their offences were triggered by the instigating speech of the accused. This seems to be a general feature of speech crimes trials. Without solid evidence of direct mental causation from insiders, the prosecutors in Šešelj relied on the chronological presentation of evidence to demonstrate a relationship of cause and effect: the accused gave a speech here, and look what happened next. When laying out the evidence for instigation, the prosecution case theory often boils down to "chronology shows causation," a theory that judges ordinarily find unpersuasive. Chapter 4 assesses the pitfalls of arguing legal causation by way of temporal proximity and chronology, and it concludes with a reflection on wider problems in criminal law's understandings of cause and effect.

Have social researchers, appearing as expert witnesses, effectively informed international courts regarding the general properties of inciting speech acts? Prosecutors and defense attorneys introduce social science research into the international courtroom as expert testimony with variable and somewhat arbitrary results, and this is the subject of Chapter 6. Social researchers often feature as expert witnesses in international criminal trials, and there has yet to be a systematic evaluation of their impact on the production of courtroom knowledge. Statistical analysis of over four hundred expert appearances reveals that international judges prefer experts using scientific methods, which coincides with their formally stated position. When social researchers are called by the parties, courts unexpectedly favor qualitative over quantitative approaches.

Comparing two international speech crimes trials, a language expert at the ICTR was preferred to a quantitative sociologist at the ICTY because the former did not challenge the sovereignty of judges and the status hierarchy of the courtroom. When the language expert appeared at the first trial for incitement to genocide at the ICTR, international jurists were receptive to assistance in grasping the social contexts of speech acts in a language (Kinyarwanda) they did not speak. Judges heard qualitative information on the cultural resonance of euphemisms from a socio-linguist, and demonstrated an openness to this kind of enhanced translation service. Qualitative experts employ the same case-based and "commonsense" approach to meaning and intention as judges, and these experts do not challenge judicial authority by pronouncing on the ultimate issue in a speech crimes trial.

Judges at international tribunals are more skeptical when presented with experts who use quantitative methods to analyze a political leader's discourse and the mechanisms through which his words prompt violence. Judges are generally well disposed towards quantitative science on ballistics and forensics, but they seldom appreciate the abstract nature of sociological theories of hate speech and the quantitative methods they employ. Quantitative findings about the causal effects of the performative utterances of the accused seem to elicit hostility from judges. Judges often perceive quantitative social science as premised on an alien (to the law) theory of causation, and as usurping the judges' axiomatic role as the trier of fact. When excluding quantitative experts, judges cite "common sense" as the basis of facticity and knowledge in the law. In these instances, social science expert testimony seems lost in translation in the international courtroom.

From the findings of the research presented in Chapter 6 on the reception of expert testimony in speech crimes trials, we can conclude that social science evidence is only of limited help in proving direct causation, the *actus reus* that underpins the charge of instigating crimes against humanity. When crimes emerge from a tangled web of causation, it is an arduous undertaking to unravel causation with the precision required to attribute direct and substantial individual criminal responsibility. Criminal law is designed to undertake this task, but social science is not. Nonetheless, social science research can have probative value when the accused is charged with inchoate speech crimes (such as incitement to genocide and hate speech) where the meaning and intentionality of the speaker are at issue, and it has potential utility when a defendant is charged with complicity, which requires only a minimal degree of direct causation.

1.4 SOCIAL SCIENCE, PART II: STUDYING THE EFFECTS OF INCITING SPEECH

This book promotes a dialogue between law and social science on the nature of international speech crimes and is propelled by the question: what would the international criminal law of propaganda and inciting speech look like if it were more fully informed by social science?

In *The Oxford Handbook of Philosophy of Criminal Law*, Sumner (2011:33) perceptively observes that whether the harm caused by hate speech is of sufficient gravity to warrant criminal regulation is a broadly empirical matter, to be decided on the basis of the evidence. Yet neither philosophers nor courts seem to be adequately informed by the social science of persuasion and political communication. One of the foremost advocates for greater regulation of hate speech, philosopher and law professor Jeremy Waldron (2012) expounds the view that inclusiveness and respect for human dignity are public goods that liberal societies are committed to upholding, and he asserts that hate speech destroys those public goods. Waldron's argument relies on powerful claims about the deleterious effects of denigrating speech, but he does not cite any empirical studies demonstrating the harm in hate speech.

Similarly, prosecutors at international criminal tribunals often rely on untested assumptions about causation and the connection between incitement and subsequent crimes. These assumptions typically rely on anecdotal observations about the case in hand, rather than systematic evidence about the phenomenon more generally. In contrast, social research on persuasion builds systematic evidence based on numerous cases to draw causal inferences about aggregate patterns of violations, and therefore it makes sense that the decisions of international courts on a specific case might be supplemented by this kind of evidence. Courts have a widely acknowledged responsibility to make reasonable efforts to obtain the current knowledge on a subject relevant to determining a case. If the information provided by the parties is inadequate, they can request further information from the parties on specific questions, or commission court-appointed experts to provide the relevant information.

In this context, some analysts such as Susan Benesch (2008, 2012) have advocated a more systematic approach to the crime of direct and public incitement to genocide, and Benesch identifies five conditions under which inflammatory speech acts are likely to cause imminent violence. Benesch's criteria are promising but, like many others in this field, she cites no social science studies on the causal role of inciting speech. By and large, there is not a great deal of social science research to support the claim that hate speech or inciting speech has a directly causal relationship to violence, and this mitigates against modes of liability like instigating/inducing/soliciting which include the element of direct causation. There is, however, extensive empirical evidence indicating that denigrating speech has (often unconscious) conditioning effects on listeners and while not attaining the level of a *sine qua non*, may contribute to a set of conditions jointly sufficient to cause crimes.

Recent neuroscience experiments by psychologists Harris and Fiske (2006, 2011) demonstrate how denigrating speech against an out-group can dehumanize and facilitate (which is different from cause) inhumane acts like torture. Economist David Yanagizawa-Drott (2014) indicates that the broadcasts of Radio Télévision Libre des Milles Collines in Rwanda in 1994 had an amplifying effect on the genocide, providing evidence that inciting speech can contribute to crimes without rising to the level of necessary and sufficient (or *sine qua non*) causation. Even though social science findings on the causal effects of speech are mixed, we should not deduce that such studies are inconclusive and therefore irrelevant. Indeed, they tell us a great deal; namely, that speech may not directly cause crimes, but it may still constitute a contributing factor and/or an enabling condition.

There is still a great deal that is unknown about the effects of inciting speech in conditions of conflict. Chapter 7 draws upon new developments in the social science of persuasion and political communication and includes new and original psychological research conducted for this book, in conjunction with psychologists Lasana Harris and Christine Lillie, and anthropologist Jordan Kiper. We constructed a survey that exposed participants to the actual speeches of Vojislav Šešelj, a Serb political leader tried at the ICTY for instigating murder, torture and deportation of Croat civilians in the early 1990s.[32]

We divided the speeches into eight subcategories: calls for revenge, extreme nationalist sentiments, stereotyping other groups, dehumanizing language, demands for justice, references to past atrocities, victimization of his own group and warnings of a direct violent threat to his group. All the speeches reduced the propensity of the US participants to empathize with the out-group and raised empathy levels for the in-group. Speeches that called for revenge or referenced past atrocities led participants to morally justify violence. Dehumanizing speech, generally seen by the courts as the most egregious type of hate speech, did not increase justifications of violence. Knowing which types of speech are most likely to instigate violence could be valuable in prosecutors' decisions about whether to charge an individual making inciting utterances, as well as in the formulation of legal and policy standards.

Chapter 8 charts a way forward by integrating the international criminal law of speech crimes with insights from the social science of persuasion and political communication. The results of our survey and other studies indicate that inciting speech has conditioning and enabling effects that could lead to a greater tolerance of, and enhanced commission of, violent acts. These findings imply that inciting speech acts should be handled firstly under the preventative doctrine of inchoate crimes (e.g., incitement to commit genocide, or hate speech). Calls for revenge condition a population to accept and justify violence to a greater degree than other forms of speech (including dehumanizing speech), and therefore their utterance in a volatile situation may warrant timely intervention by international institutions. While inciting speech is not the only factor in an ensemble of conditions jointly sufficient to cause the commission of atrocities, it is often an early contributing factor and therefore can serve as a bellwether of events to come. Preventing the persecution of minority populations and armed conflict is an often-cited weakness of the international order, and social research findings can inform policymakers as they evaluate

---

[32] The accused was acquitted by the trial chamber in 2016 and, at the time of writing, the prosecution has appealed the decision.

a deteriorating situation, as well as guide prosecutors deciding who to indict, when to indict and for what type of utterances.

When the moment for prevention has passed and international crimes have already been committed, inciting speech acts are better handled under two modes of liability: ordering, and aiding and abetting. Ordering generally occurs in the strong causal field of a military command structure where the causal nexus between the individual with authority to issue and order and the material perpetrator. Outside of the military context, complicity (also known as "aiding and abetting" in international criminal law) as a form of criminal responsibility conforms most closely to social science models of inciting speech, since complicity either does not require causation, or only requires that the speech act minimally contribute to the commission. Instigation as a mode of liability requires proof that speech directly causes crimes, but this direct nexus to violence is generally not supported by social science studies. Moreover, direct causation is much more arduous for prosecutors to prove in a criminal courtroom and ideally requires credible testimony from the material perpetrators who were instigated by the speaker to commit mass atrocities.

1.5   DEFINING THE TERMS

Both the case law and wider academic literature are characterized by overlapping and confusing nomenclature that includes, *inter alia*, hate speech, incitement, instigation, propaganda and speech crimes. To complicate matters further, international law has its own constructions of these terms that often diverges from conventional usage in domestic jurisdictions. Some clarification is therefore in order.

Hate speech is a term of art in the constitutional law of the United States and is defined as "speech designed to promote hatred on the basis of race, religion, ethnicity or national origin."[33] This is the meaning of the term as it is referenced in this book. However, hate speech plays only a limited role in the discussion, primarily because hate speech is not well established as a crime in international law. Timmermann

---

[33] Rosenfeld (2001:2). The Federal Bureau of Investigation (FBI) in the United States defines a hate crime more broadly as a "criminal offense against a person or property motivated in whole or in part by an offender's bias against a race, religion, disability, sexual orientation, ethnicity, gender, or gender identity." www.fbi.gov/about-us/investigate/civilrights/hate_crimes Hate crime is defined in the United Kingdom more broadly still as "any criminal offence which is perceived, by the victim or any other person, to be motivated by hostility or prejudice towards someone based on a personal characteristic" (Corcoran, Lader and Smith 2015).

(2015) persuasively argues for the inclusion of hate speech as an international crime, but her argument is mostly a normative and aspirational one. At present, there has only been one conviction for hate speech as a form of persecution; that of Ferdinand Nahimana at the ICTR, over a decade ago. In 2016, a high-profile defendant (Vojislav Šešelj) was acquitted of hate speech at the ICTY. Hate speech is not included as a crime in the ICC Statute and therefore it is unlikely to feature in ICC indictments going forward.

Instead, this book refers primarily to the phenomenon of "inciting speech," which I construe as hate speech combined with an appeal to attack members of a protected group; in short, hate speech plus a call to violence.[34] At international criminal tribunals, legal actors refer to these kinds of trials as "propaganda trials." The term "propaganda" is relatively modern and does not appear in common usage until after the First World War, when the techniques of consumer advertising were combined with the media of mass persuasion in an unprecedented way to exhort European and North American citizens to support the war effort.[35] Propaganda is a notoriously slippery concept, and its concrete usage tends to reflect the ideological position of the speaker. Definitions of propaganda are highly contested and there is significant controversy, for instance, about whether propaganda necessarily involves a distortion of the truth and the manipulation of symbols and individual psychology.[36]

Definitions of propaganda often suffer from being overly broad. Jowett and O'Donnell (2006:1) start their textbook with the definition "Propaganda is a form of communication that attempts to achieve a response that furthers the desired intent of the propagandist," which could conceivably apply to any and every instance of human communication. Later, they narrow their definition to "Propaganda is the deliberate, systematic attempt to shape perceptions, manipulate cognitions and direct behavior to achieve a response that furthers the desired intent of the propagandist" (2006:7).

Yet this definition could include all advertising, most media reporting, public education for health and safety, and all manner of daily communicative interactions. In addition, with respect to speech during social and/or armed conflict, an important political and collective societal element seems to be missing from the definition. More suitable is the approach of Sproule (1994) who distinguishes between collective

---

[34] *Nahimana* AC distinguishes between hate speech and inciting genocide at §692.
[35] Jowett and O'Donnell (2006:100, 160) [36] Jowett and O'Donnell (2006:4–5).

and interpersonal forms of communication, and defines propaganda as organized persuasion through the means of mass communication. In sum, most definitions of propaganda are vague and unsatisfactory, and for that reason, I do not use the term as a category to analyze the phenomenon of mass incitement.

My preference is instead to use "persuasion" and "political communication," which are more neutral analytical terms with relatively definite meanings.[37] Nevertheless, the term "propaganda" retains relevance because, at international tribunals, key defendants such as former Bosnian President Radovan Karadžić have been charged with the crime of "disseminating propaganda." Additionally, attorneys and judges commonly refer to trials where the accused is charged with crimes such as inciting genocide or instigating crimes against humanity as "propaganda trials." Propaganda is a widely used term in the ordinary speech community of international legal actors, and therefore cannot be excised entirely.

Since my focus is on international criminal law, I adopt a more precise term in the analysis, and that is "international speech crimes." This terminology encompasses a wider array of crimes than war propaganda, for instance as reviewed in Michael Kearney's (2007) excellent *The Prohibition of Propaganda for War in International Law*. In international criminal law, there are only two international speech crimes *qua* crimes, and both of them are inchoate offences: direct and public incitement to commit genocide and hate speech as a form of persecution (a crime against humanity). All other categories are modes of liability that attach to underlying offences of crimes against humanity, war crimes and genocide to complete the full conceptualization of the crime. The modes of liability addressed in this book are aiding and abetting, instigating/ inducing, joint criminal enterprise, ordering, perpetrating/co-perpetrating and soliciting.

Some of these modes of liability normally imply speech acts (e.g., ordering, soliciting), but others (e.g., joint criminal enterprise) do not. Therefore, I only introduce the latter group when a speech act is the primary evidence brought against the accused, for instance in the ICTY cases of *Gvero* and *Karadžić*, in which the defendants were charged with disseminating propaganda as a contribution to a joint criminal enterprise to commit war crimes and crimes against humanity. A final point to avoid potential confusion: in international law, inciting genocide is an inchoate crime (i.e., where the conduct is the crime), whereas the

[37] On the distinction between propaganda and persuasion, see Perloff (2010:19).

related terms of instigating, soliciting, inducing and ordering are all modes of liability for completed crimes. This contrasts with the formulation in many domestic settings such as the United States, where these terms are typically considered under the inchoate crime of "solicitation."[38]

The definition of international speech crimes adopted here leads me to review the cases against a total of thirty-five defendants at four international tribunals: eighteen cases from the ICTR, six from the ICC, nine from the ICTY and two from the International Military Tribunal at Nuremberg.[39] Of these, twenty accused were convicted of the majority of charges and had their conviction upheld on appeal. Eleven defendants were acquitted of the majority of the charges against them, or the case was dismissed before it came to trial, or the trial chamber ruled that there was no case to answer at the end of the prosecution's arguments. Of the remaining, two accused are presently still on trial, one died before the verdict was delivered and another is yet to be arrested and delivered to The Hague. This is a relatively small and defined sub-section of the over three hundred cases heard at these four tribunals, but it remains an intriguing and unsettled field that broaches some of the most intractable and complex questions in international law.

1.6 THE ROLE OF SOCIAL SCIENCE IN LAW: CONCLUDING REMARKS

In *The Role of Science in Law*, Robin Feldman (2009) observes that the law keeps going to the well of scientific knowledge in the hope of solving demanding legal problems, but in her opinion law can solve these difficulties using its own internal resources, namely legal doctrine and procedure. Rather than always turning to science, law's unique form of reasoning must be preserved. This view chimes with the opinion and practice of many international lawyers who take the view that "the law should be suspicious of statistical evidence."[40] There is a widespread view

---

[38] MPC §2.06(3)(a)(i)

[39] At the ICC: Blé Goudé, Harun, Mbarushimana, Ntaganda, Ruto and Sang. At the ICTR: Akayesu, Bagilishema, Barayagwiza, Bicamumpaka, Bikindi, Bizimungu, Gacumbitsi, Kajelijeli, Kambanda, Mugenzi, Mugiranera, Muvunyi, Nahimana, Niyitegeka, Ngeze, Ngirabatware, Ruggiu and Serugendo. At the ICTY: Babić, Blaškić, Brđanin, Gvero, Karadžić, Kordić, Krajišnik, Slobodan Milošević and Šešelj. At the IMT-Nuremberg: Fritzsche and Streicher.

[40] Enoch, Spectre and Fisher (2012:200).

in the legal profession generally that the law has all the epistemological tools it needs to handle even the most arduous challenges in adjudication. As a result, the majority of law review articles on speech crimes cite no empirical work on persuasion or the effects of inciting speech. This is understandable in part, since social science research on speech is complicated and its findings do not always provide straightforward answers to the questions that criminal law poses.

However, the law's framework for understanding human behavior will be outdated and impoverished if it is cut off from new findings in anthropology, economics, neuroscience and psychology, to mention a few. Legal scholars such as Feldman offer a false sense of security when they advise insulating law from scientific knowledge. Many others maintain a more open frame of mind. In one of the leading criminal law textbooks, Dressler and Garvey (2012:135) ask whether the criminal law that has developed over time in the United States "is consistent with modern scientific knowledge about human behavior. To the extent that it is not, should the law endeavor to conform with scientific and social research understandings, even though what we know today may prove false in the future?"

My answer to this question is reservedly in the positive. Of course, research can be unreliable and legal doctrine is often more motivated by ethical values and societal norms than scientific findings.[41] Having said this, the changing nature of science or social research is not a compelling pretext to preserve doctrinal purity, for two reasons. Firstly, it ignores the rather obvious fact that law also changes constantly, and often for highly political reasons that are rather less elevated than the trajectory of scholarly investigation and scientific discovery. Secondly, the fact that scientific knowledge revises itself over time is an advantage, not an impediment. Knowledge improves because researchers innovate technologically, explore new avenues of inquiry and revise their opinion in the light of new evidence.

Despite Feldman's comments, domestic criminal law in the United States and elsewhere has reformed itself in a number of important ways to incorporate social science insights into its understandings of human behavior. It has altered course on a range of issues as a result of new social science studies, from the reliability of eyewitness testimony to the grounds for insanity pleas.[42] Some of the most exciting and influential

---

[41] On the use of science as evidence in public policy and law, see Prewitt et al. (2012).

[42] *State v. Henderson*, 27 A.3d 872 (N.J. 2011) incorporated social science findings to revise standards on the admissibility of eyewitness identifications, particularly the finding that cross-racial identifications were often unreliable.

academic research on criminal law and evidence at present are at the intersection of law and social science, including studies that draw upon insights from cultural cognition to consider how judging might become more evidence-based.[43] In contrast, international criminal law persists in being highly doctrinal, even though in concrete trials social scientists are often called as expert witnesses at international tribunals at a rate that is higher than most municipal courts.

International law stands to benefit from being more receptive to outside knowledge, be it science, social science or other forms of expertise, as it attempts to resolve perplexing legal matters such as causation. In international law, there does not presently exist a framework based on rigorous social science research that clearly identifies the threshold criteria for inciting speech that would trigger a preventative penal response. Furthermore, when prosecuting speech acts that allegedly contributed to the commission of international crimes, judges and prosecutors appear to be grasping for a model of direct causation that is contrary to recent social research on the effects of speech acts.

Social science research can furnish courts with evidence-based understandings of the effects of incitement, and, for instance, inform international courts as they decide whether specific speech acts are likely to lead to violations of human rights. As the imperative to combat purveyors of ethnic, racial and religious violence grows, it is a decisive moment for social science research to inform legal efforts to regulate speech crimes, as well as to foster innovative political initiatives to prevent social conflict.

International criminal tribunals might make more effective use of social research on speech, persuasion and political communication. Doing so would turn international criminal law away from modes of liability such as instigating and inducing that require direct causation, to instead consider complicity (also known as aiding and abetting), which requires a low level of causation or no nexus requirement at all. Moving forward entails returning to a model of incitement employed by prosecutors over seventy years ago at Nuremberg, the topic examined in the discussion that follows.

---

[43] Prominent studies that apply the insights of cognition, psychology and neuroscience to legal problems include Kahan, Hoffman and Braman (2009), Kahan et al. (2016), Garland (2004) and Morse and Roskies (2013).

DIRECT AND PUBLIC INCITEMENT TO COMMIT GENOCIDE: AN INCHOATE CRIME

2.1 INTRODUCTION

> Several witnesses stated that during the atrocities "the Rwandese carried a radio set in one hand and a machete in the other." This demonstrates that the radio was a powerful tool for the dissemination of ethnic hatred. Radio National and RTLM freely and regularly broadcasted ethnic hatred against the Tutsis.
>
> *Kayishema & Ruzindana* TC §280.

Direct and public incitement to commit genocide (hereinafter, incitement to genocide) is an inchoate crime in international criminal law. Its underlying intended crime, in this case, genocide, need not actually occur since the inciting utterance itself constitutes the criminal conduct. It should follow, therefore, that no causal link need exist between a speech act and subsequent genocidal acts. Demonstrating that a speech, broadcast or publication constituted a public and direct call to exterminate a protected group is sufficient to establish criminal responsibility for inciting genocide.

Nonetheless, as in the quote above, ICTR judges have repeatedly advanced robust claims about the direct causal relationship between speeches and media broadcasts and subsequent public violence in their factual findings on the Rwandan genocide. Moreover, some judgments refer to causation in their legal analysis and mistakenly suggest that causation is a necessary element for establishing the crime of incitement to genocide. The ICTR's insertion of a causation element into incitement to genocide constitutes a radical departure from at least a century of the criminal law of inchoate crimes and as such, has created controversy and confusion.

The following discussion charts the development of international jurisprudence on inciting speech from the Nuremberg Trials to the ICTR judgments, highlighting the inconsistencies in contemporary legal reasoning and questioning the prominent role that ICTR jurisprudence has accorded to causation. Other observers have also noted these discrepancies and Susan Benesch (2012) has sought to remedy them by advancing a list of factors to assess the likelihood of genocide. Benesch's matrix is valuable in its emphasis on the context of speech acts, yet additional commentary is needed: first, to establish the formal legal basis for inchoate speech crimes such as incitement to genocide, and second, to separate such inchoate crimes from modes of international legal liability such as instigation that require a causal connection to the underlying crime.

Next, drawing on the speech act theory of one of the foremost philosophers of language in the twentieth century, J. L. Austin (1962), I disentangle the intention of the speaker from the consequences of speech acts and recommend various amendments to the law of incitement. In determining incitement to commit genocide, international law might usefully differentiate between three aspects of performative utterances, or what Austin (1962:94–101) terms the "locutionary" (the meaning and content), "illocutionary" (its force) and "perlocutionary" (the consequences) dimensions of speech acts. Specific intent to commit genocide is found in the content, meaning and force of speech acts, rather than in consequences, which are an unreliable guide to the intentionality of the speaker. By using this template, international tribunals could better distinguish modes of liability that require causation such as instigating, ordering, and aiding and abetting, from inchoate crimes such as direct and public incitement to commit genocide, where the meaning and the force of the speaker's public utterances is paramount. Other benefits of this approach would include refocusing attention on the prevention of genocide and clarifying and constraining the range of impermissible speech.

2.2 THE LEGACY OF NUREMBERG

A large number of the ordinary members of the German nation would never have participated in or tolerated the atrocities committed throughout Europe if they had not been conditioned to barbarous convictions and misconceptions by the constant grinding of the Nazi propaganda machine.

Captain D.A. Sprecher, "Prosecution oral presentation against Fritzsche," International Military Tribunal at Nuremberg[1]

Before delving into recent international jurisprudence on speech crimes, it is worth noting the elements of US law that have influenced international thinking on this issue. US constitutional law places well-known legal protections on freedom of speech, but there is also a fairly long tradition of First Amendment jurisprudence that limits violent speech and "'fighting' words" that "by their very utterance inflict injury."[2] The precedent-setting incitement case in US law is *Brandenburg v. Ohio* (1969), which dealt with a Ku Klux Klan leader in Ohio (Clarence Brandenburg) who was fined $1000 and sentenced to one to ten years' imprisonment for inciting violence against African Americans and Jews at a public and televised rally in 1964.[3] The US Supreme Court reversed Brandenburg's conviction, noting that while his speech was "derogatory," it merely advocated vague measures and therefore did not represent incitement to "imminent lawless action."[4]

On its own, mere advocacy of force or violence is not prohibited under US law. Under the *Brandenburg* test, public speech does not warrant First Amendment protection when three criteria are met: 1) the speech is intended to incite violence or lawlessness; 2) it "is likely to incite. . . such action"; and 3) such lawlessness is likely to occur imminently.[5] A number of questions remain unresolved, however, and Healy (2009: 655–60) notes that *Brandenburg* "does not tell us how likely it must be that speech will lead to unlawful conduct or how imminent that conduct must be." In a subsequent case, *Hess v. Indiana*, the Supreme Court reversed the conviction of a demonstrator who shouted, "we will take the fucking street later," on the grounds that the lawless advocated was not sufficiently imminent because the speaker used the word "later."[6] US law warrants a mention here because elements of the judicial reasoning motivating *Brandenburg*, and the gray areas surrounding

[1] Thomas J. Dodd, Prosecution oral presentation against Fritzsche, University of Connecticut: Archives & Special Collections at the Thomas J. Dodd Research Center, (hereinafter *Thomas J. Dodd, Prosecution oral presentation against Fritzsche*).

[2] *Chaplinsky v. State of New Hampshire*, 315 US 568, 572 (1942).

[3] *Brandenburg v. Ohio*, 395 US 444, 444–6 (1969), hereinafter *Brandenburg*.

[4] *Brandenburg*, §446, 448–9. Up until that point, the standard had been the "clear and present danger" test of the decision (1919). *Schenck v. United States*, 249 US 47, 52 (1919).

[5] *Brandenburg*, §447. [6] *Hess v. Indiana* 414 US 105 (1973).

likelihood and imminence, resurface later in the international criminal law of incitement.[7]

In international law, criminal responsibility for speech as a form of persecution was first established in 1945–6 at the International Military Tribunal (IMT) at Nuremberg in the *Streicher* case.[8] Founder and publisher of *Der Stürmer*, a vicious anti-Semitic German weekly, Julius Streicher was convicted on 1 October, 1946 of "persecution on political and racial grounds in connection with war crimes," punishable as a crime against humanity under the IMT Charter.[9] Streicher's case is exceptional in that he was the only defendant convicted and executed at Nuremberg solely on Count Four of "Crimes Against Humanity." The Tribunal justified its sentence by finding that the defendant had knowledge of Hitler's policy of extermination of the Jews and yet he continued to incite Germans "to murder and extermination at the time when Jews in the East were being killed under the most horrible conditions."[10] Nevertheless, the fleeting, almost cursory decision failed to determine unambiguously the nature of Streicher's liability. Nor, according to Margaret Eastwood (2012:203, 220), did it "specifically define the *mens rea* necessary for an act of incitement to genocide."

On what grounds did Nuremberg prosecutors seek to convict two Nazi propagandists for crimes against humanity, when no precedent existed in international law? We can learn a great deal about prosecutors' strategizing in 1945–6 from the trial briefs and memoranda held in the archives of Thomas J. Dodd, Executive Trial Counsel at Nuremberg. Dodd's papers reveal that the prosecution held the two Nazi propagandists – Streicher and Hans Fritzsche[11] – liable for crimes against humanity as accessories or abettors who incited and encouraged others. Pretrial briefs refer to Fritzsche, the deputy of Minister of Propaganda Joseph Goebbels, as "a principal conspirator in abetting aggressive wars," whose actions "create[d] in the German people the requisite psychological and political conditions for aggressive war."[12] His noteworthy role was

---

[7] Elements of *Brandenburg* also occur in other domestic criminal systems. For instance, the incitement provision in Canada's Criminal Code has a "likelihood" element, at Section 281.2(2) of Sections 318 and 319.

[8] International Military Tribunal (Nuremberg), Judgment and Sentences in *American Journal of International Law*, vol. 41: 172, 296 (1947), (hereinafter *Nuremberg Judgment and Sentences*). See also David Ohlin (2009:207, 210).

[9] *Nuremberg Judgment and Sentences*, §§294–96, 331.   [10] *Ibid.*, §§295–96, 333.

[11] Hans Fritzsche was Head of the German Home Press Department in the Ministry of Propaganda. Fritzsche was acquitted on all counts by the Tribunal. *Nuremberg Judgment and Sentences* §§327–29.

[12] Thomas J. Dodd, *The Individual Responsibility of the Defendant Hans Fritzsche*.

Figure 2.1 Defendant Julius Streicher on the stand at the International Military Tribunal at Nuremberg, 1946.
Credit: US Holocaust Memorial Museum, courtesy of the National Archives and Records Administration, College Park

"preparing Nazi Germany for aggressive war and for the barbarities committed by the Nazis both within Germany and abroad."[13]

Similarly, the prosecutors' brief on Streicher stated that "[d]efendant Streicher is an accessory to the persecution of the Jews within Germany and in occupied territories... [who] actively supported, recommended and promoted the program of extermination."[14] In an interview some twenty years after the Nuremberg trials, British prosecutor Mervyn

---

[13] *Ibid.* [14] *Ibid.*

Griffith-Jones[15] confirmed that the prosecution's case against Streicher rested upon his involvement as an accessory to genocide; Streicher's incitement and encouragement of a policy of extermination of the Jews made him "a party to the murder of millions of people."[16]

US prosecutors at Nuremberg consciously avoided introducing any causation arguments into their two "propaganda" trials. My archival research reveals that they possessed evidence of a court record of the trial of a member of the *Sturm Abteilung*, or "Stormtroopers," for the 1934 murder of a Jew, in which the defendant testified that his act was incited by a story about ritual murder published in *Der Stürmer*. After an internal debate, US prosecutors decided not to lead this evidence in the trial.[17] The prosecution team anticipated Streicher's defense rejoinder that no direct evidence had been introduced to prove that his publications and public speeches did, in fact, influence those directly participating in persecution or extermination by reminding the Tribunal that causation was "tangential to the charge brought against Streicher."[18] Instead, prosecutors concentrated the courtroom's attention on the explicit message contained in Julius Streicher's words themselves. Here, the primary exhibit was the May 1939 issue of *Der Stürmer*, in which Streicher declared, "The Jews in Russia must be killed. They must be exterminated root and branch."[19]

Prosecutors at Nuremberg also highlighted the mental states of the propagandist and the German population, asserting that Streicher "incited a fear and hatred of Jews which made persecution in the first instance, and finally, the program of mass murder which he openly advocated, a psychological possibility."[20] While the prosecution refrained from claiming that Streicher's writings and public speeches caused specific genocidal acts, time and time again prosecutors referred to how Streicher prepared the ground psychologically and rendered mass crimes thinkable. A May 1946 memo from Harriet Zetterberg Margolies to fellow prosecutor Dodd lays out the prosecution's case theory: "Streicher helped to create, through his propaganda, the

---

[15] Griffith-Jones is also famous for prosecuting Penguin books for publishing D. H. Lawrence's "Lady Chatterley's Lover" in 1960. See Vinen (2003:2–5).

[16] Eastwood (2012:220).

[17] Thomas J. Dodd, Defense of Streicher, "Office of U.S. Chief of Counsel Memorandum for Mr. Dodd," Harriet Zetterberg Margolies.

[18] Thomas J. Dodd, *Individual Responsibility of the Defendant Julius Streicher*.

[19] *Nuremberg Judgment and Sentences*, §295.

[20] See "Individual Responsibility of the Defendant Julius Streicher in Nuremberg," *Nuremberg Judgement and Sentences*.

psychological basis necessary for carrying through a program of perse-cution which culminated in the murder of six million men, women and children."[21] Captain Drexel Sprecher's oral presentation to the court-room likewise asserted that Nazi spokesman Hans Fritzsche's inciting remarks "helped fashion the psychological atmosphere of utter and complete unreason and hatred."[22]

Nuremberg judges followed the prosecution's lead in the *Streicher* decision, converging on the psychology and mental states of the German populace. They eschewed identifying a direct causal connec-tion between Streicher's speeches or publications and any particular criminal acts, but rather emphasized the relationship between his speech and the broader anti-Semitic mindset of Germans: "In his speeches and articles, week after week, month after month, [Streicher] infected the German mind with the virus of anti-Semitism, and incited the German people to active persecution."[23] Therefore the IMT deci-sion postulated a connection, not between the defendant's acts and concrete genocidal acts (or physical causation), but between the defen-dant's acts and the minds of other Germans (i.e., mental causation), through the metaphor of viral contagion. The IMT's commentary on the matter was spare and the entire decision was barely two pages, and the ICTR Trial Chamber later recognized that "the judgment does not explicitly note a direct causal link between Streicher's publication and any specific acts of murder."[24] In sum, both prosecutors and judges constructed Streicher's criminal responsibility upon accomplice liabi-lity, and upon intention and psychological states, rather than causation and a demonstrable nexus between speech acts and particular material crimes.

In the aftermath of the Nuremberg trials, on 9 December 1948, the United Nations General Assembly adopted the Convention on the Prevention and Punishment of the Crime of Genocide ("UN Genocide Convention"), which in Article III(c) declared "direct and public incitement to commit genocide" an international crime in its own right.[25] Given the brevity of judicial commentary in *Streicher* and the

---

[21] Harriet Zetterberg Margolies, *Responsibility of the Defendant Julius Streicher*, §1.

[22] Thomas J. Dodd, *Prosecution oral presentation against Fritzsche*, §23.

[23] Nuremberg Judgment and Sentences, §294. On the trial of Streicher, see also Eastwood (2012:203); and Taylor (1992:376–80).

[24] *Nahimana* TC §981.

[25] Convention on the Prevention and Punishment of the Crime of Genocide article 3(c), 9 December 1948, 78 U.N.T.S. 227 (entered into force 12 January 1951) [hereinafter Genocide Convention].

dearth of incitement cases in international courts after 1948, the ICTR – established in 1994 – had little jurisprudence to guide its reasoning on the role of the media in the Rwandan genocide. What minimal direction existed on how to interpret Article III(c) of the UN Genocide Convention lay in the Report of the International Law Commission's 48th session in 1996, during which the Commission drafted a non-binding "Code of Crimes Against the Peace and Security of Mankind."[26] Rupturing with domestic criminal codes as well as the precedent set at Nuremberg, the International Law Commission (ILC) stipulated that direct and public incitement "is limited to situations in which the other individual actually commits that crime."[27] According to the ILC's 1996 Code, criminal responsibility only applies when an individual "directly and publicly incites another individual to commit such a crime *which in fact occurs*" (my emphasis).[28]

William Schabas (2009:324) disapproves of the International Law Commission's formulation, which he says "revealed a serious misunderstanding" and "obviously departed from the spirit of article III(c)" of the UN Genocide Convention, by requiring the underlying crime of genocide to be completed. One could justifiably venture a step further: the precariousness of the ICTR's jurisprudence on incitement originated in the defective guidance provided by the International Law Commission's 1996 Draft Code, which restricted the crime of direct and public incitement to commit genocide to instances in which the crime of genocide actually occurs.[29] That ICTR Trial Chamber judges were influenced by the ILC's 1996 Draft Code is apparent: they cite it approvingly in nearly all the incitement decisions, starting with the Tribunal's very first case, that of Jean-Paul Akayesu.[30]

---

[26] Rep. of the International Law Commission, *Draft Code of Crimes Against the Peace and Security of Mankind*, 48th Sess., 17 July, 1996, UN Doc. A/CN.4/L.532; UN GAOR 51st Sess., Supp. No. 10, art. 2.3(f), *reprinted in* [1996] 2 Y.B. Int'l L. Comm'n 17, hereinafter *ILC Draft Code of Crimes*.

[27] *ILC Draft Code of Crimes*, §22.   [28] ILC, §2.3(f).

[29] *Draft Code of Crimes Against the Peace and Security of Mankind, Nuremberg Judgment and Sentence.*

[30] *Akayesu* TC §475, 556, 587. See also *Bikindi* TC §387, 96 n. 867; *Nahimana* AC §1011; *Ruggiu* TC §17; *Kayishema & Ruzindana* TC §87, 95, 229. This flawed legal formulation could have travelled from the International Law Commission to the international criminal tribunals in various ways, including through a transfer of personnel, since one Commissioner (Patrick L. Robinson) who participated in the 1996 session later became an ICTY judge in 1998 and ICTY President in 2008. Former Presidents, United Nations International Criminal Tribunal for the Former Yugoslavia, available at www.icty.org/sid/155 (last visited 13 March 2016).

Additionally, the ILC's 1996 Draft Code of Crimes exerted an authoritative influence on the drafters of the International Criminal Court's Rome Statute (1998), which unfortunately compounds the confusion on direct and public incitement to commit genocide.[31] Unlike the Statutes of the ICTY and ICTR, the ICC's Rome Statute does not list direct and public incitement as a separate crime in Article 5.1, the article that lists the four crimes within the jurisdiction of the Court: genocide, crimes against humanity, war crimes and the crime of aggression. Nor is incitement included in Article 6, which defines the crime of genocide. Because of its exclusion from Articles 5–6, direct and public incitement to commit genocide is not even addressed in the ICC's core document, *Elements of Crimes* (2011).

Instead, direct and public incitement to commit genocide is relegated in the ICC Statute to Article 25 "Individual Criminal Responsibility," which lists forms of criminal liability such as direct commission, inducing, ordering, aiding and abetting and attempting to commit a crime. Article 25(3)(e) states that a person is liable for punishment of a crime within the jurisdiction of the Court if that person, "in respect of the crime of genocide, directly and publicly incites others to commit genocide."

Legal scholars such as Werle (2007) have remarked on the odd placement of the crime of incitement to commit genocide alongside modes of criminal responsibility in the ICC Statute, which seems to have resulted less from careful deliberation than from a housekeeping error.[32] Incitement to commit genocide is unlike the other forms of participation listed in the ICC's Article 25 since they are not distinct crimes in and of themselves, and therefore they must attach to an underlying target crime under the jurisdiction of the Court. All the other modes of liability apart from attempt require completion of the crime and therefore proof of a causal connection between the act in question and the criminal consequence, a requirement that does not apply to inchoate crimes such as incitement to commit genocide and attempt. Conventionally, charges are more difficult to prove if they require evidence of causation beyond a reasonable doubt than if the crime is fully committed in the act itself.

---

[31] Davies (2009:268) also notes the malign impact of the ILC Draft Code on the formulation of incitement to commit genocide in the 1998 Rome Statute.

[32] See Davies (2009:266–8) for an account of the drafting process of the Rome Statute as it relates to incitement to genocide.

In the ICC's Statute, incitement to commit genocide has been downgraded from a standalone crime in itself to a mode of participation in genocide, possibly implying that it is not an inchoate crime. Since proof of causation is required for modes of liability for completed crimes and furnishing such proof is an arduous undertaking, the ICC's unusual formulation of incitement to genocide means that prosecutions at the ICC for the crime are less likely to succeed. They are also less likely to be used in a preventative manner, since logically, prosecutors cannot marshal evidence of causation until the crime is actually completed. Davies (2009:245) concludes that the ICC's Rome Statute undermines "the full effectiveness of the criminalization of incitement."

2.3 DIRECT AND PUBLIC INCITEMENT TO COMMIT GENOCIDE AT THE ICTR

The ICTR's case law on direct and public incitement to commit genocide was groundbreaking and represented the first application of the UN Genocide Convention's incitement provisions by an international criminal tribunal. The following discussion focuses on one key aspect of this jurisprudence: the prominent role of causation in the Tribunal's incitement rulings. In reviewing the applicable law, the rulings formally reiterated the standard legal formulation that as an inchoate crime, incitement to genocide is primarily a crime of intention as expressed in speech acts and may occur regardless of the corollaries of a speech or broadcast. The conventional view of inchoate crimes in criminal law stretches back at least to the eighteenth century when influential judges such as Lord Mansfield declared: "[t]he intent may make an act, innocent in itself, criminal; nor is the completion of the act, criminal in itself, necessary to constitute criminality."[33]

Nevertheless, a number of the ICTR judgments felt it necessary to establish a direct causal link between speeches or broadcasts and actual genocide or other material crimes in the "findings of fact" sections. Subsequent ICTR rulings went even further, and references to causation seeped into their legal findings and altered the way in which the ICTR Trial Chamber conceptualized the legal contours of incitement. Reviewing the entire corpus of ICTR case law in incitement to commit genocide, one might reasonably ask whether the emphasis given by ICTR judges to the consequence of speech acts has elevated causation

---

[33] Cited in Moenssens et al. (2003:898).

to the level of a requisite element of the crime. Reasonable grounds exist for and against the proposition, and both sides could agree that the successive trial and appeal rulings contain a great deal of ambiguity and conflicting language.

In its very first case, in 1998, the ICTR Trial Chamber convicted Jean-Paul Akayesu of direct and public incitement to commit genocide under Article 2(3)(c) of the ICTR Statute.[34] The verdict in *Akayesu* contained a novel aspect that distinguished it from *Streicher*, namely its explicit claims about the causal effects of inciting speech. In its legal findings, the Trial Chamber formally confirmed the accepted legal position that incitement to genocide is an inchoate crime that can be completed "regardless of the result achieved."[35] In its factual findings section, however, the Trial Chamber asserted conspicuously the causal effects of one of Akayesu's inciting speeches: "The Chamber is of the opinion that there is a causal relationship between Akayesu's speeches at the gathering of 19 April 1994 and the ensuing widespread massacres of Tutsi in Taba."[36] The three international judges saw it as noteworthy that Akayesu's call to arms "was indeed successful and did lead to the destruction of a great number of Tutsi in the commune of Taba."[37]

It seems that the *Akayesu* bench introduced causation as a way of shoring up the "directness" aspect of the conviction of the accused for direct and public incitement. Given the euphemistic and coded speech of the defendant, the prosecution was not able to present evidence against Akayesu as clear and direct as Streicher's exhortations, such as: "The Jews in Russia must be killed. They must be exterminated root and branch."[38] In order to conclude that Akayesu directly incited his followers to commit genocide, the judges in *Akayesu* were compelled to adopt an expansive view that encompassed implicit as well as explicit calls to exterminate a protected group. The *Akayesu* Trial Chamber based its understanding of the cultural meaning of speeches on the report, relying heavily on the testimony of Dr. Mathias Ruzindana, the prosecution's expert witness on Kinyarwanda linguistics.[39] The Trial Chamber found that Akayesu's exhortations to fight "the Inkotanyi" (literally "warriors") to a crowd of 100 people at Gishyeshye in the early

---

[34] *Akayesu* TC §§674–75.   [35] *Akayesu* TC §562.   [36] *Ibid.*, §673(vii).   [37] *Ibid.*, §675.

[38] Trial of the Major War Criminals Before the International Military Tribunal, Nuremberg 14 November 1945–1 October 1946, §303 (1947).

[39] For a summary of the expert witness report, see Ruzindana (2012:145, 145–70).

hours of 19 April 1994 "would be construed as a call to kill the Tutsi in general."[40]

Akayesu's capacious interpretation of euphemisms set a precedent that the Trial Chamber would enlarge in later cases such as *Ruggiu*, where it stated that "the term *'Inyenzi'* ["cockroach"] became synonymous with the term 'Tutsi'."[41] Over time, the Tribunal came to interpret a defendant's use of the expression "go to work" to mean, "[G]o kill the Tutsis and Hutu political opponents of the interim government."[42] In my view, the Trial Chamber made repeated references to causation in order to justify the inclusion of euphemistic speech within the "directness" element of the crime of inciting genocide.

Akayesu's treatment of causation went beyond fulfilling the directness requirement of incitement to genocide, however. The judgment seemingly elevated causation to a legal requirement to prove incitement, even though the Trial Chamber embedded its pronouncement in the factual findings part of the decision: "the Chamber feels that it is not sufficient to simply establish a possible coincidence between the Gishyeshye meeting and the beginning of the killing of Tutsi in Taba, but that there *must be proof of a possible causal link* between the statement made by the Accused during the said meeting and the beginning of the killings" (emphasis in original).[43] This demand for proof ostensibly removed incitement to genocide from the category of inchoate crimes and recategorized it among forms of completed criminal liability (such as ordering, instigating, and aiding and abetting) that require that the underlying offence actually be committed.

Subsequent incitement trials at the ICTR referred to and amplified the causal element introduced in *Akayesu*, even as they simultaneously reiterated the inchoate nature of the crime. The judgment that gave greatest prominence to the causal effects of speech acts was *Prosecutor v. Ferdinand Nahimana, Jean-Bosco Barayagwisa, Hassan Ngeze.*[44] International legal scholar Diane Orentlicher (2005:17) called *Nahimana*, also known as

---

[40] *Akayesu* TC §673(iv). The judgment notes that "Inkotanyi" means literally "warriors," and was a term commonly used to refer to soldiers of the Rwandan Patriotic Front (§147). Furthermore, "Inkotanyi" has precolonial origins and in that period had no mono-ethnic connotations. The judgment glosses the use of the term in 1994 thus: "it should be assumed that the basic meaning of the term Inkotanyi is the RPF army" (§147).

[41] *Ruggiu* Amended Indictment §44(iii).   [42] *Ibid.*, §44(iv).

[43] *Akayesu* TC §349 (emphasis added).

[44] Hereinafter, *Nahimana* TC. For legal commentary on the Media Trial, see Benesch (2004); Benesch (2008); Davidson (2004); Gordon (2012); Gordon (2010); Gordon (2005); Mackinnon (2009); Maravilla (2008); Mendel (2006), Orentlicher (2005); Schabas (2000) and Zahar (2005).

the "Media Trial," "the most important judgment relating to the law of incitement in the context of international criminal law since the judgment at Nuremberg more than fifty-seven years earlier."

The three defendants in the Media Trial all owned major Rwandan media outlets. Ferdinand Nahimana and Jean-Bosco Barayagwisa were both government ministers and founders of the main independent radio station Radio Télévision Libre des Milles Collines (RTLM). Hassan Ngeze was the owner and editor of *Kangura*,[45] a newspaper widely distributed in Rwanda before the genocide.[46] Surprisingly, all three were convicted of direct commission of genocide as a result of their leadership positions at RTLM and *Kangura* and their responsibility for publications and radio broadcasts. The judgment defended this conviction on the grounds that "[e]ditors and publishers have generally been held responsible for the media they control,"[47] itself a rather shaky proposition. As Diane Orentlicher (2005:33) explains: "the trial chamber in effect treated *Kangura* and RTLM themselves as perpetrators of genocide and convicted the defendants by virtue of their relationship to the media organs in question."

The three defendants in the Media Trial were also convicted of direct and public incitement to commit genocide, in a verdict that asserted a direct causal nexus between speeches and radio broadcasts and subsequent public violence. The ruling asserts no less than sixteen times that speech acts directly caused genocidal killings, using language such as:

> Many of the individuals specifically named in RTLM broadcasts after 6 April 1994 were subsequently killed... While the extent of causation by RTLM broadcasts in these killings may have varied somewhat, depending on the circumstances of these killings, the Chamber finds that a causal connection has been established by the evidence...[48]
>
> Without a firearm, machete or any physical weapon, he [Nahimana] caused the deaths of thousands of innocent civilians.[49]

Nahimana put a number of disparate models of causation in play. In descending order of robustness, it found a direct "specific causal connection,"[50] but also conceded that "the extent of causation by RTLM broadcasts in these killings may have varied somewhat."[51] The judgment later acknowledged that RTLM broadcasts may not

---

[45] Which according to the *Nahimana* TC glossary means, literally "wake others up."
[46] *Nahimana* TC §7 & 10.   [47] *Nahimana* TC §1001.   [48] *Ibid.*, §482.   [49] *Ibid.*, §1099.
[50] *Ibid.*, §949.   [51] *Ibid.*, §482.

Figure 2.2 Ferdinand Nahimana (L), a founder of Radio Television Libre des Milles Collines (RTLM), and Hassan Ngeze (R), an editor for the Kangura newspaper, at their trial at the UN Tribunal for Rwanda in Arusha in 2003.
Credit: Stella Vuzo/AFP/Getty Images

have been the immediate proximate cause of killings and that there may have been a number of intervening factors in addition to the communication.[52] What were the mechanisms through which the radio exerted its causal force? *Nahimana* mixed its metaphors, combining the image of spreading gasoline with Nuremberg's portrayal of a propagandist injecting poison into the mind of a civilian population:

> RTLM "spread petrol throughout the country little by little, so that one day it would be able to set fire to the whole country." This is the poison described in the Streicher judgment.[53]
>
> He [Ngeze] poisoned the minds of his readers, and by words and deeds caused the death of thousands of innocent civilians.[54]

---

[52] *Ibid.*, §952.
[53] *Ibid.*, §1078. At §981, *Nahimana* summarized *Streicher* in some detail before proceeding to gauge the consequences of the publications and broadcasts of the three accused.
[54] *Ibid.*, §1101. See also §243: "The ethnic hatred that permeates *Kangura* had the effect of poison, as evidenced by the testimony of the witnesses."

In its factual findings on RTLM broadcasts, *Nahimana* identified three types of evidence connecting the radio station's transmissions to the genocide. First, some of the Tutsi individuals specifically mentioned by name in broadcasts before and after 6 April 1994 were subsequently killed.[55] That RTLM motivated listeners to take action was proven by the testimony of one witness who reported being accosted in the street by an attacker who referred to the content of a program.[56] Finally, *Nahimana* found a nexus between broadcasts and killings in the threat perceived by individuals who had been named on RTLM.[57]

Assertions of causation, thus far confined to the factual findings section of *Akayesu* and subsequent judgments, also featured in *Nahimana's* analysis of applicable case law. In a special section on "causation" in the legal discussion of genocide, the Trial Chamber attributed a causation role generally to "the media."[58] The same section noted that while the downing of the Rwandan president's plane may have triggered the genocide, "RTLM, *Kangura* and CDR were the bullets in the gun."[59] When it turned to consider the separate charge of incitement, the Trial Chamber provided an unreliable review of the applicable law. *Nahimana* made reference to *Akayesu's* factual finding of a causal relationship between the defendant's speech and widespread massacres – but mistakenly elevated causation to an element of the legal findings section of the *Akayesu* decision.[60] A few sentences later, it reversed course, reaffirming that causation is "not requisite to a finding of incitement."

The Trial Chamber's confused understanding on causation encroached on its reasoning in other legal matters, such as *Nahimana's* formulation of incitement as a continuing crime – which, similar to the crime of conspiracy, continues in time until the target crime is fulfilled or completed. "[T]he crime of incitement. . . continues to the time of the commission of the acts incited,"[61] the Trial Chamber wrote. "[T]he Chamber notes. . . that the crime of direct and public incitement to commit genocide, like conspiracy, is an inchoate offense that continues in time until the completion of the acts contemplated."[62] As a result, the Chamber adopted the view that it could exercise its jurisdiction over "inchoate offenses that culminate[d] in the commission of acts in 1994."[63]

This view is problematic because it carries certain assumptions: first, that the inciting speech will inexorably lead to the commission of the

---

[55] *Ibid.*, §478.   [56] *Ibid.*, §479.   [57] *Ibid.*, §480.   [58] *Ibid.*, §952.   [59] *Ibid.*, §953.
[60] *Ibid.*, §1015.   [61] *Ibid.*, §104.   [62] *Ibid.*, §1017.   [63] *Ibid.*, §104.

encouraged acts, and second, that such commission is relevant to the adjudication of incitement to genocide, even though the formal legal position is that the target crime need not be completed for incitement to genocide to constitute a crime. I share Orentlicher's (2005:45) observation that:

> [t]his characterization is hard to reconcile with the trial chamber's view that, as an inchoate offense, incitement is a crime regardless of whether it has its intended effect (in the case of incitement to commit genocide, provoking listeners to commit genocide). If the criminality of incitement does not turn upon its impact, it is not readily apparent that this offense should be considered to have 'ended' when it achieves its aim.

In 2007, the Appeals Chamber in *Nahimana* corrected some of the more egregious mistakes of fact and law in the Trial Chamber judgment and reversed a number of its findings. As for the genocide charge (that is, the charge of its direct commission), the Appeals Chamber acquitted all three defendants of genocide convictions resulting from their leadership positions at RTLM and *Kangura*. The Appeals Chamber found that there was "no evidence that Appellant Nahimana played an active part in the broadcasts after 6 April 1994 which instigated the commission of genocide. Furthermore, the appeal record contains no evidence that Appellant Nahimana had, before 6 April 1994, given instructions to RTLM journalists to instigate the killing of Tutsi."[64] In acquitting Nahimana on the separate charge of instigating genocide, the Appeals Chamber rejected the Trial Chamber's evidence of a link between RTLM broadcasts and acts of genocide, declaring such evidence, "at the very least, tenuous."[65] In short, the evidence for causation was too unconvincing to support a conviction for commission of genocide.

In defining the crime of incitement to genocide, the ICTR Appeals Chamber seemed to introduce a new criterion of contemporaneousness, in which genocidal speech acts had to be uttered very near or simultaneous with the onset of an actual genocide. The Appeals Chamber upheld the incitement convictions against Nahimana for speeches and broadcasts after 6 April 1994 and against Ngeze for publications of *Kangura* in early 1994 before the start of the genocide.[66] It overturned

---

[64] *Nahimana* AC §597.
[65] *Ibid.*, §513. This comment refers specifically to prosecution evidence for the time period before 6 April 1994, although Nahimana was also acquitted of incitement for the period after 6 April. *Ibid.*, §346.
[66] *Ibid.*, §§346–347.

the conviction of defendant Barayagwisa for inciting genocide, however, on the grounds that he was no longer in a position of superior responsibility at the station after 6 April 1994, when the genocide began. The Appeals Chamber found that "although it is clear that RTLM broadcasts between 1 January and 6 April 1994 incited ethnic hatred, it has not been established that they directly and publicly incited the commission of genocide."[67]

Successive ICTR verdicts reaffirmed the *Nahimana* Appeals Chamber's contemporaneity criterion. In 2008, for example, Rwandan pop musician Simon Bikindi was convicted on the basis of his appeals to Hutus, "You know the minority population is the Tutsi. Exterminate quickly the remaining ones," made over a public address system while genocide was occurring.[68] According to Gordon (2010:262), the Tribunal implicitly confirmed the contemporaneity criterion formulated in *Nahimana* by absolving Bikindi of liability for anti-Tutsi songs written before the genocide on the grounds that only words uttered by the accused at or near the time of genocidal violence may constitute incitement.[69]

The ICC's *Elements of Crimes* (2011) lends support to the notion that there is a contemporaneousness requirement to incitement to genocide, insofar as Article 6(a)(4) (Genocide by killing) stipulates that "The conduct took place in the context of a manifest pattern of similar conduct directed against that group or was conduct that could itself effect such destruction." Obviously, a single act of inciting genocide alone could likely not, in the absence of any other factors, cause genocide. In parsing "in the context of a manifest pattern," we must start by recognizing that no defendant at the ICC has been charged with incitement to genocide, so we do not yet know how the contextual requirement will be interpreted. One could reasonably expect it to mean that the incitement to commit genocide would have to occur in the context of genocide against a protected group, or, at a minimum, in the context of crimes against humanity which themselves demand a widespread or systematic attack against a civilian population.

Furthermore, the ICC's *Elements of Crimes* at Article 6 (a–b) contains the following provisions: "The term 'in the context of' would include the initial acts in an emerging pattern," and "The term 'manifest' is an objective qualification." This wording could support an interpretation that isolated, and highly preliminary acts are not within

---

[67] *Ibid.*, §636, 754.   [68] *Bikindi* TC §422, §426. The quote is cited in the judgment at §266.
[69] For the relevant section, see *Bikindi* TC §255, 421.

the scope and jurisdiction of the ICC, and it makes it less likely that a defendant would be convicted of inciting genocide in a situation where neither a full-blown genocide nor an objectively manifest pattern of genocidal acts are underway. Such an interpretation would obviously undermine the preventative potential of the inchoate crime of incitement to genocide.

On the question of the Trial Chamber's construal of incitement as a "continuing crime," the ICTR Appeals Chamber pronounced that the Trial Chamber had made an error in law in considering that incitement continues in time until the completion of the crime's intended purpose, and therefore inciting genocide cannot be considered a "continuing crime" like conspiracy.[70] Instead, the Appeals Chamber correctly reaffirmed that the crime of incitement to genocide "is completed as soon as the discourse in question is uttered or published, even though the effects of incitement may extend in time."[71]

While the *Nahimana* Appeals Chamber cleared up a number of irregularities in the Trial Chamber judgment, it did not overtly address the Trial Chamber's reasoning on the relevance of causation in determining whether incitement to genocide had been committed. In some cases, however – for instance, insofar as it introduced a new criterion of contemporaneousness – it implicitly confirmed the centrality of causation and the need for prosecutors to show a proven chronological nexus with the target crime.

A great deal is at stake in the ICTR case law on causation and direct and public incitement to commit genocide. Because the Tribunal issued the first judgments since Nuremberg, the ICTR's flawed reasoning on causation is likely to influence the international criminal law of incitement to genocide for some time to come. This is exacerbated by the fact that the ICC Statute, the prevailing benchmark of international criminal law, has seemingly downgraded incitement to genocide to a mode of liability rather than a standalone crime, and thereby left room for ambiguity on the role of causation in incitement to genocide.

It is fair to say that this has been one of the most controversial areas of international criminal law in the last twenty years, and several leading legal commentators have found the ICTR's reasoning on incitement sorely wanting. *Nahimana* is perhaps the most contentious of all the ICTR's judgments, and both its Trial Chamber and Appellate

[70] *Nahimana* AC §723.   [71] *Ibid.*, §723.

Chamber opinions have sparked controversy. Diane Orentlicher (2005:558–9, 576), for example, calls the Trial Chamber decision "problematic," characterized by "unpersuasive reasoning," and representing such a rupture with existing law of hate speech and incitement that it potentially violated the legal principle of non-retroactivity. Alexander Zahar (2005:33–4, 48), an attorney at both the ICTR and ICTY, pronounces the same ruling "a very poor precedent," and states that the judges drifted into "legal activism, at worst legal absurdity."

Perhaps most damning of all is Judge Theodor Meron's partly dissenting opinion in the *Nahimana* Appeals Chamber judgment. Meron felt that there were so many errors of fact and law in the *Nahimana* Trial Chamber judgment that "remanding the case, rather than undertaking piecemeal remedies, would have been the best course."[72] Perhaps Meron's call to send *Nahimana* back to the Trial Chamber for a complete retrial was justified. Even though the *Nahimana* Appeals Chamber corrected many mistakes in the trial ruling, it glossed over others and left room for future misinterpretation – especially given that it did not explicitly overturn the International Law Commission's view that the UN Genocide Convention's article III(c) on direct and public incitement only applies when an act of incitement "in fact occurs." The exact role of causation in determining incitement to genocide was not fully presented and worked through, and it continues to cast a shadow over incitement jurisprudence, even after the *Nahimana* Appeals Chamber judgment.

The inconsistency both within the ICTR's incitement jurisprudence and between the Appellate Chamber ruling and other sources of international law thwarts the imperative to formulate unambiguous provisions in this new field of international criminal law. That future tribunals such as the ICC, with its own irregular framing of incitement, will encounter such contradictory characterizations of incitement destabilizes the legitimacy of international criminal law. It may also violate the due process rights of the accused to have their case adjudicated according to a coherent corpus of legal precedent.

---

[72] *Ibid.*, §375 (Meron, J., dissenting). A year later, Judge Meron was a member of an Appeals Chamber bench that quashed the defendant's conviction for direct and public incitement to commit genocide and ordered a retrial pursuant to Rule 118(C) of the Rules of Procedure and Evidence of the Tribunal (*Muvunyi* AC §171). The accused, Tharcisse Muvunyi, was retried by the Trial Chamber, and his conviction for incitement to genocide was upheld on appeal, albeit with a sentence reduced from twenty-five to ten years.

2.4 REVERSE ENGINEERING SPECIFIC INTENT FROM CONSEQUENCES

It is worth considering the factors that would induce professional judges to abandon centuries of convention on the law of inchoate crimes to claim a causal connection between speech acts and the crime of genocide – and even to include causation in legal discussions of incitement without a doctrinal reason to do so. Initially, the causation claims proposed in *Akayesu* were a way of establishing the directness aspect of the defendant's inciting speech, but the causation element has plagued a succession of judgments and even been elevated from the factual findings to the legal discussion of judgments. In looking for clues to explain a sudden rupture in legal reasoning, it can be fruitful to look for the places in the text of judicial decisions where logical argumentation breaks down. In venturing a new legal precedent on the role of causation in inchoate crimes, the trial chamber in *Nahimana* tied itself in analytical knots:

> With regard to causation, the Chamber recalls that incitement is a crime regardless of whether it has the effect it intends to have. In determining whether communications represent an intent to cause genocide and thereby constitute incitement, the Chamber considers it significant that in fact genocide occurred. *That the media intended to have this effect is evidenced in part by the fact that it did have this effect.*[73]

The *Nahimana* Appeals Chamber did not find the trial chamber's above reasoning erroneous, on the grounds that in some circumstances, the fact "that a speech leads to acts of genocide could be an indication that in that particular context the speech was understood to be an incitement to commit genocide, and that this was indeed the intent of the author of the speech."[74]

However, sentence two of the above paragraph appears to be a non-sequitur, or at the very least contradicts the sentence before it. Either way, placing the two statements sequentially defies standard conventions of logical inference. Sentence three engages in a perplexing reverse logic, where proof of intention is discovered ("in part") in the putative consequences of a speech act. The quote is an illustration of *post hoc ergo propter hoc*[75] or what is known as the "post-hoc fallacy." In this instance, the fallacy in the trial chamber's reasoning can be

---

[73] *Nahimana* TC §1029 (emphasis added).   [74] *Nahimana* AC §709.
[75] Latin: "after this, therefore because of this."

stated thus, "since event z followed speech act y, speech act y must have been motivated by the intention to cause event z."

Speech crimes, like other inchoate crimes, are primarily crimes of intention, yet can intentions legitimately be deduced from subsequent acts? At times, yes: for instance, when individual A encourages individual B to commit a crime, and B commits the crime in the way that A intended. However, not all events related temporally are causally related, and there might exist other causal factors that would rule out a connection between events. A speech act could lead to one outcome when the speaker in fact intended another, or the causal sequence was already in train and the speech act did not causally affect the outcome.

What matters here, however, is not whether effects (always, or even sometimes) prove intentions beyond reasonable doubt, but that the ICTR judges contended that this was the case and felt the need to repeatedly accentuate this point as they justified the centrality of causation in incitement to genocide. The causation element may have been a method for the ICTR to compensate for tenuous evidence for specific intent – allowing judges to reverse-engineer the intentionality of the accused on the faulty basis of genocidal acts that occurred after a speech or broadcast.

The key to understanding how causation functioned in judicial reasoning at the ICTR can be found in the problem of proving specific intent to commit genocide, a particularly arduous exercise that has vexed jurists for decades at international tribunals. This is relevant because the type of intention in direct and public incitement to commit genocide is not a standard type of criminal intention where the intention to commit the immediate crime is sufficient. Direct and public incitement to commit genocide requires the specific intent ("*dolus specialis*") to eliminate a protected group as such, in whole or in part.[76] Under international criminal law, specific intent calls for proof of a higher-order purpose, above and beyond the standard intention merely to commit a prohibited act.[77]

There are times when the ICTR judges' deliberations on specific intent border on ulterior intent and even motive, where the intent transcends a wrongful act to target a larger objective for the sake of which the act is done. For instance, the *Akayesu* Trial Chamber

---

[76] That any genocide charge requires proof of specific intent is established in *Krstić* AC §140.

[77] For specific intent in genocide jurisprudence, see Schabas (1999:260–4).

introduced "ulterior motive"[78] into its definition of specific intent. Subsequent ICTR judgments continued with this conflating of motive and intent, misguidedly referring to an "ulterior purpose" and "ulterior motive" to destroy a group during discussions of intent.[79] Motive is generally irrelevant in a criminal trial: all that is necessary for a guilty verdict is a finding that the defendant intended to commit the offence.

The heightened burden of proof for specific intent constitutes the main reason why many defendants have been acquitted of genocide, especially at the International Criminal Tribunal for the Former Yugoslavia.[80] Proving specific intent therefore emerges as the judicial motivation to explain why causation featured in the way it did in ICTR judgments on incitement to commit genocide. The central issue that the judges faced in the early incitement cases like *Akayesu* and *Nahimana* was the yawning gap between the high threshold of specific intent to commit genocide and the paucity of prosecution evidence for specifically genocidal intention. Despite the conventional wisdom in journalistic and human rights circles that the pro-government radio and press was full of daily calls for genocide in 1994, strong evidence for genocidal *mens rea* was not presented by the prosecution in *Nahimana*.

Former ICTR attorney Zahar (2005:37–8) finds himself "puzzled by the court's inability to come up with a single example – broadcast on RTLM or printed in *Kangura* – of a blatant call on Hutu to hunt down and destroy the Tutsi ethnic group." He notes that while the thirty-seven fragments of RTLM cited in the judgment are "brutal," full of ethnic animus, and likely deserving of a penal response, "the fragments do not read like direct and public incitement to commit genocide" (p. 38). Zahar finds it remarkable that "the prosecutor was not able to arrange for a single witness to testify that he or she was incited by appeals or hints... to commit genocide" (p. 41). The allure of causation for international judges was that it compensated for the fragility of the prosecution evidence for specific intent, and allowed judges to reverse-engineer intention from the acts occurring after a speech or broadcast.

This line of argumentation finds additional support when we consider the negative examples that exist in incitement case law – that is, those trials in which causation made no appearance at all in the final

---

[78] *Akayesu* TC §522.   [79] *Akayesu* TC §522; *Musema* TC §165; *Rutaganda* TC §§59–60.

[80] ICTY cases where the accused was acquitted of genocide (direct commission) at the ICTY include *Brđanin* AC §3; *Popović et al.* TC §1834; *Jelisić* AC §5; *Krajišnik* AC§280; *Krstić* AC §268; *Stakić* AC §55.

judgment. Two trials at the ICTR warrant mention here: Rwandan pop star Simon Bikindi and politician Augustin Ngirabatware. In each instance, the inciting words of the accused were much more explicitly, purposefully and precisely genocidal. Even though the Trial Chamber attested that Bikindi's "songs inspired action,"[81] and that "broadcasts of Bikindi's songs had an amplifying effect on the genocide,"[82] the defendant was convicted solely for his unequivocal calls to eliminate Tutsis, delivered in person over a public loudspeaker system.

The plain and unvarnished bluntness of Bikindi's speech formed the basis of the Trial Chamber's determination of specific intent, rather than any putative causal effects of his words. In fact, the *Bikindi* judgment openly acknowledges that one witness did not testify to any causal link between Bikindi's speech to a crowd and a subsequent killing, as the prosecutors' indictment had claimed.[83] In the subsequent case of *Ngirabatware*, the Trial Chamber makes no reference to causation whatsoever in the judgment, in strong contrast to *Akayesu*, *Nahimana* and *Ruggiu*. Instead, it arrives at its conclusions regarding the genocidal state of mind of the accused solely on the basis of the content of Ngirabatware's speech at a roadblock in 1994:

> His instruction to "kill Tutsis" objectively and unambiguously called for an act of violence prohibited by Article 2(2) of the Statute, and the Chamber has no doubt that Ngirabatware made this statement with the intent to directly incite genocide.[84]

As a working hypothesis, we might posit that in judgments where the prosecution's evidence of specific intent is incomplete and precarious, then causation language performs the function of filling the evidentiary gaps in proving specific intent to commit genocide. But where a defendant's words are direct and explicitly genocidal – Ngirabatware's "kill Tutsis," for instance – then causation fades away entirely in the judgment.

Having diagnosed the reasons why causation has been such a feature of incitement jurisprudence at the ICTR, it is worth weighing the long-term significance of the Tribunal's jurisprudence. In my view, one negative result relates to the challenging issue of genocide prevention.

---

[81] *Bikindi* TC §253.   [82] *Ibid.*, §264.   [83] *Ibid.*, §126.

[84] *Ngirabatware* TC §1368. Similarly, the accused Juvénal Kajelijeli uttered "exterminate the Tutsis" and this was sufficient to convict him of direct and public incitement to commit genocide; see *Kajelijeli* TC §856 and *Kajelijeli* AC §90, §105.

Prevention is the principle underlying inchoate crimes like incitement to commit genocide, yet thus far, no defendant has been indicted for inciting genocide in the absence of an actual genocide.[85] This is perplexing. The overriding motivation of the drafters of the UN Genocide Convention for including incitement to commit genocide as one of the five[86] distinct crimes, each of which is punishable in its own right, was genocide prevention. In proscribing incitement to commit genocide, the objective was to interdict the first steps in a deadly chain of events.[87] An early draft of the Genocide Convention, prepared by the Ad Hoc Committee on Genocide in April and May 1948, criminalized "direct incitement in public or in private to commit genocide, whether such incitement be successful or not,"[88] and the *Akayesu* Trial Chamber noted that the "specific crime" of direct and public incitement to commit genocide was established in the Convention "in particular, because of its critical role in the planning of a genocide."[89]

In this light, the ICTR's elevation of causality in the determination of incitement to commit genocide thwarts the prevention clauses of the UN Genocide Convention.[90] By finding directness and specific intention in outcomes, by insisting on "proof of a possible causal link," and by introducing a criterion of contemporaneousness that demands that incitement to commit genocide can only occur at or near an actual genocide, the existing case law could hinder a range of preventative international responses to early genocidal speech. These might range from destroying the antennae of radio stations transmitting messages of violence, to jamming radio transmissions, to issuing an indictment against those most responsible as they launch a campaign of inciting genocide.[91]

According to Jean-François Gaudreault-DesBeins (2000:121–5), the concern with causation at the ICTR "forces the potential victims of

---

[85] To date, there have been no indictments for direct and public incitement to commit genocide at the ICC or ICTY, or at hybrid tribunals such as the Special Court for Sierra Leone and the Extraordinary Chambers in the Courts of Cambodia. On the preventative aspects of criminal justice, see Ashworth and Zedner (2014).

[86] The UN Genocide Convention's five crimes related to genocide are: commission of genocide, conspiracy to commit genocide, incitement to genocide, attempting genocide and complicity in genocide.

[87] See Schabas (1999:521) and Davies (2009:247).

[88] Rep. of the Ad Hoc Comm. on Genocide to the Econ. & Soc. Council, 5 April–10 May 1948, UN Doc. E/794, Annex, art.iv(c), §55 (1948).

[89] *Akayesu* TC §551.   [90] UN Genocide Convention, §1, 8.

[91] On the prevention options weighed by the United States and international community during the Rwandan genocide, including radio jamming, see Metzl (1997) and Power (2002:371).

hate propaganda to bear or absorb all risks" of inciting speech. If there is an unspoken condition that courts will find incitement to genocide only in the context of actual genocide, and prosecutors therefore feel they must prove a causal nexus between inciting speech and genocidal acts, then such prosecutors are likely to wait until genocide is underway before charging an individual for inciting genocide. This formulation precludes any preventive force that criminalizing incitement to genocide could have, and encourages the international community to adopt a "wait and see" approach.

The central rationale of the crime of direct and public incitement to commit genocide is to deter the kind of public exhortations to commit genocide that ordinarily precede the onset of violence. International criminal tribunals have been criticized for being reactive and failing in their prevention and deterrence functions,[92] and the ICTR's incitement jurisprudence, combined with the relegation of incitement to genocide to a mode of liability, only exacerbates this shortcoming.

2.5 THE "GHOST OF CAUSATION" IN INTERNATIONAL SPEECH CRIMES CASES

> Causation slips into judicial rulings on incitement to genocide for several reasons, all of which are signs of systemic difficulties in international criminal law. First, there is a void to fill. Causation stands in for a tool that courts are lacking: a systematic method for identifying incitement to genocide. That crime, like other speech crimes in international law, has not clearly been defined.
>
> Susan Benesch (2012:257)

Legal scholars and speech crimes experts have made various attempts to resolve the contradictions in the formulation of incitement to commit genocide at the ICTR. In the noteworthy collection *Propaganda, War Crimes Trials and International Law*, leading international speech crimes expert Susan Benesch (2012:254) lucidly identifies the ways in which the "ghost of causation" has haunted the international law of incitement to genocide. She observes that in incitement cases, ICTR judges have made stirring pronouncements on causation, even when such pronouncements are neither required by law nor justified by the

---

[92] See, for example, Osiel (2009) and Schabas (1999:529), who reviews criticisms of the Clinton Administration and the international community for failing to act in the Rwandan genocide. For a contrasting view, see Akhavan (2001), who defends the prevention capabilities of international tribunals.

circumstantial evidence presented before the Tribunal. On the causal connection between speech acts and subsequent violence, she recognizes that "[i]t is difficult to prove such a nexus, since the effect of speech on large groups of people is hard to measure, poorly understood, and is only one of a constellation of forces that affect why people act as they do" (p. 257).

In the place of unfounded claims about the corollaries of speeches and broadcasts, Benesch (2012:262–4), following *Brandenburg*, advances a framework for assessing the *likelihood* that a speech act could have resulted in genocide, based upon the context of the speech act and the foreseeability that the speech act would have genocidal consequences. Her matrix for evaluating the gravity of a speech act is composed of five indicators. I summarize her proposed criteria below and encourage readers to consult Benesch's publications for a fuller and more detailed rendition:

1. The degree of authority and influence of the speaker
2. The disposition of the intended audience of the speech and its capacity to commit violent acts
3. The content of the speech acts and the degree to which they were repetitive, dehumanized the victims and were understood as a call to violence.
4. The socio-historical context and history of intergroup relations
5. The form of transmission of the speech and degree of persuasiveness of the form.

These criteria, Benesch is careful to say, would not replace the existing law of incitement to genocide. Rather, they are formulated principally to assist prosecutors at international tribunals, and to guide international agencies and governments as they decide whether to intervene or prevent genocide.[93] Instead of determining direct causation, Benesch's criteria assess the likelihood that a speech act could have foreseeable genocidal consequences. By offering more nuanced and specific guidance on the contextual conditions and likelihood that a speech act could incite violence, Benesch's framework complements and enhances existing ICTR case law. At first glance, Benesch seems to have identified the most appropriate "conditions of satisfaction"[94] for potentially harmful

---

[93] Benesch (2012:262). See also Dale (2001) on jamming radio broadcasts during genocide by the international community.

[94] To borrow a phrase from John Searle (2010:29) which refers to "the conditions in the world which must be satisfied if the intentional state is to be satisfied."

utterances. Her risk assessment model presents an advance on mere supposition and opinion by prosecutors about whether a speech act is likely to incite violence.

Benesch's framework also prompts a number of questions. It would be useful to know, for example, whether – and if so, then how exactly – the five criteria are grounded in any empirical research on the causal effects of speech acts, so that the reader might assess the criteria on the basis of rigorous social science studies. Benesch only sparsely references social science research to support her model, even though there are many studies that would support particular elements, for instance, her contention that the authority of the speaker is a substantial factor in persuasion.[95] Other items on her list are unsupported; for instance, dehumanizing language may not be the most likely to incite violence. Social psychological research conducted for this book and presented in Chapter 7 finds that other forms of speech such as revenge speech and references to past atrocities may have more significant measurable effects. Research on inciting speech also points towards other factors not included by Benesch that, according to social psychologists, also demand consideration, such as the role of moral disgust as the mechanism of dehumanization.[96] A central aim of this book is to bring law and social science into dialogue with one another so that the tests created by lawyers to evaluate inciting speech bear some relationship to the present state of social science research on the subject.

Additionally, Benesch's model for evaluating speech acts merits further evaluation because recent empirical social science studies have cast doubt upon the international tribunal's account of the role of the media in 1994 Rwanda.[97] On the basis of 100 interviews of convicted perpetrators in a Kigali prison, Rwandan cultural anthropologist Charles Mironko (2007:125, 129–30) found that many ordinary villagers either did not receive genocidal radio transmissions or did not interpret them in the way they were intended. Mironko (2007:134) therefore urges caution in ascribing a causal link between RTLM broadcasts and genocidal killings: "[T]his information <u>alone</u> did not cause them to kill." Scott Straus's (2006, 2007) quantitative study of the relationship between radio and violence in Rwanda both corroborates and extends Mironko's study. Straus (2007:616–20, 622) identifies a number of flaws in the ICTR's reasoning and fact-finding:

---

[95] On authority and the behavior of subordinates, see Milgram (1974) and Zimbardo (2007).
[96] See, for example, Harris and Fiske (2011).   [97] See, for example, Carver (2000).

RLTM's coverage was very uneven, especially in rural areas, and only ten percent of the population owned a radio in 1994; the initial violence did not correspond with areas of broadcast coverage, and the most extreme and inflammatory broadcasts came after most of the killings had been carried out. Straus (2007:626) complements his quantitative analysis with 200 perpetrator interviews, and these revealed that radio listeners did not necessarily internalize the elements of anti-Tutsi rhetoric. Perhaps most crucially, no respondent cited the radio broadcasts as the most important reason for their participation in the genocide.

Both Mironko's (2007) and Straus's (2007:628–9) respondents reported that that peer pressure from male neighbors and kin exerted more influence on their decision to participate in the killing than did government and radio broadcasts.[98] In concurrence with Mironko, Straus (2007:631) infers that the radio broadcasts functioned as a device to coordinate attacks and were meant primarily for local authorities, who played the main role in mobilizing citizens directly: "Radio did not cause the genocide or have direct, massive effects. Rather, radio emboldened hard-liners and reinforced face-to-face mobilization." Richard Carver (2000:190–1), an expert on Africa formerly employed by Amnesty International and Human Rights Watch, comprehends the Rwandan genocide as prearranged by Hutu hardliners in conjunction with their militias, rather than incited by RTLM broadcasters,

> [A]ll the evidence is that the genocide was a meticulously planned and well-organized affair, with the Hutu extremist militias acting under strict orders according to a prearranged strategy. The apparatus of militias, hit squads, arms caches and death lists was put in place in the months before April 1994. In other words, the radio may have produced propaganda for the genocide but it did not incite it.

Carver (2000:190) questions the causal relationship established by observers and the ICTR, "Most commentary on Rwandan hate radio has worked on the simple assumption that since RTLM broadcast propaganda for genocide did indeed occur, there must have been a causal relationship between the two." Nevertheless, he asserts that "The massacres would have taken place with or without the RTLM broadcasts" (p. 192). This body of research offers quite a different model of violence than that asserted by the ICTR judges: instead of positing

[98] See also the work of psychologists Harris and Fiske (2011).

52

a direct and causal relationship between leaders' speeches and genocidal acts, it points towards an indirect and enabling role, in which political speeches and radio broadcasts created an atmosphere of popular tolerance for mass atrocities, and constituted a form of nationwide communication between elites, who then recruited followers on a personal or kin basis. In Mironko's and Straus's studies, inciting speech was a background condition rather than a necessary or sufficient cause of the genocide.

There also exists a smaller body of social science research confirming a more substantial connection between the media and genocide in Rwanda. Economist David Yanagizawa-Drott (2014), the only social science researcher cited by Benesch, claims that RTLM coverage increased participation in violence by a statistically significant margin. Media effects were most marked where the Hutu population was large and the Tutsi population relatively small,[99] and where a village or town had full, rather than partial, radio coverage.[100] There were also spillover effects – such that full radio coverage in one village increased participation in surrounding villages. RTLM emerges in this study as a significant driver of genocidal violence. Yanagizawa-Drott (2014:43) estimates that the radio broadcasts caused approximately ten percent of overall popular participation and one-third of violence by militias and other armed groups. Using a qualitative methodology, the ethnographic research of Darryl Li (2004) largely corroborates aspects of Yanagizawa-Drott's findings regarding mass participation in genocide. At this point, we can only reliably say that the empirical evidence on the effects of incitement is mixed, although we now know enough to approach with circumspection ICTR judges' forceful claims about a direct causal connection between speech acts and violence.

In evaluating Benesch's model, other questions arise related to the adversarial process of the international criminal courtroom. If the prosecution is to build its theory of an incitement case on probable causation, then it is not at all evident what type and threshold of probability the prosecution is aiming for. The standard of causation for international speech crimes is the subject of the next chapter, but here it is worth simply noting that ICTR case law has set the threshold of proving causation for incitement to genocide quite a bit lower than the conventional *sine qua non* or "but-for" standard of causation in

---

[99] Yanagizawa-Drott (2014:41).   [100] *Ibid.*, p.32.

criminal law.[101] Under the "but-for" standard, the defendant's conduct is a cause in fact of the particular prohibited result if the result would not have occurred in the absence of the defendant's conduct.[102] No international criminal tribunal has yet provided a definitive statement on how a standard of probable causation could, in incitement to commit genocide cases, relate to the general criminal law requirement to prove a crime beyond a reasonable doubt. Until it does, we are in uncharted waters.

Additionally, Benesch's matrix is explicitly designed as a tool of analysis to guide the prosecution in identifying the crime of incitement to genocide. But if it can confirm incitement, then so, too, must it be able to refute incitement if it aspires to be a testable and verifiable theory. However, Benesch does not elaborate on the conditions under which a particular speech act would *not* meet the requirements for incitement to genocide, and this suggests a worrying potential bias in the model. The proposed framework appears overly directed towards making a finding of incitement to genocide: it leads the user into a spectrum of criminal liability where the answer to the question, "Does this particular speech act constitute direct and public incitement to commit genocide?" will likely vary from "a little bit" to "a lot." Benesch does not assist a court to identify the conditions in which the response might be "not at all." In addition, it is a cause for concern that Benesch does not acknowledge how the context can cut both ways, and how listeners may hear an inciting message, but reject it and turn away.

If Benesch's model is consciously designed to guide the prosecution at an international tribunal, then we can expect it to be challenged by defense counsel as neither neutral nor objective. Experienced criminal

---

[101] International criminal tribunals do not apply the "but-for" test of causation as a matter of course. This is generally stated in *Kordić and Čerkez* TC §391. Reviewing key speech crimes cases such as *Nahimana* AC we learn that for indirect modes of liability such as instigation: "The *actus reus* of instigating implies prompting another person to commit an offense. It is not necessary to prove that the crime would not have been perpetrated without the involvement of the accused" (§480). This position on the *actus reus* of instigation was refined further in *Blaškić* TC: "Although it must be proved that the instigation was a clear contributing factor to the commission of the crime, it need not be a *conditio sine qua non*" (§270).

[102] Moenssens (2003) observes that in rare instances if the "but-for" test of causation-in-fact fails, then US criminal courts may use a "substantial factor" test in which, for instance, two separate defendants acting independently, commit two separate acts, each of which alone will not bring about the prohibited result, but when considered together, will. See also *Velazquez v. State*. District Court of Appeal of Florida, 1990. 561 So.2d 347. Turner (1958:18) traces the origins of the "but-for" test to an 1874 English manslaughter/murder case, *R. v. Towers* (1987) 12 Cox 530 (T.A.C.). See Moenssens, (2003:119); Dressler and Garvey (2012).

defense attorneys may reasonably ask a series of thorny questions such as, "Why should a court or international body use these five criteria and not another five? Are not these criteria avowedly created to assist the prosecution side of the case, and would this not lead defense counsel and possibly the court to question their neutrality and objectivity? How are these criteria grounded in legal precedent, and – invoking the *Frye* test ... to what degree are they accepted within a community of scholars who study persuasive speech and political communication?"[103]

My concern is that Benesch proposes a model that aims to be predictive of risk, without actually being testable. A probabilistic framework needs to clearly identify the threshold of probability to be employed, as well as its criteria of falsifiability, and Benesch's model does neither. In this way, it suffers from the same ambiguity that afflicts ICTR rulings: while the *Akayesu* Trial Chamber requires proof of a "possible causal link," Benesch (2012:256) proposes a similar method that relies upon "the likelihood that the speech could have caused genocide."[104] Insofar as Benesch does not explain how her model is testable and falsifiable on an evidentiary basis, it occupies the same uncomfortable halfway house of potential causation as the ICTR decisions themselves. This book reviews the social science of persuasion and political communication in detail in Chapter 7 and conducts original research using the speeches of an accused at the ICTY, and proposes a testable risk assessment model in Chapter 8.

Instead of being concerned with likely causation and immediacy (as we find in *Brandenburg* and Benesch), we might instead refocus on the intentionality of the speaker and how intention is expressed in the utterance itself. This time-honored approach was advocated by US jurists Learned Hand at a time in US history (the First World War and its aftermath) when legal constraints on inciting speech were being hotly debated. Hand wrote a letter on 8 January 1920 to Zecharaiah Chaffee, Harvard law professor and author of a law review article on "Freedom of Speech in War Time," in which he held that:

> The State ... must regard with disapproval all conduct which tends to produce a violation of its laws. It may, and in my judgment must, permit a great deal of such conduct-utterances ... notwithstanding the probability that it may produce a violation of law. This toleration, however, depends upon the fact that the utterances in question may have some

---

[103] *Frye v. United States*, 293 F. 1013 (D.C. Cir. 1923).
[104] The citation to the quote in the Akayesu case is *Akayesu* TC §349.

other result than to produce the evil against which the law is directed. Utterances which can have no other results than to do this may be unconditionally forbidden . . . the test of immediacy and directness . . . is not strictly speaking correct; I say this with genuine diffidence. I prefer a test based upon the nature of the utterance itself.[105]

2.6 THE NATURE OF THE UTTERANCE ITSELF: INCITEMENT AND AUSTIN'S THEORY OF SPEECH ACTS

There is something which is at the moment of uttering being done by the person uttering.

J. L. Austin (1962:60)

Scholars typically define or categorize inchoate crimes only in the negative, as crimes that are not consummate, and even this distinction is unexplained. What is needed instead is an affirmative account of the inchoate category. . . a conceptual framework to support the claim or intuition that recognizing this category is useful.

Michael T. Cahill (2012:751, 754)

Cahill's quote is symptomatic of the critical legal commentary on inchoate crimes, which are often considered by legal scholars to be theoretically wobbly compared with completed or "consummated" crimes. Over seven decades at international tribunals from Nuremberg to the International Criminal Court, defendants charged with inchoate speech crimes are often acquitted, in part due to the conceptual frailty of the crimes.[106] Even when the accused is convicted, the incomplete nature of inchoate crimes makes them vulnerable to logical fallacies and eccentric judicial reasoning. As we have seen at the ICTR, when international criminal tribunal judges are presented with evidence regarding the causal effects of inciting speech, they seemingly cannot resist invoking them in their factual findings, and they even weave causation and consequences into the fabric of their legal reasoning about inchoate crimes.

Taking up Cahill's challenge, international law still lacks a proper philosophical grounding for direct and public incitement to commit genocide. In resolving the confusion surrounding causation in the international law of incitement to genocide, I turn to the theories of

[105] Quoted in Jordan (2013:83–4).
[106] Including Fritzsche at Nuremberg and Šešelj at the ICTY.

British philosopher of language J. L. Austin. As one of the more influential philosophers of the twentieth century, the literature on Austin's theory of speech acts is too vast to review here, yet fortunately some excellent retrospectives of his work are available.[107] In my engagement with speech act theory, I primarily rely upon Austin's own writings, augmented by those of John Searle, the leading modern proponent of Austin's philosophy.

Austin's theory of speech acts disaggregates three aspects of each utterance and orders them chronologically. By breaking a speech act into three dimensions, we can differentiate the aspects of the meaning and the persuasive force from the subsequent effects of a speech act. By differentiating the meaning and persuasive force dimensions from any presumed consequences, we can see how an inchoate speech crime like incitement to commit genocide might pertain to what a speaker meant and what he was encouraging others to do, rather than the consequences of his or her words. What matters are the content and force of a speech act, rather than its subsequent effects in the world, an emphasis intended to suppress incitement to genocide and thereby assist in the prevention of genocide. Subsequent effects of the inciting speech act, including any potential uptake and criminal acts committed by listeners, are only relevant to modes of liability for completed crimes such as ordering, instigating/inducing and aiding and abetting.

Austin's theories are germane to inciting genocide because they have featured prominently in debates on the relationship between language and the law over the last fifty years. Austin had a profound impact on one of the foremost philosophers of law in the twentieth century, H. L. A. Hart, as Nicola Lacey (2004:133) has noted. Hart and Austin were at Oxford at the same time and Hart (1961:vii) acknowledged Austin's influence on his thinking in the preface of his groundbreaking book, *The Concept of Law*.[108] More recently in the United States, speech act theory has featured prominently in the writings of feminist legal scholars seeking to establish ordinances recognizing pornography as a civil rights violation.[109] Austin has inspired many advocates of heightened legal regulation of hate speech. For example,

---

[107] See, for example, Gustafsson and Sørli (2011); Loxley (2007). For classic philosophical texts inspired by Austin, see Cavell (2005:177–98), Goodman (2005), Cavell (1979), Grice (1986), and Searle (1969).

[108] For an application of ordinary language philosophy to the law generally, and criminal law in particular, see Constable (2014:1–2, 138–40) and Yeager (2006:137–9).

[109] See, example, MacKinnon (1993); Langton (1993:293).

in his influential book *Speech, Crime, and the Uses of Language*, Kent Greenawalt (1989:57–9) observes that some kinds of speech go beyond mere assertions of fact and, in threatening, ordering or exhorting, become "situation-altering utterances" that change the social context in which we live. Given their practical and decisive effects, such as changing a person's status, or enforcing contractual obligations, Greenawalt (1989:58) argues that some such utterances lie outside the scope of the principle of free speech and therefore are "subject to regulation on the same bases as most non-communicative behavior."[110]

While they might be similar in some ways – that is, they are forms of speech that cause or may have the potential to cause harm *per se* – hate speech, pornography and inciting genocide are quite distinct as categories of criminal law. Direct and public incitement to commit genocide is always and everywhere illegal and has achieved the *jus cogens* status globally, whereas hate speech and pornography are illegal only to varying degrees, and are legal in many settings. To my knowledge, no scholars of international criminal law have thus far employed speech act theory to analyze the crime of incitement to genocide, which is perhaps surprising given its ubiquity in domestic hate speech debates. Predrag Dojčinović (2012:71–117), a linguist at the ICTY, has creatively applied the theories of John Searle to the mode of liability of instigation, as well as to the crime of hate speech as a form of persecution. However, Austin's theory of speech acts has not yet been employed to distinguish between forms of criminal liability that require proof of criminal outcomes (such as instigating persecution and deportation) and non-causal speech crimes (such as incitement to genocide and hate speech as a form of persecution).

Now, to the argument itself. A direct call for the destruction of a group protected by the 1948 UN Genocide Convention in a public setting, even if utterly ignored by its intended audience, is a criminal act. This type of "genocidal speech" is a crime *per se*, by virtue of what it itself does.[111] Standard theories justify the category of inchoate crimes by conceiving of the proscribed crime as an initial step towards a grievous target crime.[112] In order to provide firmer foundations for these classic criminal law arguments, we need to delve deeper into the

---

[110] Defenders of unfettered free speech such as Franklyn Haiman (1992:1–4) charge Greenawalt with conflating words and deeds, arguing instead that language is largely symbolic and devoid of any subsequent effects. Another renowned critic of the movement to curtail pornography, sexist language and "hate speech" is Stanley Fish (1994).

[111] UN Genocide Convention, Art. 3(c).   [112] See Cahill (2012:754–5).

philosophy of language to grasp how speech acts are specifically acts, and how words do things. We might profitably start with J. L. Austin's (1962) *How to Do Things with Words*, a groundbreaking treatise that transformed both philosophy and linguistics.

Austin was part of a mid-twentieth century movement in the philosophy of language that discovered meaning in concrete usage of language rather than through theories of semantics. Austin's (1962:12) famous credo was, "To *say* something is to *do* something." Austin (1962:100) challenged the "descriptive fallacy" of prevailing philosophical orthodoxy, which held that sentences could be evaluated on the basis of the accuracy of their referential account of the world.[113] Instead, speech acts are acts – deeds in and of themselves – and therefore can be assessed according to what each individual speech act does: that is, according to its function. In *How to Do Things with Words*, Austin draws our attention to a category of language that had been overlooked by the descriptive model of language. In a class of sentences that Austin (1962:6) calls "performative utterances," the utterance is the act itself. Examples include, "I marry you," "I warn you the bull is dangerous," "I apologize," "I find you guilty," "I congratulate you," "I welcome you," and so on.

Austin (1962:94–101) identifies three aspects of performative utterances: the locutionary, the illocutionary and the perlocutionary aspects. The locutionary aspect, or locution, contains the semantic and grammatical attributes that together denote the meaning of a proposition. That is, they convey the utterance as one "with a certain sense and a certain reference" (p. 94). One of the leading modern interpreters of Austin, John Searle (1998:137), glosses the locutionary attribute as the "content of the act... the propositional content."[114] The illocutionary element of a speech act, or illocution, denotes the use or function of the sentence: that is, its force and the degree to which it urges, advises, or orders.[115] Loxley (2007:168) defines the illocutionary force of an utterance as "the function it performs" in, for example, "promising, threatening, ordering, or persuading."

---

[113] Here, Austin got a little carried away. Just because some sentences are performative utterances that achieve a result in their very utterance ("I promise"), does not mean that all sentences are of this kind. John Searle (2010:11–12), Austin's foremost successor in philosophy, accepts that many speech acts aim to match an independent existing reality and can be evaluated on this basis.

[114] In this quote, Searle (p. 137–8) breaks down the "illocutionary act" into two dimensions; the propositional content, which refers to the locutionary aspect, and the type of act it is and the force it has, which refers to the illocutionary aspect.

[115] Austin (1962:98).

Austin (1962:108) dedicates most of his energy in *How to Do Things with Words* to dissecting the illocutionary quality of speech acts such as informing, ordering, warning and threatening: that is, those "utterances which have a certain (conventional) force." Illocutionary acts have been further differentiated by Searle (1998:148–9) into five different types which he terms assertive, directive, commissive, expressive and declarative and the criminal law of inciting speech is primarily concerned with directive illocutionary acts such as orders, commands and requests.

The third or perlocutionary property of a performative utterance, or perlocution, invites analogy to the causation analysis that plagues incitement jurisprudence. A perlocution refers to the consequences that a speech act has for the feelings, thoughts, or actions of a listener.[116] The concrete effects of a perlocution may be, *inter alia*, to convince, persuade, deter, surprise, or mislead.

Austin (1962:116–17) is careful to say that speech acts do not always persuade in the way they are intended, as this depends on the "uptake" by the listener. Austin (1962:14, 101, 106) points out that there may be "[i]nfelicities," or conditions under which performative utterances are unfulfilled or invalid, and that speech acts may also have unintended consequences. Loxley (2007:169) says of the perlocutionary aspects of an utterance: "[T]hey are not predictable or regular." To summarize, then, Austin (1962:122) distinguishes between the three orders of a speech act thus: "the locutionary act... which has a *meaning*; the illocutionary act which has a certain *force* in saying something; the perlocutionary act which is *the achieving of* certain *effects* by saying something." In the argument that follows, I follow attentively Austin's distinctions between the meaning, the force and the effects of a speech act.

Speech act theory is directly applicable to the legal regulation of inciting speech, a fact that Austin (1962:7) was quite cognizant of, observing that performative speech acts comprise the operative or contractual element of a legal instrument that serves to effect an authorized transaction.[117] Furthermore, Austin (1962:57–8) included as "performative utterances" a number of examples that authorize, sanction, warn or threaten, and so it seems fair to include incitement under the general category of illocutionary performative utterances.

---

[116] Loxley (2007:169) defines the perlocutionary aspect as follows: "[t]he perlocutionary aspect of an utterance is any effect it achieves on its hearers or readers that is a consequence of what is said."

[117] One example could be, "Upon my death, I hereby bestow my entire estate to my Schnauzer, Pepper Pot."

The appropriateness of Austin's model of language to incitement to genocide is apparent in the example he used to illustrate the distinction between locutions, illocutions and perlocutions. This is reproduced below, as it appears in the original text:

> Act (A) or Locution
> He said to me "Shoot her!" meaning by "shoot" shoot and referring by "her" to *her*.
> Act (B) or Illocution
> He urged (or advised or ordered, &c.) me to shoot her.
> Act (C.a) or Perlocution
> He persuaded me to shoot her.
> Act (C.b) [or Perlocution]
> He got me to (or made me, &c.) shoot her.[118]

Distinguishing between the three orders of speech acts helps to justify and explain incitement as an inchoate crime, and to provide grounds for my questioning of the causal language that characterizes the ICTR's incitement rulings. Since it is an inchoate crime, intent to commit genocide focuses upon the locutionary and illocutionary aspects of a speech act, not on the perlocutionary dimensions. Notwithstanding ICTR jurisprudence that would suggest otherwise, direct and public incitement to commit genocide criminalizes steps A and B, regardless of, and ideally in advance of and with the aim of preventing, steps C.a. and C.b. In the law of incitement to genocide, the specific intent to commit acts C.a. and C.b. can be found in the logically prior stages A and B.

Moreover, Austin's emphasis on illocutions assists in our comprehension of incitement as a crime that is constituted on the basis of its meaning and what exactly it is urging or encouraging others to do. Parallel arguments have been made with regard to hate speech.[119] One thesis that is directly based on Austin's philosophy of speech acts is advanced by philosopher Rae Langton (1993), who makes the case that pornography is in itself an act of discrimination and therefore constitutes unprotected speech that may be subjected to statutory limitations. Langton (1993:305) emphasizes what she calls *"authoritative* illocutions;"* that is, speech acts whose force can officially justify, promote, condone, and legitimate acts of subordination and discrimination.[120] One such speech act she considers is "Blacks are not permitted to vote,"

---

[118] Austin (1962:101–2).
[119] See, for example, Waldron (2012:4–6); Maravilla (2008); Rikhof (2005:1121, 1126).
[120] See also Benesch (2012:262).

as uttered by a legislator in apartheid South Africa.[121] In this instance, Langton (1993:304) observes that "[t]he authoritative role of the speaker imbues the utterance with a force that would be absent were it made by someone who did not occupy that role." Langton helps us to understand how inciting genocide is a crime because of what it *itself* does: namely to legitimate, authorize and condone genocidal behavior.

Speech act theory conventionally draws sharp lines among the meaning, the force and the effects of a speech act. To what degree are these three orders in fact distinct and chronological? Austin's illustration of an inciting speech act above presents the three orders sequentially, listing them as "A, B, C.a, C.b" and indicating a series progression. It stands to reason that locutions precede perlocutions, since logically a proposition cannot have a consequence until a listener has heard and comprehended the proposition. However, the locutionary and illocutionary aspects of a speech act may occur almost simultaneously; the propositional content and the force may be conveyed in the same moment. Similarly, some speech acts may have aftereffects that arrive within moments of, or even simultaneously with, the statement itself. For instance, a listener might be convinced or repelled by an inciting utterance in the instant that it is delivered – although again, since humans are not simple automatons, they may come to question and even repudiate their initial response.

Refocusing on the conundrum of the role of causation in incitement to genocide helps to resolve these matters somewhat. While morally reprehensible, simply believing that the speaker is justified in his or her public and direct call for genocide is not in itself a crime under international criminal law, which does not proscribe mere thoughts. All the specifically criminal perlocutions which may or may not follow an inciting speech act (for example, extermination or deportation of a protected group, in whole or in part) must both logically and practically come after the utterance is completed. Therefore, while some perlocutions could be more or less simultaneous with illocutions, all specifically *criminal* perlocutions, and especially those which require widespread and systematic collective orchestration such as genocide, logically occur after locutions and illocutions.

Austin's (1962:23, 111) writings provide firm foundations for this interpretation, and he insists at various points on the distinction between the performative utterance and its consequences, stating, "We have then to draw the line between an action we do (here an

---

[121] Langton (1993:304).

illocution) and its consequences." Austin (1962:112) asserts there is "a break at a certain regular point between the act (our saying something) and its consequences (which are usually not the *saying* of anything)," and he finds a "regular natural break in the chain" between illocutions and their consequences (p. 113). While Austin accepts that a connection may be identified between a speech act and its physical consequences, this chain of causation "does not seem to prevent the drawing of a line... between the completion of the illocutionary act and all consequences thereafter" (p. 114). Additionally, Austin's logical distinction between the meaning and force of a speech act on the one hand, and their consequences on the other, is endorsed in the post-Austin philosophical literature, with Searle (2010:136) reaffirming that "[w]e need to distinguish illocutionary acts... from the effects or consequences that illocutionary acts have on hearers."

More remains to be said about how speech act theory relates to criminal intention. The speaker's intention is the ultimate issue in an incitement trial, and it is standard orthodoxy in both speech act theory and the law of inchoate crimes[122] that the subjective intention of the speaker can be found in what Austin terms the locutionary and illocutionary attributes of an utterance. Searle (2010:137–9) draws our attention to the "theory of intentionality" built into the distinction between the locutionary, illocutionary and perlocutionary aspects of a speech act – in which the speaker's intention is concentrated in the meaning and force of a speech act, and not in its effects, which are unpredictable and heavily dependent on the disposition and subsequent behavior of the listener. Searle (2010:137) writes:

> Typically, illocutionary acts have to be performed intentionally. If you did not intend to make a promise or statement, then you did not make a promise or statement. But perlocutionary acts do not have to be performed intentionally... The fact that illocutionary acts are essentially intentional, whereas perlocutionary acts may or may not be intentional, is a consequence of the fact that the illocutionary act is the unit of *meaning* in communication... Illocutionary acts, meaning, and intention are all tied together.

Only the locutionary and illocutionary aspects of the speech act are entirely under the control of the speaker. Where direct and public incitement is charged, only the utterances of the speaker can justifiably

---

[122] On *mens rea* for inchoate crimes, see Alexander and Kessler (1997).

come under legal scrutiny for the evidence they might contain of intention to commit genocide. In most situations, the hearer may decide whether the illocutionary force of a statement is convincing or not, and even if it is persuasive, then the listener still can decide not to act. Context and the nature of the speaker–listener relationship matters here. When the speaker is a civilian politician or radio broadcaster speaking in the media to the general public, perlocutions are not under the control of the speaker. As John Searle (2010:190) observes, with speech acts where the listener is not coerced, "the perlocutionary effects on the hearer are in large part up to the hearer."

The situation is more complicated when the listener is constrained, as when a superior issues an order to a subordinate in the command and control structure of a military unit. There are a range of punitive sanctions to ensure that the intention of the superior becomes the intention of the subordinate and as an example, the US Army's *Uniform Code of Military Justice*, under "10. Punitive Articles," includes the following violations of the code: desertion (885.85), disrespect towards superior commissioned officer (889.89), and failure to obey an order or regulation (892. 92). As a result, perlocutions follow on strongly from locutions and illocutions in the military setting, which is why a superior officer adding, "and that's an order" to his or her request has such illocutionary force. I address the difference between the speech contexts of the two modes of liability of "instigating" (where the speaker need not be in a hierarchical relationship) and "ordering" (where the speaker is a commanding officer) in the final chapter.

If an international court does not distinguish between the three aspects of a speech act, then it may be prone to mistaken suppositions about where the intention of speech acts lies. Dressler's (2009:185) *Understanding Criminal Law* observes that actual causation and *mens rea* (criminal intention) are "independent concepts, each of which must be proven in criminal prosecution. Frequently, however, these doctrines are confused." Motivated by a similar aim to separate intentions from outcomes, Austin (1962:106) exhorted us to distinguish between the intended and unintended consequences of speech acts:

> Since our acts are actions, we must always remember the distinction between producing effects or consequences which are intended or unin-tended; and (i) when the speaker intends to produce an effect it may nevertheless not occur, and (ii) when he does not intend to produce it, it may nevertheless occur.

Sociolinguist Roger Shuy (2005:4) documents extensively how overzealous US prosecutors regularly manipulate language evidence (including in solicitation to murder cases) to construct the illusion that the defendant has committed a crime. Once the evidence is subjected to closer scrutiny by a professional linguist, the allegation is often not supported. A famous case from the United Kingdom where a defendant was convicted and hanged on the basis of ambiguous speech illustrates how perlocutions can be a false guide to meaning and intention. In 1953, British teenager Derek Bentley was hanged for the murder of a police officer during a burglary attempt, even though the officer was shot by Bentley's friend and accomplice, Christopher Craig, then aged 16.[123] When confronted by police officers during the burglary of a warehouse, Bentley was alleged to have called out to Craig, "Let him have it, Chris." Bentley, who did not possess a gun, was at that moment overpowered and docile, and he had warned police about the dangerous mental state of his accomplice. Fifteen minutes later, after Bentley had already been arrested and handcuffed, Craig shot Police Constable Sidney Miles dead while resisting arrest.

The prosecutor's opening words claimed that Bentley "incited Craig to begin the shooting and, although technically under arrest at the actual time of the killing of Miles, was party to that murder and equally responsible in law."[124] The jury, as directed by Judge Goddard in his summing up, interpreted Bentley's "Let him have it" statement as deliberate incitement to murder rather than a call to surrender the weapon, a line of reasoning based in part upon the actual outcome.[125] Over time, however, the British legal establishment found fault with Judge Goddard's direction to the jury regarding Bentley's alleged incitement.[126] The Bentley case became a cause célèbre in the eventually successful campaign to ban the death penalty in Great Britain. In 1998, Derek Bentley was granted a posthumous pardon by the highest criminal appeals court in England and Wales.[127]

Austin's framework also has implications for the directness aspect of the crime of direct and public incitement to commit genocide. Krauss and Chiu (1997:44) write, "When the locutionary and illocutionary force of an utterance (that is, its literal and intended meaning) are the same, the result is termed a *direct speech act*; when an utterance's locutionary and illocutionary force are different. . . the result is termed

---

[123] *R v. Derek William Bentley*, [2001] 1 Crim. App. R. 307 (Eng.), hereinafter *Bentley*.
[124] *Bentley*, §1. [125] *Bentley*, §II(3). [126] And the standard of proof applied in the case.
[127] Campbell (1998).

an *indirect speech act.*" So, for the incitement to be direct, the meaning and force of the utterance must coincide. If the two are not aligned in this way, then the speech act is indirect – which, depending on the facts, may be reprehensible and constitute a moral transgression or even another international crime (such as persecution as a crime against humanity) – but falls short of inciting genocide.

The distinction between direct and indirect speech acts has practical applications in the criminal law. The ICTR Trial Chamber erroneously cited an indirect speech act by Prime Minister Jean Kambanda as evidence of his direct and public incitement to commit genocide; "you refuse to give your blood to your country and the dogs drink it for nothing."[128] This statement, while repugnant, does not, in my view constitute incitement to genocide since it does not make a call for violence, much less genocide, against a protected group. It is a bloodthirsty but familiar wartime exhortation from a politician that the citizens of one's country are being murdered by an external aggressor and the situation calls for sacrifice, including the blood of those citizens fighting the aggressor. Again, the speech act may be morally objectionable and even criminal under certain circumstances, but the relevant category of crime in international law does not appear to be direct and public incitement to commit genocide. The implication of Austin's philosophy of speech acts for international criminal law is to narrow the range of impermissible statements to those that are comparable to Julius Streicher's "The Jews in Russia must be killed. They must be exterminated root and branch,"[129] or ICTR defendant Augustin Ngirabatware's "kill Tutsis" or Simon Bikindi's public address to "exterminate quickly"[130] the minority Tutsis.

Limiting the range of utterances that would qualify as incitement does not *a priori* exclude euphemisms,[131] if the prosecution can show that the overwhelming majority of listeners understood a euphemistic form of speech as a direct (rather than circuitous, oblique or veiled) call to commit genocide.[132] Readers familiar with the hate speech literature

---

[128] *Kambanda* TC §39(x).   [129] *Nuremberg Judgment and Sentences*, §295.
[130] *Bikindi* TC §266.
[131] *Bikindi* TC discusses the use of euphemisms such as "accomplices" and "cockroaches" during inciting radio broadcasts: "A reading of the RTLM transcripts reveals assimilation between the Inkotanyi – designation used for the 'enemy,' the Rwandan Patriotic Front (RPF) – and, on some occasions, the Tutsi ethnic group. It also reveals that the derogatory term 'Inyenzi,' meaning cockroach, was used for the assailants and, more generally, the Tutsi ethnic group. From April to June 1994, RTLM journalists called on listeners to seek out and take up arms against Inkotanyi and Inyenzi, the RPF, and its 'accomplices,' the Tutsi ethnic group" (§114).
[132] Mere comprehension is not in itself a perlocutionary aspect of an utterance, it is simply an indication that the locutionary and illocutionary aspects have been heard and understood by

in the United States might find this outcome somewhat surprising, since advocates of hate speech regulation such as Greenawalt (1989: 57–9) and Langton (1993) have tended to use ordinary language philosophy to expand the range of speech acts not protected by the First Amendment to the US Constitution. In the international law of incitement to genocide, speech act theory has the reverse effect as a result of the uniqueness of the specific intent element of the crime of genocide. While references to causation in the incitement to genocide judgments of the ICTR Trial Chamber have compendiously widened the scope of utterances that would qualify as inciting genocide, speech act theory narrows the aperture.

2.7   CAUSATION IN COMPLETED SPEECH CRIMES

Thus far, I have sought to demonstrate the relevance of J. L. Austin's speech act theory for international courts tasked with determining whether the crime of incitement to genocide has occurred. An international court can find evidence of specific intent in the locutionary and illocutionary aspects of the utterances of the accused, and not in their consequences. This shift in emphasis has a number of ramifications, the first being that it augurs a move towards prevention – and the possible emergence of international criminal tribunals as a mechanism of proscribing early calls for genocide by political leaders, and thereby standing a better chance of preventing humanitarian catastrophes.

If the clarifications given here regarding causation are persuasive, then what about situations where an individual encourages an audience to commit genocide and then the crime of genocide actually occurs, and where prosecutors possess clear and compelling evidence that certain speech acts led to specific criminal acts that may amount to genocide? My recommendation is that prosecutors and judges refrain from attempting to incorporate the perlocutionary aspects of speech acts into the category of incitement to genocide. Instead, they are advised to charge separate modes of criminal liability in international criminal law that are more appropriate for completed crimes. I refer specifically to aiding and abetting, instigating/inducing/soliciting, joint criminal enterprise (JCE), co-perpetration and ordering.[133]

---

the listener. Perlocutions entail responses, that is, being convinced, taking alarm, and in Austin's view, mostly the undertaking of non-verbal physical actions.

[133] International criminal law defines and differentiates planning, instigating, ordering and aiding and abetting in a number of places, including the *Brđanin* Trial Judgment. *Brđanin*

The need for consummation of the underlying crime distinguishes these crimes unambiguously from direct and public incitement to commit genocide. In international law there is no dispute that each of these modes of liability require that the crime be completed or attempted. Article 25 of the 1998 Rome Statute of the International Criminal Court, which addresses individual criminal responsibility, states:

> 3. . . [A] person shall be criminally responsible and liable for punishment for a crime within the jurisdiction of the Court if that person: . . .
> (b) Orders, solicits or induces the commission of such a crime which in fact occurs or is attempted;
> (c) For the purpose of facilitating the commission of such a crime, aids, abets, or otherwise assists in its commission or its attempted commission, including providing the means for its commission.[134]

Note the reference to "a crime which in fact occurs or is attempted": in each instance the assistance, support, command, encouragement, or solicitation must have a defined perlocutionary dimension: that is, an effect on the commission of the offense commensurate with the mode of liability charged.[135] Where genocide is in fact carried out, or a serious attempt is made to commit genocide, a range of modes of liability may apply – running the gamut from high (e.g., ordering) to low (e.g., aiding and abetting) levels of criminal responsibility.[136]

The majority of defendants at the ICTR charged with inciting genocide were also charged with the completed crime of instigating genocide and crimes against humanity. Instigating is a type of criminal responsibility that is commonly glossed as "prompting another to commit an offense" and which is conceptually related to incitement.[137] In US criminal law, instigation and incitement are routinely equated and subsumed under the wider crime of "solicitation."[138] By creating

TC §267–74. The literature on international criminal law's "modes of liability" is vast, and one might start with chapters 9–11 of Antonio Cassese's (2013) International Criminal Law.

[134] Rome Statute of the International Criminal Court art. 25.3(b)–(c), 17 July 1998, 2187 U.N.T.S. 90).

[135] See Cassese (2013:214).

[136] Here, I do not include the mode of liability of JCE on the grounds that, following Schabas's (2009:355) lead, "the role of joint criminal enterprise complicity in genocide has to date remained largely theoretical. . . any genuine utility of joint criminal enterprise in genocide prosecutions remains unproven."

[137] *Nahimana* AC §480. See Agbor (2013) on instigation jurisprudence at the ICTR.

[138] In the American Law Institute's Model Penal Code, a person is guilty of the crime of solicitation if "he commands, encourages or requests another person to engage in conduct which would constitute such crime or an attempt to commit such crime or would establish his complicity in its commission or attempted commission." Model Penal Code § 5.02(1) (1985).

two distinct categories, international tribunals have differentiated incitement from instigation, defining the former as a direct and public inciting speech act, whereas the latter may take many forms (that is, not only speech) and may be expressed or implied, private or public.[139] In all cases, the instigation must have substantially contributed to the physical element of the crime, and the *Brđanin* Trial Judgment demands that "[t]he *nexus* between instigation and perpetration requires proof."[140] Causality is a central element of instigation; the ICTY Trial Chamber in *Blaškić* stated that "[t]he essence of instigating is that the accused causes another person to commit a crime."[141]

Even though there are clear grounds upon which to separate inchoate speech crimes such as incitement from modes of criminal liability for completed crimes such as instigating, the genocide case law of the ICTR has unfortunately conflated incitement and instigation. Timmermann (2006:840) points out this confusion, noting that incitement to genocide is defined in terms of instigation in two cases at the ICTR: the Trial Chamber in *Rutaganda* and *Musema* opined that "incitement... involves instigating another, directly and publicly, to commit an offense."[142] This statement is misguided because instigation is not a crime but rather a form of responsibility for manifold different crimes, whereas incitement to genocide is a crime in and of itself.[143] Timmermann (2006:848–50) recalls that German law and Swiss law sharply differentiate incitement and instigation, and both domestic systems define incitement as an inchoate crime and instigation as a mode of liability for crimes that are attempted or completed.

To be clear: while I have sought to clarify the confusion on causation for the inchoate crime of direct and public incitement to commit genocide, causation is absolutely necessary for the modes of liability for consummated crimes.[144] Of course, the devil is in the details, and I do not presume that it

[139] In distinguishing between instigation as a mode of liability and incitement as an inchoate crime, ICTR judges declared in *Prosecutor v. Kalimanzira*, Trial Chamber Judgement, ICTR-05–88-T, 20 June 2009, §512, "Instigation under Article 6 (1) is a mode of liability; an accused will incur criminal responsibility only if the instigation in fact substantially contributed to the commission of one of the crimes under Articles 2 to 4 of the Statute. By contrast, direct and public incitement is itself a crime, requiring no demonstration that it in fact contributed in any way to the commission of acts of genocide."

[140] *Brđanin* TC §269. On instigation in international criminal law, see Cryer et al. (2014:376–9).

[141] *Blaskić* TC §270.

[142] Referencing *Rutaganda* TC §38; *Musema* TC §120. This point is also noted by Agbor (2013:23).

[143] *Kalimanzira* TC §512.

[144] Where speech crimes are alleged, prosecutors may indict either the inchoate crime (incitement to genocide) or the consummated crime (e.g., instigating genocide), but not both

is a straightforward matter to connect an inciting speech act to a criminal offense in any actual criminal case before an international criminal tribunal. To the contrary, as we will see in subsequent chapters. Causation has been defined in centuries of criminal law and jurisprudence, and genocide convictions for speech acts using a "completion" mode of liability (e.g., aiding and abetting, inducing, instigating, JCE, ordering, soliciting) must satisfy the standard conventions of criminal law and prove their case beyond reasonable doubt. For an illocutionary act to be effective, the speaker must, in Austin's (1962:117–18) words, "secure uptake" of the audience – wherein the audience members comprehend what the speaker is urging or ordering them to do, and are successfully persuaded to act to achieve the speaker's intended goal. To function as intended, a speech act must go beyond the locutionary and illocutionary aspects and have demonstrable perlocutionary effects. Whether this occurs depends upon context and convention, requiring "the uttering of certain words by certain persons in certain circumstances" (Austin 1962:14).[145] Langton (1993:301) correctly notes that "the context determines the uptake secured," and Chapter 7 on the social science of persuasion addresses the influence of context on the uptake of inciting speech acts.

In sum, the ICTR confounded matters by introducing causation into its jurisprudence on an inchoate crime, direct and public incitement to commit genocide, and the ICC Statute has only compounded the confusion. The nexus requirement is, however, an essential element of modes of liability in completed crimes such as instigating genocide. The prevailing international criminal law of incitement to genocide is problematic for a number of reasons, and I have sought to clarify matters using Austin's ordinary language philosophy. Performative speech acts are acts, and they can be evaluated according to what they mean, what they encourage others to do and what corollaries they have. In what they mean and what they urge, certain speech acts can be criminal acts in and of themselves.

---

simultaneously. Citing the US Model Penal Code, Cahill (2012:753) observes that most criminal codes "prohibit imposition of liability for both an inchoate crime and the target offense of that crime."

[145] Austin (1962:23) uses the naming of a ship as an example, and explains that the person naming a ship must be authorized to do so. He illustrates this by reflecting that if he himself walked idly by a ship and named it the "Mr. Stalin," it would be an ineffective speech act, since it was not uttered by the right person in the right circumstances.

CHAPTER THREE

CAUSATION IN INTERNATIONAL SPEECH CRIMES

3.1 INTRODUCTION

> [T]he word "cause" is so inextricably bound up with misleading associations as to make its complete extrusion from the philosophical vocabulary desirable.
>
> Bertrand Russell (1965:163)

Whereas inchoate speech crimes rely on proof of the criminal intention (or *mens rea*) contained in the speech act itself, completed crimes require a cause-and-effect relationship between the speech acts of the accused and the target crime(s). Establishing a causal nexus between a speech act and a subsequent criminal act is an essential element when the crime being encouraged is actually committed, and where the defendant is charged with forms of international criminal responsibility such as ordering, instigating/inducing, aiding and abetting and co-perpetrating crimes against humanity, genocide and war crimes.

Demonstrating causation in international speech crimes presents distinct challenges and requires a general understanding of how causation is defined and interpreted in both domestic and international criminal law. In all modern criminal law systems, a crime conventionally has two elements: a mental or subjective element (*mens rea*, or "guilty mind") and a material element (*actus reus*) which refers to the physical part of the crime. *Actus reus* itself has two aspects: the conduct (*actus*) and the harm caused (*reus*). A casual nexus connects the conduct and the harm, fusing them into a single conception.[1] Stated plainly, the challenge for prosecu-tors in cases involving inchoate speech crimes is proving *mens rea*, whereas for completed crimes the challenge is demonstrating *actus reus*. In trials where the accused is charged with, say, instigating crimes against humanity, the stakes are high: if the prosecution is unable to demonstrate beyond a reasonable doubt that there existed an identifiable causal link between a specific speech act and subse-quent felonies, then a court cannot justifiably attribute criminal responsibility to the defendant. Establishing a causal nexus is a complicated matter, and requires a fuller understanding of how international prosecutors construct their theory of a case and what evidence they present to the court to claim that the defendant's words had verifiable and deleterious consequences.

Before we get to that, however, we need to fully understand how causation is defined in both Anglo-American and international crim-inal law, and how each legal system has its own unique tests for determining relations of cause and effect, tests that are unlike any other branch of human knowledge. The next section reviews causation in the common law, in order to establish a basis of comparison with international criminal law. Addressing causation at international tri-bunals is a more involved undertaking, since causation has not been adequately addressed in their judgments. Former international prose-cutor James G. Stewart (2012a:1194) observes correctly, "There is something quite peculiar about international criminal justice as a discipline: causation has escaped direct treatment by almost all courts and scholars." This chapter closely reviews the ways that international law has conceptualized causation so as to better comprehend why the nexus requirement has proved to be such a persistent stumbling block for prosecutors in speech crimes trials.

3.2 CAUSATION IN ANGLO-AMERICAN CRIMINAL LAW

> Nobody cares about criminal law except theorists and habitual criminals.
> Sir Henry Maine[2]

The idea of causation, glossed by philosopher John Searle (1983:112) as "a natural relation between events in the world," is a foundational

---

[1] On *actus reus* and causation, see Dressler and Garvey (2012:127).
[2] Quoted in Dressler and Garvey (2012:465).

concept in law, science, social science and the humanities, yet each discipline has its own formulations and proofs for verifying a relationship of cause and effect.[3] Causation is not only one of the fundamental axioms of law and science, it is arguably an indispensable component of human reasoning more generally.

The academic literature on causation is vast and the discussion that follows must therefore have modest aims, namely to review how causation is construed in domestic Anglo-American criminal law, and to compare and contrast with international criminal law in order to understand the distinctiveness of the latter system. This section may benefit social scientists and others who are unfamiliar with legal conceptions of causation. Despite the emphasis in the Introduction on the benefits of using a legal realist approach to understand legal process, one must grasp enough of the doctrine of municipal and international criminal law to appreciate how legal causation departs from other understandings of cause and effect, say in economics or political science. By understanding the rules of the game and where the areas of doctrinal and procedural uncertainty and ambiguity lie, we can better comprehend the exigencies placed on legal actors, and the strategies they adopt at international tribunals.

For legal scholars, the following discussion offers an analysis of the distinctive features of international criminal law that have thus far not received adequate attention. It is worth noting at the outset that scholarly treatises on international criminal law do not typically engage in extensive comparisons with domestic criminal law, for the reason that international is often seen as operating autonomously in its own separate legal universe.[4] The comparison with Anglo-American criminal law is warranted for several reasons. First, international criminal law was influenced at the outset more by the adversarial system[5] than any other municipal tradition, and common law continues to be regularly cited in judgments and the briefs of the parties in international trials. Second, such a comparison offers a baseline of evaluation. Taking US law into consideration throws into relief both the similarities and distinctiveness of international criminal

---

[3] This discussion relies primarily on Hart and Honoré's (1985) classic text, *Causation in the Law*. On causation in the law, see Robinson and Cahill (2012), and in philosophy, see Paul and Hall (2013). For a magisterial application of analytical philosophy to causation and legal responsibility, see Moore (2009).

[4] There are exceptions to this pattern of course, and one notable exception is Van Schaack and Slye's (2014) excellent textbook *International Criminal Law and Its Enforcement*.

[5] Reasonable minds may differ on this question. The view adopted here is supported by many international law scholars and practitioners (albeit with various qualifications), including, *inter alia*, Langer (2005), Mundis (2001) and Wald (2001, 2004).

law, and holding domestic law in the frame helps to answer the perennial question, "compared to what?" Finally, international judges interviewed for this book often maintain that international and domestic criminal law are not so radically dissimilar, as one reflected:

> Causation in international criminal law is the same as in the domestic setting. We couldn't invent something new here that hadn't been thought of earlier. Sometimes observers want international criminal law to be more new and innovative than it is. Sure, we have joint criminal enterprise (JCE), but most of our law and procedure is the same as you would find in a domestic court.[6]

Questions of cause and effect are central to law everywhere, and are addressed in modern state criminal law under the *actus reus* component, and they denote a causal connection between the defendant's conduct and the end result, usually a harm or injury. Criminal law everywhere is constructed on the concept of causation and could not function in any meaningful way without it. This is reflected in the number of different categories of causation that exist, and Black's Law Dictionary contains definitions for eight different types of cause, from "but-for" cause to "superseding" cause, each with its own specific legal connotations. Causation is such a fundamental feature of the legal environment attorneys inhabit that it is tempting to say that attorneys speak about the many fine gradations of causation with the precision that Inuit speakers of Baffin Island speak about the many types of snow.[7]

In Anglo-American (and, as it happens, German) criminal law, the question of whether a certain conduct is the cause of an injury is bifurcated[8] into two aspects, which criminal courts address sequentially: the material cause and the legal cause. The material cause, or "cause-in-fact," is understood as the actual cause of an event. Establishing cause-in-fact conventionally requires evidence of direct causation that passes the "but-for" or *sine qua non* test,[9] a counterfactual method of proof to identify the cause without which the event could not have occurred: "Under this test, a defendant's conduct is

---

[6] Author interview, 2015.   [7] At least according to Franz Boas.
[8] The American Law Institute's Model Penal Code bifurcates causation into "but-for" and "legal" causation at Section 2.03. For further elucidation of this topic, see Hart and Honoré (1985: 110–4).
[9] English criminal law, from whence common law approaches to causation originate, generally prefers the Latin expression "*conditio sine qua non*." Kenney's *Outlines of Criminal Law* (Turner, 1958:18) traces the origins of the but-for test to an 1874 English manslaughter/murder case, *R. v. Towers* (1987) 12 Cox 530 (T.A.C.).

a cause-in-fact of the prohibited result if the said result would *not* have occurred 'but-for' the defendant's conduct."[10] Ascertaining the but-for cause necessarily involves paring down the tapestry of potential factors to isolate a singular and continuous X→Y→Z sequence of cause and effect. A metaphor commonly used by criminal courts is the "chain of causation," which invokes an image of billiard balls striking one another in succession, or, in the words of Hart and Honoré (1985:72) "a series of single events each of which is dependent upon (would not have occurred without) its predecessor in the 'chain' and so is dependent on the initiating action or event."

The but-for test is the gold standard for determining cause-in-fact, and criminal courts in the common law tradition endeavor to apply it in the first instance. That said, criminal law recognizes at least two major limitations; multiple causation and infinite regress. In situations where a harm or injury is preceded by multiple sufficient conditions and each of a number of separate acts are enough to cause the harm, identifying the *sine qua non* may be impossible, or at least exceedingly difficult. In such circumstances of over-determination, criminal courts may recognize the existence of "multiple causation" or "concurrent sufficient causes."[11] The textbook scenario commonly used to illustrate the dilemmas of multiple causation is one where two hunters are charged with man-slaughter on the basis that the two defendants, acting independently and not in concert with one another, committed two separate acts (i.e., shooting their guns), each of which alone would have been sufficient to inflict mortal injury on a third person walking in the woods.[12]

The predicaments engendered by multiple causation are not confined to law-school hypotheticals, however, and US courts wrestle with multiple causation on a daily basis, especially in incidents of "vehicular homicide" (usually involving drag racing),[13] or death by drug overdose where a number of illicit substances are found in the victim's body and no one substance on its own would likely have caused a fatality.[14] When there exist a number of independent events sufficient to produce

---

[10] *Velazquez v. State.* District Court of Appeal of Florida, 1990. 561 So. 2d 347.

[11] Hart and Honoré (1985:19 *et passim*) and Moore (2009:510–12) discuss the problems that multiple causation raises for singularist theories of a continuous causal chain.

[12] See Dressler (2009:187) on concurrent sufficient causes in US criminal law.

[13] In the negligent vehicular homicide case of Commonwealth v. Berggren (1986), the Massachusetts Supreme Court ruled that state courts will apply the standard of causation employed in tort law.

[14] Although contrary examples can be found, such as the US Supreme Court decision in *Burrage v. United States*, No. 12–7515, a case where a heroin dealer was held criminally liable for the death of one of his clients who had also ingested a large amount of other illegal drugs.

a harm, a criminal court may replace the *sine qua non* standard with the "substantial factor" test, which lowers the threshold of proving causation by asking, simply, was the defendant's act a substantial factor in causing the prohibited result?[15] The substantial-factor test has become routine in torts cases and those criminal cases in which the but-for standard is inappropriate because the harm under scrutiny is the result of two or more separate causal chains.

The second main drawback to the but-for test is that there is no rational cutoff point for allocating responsibility in the chain of causation. US courts noted the problem of infinite regress over one hundred years ago, noting wryly that "a reduction *ad absurdum* may be promptly established by calling to mind that if the injured person had never been born, the injury would not have happened."[16] As a practical necessity, then, Anglo-American criminal courts have felt compelled to identify a limiting or restraining principle so as to exclude those causes that are considered too remote and thereby to constrain criminal liability to the immediate action or actions that produced the injury.

Criminal law handles these limiting theories under the heading of "legal causation." The concept of legal causation in the criminal law is dedicated to one sole function: to assess causes and effects with a view to attributing criminal responsibility, a policy consideration that in reality may have little to do with actual material causation. In considering whether a driver-participant in an illegal drag race can be held criminally liable for the death of another driver-participant, *State v. Petersen* (270 Or. 166, 526 P.2d 1008, 1974) held that "The question of legal causation thus blends into the question of whether we are willing to hold a defendant responsible for a prohibited result. Or, stated differently, *the issue is not causation, it is responsibility*"[17] (my emphasis).

In order to distill criminal liability from a collection of competing causes, US law introduced the notion of "proximate cause." Stated plainly, the proximate cause is the cause *legally* sufficient to establish

---

[15] On the "substantial factor" test, see Dressler and Garvey's *Criminal Law* (2012:213–4). As is the case with many conceptions of causation in criminal law, the substantial factor test is derived from the law of torts. Here the reader might also profitably consult one of the original sources, namely Prosser and Keeton (1984). According to Hart and Honoré (1985:123), Prosser understands substantial factor as a test for cause-in-fact, whereas Hart and Honoré see it as a test for determining proximate cause. Prosser's formulation is conventionally upheld by US appellate court judges (e.g., *Velazquez v. State*. District Court of Appeal of Florida, 1990. 561 So. 2d 347, Section IIA).

[16] *Atlantic Coast Line Railway Company v. Daniels* (1911) 8 Ga. App. 775, 70 SE 203.

[17] Cited in Moenssens (2003:121).

liability.[18] Here, "proximate" denotes an immediate, contiguous or adjacent cause, and generally it refers to cause Y in the causal sequence X→Y→Z, where Z is the resultant harm or injury. However, the proximate cause need not be the last act in a chain of causation, and there are times when causal factor X is identified as the proximate cause. Proximate cause is determined primarily by a legal judgment of the significance of an event, rather than the event's straightforward factual significance. Thus, in the concept of proximate cause, the law's initial pursuit of an unmediated "cause-in-fact" is subordinated to the imperatives of policy, statutes and legislation. Dressler and Garvey's *Cases and Materials in Criminal Law* (2012:219) explains:

> Proximate cause analysis is not a matter of applying hard and fast rules leading to some scientifically "correct" outcome; instead it is an effort by the factfinder to determine, *based on policy considerations or matters of fairness*, whether it is proper to hold the defendant(s) criminally responsible for a prohibited result [emphasis in original].[19]

Which act in a causal sequence constitutes the proximate cause, and how adjacent the act is to the prohibited result is highly variable, and represents "nothing in the facts or in the meaning of causation, but expresses fluctuating legal policy or sentiments of what is just or convenient."[20] Policy, not facticity, is the weathervane of proximate cause. In order to constrain the potentially arbitrary character of proximate cause, US criminal law has refined the concept with a number of special rules and tests.[21] In addition to the substantial factor test, courts have excluded remote and improbable causes by requiring that there be a "reasonable foreseeability" that the action in question would cause the prohibited result or harm.[22] Further, courts may acquit defendants if they

---

[18] On legal causation and proximate cause, see Dressler and Garvey's Criminal Law (2012: 218–24) and Hart and Honoré (1985:86–7, 90 et passim).

[19] Justice Andrews in Palsgraf, the groundbreaking case in the US law of torts is even more blunt: "What do we mean by the word "proximate" is that because of convenience, of public policy, of a rough sense of justice, the law arbitrarily declines to trace a series of events beyond a certain point. This is not logic. It is practical politics."

[20] Hart and Honoré (1985:69).

[21] Moore (2009:107–8) provides a helpful table of proximate cause tests.

[22] *Palsgraf* established the element of foreseeability in proximate cause. See Hart and Honoré (1985:97–8) and Moore (2009:98–9) for philosophical examinations of the foreseeability test. The State of Connecticut Judicial Branch recommends to judges the following standard criminal jury instructions on this topic: "When the result is a foreseeable and natural result of the defendant's conduct, the law considers the chain of legal causation unbroken and holds the defendant criminally responsible." Revised 1 December 2007. www.jud.ct.gov/ji/criminal/Part2/2.6–1.htm#1

can establish the existence of an "intervening cause;" an act or omission between the initial event in the sequence and the resulting injury that breaks the sequence of cause and effect and thereby relieves the defendant of liability.[23]

In formal legal theory, "material (or actual) cause" and "legal cause" are discrete concepts. However, as a practical matter, US criminal courts treat causation as a hybrid, even composite concept that embraces both actual cause and legal cause.[24] For example, the standard criminal jury instructions on proximate cause in homicide cases in the US state of Connecticut include both the but-for and the substantial factor tests, and append an additional concept to this heady mix, "predominating cause:"

> An act or omission to act is a proximate cause of the (death/injuries) when it substantially and materially contributes, in a natural and continuous sequence, unbroken by an efficient, intervening cause, to the (death/injuries). It is a cause without which the (death/injuries) would not have occurred. It is a predominating cause, a substantial factor from which the (death/injuries) follow[s] as a natural, direct and immediate consequence.[25]

Complex formulae for determining criminal causation like this one have provoked objections by a succession of legal commentators, from Leon Green (1927) in the 1920s to present-day scholars such as Richard W. Wright (1985, 1988) and Jane Stapleton (1988, 2001, 2008). These writers maintain that only causally relevant conditions that pass the stringent but-for test are genuinely causal. All else is policy, and therefore not directly causal, and to call it so is inaccurate and misleading. In the words of Wright (1985:1737), "the misleading label of 'proximate cause' or 'legal cause,' served as a smokescreen for policy judgments on whether the defendant ought to be held liable for an injury to which his conduct had clearly contributed."

While the concepts developed to determine legal causation attract the most criticism, even the most common tests for material causation are not insulated from challenge, and not only from within the academy. The substantial factor test has been increasingly disputed, and the influential American Law Institute has declared that,

---

[23] On intervening and superseding causes, see *People v. Acosta*, 284 Cal. Rptr. 117 (1991).

[24] The US Supreme Court opinion in *Burrage v. United States* (at III.A.) states, "The law has long considered causation a hybrid concept, consisting of two constituent parts: actual cause and legal cause."

[25] Citing *State v. Griffin*, 251 Conn. 671, 712–13 n. 17 (1999). Criminal jury instructions on 2.6-1 "Proximate Cause" are issued by the State of Connecticut Judicial Branch. Version revised 1 December 2007. www.jud.ct.gov/ji/criminal/Part2/2.6-1.htm#1

"The substantial-factor test has not, however, withstood the test of time, as it has proved confusing and been misused," and it recommends adherence to the more widely accepted and comparatively more straightforward but-for standard.[26] Causation has been an "especially troublesome"[27] matter for domestic courts, and the inconsistencies in international criminal law are not unique to international law.

3.3   CAUSATION IN INTERNATIONAL CRIMINAL LAW

> Anyone who asks for the cause of an event faces an *embarrass de choix* of literally cosmic proportions.
>
> Hart and Honoré (1985:110)

The concept of causation has received extensive deliberation in Anglo-American criminal law, and a variety of diverging opinions are in play. The knotty logical and moral issues arising from the imperative to identify a sequence of cause and effect and on the basis of this, to attribute criminal responsibility, have taxed the most gifted legal minds of the nineteenth and twentieth centuries.

The same degree of legal reflection and elucidation cannot be found in international criminal law. There is very little in the way of explicit guidance on causation in the statutes, rules of procedure and evidence or trial and appeals decisions of international criminal tribunals. This lacuna is surprising, especially given the fact that international crimes such as war crimes and genocide tend to be exceptionally complex in their planning and execution, and involve many agents and organizations acting in concert. As a practical matter, teasing out a single thread of causation is a more demanding exercise in the international setting because the crimes often occur in the context of genocide and/or armed conflicts in which armies, states and multiple actors are involved.

Nor has there been much reflection in the academic and scholarly literature on this necessary element of criminal responsibility. One of the leading textbooks in international criminal law, *Cassese's International Criminal Law* [Cassese and Gaeta (2013:38–9)] offers less than a page on causation and cites no relevant cases. Cryer et al.'s (otherwise excellent)

---

[26] American Law Institute (2010) 26: Factual Cause (1)(c). *Restatement Third* proposes the following jury language on causation: "700.3 Cause—Defined. The conduct of a party is a cause of damage when the damage would not have happened except for the conduct." It also proposes replacing substantial factor with "scope of liability" (§6, §29). My thanks to Paul Chill for bringing this development in the law of torts to my attention.

[27] National Research Council (2002:2).

An Introduction to International Criminal Law and Procedure (2014:392–3) contains no overall discussion of causation, and only touches on the subject briefly when reviewing the law of command responsibility and whether omissions by a superior officer could constitute sufficient cause to hold a commanding officer criminally liable. Stewart (2012a:1194) is one of the few legal commentators to point out this peculiar lacuna in international criminal justice. Despite the invisibility of causation in the judicial judgments and the secondary international criminal law literature, causation is a live issue that preoccupies, even consumes, the parties in an international criminal trial. According to my interviews, when behind closed doors, and in the company solely of members of their own team, defense and prosecution teams deliberate the causation issues in their case *ad finitum.*[28]

Despite the relative absence of explicit judicial reflection on causation, what we can glean from the case law is that international criminal tribunals do not apply the *sine qua non* test of causation as a matter of course. Reviewing key speech crimes cases such as *Nahimana*, we learn that for modes of liability such as instigation: "The *actus reus* of instigating implies prompting another person to commit an offense. It is not necessary to prove that the crime would not have been perpetrated without the involvement of the accused."[29]

The ICTY Trial Chamber in *Blaškić* further refined the position on the *actus reus* of instigation: "Although it must be proved that the instigation was a clear contributing factor to the commission of the crime, it need not be a *conditio sine qua non*" (§270). If the Tribunal had stopped there, then international law might have settled on the sound and sensible standard of "clear and contributing factor." A year or so later, however, *Kordić and Čerkez* lowered the bar of causation to such an extent that it is hard to imagine any defendant ever escaping conviction, "Although the accused's conduct need not have been a *conditio sine qua non* of the commission of the crime, it must have made a difference" (§391).[30]

---

[28] Supporting Stewart's (2012a:1207) contention that "Frequently, difficult causal problems are simply abandoned under the guise of prosecutorial burdens of proof."

[29] *Nahimana* AC §480. For a critical view of ICTR jurisprudence on instigation, see Agbor (2013).

[30] The *Čelebići* TC clarified the *actus reus* standard when considering omissions by commanding officers, "Notwithstanding the central place assumed by the principle of causation in criminal law, causation has not traditionally been postulated as a *conditio sine qua non* for the imposition of criminal liability on superiors for their failure to prevent or punish offences committed by their subordinates" (§398).

Given this inconsistency on the standard of causation for instigation, one might expect more discussion of the topic, but none presently exists. The explanation for this might lie in how causation is conceptualized in international law. In contrast to the common law, international criminal law does not explicitly bifurcate causation into material causation and legal (or proximate) causation. In fact, it does not employ the concept of "proximate cause" at all, a fact that is rather intriguing. Even though no international criminal court has ever had recourse to proximate cause, the prior discussion of material and legal causation in US criminal law is germane because it compels us to recognize that what counts as a "cause" is as much policy as it is brute "fact." Attorneys trained in the Anglo-American tradition do not conceal this fact; to the contrary, they openly acknowledge it. The bifurcation of causation in Anglo-American law, for all its complications, at least formally distinguishes between the aspects of causation that are considered "cause-in-fact" and those that result from legislative and policy decisions.

In international criminal trials, by way of contrast, it is not apparent where the determination of the material facts ends and the policy (or "scope of liability") considerations begin. International criminal law welds the two together into a single indivisible amalgam. This could be one reason why international law textbooks are so reticent to broach the subject of causation and dissect its constituent elements.

In place of the concept of proximate cause, international criminal law utilizes categories that are commonly used in, or analogous to, Anglo-American domestic law as guides or tests for determining prox-imate cause.[31] The forms of criminal liability used at the ICC, ICTR and ICTY that have most bearing on completed speech crimes are an assortment of standards of causation, including "essential contribu-tion," "significant contribution" and "substantial contribution." Some of these modes of liability were already introduced in a previous chapter and appear again later in the book, so the discussion here primarily refers to the threshold of proof of causation in each mode:

> *Instigating*, or prompting another to commit a crime, requires proof that the exhortations of the instigator made a "substantial contribution" to the conduct of the principal perpetrator who commits the crime.[32]

---

[31] See Hart and Honoré (1985:97) for a fairly critical discussion of substantial factor and foreseeability as they relate to determining proximate cause.

[32] *Kordić and Čerkez* AC §27. Instigating is listed as a mode of liability in Art. 7(1) of the ICTY Statute and Art. 6(1) of the ICTR and SCSL Statutes. The ICC Statute does not include a specific listing for "instigating," but will likely hear such types of cases under Art. 25(3)(b)

Nahimana AC confirms that "it is sufficient to demonstrate that the instigation was a factor substantially contributing to the conduct of another person committing the crime" (§480). Instigating does not require that the instigator stand in a position of command or superior responsibility in relation to the material perpetrator,[33] or even have "effective control" over those instigated.[34]

Aiding and abetting involves providing "practical assistance, encouragement or moral support"[35] with the knowledge that it assists the perpetrator in the commission of the crime. When applied to speech acts, the threshold of demonstrating causation would require that speech act(s) in question have a "substantial effect" on the perpetration of the crime.[36] While the "substantial" part of the equation connotes a relatively high standard, "effect" appears to be a lower measure of causation than "contribution." Affirming this interpretation, Cryer et al. (2014:371) notes that the ICTY has interpreted "substantial effect" to mean "any assistance which is more than *de minimis*." However, courts have also used the expression "substantial contribution" as well as "substantial effect" to refer to the threshold of causation, creating a certain amount of ambiguity.[37]

Joint Criminal Enterprise (or JCE) is a mode of liability that originated, and has been used most extensively at the ICTY and Special Court for Sierra Leone, but is not listed in the Rome Statute of the ICC. With the closing of the ICTY, the future applicability of JCE in international criminal trials is uncertain.[38] JCE is similar to the common law crime of conspiracy insofar as it involves a plurality of persons who share a common plan or purpose to commit a crime, and it permits a court to hold responsible all the individuals within a group for the crimes committed by the group.[39] JCE diverges from conspiracy in that conspiracy

---

which refers to soliciting and inducing. For further discussion of instigation, see Cassese and Gaeta (2013:197) Cryer et al. (2014:376–9).

[33] *Orić* TC at §272; *Popović* TC at §1008.   [34] *Milutinović* TC at §83.

[35] *Ruzindana* TC §126.

[36] *Tadić* AC §192, *Blaškić*, AC §46, *Karadžić* TC 576. For further discussion, see Cassese and Gaeta (2013:193–6) and Cryer et al. (2014:370–5). The ICC Statute establishes the crime of aiding and abetting at Article 25(3)(c).

[37] *Mbarushimana* PTC "Confirmation of Charges" (2011), §281, §281 fn. 663.

[38] Although defendants such as Nuon Chea and Khieu Samphan have been convicted in 2014 of JCE at the Extraordinary Chambers in the Courts of Cambodia (ECCC). As for its applicability at the ICC, Cassese and Gaeta (2013:175) state that JCE is not a form of criminal liability included in, or even identifiable through a broad interpretation of other provisions in, the ICC Statute.

[39] JCE was not established in the ICTY Statute, but was introduced in the 1999 *Tadić* AC judgment at §185 *et passim*. The most succinct definition of JCE in the ICTY case law can be found in *Brđanin* AC at §364, "There are three requirements for such a finding. First, a plurality of persons. Second, the existence of a common purpose (or plan) which amounts to or involves the commission of a crime provided for in the Statute. Third, the participation of the accused in this common purpose."

may be found even if the intended crime is not committed, whereas JCE requires completion of the crime and therefore proof of causation.[40] With regard to speech crimes, Bosnian Serb leader Radovan Karadžić was convicted in 2016 for disseminating propaganda as part of a JCE.[41] With JCE, the burden lies with the prosecution to show that the words of the accused made a "significant contribution"[42] to the actual commission of the crime.[43] Like conspiracy, JCE is a controversial notion, and has ardent proponents and detractors.[44]

Perpetration Jointly with Another or "Co-Perpetration:" The ICC has replaced JCE with co-perpetration, a form of collective criminal responsibility that, like JCE, involves two or more persons who have devised a common plan to commit a crime.[45] The *Lubanga Decision on the Confirmation of the Charges* sets out the elements of the crime of co-perpetration, and the *actus reus* requirement necessitates a "co-ordinated essential contribution made by each co-perpetrator resulting in the realization of the objective elements of the crime."[46] Essential contribution is equivalent to *sine qua non*, or "but-for" causation. Whether a speaker is found guilty of co-perpetrating crimes against humanity on the basis of speech acts will be evaluated under the "essential contribution" standard of causation. Given that this is a very high threshold of causation for the prosecution to attain, it is unlikely that an inciting speaker would be charged under this mode of liability, in the absence of other contributions to the commission of the crime.

Ordering: in which a *de facto* or *de jure* superior issues a written or verbal command to a subordinate to commit a criminal offense, when that superior is in position of superior (or command) responsibility within a military or political hierarchy or organization,[47] and where the order has a "direct and substantial effect" on the commission of the

---

[40] Cassese and Gaeta (2013:163). *Kenny's Outlines of Criminal Law* (Turner 1958:89) states that "the gist of conspiracy is the agreement, whether or not the object is attained."

[41] *Karadžić* TC §3487, §3514.

[42] On significant contribution in JCE, see *Brđanin*, AC §430. Cassese and Gaeta (2013:163–4).

[43] On disseminating propaganda as a contribution to a JCE, see *Karadžić* TC §§3470–1; *Popović* TC §1822.

[44] For the contours of the debates regarding JCE, refer to Cassese and Gaeta (2013:163–75) and Cryer et al. (2014:356–63). The objections to JCE are much the same as historically have been made against the crime of conspiracy. *Kenny's Outlines of Criminal Law* (Turner, 1958:89) remarks that "in the hands of common law judges conspiracy was maintained as a vague offence capable of almost indefinite extension."

[45] Perpetration "jointly with another" is listed in the ICC Statute at Article 25(3)(a).

[46] ICC-01/04-01/06-803-tEN, para. 346. This standard of causation was reaffirmed in the *Lubanga* trial chamber judgment at §923. For a succinct review of the co-perpetration model, see Cassese and Gaeta (2013:176–8) and Cryer et al. (2014:363–7).

[47] On the relationship of authority in ordering, see *Karadžić* TC §573. For legal scholarship on ordering, see Cassese (2013:204–5); see also Cryer et al. (2014:375).

offence.[48] Ordering requires a positive act of instructing a subordinate and cannot be committed by omission.[49]

When asked outright, prosecutors and judges usually balk at ranking or grading the modes of liability, repeating the official position in international criminal law that each mode has such a distinctive array of elements of intention and causation that they are incomparable along a single continuum. However, from my interviews it is evident that most legal actors at international tribunals have a mental schema that they use to classify causation problems in the immediate case in which they are involved. And occasionally, a trial decision will provide an opinion on the threshold of contribution for the various modes of liability and establish a hierarchy between them, as the ICC Pretrial Chamber did in *Mbarushimana* when it indicated that JCE requires a lower level of contribution (namely, "significant contribution") than aiding and abetting ("substantial effect/contribution").

Practically, in actual trials, one wonders how attorneys differentiate between these various tests for causation, and more specifically how international criminal courts parse the gossamer-thin gradations between, say, "significant effect" (for aiding and abetting), "significant contribution" (for JCE) and "substantial contribution" (instigating). The answer, thus far, is inconsistently. Robert Cryer (2014:358, fn. 46) observes that "the exact difference between "substantial" and "significant" is not entirely clear, but has been repeated." Repeating the distinctions between levels of contribution or effect has thus far not produced a systematic and rigorous framework that is widely understood and accepted. Stewart (2012a:1216) goes a step further and finds international criminal judges' guidance on matters of causation "at best unhelpful and at worst fundamentally incoherent."[50]

Interviews conducted for this book revealed that most judges, prosecutors and defense attorneys at three international tribunals are not especially confident about their grasp of the *actus reus* standards, and some remain unconvinced that the standards make any sense at all. Criminal defense attorneys openly express their frustration with international

---

[48] *Kamuhanda* AC §75; *Karadžić* TC §573, *Milutinović* TC §88. The ICC Statute lists ordering as a mode of responsibility under Article 25(3)(b). For further discussion, see Cassese and Gaeta (2013:196–7) and Cryer et al (2014:375–6).

[49] *Galić* AC §176; *Milutinović* TC §87.

[50] In specific reference to the Trial Chamber's formulation in *Kordić and Čerkez* at §391, "Although the accused's conduct need not have been a conditio sine qua non of the commission of the crime, it must have made a difference."

tribunals' tests of causation, finding them to be artificial to the point of affectation and erratically applied. Prosecutors, while generally more reticent to criticize court standards of proof, admit that the tests are not easily fathomed. One prosecuting attorney spoke for many when she referred to the distinction between "significant" and "substantial" contributions as "a squishy standard."[51]

During an interview with one ICTY judge, I asked about the difference between significant contribution and substantial contribution. The judge gave a vague answer which I could not follow, so I asked him again. Again, an elusive and roundabout response. I indicated my continued puzzlement and he narrowed his eyes and countered flatly, "You look at the facts and examine all the evidence and decide the case one way or another." Such encounters led me to conclude that while theorists of international criminal law and authors of international criminal law textbooks expend a great deal of energy in precisely defining and distinguishing the thresholds of causation for various modes of liability, many practitioners at international criminal tribunals neither comprehend the fine gradations of legal scholarship, nor apply them rigorously.

In a few rare instances, international jurists are willing to entertain such uncertainties. When I asked the experienced German Judge Wolfgang Schomburg whether it was possible to distinguish between substantial and significant contribution, he replied bluntly, "No. It never was." Given that he served as a respected trial and appeals chamber judge at two international tribunals, this is a rather unfavorable evaluation of the standards of causation in international criminal law. Yet even more damning was Schomburg's explanation for how the various standards of proof emerged,

> The reason why they came with these categories of significant or substantial contribution was to cure the negative effects of the third and extended version of JCE [Joint Criminal Enterprise], because it was a category that, as William Schabas said, implied "Just Convict Everyone," and because there was no clear contrast regarding the objective elements of the crime. Seeing this gap and a flawed definition of Joint Criminal Enterprise, they added standards like substantial and significant contribution. To this day, I don't understand the difference between a significant contribution and substantial contribution. They had to provide a clear contrast between Joint Criminal Enterprise III and aiding and abetting. Normally we would speak about a reasonable contribution to achieve the goal of the perpetrator

---

[51] Author interview, 2014.

as a definition of aiding and abetting. But they couldn't just propose "contribution" as the standard anymore so they added these other tests of significant and substantial contribution in order to distinguish JCE III from aiding and abetting.

This admission is a bombshell coming from a senior judge at an international criminal tribunal. Those familiar with international criminal law will immediately understand why, but for others, Judge Schomburg's remarks require some elucidation. Judge Schomburg refers to the doctrine of JCE created at the ICTY to address the collective nature of many international crimes. JCE has proved highly contentious from the outset and its stock in international law seems to be falling. JCE was not listed in Article 7(1) as a doctrine of criminal responsibility in the original 1993 United Nations Statute that founded the ICTY and set out its mandate and powers. Instead, this new doctrine was invented, more or less *ex nihilo*, in 1999 by the *Tadić* Appeals Chamber and became the prevailing mode of liability at the ICTY.

Nearly every ICTY defendant post-*Tadić* has been charged with JCE in addition to the other relevant modes of liability. Like the capacious crime of conspiracy in the domestic setting, prosecutors favored JCE as the widest available dragnet for securing a conviction. The doctrine has three categories, and the third "extended" version of JCE that Judge Schomburg refers to is the most controversial of all, and has been unequivocally rejected by other war crimes tribunals, most notably the International Criminal Court and the Extraordinary Chambers of the Courts of Cambodia.[52]

JCE III provided the basis for holding a defendant responsible for a wider program of genocide, war crimes or crimes against humanity even if the perpetrator "commits an act which, while outside the common design, was nevertheless a natural and foreseeable consequence of the effecting of that common purpose."[53] This means that the prosecution need not show that a defendant shared the necessary *mens rea* for the defendant to be considered a member of the JCE.[54] Under the doctrine of JCE III, an individual could be convicted of genocide, war crimes and/or crimes against humanity even if they were not aware of a wider genocidal program and did not consciously commit

---

[52] *Prosecutor v. Lubanga*, ICC-01/04-01/06, Decision on Confirmation of Charges, 29 January 2007, §322–40 rejected the doctrine of JCE in its entirety. Case of *Nuon Chea et al.*, 002/19-09-2007-ECCC-TC Decision on the Applicability of Joint Criminal Enterprise, 12 September 2011, §33–5, rejected just JCE III.
[53] *Tadić* AC §204. [54] An approach confirmed in *Brđanin* AC §410.

acts in furtherance of genocide, but genocide was a "natural and foreseeable consequence" of their actions. This is problematic in that it
removes the special intent (or purpose) requirement of genocide and
replaces it with a lower *mens rea* standard similar to recklessness.[55]
As Schomburg notes, JCE III also makes an undesirable incursion
into the terrain of complicity.

The various causation standards of international criminal law emerged
not out of a rational and coherent process of judicial deliberation, but as
a quick fix to disentangle JCE from other forms of criminal responsibility
such as aiding and abetting. Modes of liability are typically distinguished
from one another by the type of contribution made by an actor, and by his
or her state of mind and intention. JCE III unsettled these conventional
distinctions and swept up individuals who acted without a full awareness
of a wider criminal plan or program, and who normally might have been
not held responsible for the overarching criminal enterprise or only
charged under aiding and abetting. The different levels of significant,
essential, or substantial contribution emerged as a way of distinguishing
the modes of liability from one another, but the variances are so small that
they only generated more bewilderment. Schomburg's account of how this
situation arose seems plausible, and goes some way to explaining how so
many standards of causation came into being, why they persevere to
this day and why so many judges, prosecutors and defense attorneys at
international tribunals are confounded by them.

International criminal law presently construes causation in a way
that departs from the time-honored *sine qua non* standard in favor of
a number of secondary tests for legal cause, and I have outlined the
complications inherent in distinguishing between the various standards. Here, it is worth considering the possible justifications for the
path followed by the international criminal tribunals. First, in the
context of armed conflict surrounding most of the crimes adjudicated
at international criminal tribunals, multiple causation or overdetermi-
nation is the rule rather than the exception. Widespread and systematic
war crimes, crimes against humanity and genocide require planning by
a collectivity of actors who typically act in concert and who orchestrate
mass crimes through state and/or state-like military organizations and

---

[55] Scheffer and Dinh (2010:3) defend the use of JCE at international tribunals, but they concede
that JCE III "is akin to recklessness in domestic criminal law." That any genocide charge
requires proof of special intent stated as "proof that the defendant knew about the principal
perpetrator's genocidal intent" is conventionally established in *Krstić* AC §140.

more loosely structured paramilitary organizations (e.g., the *interahamwe* of Rwanda, or "Arkan's Tigers" in Bosnia-Herzegovina).

In these circumstances, isolating a single thread of cause and effect that could satisfy the but-for standard is an exceedingly arduous undertaking. Addressing the problem of "overdetermined atrocities," James Stewart (2012a:1190) correctly remarks, "This moral quandary is, by and large the leitmotif for international criminal law. Very few atrocities are so dependent on the acts of any one individual that we can say with confidence that they would certainly *not* have transpired absent any one accused's individual agency."

The second justification for departing from the *sine qua non* standard is that speech crimes do not generally or solely involve direct causation of the billiard-ball type. Instead they result from comparatively indirect relations of cause and effect. A unifying feature of speech crimes cases is that the defendant is primarily acting through other persons who are the actual material perpetrators, recalling the *Blaškić* Trial Chamber's definition of instigating, the essence of which is "that the accused causes another person to commit a crime" (§270).

The role of intermediaries in the material commission of crimes is a complicating factor that may constitute an "intervening cause" and may rupture the prosecutors' theory of a chain of causation linking the speaker to the crimes. In the realm of speech crimes, we are less in the realm of physical causation than we are in mental causation, in which the intention of the speaker is communicated to the listeners, who then take the speaker's intention to be their own and act upon it. As noted previously, speech crimes rely heavily on the intentionality and mental states of the actors, and the usual linear $X \rightarrow Y \rightarrow Z$ model of direct causation[56] is inadequate for grasping the conditioning effects of denigrating and inciting speech, and the often unconscious nature of mental causation.

These points notwithstanding, there are serious drawbacks to international law's abandonment of the distinction between material and legal causation. The main one is this: given the myriad of "squishy" legal causation standards (e.g., "substantial effect" or "significant contribution"), it is unclear which *actus reus* elements relate to the facts of the matter and which result from policy decisions. This fosters the perception that the legal causation standards in international criminal

---

[56] Legal adviser to the International Committee of the Red Cross Nils Melzer (2009:53) defines direct causation in international criminal law as "meaning that the harm in question must be brought about in one causal step" which makes it akin to "proximate cause."

law are matters of policy "all the way down."[57] The relative silence on the fact/policy distinction leaves international criminal law exposed to the charge that international judges are exercising policy decisions in a manner that is unpredictable and less than fully transparent. Charges abound that the decisions of international criminal courts are based more on politics than law, and the uncertainty surrounding causation undermines the ability of international courts to provide a convincing rejoinder.

At international criminal tribunals, judges, prosecutors and defense attorneys are operating in the realm of legal, not factual, causation. This condition may be justified, but it would benefit from more explicit justifying in the case law and scholarly literature. Instead, legal commentators have been sidetracked into byzantine and unproductive discussions about the manifold "modes of liability" that exist in international criminal law. Intricately technical formulations of the modes of liability have dominated this nascent field of international law for over a decade and they show no signs of abating.[58] The interminable disagreements about modes of liability such as JCE, or how to differentiate between the standards of proof for aiding and abetting and co-perpetration "in any other way" are, in my view, surface manifestations of the more profound lack of clarity on the matter of causation.[59]

3.4 CAUSE AND EFFECT BEYOND A REASONABLE DOUBT

> In order to convict the accused, the Court must be convinced of the guilt of the accused beyond reasonable doubt.
> Article 66(3) of the Statute of the International Criminal Court

An appraisal of legal standards of causation at international tribunals is not complete until it has addressed the standard of proof to establish a relationship of cause and effect. The prevailing burden of proof of causation in both US domestic criminal courts and international

---

[57] To employ the "turtles all the way down" metaphor of the universe, conventionally attributed to an elderly English woman challenging the scientific account of the cosmos presented by Bertrand Russell at a public lecture.

[58] On being invited to give a presentation to the Office of the Prosecutor (OTP) at the ICC in 2013, the staff contact requested that I speak about any topic except modes of liability, since this was a topic that the OTP had been lectured on previously to their full satisfaction and, indeed, ennui.

[59] Stewart (2012a:1194, fn. 20) arrives at similar conclusions, writing that the modes of liability rubric "is conceptually misleading and of uncertain historical pedigree."

criminal tribunals is "beyond a reasonable doubt."[60] While in theory international and domestic criminal systems are in congruence, in practice they diverge from one another in key respects.

In the adversarial common law system, judges direct juries on how they should understand the reasonable-doubt standard as a matter of course. Jury instructions vary and Dressler and Garvey's casebook in US criminal law (2012:9–13) lists eight discrete types of jury guidance, including, *inter alia*, that the jurors should feel "near certitude" "moral certainty," "no real doubt," "firmly convinced of the defendant's guilt," that they should not "waver or vacillate" and should feel "thoroughly convinced" and that "the truth has triumphed." The most common instruction given to juries by judges is that the meaning of reasonable-doubt is "self-evident," and jurors ought to just use their ordinary judgment.[61] Each definition connotes distinct shades of meaning, and trial attorneys are sensitive to how each formulation may tilt the scales of adjudication in the direction of the prosecution or defense.

At bottom, what matters is the juror's own belief based upon their ordinary, everyday reasoning. It is worth observing that none of the jury instructions on the reasonable-doubt standard refer to science, the scientific method of hypothesis-evidence-deduction or the statistical probability that the defendant's actions caused the harm. Hart and Honoré (1985:9) articulate the view of Anglo-American law generally when they contend that "the lawyer's causal problems are not 'scientific inquests' but are to be determined on 'common-sense principles'." This stance is in part shaped by John Stuart Mill's influential claim that when faced with a set of jointly sufficient conditions, law and philosophy can single out the principal cause in an invariable causal sequence using common sense principles.[62] Despite the fact that all manner of beliefs about cause and effect (witches causing misfortune, vengeful gods causing the waters to flood, etc.) have been, and possibly still are, considered a matter of "common sense," it has been a consistent position of US criminal courts that the reasonable doubt standard is

---

[60] The reasonable doubt standard is a foundational constituent of US law, articulated in the Due Process Clause of the United States Constitution and was upheld as a general principle of criminal law by the US Supreme Court in *Winship* (1970). In international criminal law, it is stated in Rule 87(a) of the Rules of Procedure and Evidence of the ICTR and ICTY, and in *Kordić and Čerkez* AC §833. The reasonable doubt standard is listed, but not defined, in Article 66(3) of the ICC Statute, nor is it defined in the Regulations of the Court, the Rules of Procedure and Evidence or the Elements of Crimes.

[61] *State v. Portillo*, 182 Ariz. 592, 898 P.2d 970 (1995).

[62] See Hart and Honoré (1985:28–32, 44).

essentially qualitative and grounded in personal belief and "common sense."[63]

What is generally prohibited is any quantification of the reasonable doubt standard. This has a significant bearing on our understanding of how both law and science understand proof of causation. One Nevada judge attempted to quantify reasonable doubt as a seventy-five percent chance that the defendant is guilty, and this was ruled as improper by the Nevada Supreme Court on the grounds that "[t]he concept of reasonable doubt is inherently qualitative. Any attempt to quantify may impermissibly lower the prosecution's burden of proof, and is likely to confuse rather than clarify."[64] Wright (2011:6) observes that the situation is much the same in Europe and in the "inquisitorial" civil law tradition, and he quotes a decision of the Italian Supreme Court of Cassation confirming that "The [European] Court of Justice CE has recently stated that causation cannot be based on probabilities."

We can therefore conclude that historically, US, European and international criminal law are resolutely resistant to quantifying the burden of proof. In criminal law, certainty remains a qualitative term, based on personal beliefs and inner convictions regarding the facts at issue. In contrast, in qualitative historical and social science research, "beyond a reasonable doubt" is not a term of art any researcher is likely to use, on the grounds that it is far too settled and determinate. Any claim by an historian or anthropologist that his or her evidence proved a relationship of cause and effect between two social events beyond a reasonable doubt would be considered either as embarrassingly simplistic or as excessively overconfident of the status of the evidence and interpretation.

As with the concept of causation, there is very little in the way of judicial reflection on the reasonable doubt standard in international criminal law. In fact, in most trials there is complete silence on this topic, partly because there is no jury to instruct in the bench trials at international criminal tribunals. Instead, rulings emanate from an invisible process of negotiation behind closed doors between three international judges and their clerks who come from different countries and myriad legal traditions. Judicial deliberation on the exact meaning of this or that term of legal art is seldom openly aired. As one ICTY judge commented wryly when I asked him about judges' discussions in

---

[63] Dressler (2009:181). [64] *McCullough v. State*, 99 Nev. 72, 657 P.2d 1157 (Nev. 1983).

chamber regarding reasonable doubt, "You'll never know what we talk about before a judgment, because there is no jury to instruct."[65]

There are only a few instances of reflection on the reasonable doubt standard in the case law, and these are not especially illuminating. The ICTR Appeals Chamber in *Rutaganda* opined that "the reasonable-doubt standard in criminal law[...]must be based on logic and common sense, and have a rational link to the evidence, lack of evidence or inconsistencies in the evidence."[66] This tells us that the legal standard must be rigorous, but does not actually tell us what "beyond reasonable doubt" is, and therefore it leaves us none the wiser. In 2004 in *Brđanin*, an ICTY Trial Chamber did not tackle defining the reasonable doubt standard head on, although it left little doubt as to its operational definition, repeatedly referring to what I term the "only reasonable inference" test of reasonable doubt. It used this expression over a dozen times in the judgment in phrases beginning with the statement that "the Trial Chamber is satisfied beyond reasonable doubt that the only reasonable inference that may be drawn is that ..."[67] At the end of *Brđanin*, the judgment states categorically that "Where an inference needs to be drawn, it has to be the only reasonable inference available on the evidence" (§970).

The "only reasonable inference" test was expanded in *Halilović* (2005) where the Trial Chamber judgment held that it "has carefully considered whether there is any reasonable interpretation of the evidence admitted other than the guilt of the Accused. Any ambiguity or doubt has been resolved in favour of the Accused in accordance with the principle of *in dubio pro reo*" (§12). One ICTY judge interviewed for this book confirmed that the "only reasonable inference" standard was the one most commonly used by judges at the ICTY. Prosecutors might reasonably object that this threshold tilts the scales in favor of the defense and that the mere identification of another reasonable interpretation of an event does not logically preclude the fact that a defendant might still have caused the harm in question.

The ICTY Appeals Chamber in *Delalić* advanced yet another criterion; that the accused need only bring evidence "to suggest a reasonable possibility" of reasonable doubt. On any other matters that the accused might raise, judges were to determine their probative value "on the balance of probabilities" (§582–603). The *Delalić* Appeals Chamber thus created precedent by introducing two separate standards, in which the prosecution evidence shall be weighed on a reasonable doubt standard

[65] Author interview, 2015. [66] *Rutaganda* AC §488. [67] *Brđanin* TC §532, §667.

92

whereas defense evidence would be accepted on a much lower "balance of probabilities" threshold. To my knowledge, this formulation has no parallel in any domestic system of criminal law, since all evidence introduced in a criminal trial is generally evaluated according to the same reasonable doubt standard.

International criminal trials continue to be stymied by uncertainty on the reasonable doubt standard, and the confusing standards articulated in *Delalić* and *Brđanin* and *Halilović* periodically resurface they did recently at the ICC in the Ngudjolo case. In 2012, an ICC trial chamber acquitted the defendant on the grounds that it was "possible" that Mathieu Ngudjolo had confessed his role in the slaughter of a village in the Democratic Republic of the Congo in 2003 in order to inflate his standing within the Congolese Army. The ICC Trial Chamber applied the "only reasonable inference" standard in a number of instances in the Ngudjolo judgment in disallowing the prosecution evidence. The prosecution energetically appealed on the basis that:

> The Chamber misinterpreted the legal standard of "guilt beyond a reasonable doubt," and effectively required demonstration of guilt beyond *any* doubt by the Prosecution. It rejected evidence on hypothetical and fanciful grounds that are completely unsupported by the record [original emphasis].[68]

The prosecution offered the following rebuttal of the only reasonable inference test of the reasonable doubt standard:

> A number of key findings in the Judgment demonstrate a pattern whereby the Trial Chamber concluded that facts alleged by the Prosecution had not been established beyond reasonable doubt based on a possible alternative or competing inference or on other grounds. But, neither the competing inferences nor the grounds purportedly establishing a reasonable doubt are based on evidence, logic, reason or common sense. At best, they establish a hypothetical alternative reading of the evidence. This demonstrates that the Trial Chamber, rather than applying the standard of proof beyond reasonable doubt, effectively required proof of the relevant facts to a degree of absolute certainty (i.e. beyond *any* doubt) [original emphasis].[69]

In appealing the acquittal, the prosecution made only scant reference to international case law on the reasonable doubt standard, and instead built

---

[68] *Ngudjolo* AC, Prosecution's Document in Support of Appeal, 15 October 2014, §29.
[69] *Ngudjolo* AC, Prosecution's Document in Support of Appeal, §38.

its argument on the legal standards found in the municipal systems of Canada, the United States, Scotland and Germany.[70] The prosecution's recourse to interpretations found in domestic jurisdictions was necessitated by the lack of a clear definition of "beyond a reasonable doubt" in international law, and the dearth of well-reasoned opinion on the matter.

The ICC appeal chamber was unmoved, however, and denied the grounds of the prosecution's appeal and upheld the acquittal of Ngudjolo. The appeals chamber judgment referred only to the immediate facts of the case, including the confession of the accused and the credibility of witnesses. It endorsed the trial chamber's interpretation of the reasonable doubt standard, but did not discuss that interpretation in any depth.[71] The appeals chamber judgment in *Ngudjolo* vindicated the "only reasonable inference" test, but offered no definition, discussion or meaningful elucidation of it.

A year later at the ICC, the lack of a settled opinion on the reasonable doubt standard became a central matter of dispute in *Ruto and Sang*, a trial where the charges included criminal liability for speech acts. In June 2014, the trial chamber issued a decision on the principles and guidance on "no case to answer" motions, in which it responded to the defense argument that the chamber ought to employ the reasonable doubt standard to weighing evidence at the stage in the trial when the prosecution has completed its case.[72] Given the allegations of witness bribery and coercion and the question mark hanging over the credibility and reliability of prosecution witnesses in *Ruto and Sang* (and many other international speech crimes trials), accepting the defense arguments would have effectively dismantled the prosecution case.

The trial chamber, however, indicated that it was using a lower threshold of proof than beyond reasonable doubt at the "no case to answer stage" although it indicated that the final judgment in a case must apply the reasonable doubt standard in its fullest sense (which it neglected to fully define). The trial chamber recognized that there are various thresholds of proof at play during the successive stages of an international trial:

> the test to be applied for a "no case to answer" determination is whether or not, on the basis of a prima facie assessment of the evidence, there is a case, in the sense of whether there is sufficient evidence introduced on which, if accepted, a reasonable Trial Chamber could convict the

---

[70] *Ibid.*, §§40–8 [71] *Ngudjolo* AC §§57–63, §104.
[72] *Ruto and Sang* TC, "Decision No. 5 on the Conduct of Trial Proceedings (Principles and Procedure on 'No Case to Answer' Motions)," 3 June 2014, §20.

accused. The emphasis is on the word "could" and the exercise contemplated is thus not one which assesses the evidence to the standard for a conviction at the final stage of a trial. For the present purposes, the Chamber therefore need not elaborate on the standard of proof for conviction at the final stage.[73]

Surprisingly, given the judicial inconsistency on the reasonable doubt standard, there is little in the way of scholarly elucidation on the topic in international criminal law. One of the leading textbooks, *Cassese's International Criminal Law* (Cassese and Gaeta, 2013:38–9), contains no discussion whatsoever of the reasonable doubt standard. Cryer's (2014:439–40) *An Introduction to International Criminal Law and Procedure* offers just an unembellished paragraph. This discussion raises the deeper question, why has there been such relative reticence on the part of scholars and international judges to provide transparent guidance on the burden of proof in international law, and why do the few expositions that exist only generate more irregularity?

One answer focuses on the uncertainties created by fusing the civil and common law models together into a "hybrid" model of international criminal justice.[74] Specifically, international criminal law's reasonable doubt standard, originally derived from US criminal law, is quite dissimilar to the standards commonly applied in the inquisitorial system – the tradition that shaped the legal systems functioning in a majority of the world's countries. While civil law judges may be in principle aware of the reasonable doubt standard, they may not have actual experience applying it on a regular basis. In France, the trier of fact must conventionally be in possession of *une intime conviction*, that has been interpreted to mean "an inner, deep-seated, conviction of the judge" (Clermont and Sherwin 2002:246), and also "reasonable conviction, reasonable certainty; state of being satisfied beyond reasonable doubt (personally convinced)."[75] In German law, "the judge may and must always content himself with a degree of certainty that is appropriate for practical life which silences doubts, without entirely excluding them" (Clermont and Sherwin 2002:243).

---

[73] *Ibid.*, §23.
[74] See the memoirs of ICTY/ICTR Chief Prosecutor Carla Del Ponte (2008) on the procedural and conceptual difficulties created by the hybrid model of justice. Mundis (2001) also provides an insider's critical eye on the practical effects of the combining of common and civil law elements.
[75] Wright (2011:1, fn. 2) quoting *The Council of Europe French–English Legal Dictionary*.

This brief review of three countries (the US, France and Germany) that have contributed many judges to international criminal tribunals identifies three competing standards of certainty: beyond a reasonable doubt, silencing practical doubts and an inner personal conviction. More could be found in the dozens of other jurisdictions that send judges to international criminal tribunals. The situation in international criminal courts is not so different from municipal criminal law, especially in federal nation-states like the USA and Germany, where, as we have seen, juries regularly provide diverging instructions to juries in different trials on the exact meaning of "beyond a reasonable doubt." However, a counterpoint would be that the variation at the domestic level occurs at the level of the states in a federation, and the diverging standards tend not to intermingle in the same trial as they do in the international setting.

Given that judges at international criminal tribunals approach the reasonable doubt standard from different starting points, then how do international judges know how to apply it consistently, especially given the absence of a secondary literature on the topic? My sense is that this standard is still unsettled and that in practice, international judges do not apply it evenly. Instead, international judges assemble an *ad hoc* hybridized construction of the reasonable doubt standard in each trial, based upon the domestic backgrounds and the prior experience of the three judges on the bench. This could be one reason why clear articulation of the reasonable doubt standard is undeveloped in the case law and the secondary literature.

This interpretation did not find favor with one of the international judges interviewed for this book. Judge Schomburg, who served as a judge at the ICTY and ICTR insisted that the same standard of beyond reasonable doubt was applied at both of the international tribunals at which he served. When asked whether an underlying consensus united the variations in national traditions, he replied, "Absolutely there is a consensus ... there was never any disagreement between the judges on beyond reasonable doubt in either the trial chamber or appeals chamber."[76]

Nevertheless, Schomburg expressed concern at a recent judgment of the ICTR Appeals Chamber, "The ICTY has upheld beyond reasonable doubt from the beginning. The only case where the Appeals Chamber has departed from beyond reasonable doubt was in the

---

[76] Author interview, 2014.

'Government II' case[77] where the ICTR Appeals Chamber acquitted the defendant Mugenzi of genocide and incitement to genocide and this led to protests in Kigali." Judge Schomburg drew cited the ICTR Appeals Chamber decision in Government II which reads,

> The Appeals Chamber is not convinced ... that the considerations identified by the Trial Chamber *eliminate the reasonable possibility* that Mugenzi and Mugiraneza agreed to remove Habyalimana for political or administrative reasons rather than for the purpose of furthering the killing of Tutsis in Butare Prefecture. Consequently, the Appeals Chamber finds, Judge Liu dissenting, that the Trial Chamber erred in concluding that the *only reasonable inference* that could be drawn from the circumstantial evidence is that Mugenzi and Mugiraneza possessed the requisite *mens rea* for a conviction for conspiracy to commit genocide [§91, my emphasis].

The Trial Chamber judgment relied in part on the prosecutions' claim that the defendants had removed a Tutsi official, Habyalimana, so they could more effectively pursue their genocidal extermination of Tutsis in their municipality. In overturning the convictions in Government II, the Appeals Chamber drew upon the two deviations from the reasonable doubt standard that we saw previously in *Delalić* and *Brđanin* at the ICTY, namely the "reasonable possibility" of doubt test (*Delalić*) and the "only reasonable inference" standard (*Brđanin*). Judge Schomburg indicated that he concurred with Judge Liu's dissenting opinion and added that the Appeals Chamber judgment was "outrageous" and "stood in stark contrast to which the Trial Chamber has decided in the past [. . .] and on this basis you can acquit anyone since another Trial Chamber could always come to another conclusion [. . .] This is extremely counterproductive."[78]

3.5 HOW INTERNATIONAL LAW KNOWS ABOUT CAUSES

The burden of proof required to demonstrate a relationship of cause and effect beyond a reasonable doubt is utterly unique to criminal law. Criminal courts have developed their own inimitable standards and tests for determining relations of cause and effect that are not used in any other fields of human understanding. Concepts such as "legal

---

[77] *Prosecutor v. Justin Mugenzi and Prosper Mugiraneza*, Case No. ICTR-99-50-A. 4 February 2013.
[78] Author interview, 2014.

causation" and "beyond a reasonable doubt" have been formulated in specialized ways over centuries, such that the criminal courtroom inhabits its own self-contained universe of knowledge, understanding and truth-finding.

All criminal courts do not apply the same criteria, however. Whereas Anglo-American law conventionally distinguishes between the factual and policy criteria used to determine causation, international law combines these two together and favors tests of causation that are commonly found in the policy arena of "legal causation" rather than "cause-in-fact." It does so with little explicit reflection on the fundamental concepts of *actus reus*. The absence of precision in defining causation in international law, and the use of quick fixes to repair the tears in the legal fabric caused by excessive judicial creativity has led to a proliferation of modes of liability, each with their own contribution requirements. This variation exists both internally within one tribunal and between tribunals, thus exacerbating the discrepancies. Thus, there is still great flux and internal contestation over even the most basic norms of adjudication in international criminal tribunals.

This stands in contrast to most domestic jurisdictions which have generally sought to recognize and address conceptual ambiguities, however imperfectly and however much their recognition was motivated primarily by public outrage at miscarriages of justice.[79] After over twenty years of case law at modern international criminal tribunals, it is perplexing that fundamental legal concepts such as causation and beyond reasonable doubt remain so overlooked, nebulous and downright mystifying. Of course, domestic criminal law in the United States and elsewhere also suffers from conceptual contradictions and profound procedural shortcomings. Yet some of the challenges confronting international criminal law are singular and even unique, emanating as they do from a complex process of melding distinctive legal traditions into a functioning framework to adjudicate mass atrocities, in a compressed time period and in the absence of higher judicial review and legislative oversight found at the nation-state level. Its rules of procedure and evidence are not drawn entirely from either the common law or civil

---

[79] The classic case here is the 1843 trial of Daniel M'Naghten [M'Naghten's Case, 8 Eng.Rep. 718 (1843)] who attempted to assassinate Sir Robert Peel, the Prime Minister of England. After his acquittal on grounds of insanity led to a storm of protest from both the Crown and the general populace, the Judges of England were summoned to the House of Lords and compelled to justify their decision, resulting in the M'Naghten Test for cognitive incapacity. See Dressler and Garvey (2012:600–8).

law system, and tribunal statements appropriately define the ICTY and ICTR as a "hybrid system."[80] Such hybridization, while comprehensible given the international nature of international criminal tribunals, gives rise to profound uncertainty and unpredictability since it creates a new language of law that no legal actor speaks fluently (at least at the outset) and in which the rules of the language game are inscrutable, even to its proponents.

There are several inferences of a normative or policy kind that could be drawn from this review of causation in international criminal law. There is a pressing need, addressed more fully in later chapters, to re-establish the distinction between material cause and legal cause, and to clarify the confusion on the standards of causation by using one clear standard to delineate the scope of liability. This is a book about international speech crimes and such crimes raise a number of demanding questions about causation, but these cannot be resolved until the wider issue of causation in international law is settled.

---

[80] ICTY Press Release. "Blaskic Case: Defense Objection to the Admission of Hearsay is Rejected." The Hague, 23 January 1998.

CHAPTER FOUR

INSTIGATING PERSECUTION: THE PROSECUTION CASE AGAINST VOJISLAV ŠEŠELJ

> Propaganda is based on the fact that the vast majority of people are naturally ready to believe indiscriminately in everything they read, hear, or see on television.
>
> *Vojislav Šešelj*[1]

4.1 INTRODUCTION

Having reviewed the legal and theoretical issues relating to causation in domestic and international criminal law, we now turn to more tangible questions such as, what form do debates about causation take during international criminal trials? Specifically, how do international prosecutors seek to demonstrate beyond a reasonable doubt that there exists a causal connection between a public speech and subsequent crimes that is sufficiently direct to warrant imposing criminal liability? What case theory do prosecutors adopt and how do they marshal their evidence for causation? How do judges evaluate the prosecution's claims of cause and effect, and what evidence persuades them that words are causally connected to deeds?

This chapter examines in detail the prosecution case against the Serb political leader Vojislav Šešelj at the International Criminal Tribunal for the Former Yugoslavia in The Hague (ICTY). The analysis is based on my review of the indictment, the trial transcripts, exhibits and briefs submitted by the prosecution, an expert witness report, as well as

---

[1] Exhibit P1337, referred to in the Prosecution's closing arguments on 5 March 2012 (T.17157).

lengthy interviews with many of the main protagonists in the trial, including six members of the prosecution team, three judges and two prosecution expert witnesses. Since Vojislav Šešelj represented himself, there was no criminal defense counsel to interview.[2]

Since it is primarily concerned with the trial process, a substantial portion of this chapter was written before the 2016 judgment that acquitted the accused of all nine counts of war crimes and crimes against humanity. This may sound like a risky strategy, but the aim all along was to closely examine the prosecution's efforts to prove instigating as a mode of liability for speech crimes. As it turned out, this legal realist method explains why the prosecution case failed, whilst also acknowledging that prosecutors presented compelling evidence against the accused and the trial chamber acquittal may still be reversed on appeal.

Prosecutors refer to the Šešelj case as the only clear-cut "propaganda trial" at the Tribunal, and they often equate it to the "Media Trial" (*Nahimana*) at the International Criminal Tribunal for Rwanda.[3] As we will see, demonstrating that a leader's public utterances prompted his followers to murder and deport members of other national, religious, ethnic or racial groups is an arduous undertaking, for reasons of both law and logistics. Even though there may be a surfeit of *mens rea* evidence against political leaders who mobilize their base through public expressions of discriminatory animus against the out-group, there is seldom much in the way of evidence of *actus reus*, or what prosecutors call "linkage evidence," that connects the accused to the actual crimes committed. Political leaders in conflict situations, including the most ostensibly irresponsible of demagogues, generally steer clear of issuing direct orders for, or participating in, physical acts of violence. Leaders like Šešelj are rarely accused of materially perpetrating murder, torture or other offenses beyond the use of their words to instigate and encourage their followers, who may only loosely be described as their "subordinates."

4.2   INSTIGATING CRIMES AGAINST HUMANITY

The 2007 prosecution indictment charged Vojislav Šešelj with nine counts of war crimes and crimes against humanity for acts committed

---

[2] Attempts to interview the accused while in custody at Scheveningen were unsuccessful.

[3] While there might arguably be some ICTY antecedents such as *Brđanin, Gvero, Krajišnik, Kordić and Čerkez*, none had the prominence of the Šešelj case, nor the reliance on speeches as the basis of the charges against the defendant.

between dates of August 1991 and September 1993.[4] The indictment alleged that, acting individually or as part of a JCE with high-ranking Serb political and military leaders such as the late Serbian President Slobodan Milošević,[5] Vojislav Šešelj, "planned, ordered, instigated, committed or otherwise aided and abetted in the planning, preparation or execution" of crimes against humanity and war crimes that including persecutions, murder, sexual assaults, torture, deportation and forcible transfer of non-Serbs in Croatia and Bosnia.[6]

Compared with other cases at the Tribunal, the indictment was unusual in the degree to which the charges involved indirect forms of participation that occurred at a distance from the actual crimes. The indictment largely conceived of the accused's participation and criminal responsibility as vicarious; that is, as resulting from public speeches that prompted proxies to perpetrate the material crimes. "Instigating" and "aiding and abetting" in particular invoke vicarious forms of liability that allow the accused to be held responsible for crimes carried out by other perpetrators.[7]

More than any other recent case at international tribunals, *Šešelj* foregrounds the form of criminal responsibility that most directly bears on the problem of causation in international speech crimes; instigating persecutions on political, racial or religious grounds (a crime against humanity). The indictment defined this form of criminal responsibility thus: "By using the word 'instigated', the Prosecution charges that the accused Vojislav Šešelj's speeches, communications, acts and/or omissions contributed to the perpetrators' decision to commit the crimes alleged."[8] More concretely, the indictment alleged that "In public speeches Vojislav Šešelj called for the expulsion of Croat civilians from parts of the Vojvodina region in Serbia and thus instigated his followers and the local authorities to engage in a persecution campaign against the local Croat population."[9] Persecuting a civilian population and forcibly displacing civilians from a territory was a widespread and

---

[4] While the first indictment was issued in 2003, this discussion references the indictment used in the actual trial beginning in 2007; that is, the Third Amended Indictment of 7 December 2007, Case No. IT-03-67-T.

[5] *Šešelj*, "Third Amended Indictment of 7 December 2007", IT-03-67-T (hereinafter, TAI), §8(a).

[6] TAI, Count 1, §15.

[7] This statement also applies to the mode of liability of JCE, as the indictment makes clear: "Vojislav Šešelj is responsible for all the crimes the *actus reus* of which was carried out by a person used by him or any other participant in the joint criminal enterprise." TAI, §8(c).

[8] TAI, §5.   [9] TAI, §10(d).

systematic practice used by all sides in the Balkans conflict of 1991–5, a conflict that resurrected a disconcerting euphemism used in earlier conflicts, "ethnic cleansing."

One of the most notorious speeches the defendant gave in the Vojvodina region in northern Serbia was at an election rally in the village of Hrtkovci on 6 May 1992. According to the prosecution, the speech allegedly triggered the ethnic cleansing of 700–800 Croats in the community of less than two thousand persons. Indeed, it is fair to say that the speech at Hrtkovci is the heart of the prosecution case against Vojislav Šešelj, and Hrtkovci is mentioned forty-two times in the indictment, more than any other "crime base" in the trial. Šešelj's Hrtkovci speech is the mainstay of the charge of "direct and public ethnic denigration through 'hate speech' of the Croat, Muslim and other non-Serb populations in Vukovar, Zvornik and Hrtkovci on the basis of their ethnicities."[10] The indictment considers the speeches in those locales as hate speech, material acts of persecution in and of themselves that constituted full participation in the international crime of persecution of a civilian population.

Like the crime of direct and public incitement to commit genocide examined in Chapters 2–3, hate speech is an "inchoate crime," a form of direct material commission where the harm is the conduct itself, and no further harms or injuries need follow. This was the first and only time at the ICTY that an accused faced charges of direct commission primarily on the basis of their speech acts. When the trial began, there existed only one prior legal precedent in international criminal law, and that had been issued at the International Criminal Tribunal for Rwanda in *Nahimana* only weeks before the prosecution submitted their final indictment against Šešelj.[11]

Given the centrality of the 6 May 1992 Hrtkovci speech in the Šešelj trial, it is worth reproducing a passage from it here:

> In Hrtkovci . . . there is no room for Croats . . . (they) must clear out of Serbia . . . Serbian refugees will move into their houses . . . We have to give those Serbs a roof over their heads and feed the hungry mouths. We have no money to build new housing. We do not have the capacity to create new jobs for them. Very well, then, if we cannot do that, then we

---

[10] TAI, §17(k).

[11] The Appeals Chamber in *Nahimana* upheld the Trial Chamber decision that in certain circumstances, hate speech in the broader context of discriminatory violence towards a civilian population could constitute an act of persecution in and of itself (*Nahimana* AC §995).

should give every Serbian family of refugees the address of one Croatian family. The police will give it to them, the police will do as the government decides, and soon we will be the government. Fine, then. Every Serbian family of refugees will come to a Croatian door and give the Croats they find there their address in Zagreb or other Croatian town. Oh, they will, they will. There will be enough buses, we will drive them to the border of Serbian territory and they can walk on from there, if they do not leave before of their own accord.[12]

The message is fairly explicit, indicating the accused's intention that Croats in the village of Hrtkovci be forcibly transferred, against their will if need be, to Croatia to make room for the Serb refugees recently deported from that country. Seldom at an international criminal trial is there such unambiguous evidence of the intentionality of the accused encouraging the commission of crimes. Šešelj declared that Croats "must clear out" and just afterwards, in an atmosphere of extreme intimidation, they cleared out. This speech occurred in an extreme context – during the deadliest armed conflict in Europe since the Second World War. The Balkans conflict claimed approximately 130,000 lives, and most the fatalities were civilians murdered during forcible removals known as "ethnic cleansing."[13]

Given this setting, and with plausible evidence of the defendant's intentionality to commit widespread and systematic crimes against a civilian population, it may seem that prosecutors had a straightforward task in convicting Šešelj of crimes against humanity and war crimes. This impression, however, was not widely held at the Tribunal and the Šešelj trial was generally viewed as one of the weakest cases against a political leader at the ICTY from an evidentiary point of view. As noted previously, in most international trials, there is ample evidence of *actus reus*, and the primary responsibility of the prosecution is to prove that the defendant had the requisite intent and shared the purpose of the material perpetrators. In the Šešelj trial, the challenge was the reverse: the prosecution possessed an abundance of evidence of discriminatory animus and *mens rea*. Šešelj openly used denigrating language towards

---

[12] Prosecution's Closing Brief, IT-03–67-T, 5 February 2012 (hereinafter Prosecution's Closing Brief), §496.

[13] The most widely accepted estimate of deaths during the armed conflict come from demographers Tabeau and Bijak (2005:207). Based upon voting registers and municipal and census records, they estimate 100,000 dead in Bosnia and Herzegovina alone, with civilians making up the majority (fifty-four percent) of the fatalities.

Croats, such as the ethnic slur, "Ustaše" or "Ustashas"[14], and Muslims during the conflict. Some of it openly encouraged *ex ante*, or condoned *ex post facto*, the persecution and deportation of non-Serb civilians, as in the paragraph from the Hrtkovci speech cited above.

Throughout the trial, the prosecution turned the defendant's own words against him, and during the Prosecution's closing arguments, each assertion about the defendant's actions or intentions was accompanied by a colorful proclamation from Šešelj that matched their claim.[15] Additionally, the accused was predisposed to outbursts of ethno-nationalist hatred during the trial proceedings, for instance stating, "As far as I am concerned, I really would like all Ustashas to be dead because Ustashas are such an evil, they are even worse than Hitler's Nazis."[16]

Moreover, the prosecution possessed ample evidence of the *actus reus* of crimes against humanity and war crimes. In the period of the indictment (1991–3), hundreds of non-Serbs had been murdered, ethnically cleansed, sexually assaulted and tortured by self-styled ultra-nationalist followers of Šešelj. What the prosecution struggled to present to the courtroom was "linkage evidence," evidence that could connect the gushing fire hose of Vojislav Šešelj's animus to the commission of concrete material crimes on the ground in Serbia. Did the defendant's words of ill will, malice and spite have verifiable consequences of a magnitude that would justify imposing criminal liability, or was it all just empty rhetoric, ethnically charged hot air of the kind that is commonplace in the Balkans, and indeed elsewhere, including the location of the trial, the Netherlands?

Here, it merits acknowledging the uncertainty and doubt hanging over the category of speech crimes, as staff interviewed expressed a generalized lack of confidence in securing convictions for instigation, JCE (joint criminal enterprise), ordering and other modes of liability based on speech acts. I began all my interviews with the question, "Is this an unsettled area of law and is there is greater uncertainty in demonstrating speech crimes compared with war crimes and other crimes against humanity?" All the prosecuting attorneys and a majority

---

[14] The Ustaša ("Insurgence") was a fascist group created by Croatian separatist Ante Pavelić in Italy in 1929 that later established a pro-Nazi regime in Croatia during World War II. Ustaše, or Ustashas, refers to members or supporters of the Ustaša. The term Ustaše has also been used by some Serbian nationalists as an ethnic slur against all Croats. Prosecutors provided evidence of the accused's use of this term in the Prosecution's Closing Brief, 2012, §§51–3 and §162.
[15] See, for example, T.17143, 5 March 2012.   [16] T.16624, 7 March 2011.

of criminal defense attorneys and judges acknowledged that there was less predictability in the law of speech crimes than say, murder as a war crime, in part because the standard for causation in instigating was less well established in the case law.

As a general proposition, all the prosecutors who I interviewed acknowledged that it is hard to substantiate the claim that a specific speech or broadcast led to specific crimes. ICTY Senior Trial Attorney Hildegard Uertz-Retzlaff responded that the investigation and evidence gathering process is the same for all kinds of cases, however as a practical matter it is more difficult to persuade the judges, "When we speak about speech crimes, we have to recognize that this is an unsettled and new area of law. We prosecutors are learning about what we need to prove the crimes and what elements of the OTP [Office of the Prosecutor] case the judges will accept."[17]

ICTY Senior Trial Attorney Dan Saxon pointed to an unpredictability in how judges assess speech acts, based upon their national backgrounds.[18] From my interviews with prosecutors, it seems that the spoken words of political leaders are viewed in much more variable ways than other forms of evidence, in part because of the exceptionally diverse traditions of freedom of speech worldwide. Hildegard Uertz-Retzlaff felt that the influence and relative permissiveness towards speech of Anglo-American law explained why judges can be skeptical of prosecution evidence regarding the effects of speech acts, whereas in Germany it is commonly accepted that certain forms of speech (e.g., Holocaust denial) may be legitimately regulated by criminal law.[19] Prosecutors are keen observers of the proclivities of judges, motivated as they are to persuade them of the reasonableness of their arguments, and their views were largely borne out in my interviews with judges. When asked, "Is a speech act like other acts when determining causality?" one international criminal tribunal judge replied:

> It is similar to other acts, but the quest to establish a causal relationship might be a bit more abstract. I have concrete things to consider if a person drives their car erratically and causes a crash. It's all concrete – the speed of the car, its direction and so on. I don't have to fill in the gaps. Whether a speech act is causal or not is mainly an evidentiary problem ... the problem with speech is that its effects are difficult to

[17] Author interview, October 2013.   [18] Author interview, October 2013.
[19] Author interview, October 2013.

106

measure, they're not usually visible. Whereas if I hit a table with a hammer [pounds the table], it leaves a mark.[20]

There is also uncertainty regarding where the prosecution must begin its case – with causation and *actus reus*, as is customarily the case, or with intention. The judge just answered my question, "how do judges determine whether a speech instigated a crime?" thus,

> If we start with the speech, then we get a different answer than if we start with the crime committed. If we start with the crime, then we look at the criminal act and work outwards to other factors, we need to commence with the intention to commit the crime and ask, did the speech add to this? Which is different from a mono-causal approach that starts with the speech and asks was it the causal act, did this speech cause the crime to happen and without the speech would it not have happened? It is difficult to isolate the speech as the main or primary cause.[21]

Given the novelty of an international trial based primarily on evidence of speech acts, and the uncertainty of the status of the evidence and the variety of judicial approaches to proving causation beyond a reasonable doubt, speech crimes cases emerge as among the most demanding cases facing prosecutors at international criminal tribunals. What evidence might convince an international criminal court of a nexus between words and crimes? What case theory could the prosecution construct to show that Vojislav Šešelj successfully instigated his followers and local Serb authorities to persecute Croats? Demonstrating that causal link is especially tricky when the accused exercises major political authority over material perpetrators and visits them frequently on the battlefield, but does not clearly occupy an official position of superior or command responsibility. When the integrity of the legal process is undermined at every step by a filibustering defendant who enjoys uncommon tolerance from the presiding judge, the task only gets more onerous.

4.3   CIRQUE DU ŠEŠELJ

> For if we have no evidence of fact supporting our own case or telling against that of our opponent, at least we can always find evidence to prove our own worth or our opponent's worthlessness.
>
> Aristotle (2004:54) *Rhetoric*

---

[20] Author interview, October 2013.   [21] Author interview, October, 2013.

Vojislav Šešelj took a long and winding path to the International Tribunal for the Former Yugoslavia in The Hague. He was born in 1954 in Sarajevo, Bosnia-Herzegovina, then part of Yugoslavia.[22] Sarajevo was at that time a multicultural city where persons of Croat, Muslim and Serb backgrounds mixed freely, intermarried, worked together and mostly got along without a pronounced sense of political identity based upon religion or national group. Šešelj was considered a talented doctoral student in political science and, in 1981, he became one of youngest faculty members at Sarajevo University. Although initially a communist, he developed close relations with Serb nationalists at the university, and his promising academic career was derailed when he was convicted in 1984 of "counterrevolutionary activities" by a Sarajevo court. Sentenced to eight years in jail, he was released after serving nearly two years of his sentence. He then moved to Belgrade where he intensified his involvement in the nationalist circles opposing the communist regime.

Šešelj gravitated to the "Chetniks," Serbian nationalists who in the Second World War waged a brutal campaign against Josip Broz Tito's communist partisans. At various points in the war, the Chetniks both resisted and collaborated with the occupying Germans. In 1990, having received the endorsement of the elder statesmen of Serbian nationalism, Šešelj founded his own proto-political party, the "Serbian Chetnik Movement" (SCP). In 1991, as the communist one-party system disintegrated in Yugoslavia, he founded a far-right nationalist party, the Serbian Radical Party (SRS)[23] and was elected a member of the Assembly of the Republic of Serbia.

At that point, the SRS only had one Member of Parliament, Vojislav Šešelj, who was still a relatively marginal political figure. Šešelj vaulted to political prominence during the 1991–5 armed conflict in Yugoslavia, as the state media under the control of President Slobodan Milošević actively cultivated his reputation. The SRS's radical ethno-nationalist platform gave voice to a growing constituency of Serbs who were fearful about the disintegration of Yugoslavia, a state that they had controlled for much of the twentieth century.

In the 1992 general election, Šešelj's party took 73 seats out of 250 and become the second largest parliamentary party.[24] Radical nationalists

---

[22] Much of this biographical section is drawn from the Third Amended Indictment and corroborated by references in the international and local Balkans press.

[23] The SRS incorporated the pre-existing SCP into its party structure.

[24] http://en.wikipedia.org/wiki/Serbian_general_election,_1992

projected nationalist pride, and promised to seize territory and protect the rights of Serb minorities. They revived the nineteenth-century idea of a state that included all Serbs, or a "Greater Serbia."[25] To achieve this aim, the Chetniks were willing to go to war against Serbia's "historic enemies,"[26] namely the Croat, Muslim and Albanian populations within the former boundaries of Yugoslavia.

As the armed conflict intensified in 1992, Šešelj showed himself to be an effective mobilizer of volunteers for the Serbian war effort. Šešelj inspired Chetnik volunteers called the "Šešeljevci," or "Šešelj's Men," who were attached to various military and paramilitary units. During the trial, the prosecution cited Šešelj's own estimate that there were 30,000 Šešeljevci active during the conflict.[27] Fighters described as "Šešelj's Men" were notorious for attacking villages and towns across eastern Croatia and Bosnia, murdering, sexually assaulting, robbing and torturing Croat and Muslim civilians. Šešelj himself simulta-neously condoned and disavowed the Šešeljevci, and he studiously cultivated the ambiguity of his position of authority and military command.

Despite the fact that his followers revered him as the anointed "Vojvoda," or "Duke" and supreme Chetnik military and political leader,[28] the prosecution acknowledged that this title did not denote any official rank in the Yugoslav National Army (JNA) or Bosnian Serb Army (VRS),[29] and that Šešelj himself did not exercise conven-tional command responsibility over the men who acted in his name.[30] At the same time, the prosecution team reiterated throughout the trial that Šešelj's criminal liability stemmed from his position of political authority, "As the undisputed and revered leader of the SRS and SCP,

---

[25] Greater Serbia is a political principle that calls for an expansion of the Serbian state into all territories inhabited by Serbs. It is conventionally traced back to articulations of Serb nation-alism in the mid-nineteenth century. One of the founding documents proposing the concept of Greater Serbia was Načertanije (defined variously as "Program", "Outline" or "Principles"), produced in 1844 by the Serb Minister for Internal Affairs, Ilija Garašanin. Accompanying this was a panoply of other plans, documents and historical factors that contributed to the emergence of the Greater Serbia nationalist ideal. I thank Predrag Dojčinović for his thought-ful comments on this concept.

[26] TAI, §4.   [27] T.17185, 6 March 2012.

[28] "Vojvoda" is a military title traditionally conferred by Momcilo Djujić, the Second World War Chetnik leader. Šešelj was named Vojvoda in 1989 and the discussion of the significance of this during the trial can be found at T.17122, 5 March 2012.

[29] See the testimony of prosecution expert witness Theunens, 19 February 2008, T. 3815.

[30] "Prosecutors Seek 28-Year Jail term for Šešelj." Rachel Irwin. Institute for War and Peace Reporting. 9 March 2012. http://iwpr.net/report-news/prosecutors-seek-28-year-jail-term-seselj

Šešelj exercised ideological and moral authority over the Šešeljevci sent to the front by his politico-military organization."[31]

In 1998, the Serbian Radical Party entered a coalition with the ruling Socialist Party of Slobodan Milošević and Šešelj became vice-president of the Serbian government. According to some commentators, he allegedly participated in formulating and executing the Serb government's policy to expel ethnic Albanians from the part of Kosovo claimed by Serbs, a policy that led to NATO bombing of Serb positions in 1999. It is unclear why Šešelj's activities during this period, when he occupied a high-ranking and official position of superior responsibility in the government, were not included in the ICTY indictment, which only charged Šešelj with crimes up until 1993.

By 2000, the Balkans wars had ended, with mixed results for the advocates of Greater Serbia. Šešelj himself seemed washed up. He was out of government and his party held only a few seats in the Serb Assembly. He voluntarily surrendered in 2003 after his indictment was issued by the ICTY. The actual trial did not begin until late 2007, after a prolonged period of obstructionism by Šešelj, who engaged in hunger strikes and filed frivolous motions to disqualify judges and prosecuting attorneys on grounds of bias and ethics violations.[32] Even after the official trial got formally underway, the defendant was convicted three times for contempt of court[33] and sentenced to a total of four years and nine months for revealing the identities of protected witnesses on his personal website and in his published books.

After the proceedings ended, and only a few months before the Trial Chamber's judgment was expected, one of the judges in the trial, Danish Judge Frederik Harhoff was disqualified and removed in August 2013 for demonstrating "an unacceptable appearance of bias in favour of conviction" after sending a private letter to over fifty friends that shared his concerns about the integrity of recent war crimes acquittals at the ICTY.[34] The Tribunal replaced Harhoff with Senegalese Judge Mandiaye Niang who had to familiarize himself with the trial, delaying the judgment by eighteen months.

---

[31] *Šešelj* Prosecution's Closing Brief, §593.

[32] These accusations were investigated by the Tribunal. All were dismissed.

[33] In 2010, 2011, 2013.

[34] ICTY Press release "Judge Harhoff disqualified from Šešelj case." The Hague, 29 August 2013. www.icty.org/sid/11357

Characterized as a "series of unfolding disasters" by one legal analyst,[35] the trial finally ended with an acquittal on 31 March 2016, thirteen years after the first indictment and nine years after the commencement of the trial proceedings, making it the longest running trial thus far in war crimes history. The Tribunal released the defendant on compassionate and medical grounds in early 2015 and he returned to Belgrade to give press conferences that were more bellicose than ever. The length of the trial resulted in various negative consequences for both the individual accused and due process in international tribunals, and it undermined the ICTY's aspirations to international rule of law.

The Šešelj trial is a classic illustration, if any were needed after the trial of Slobodan Milošević,[36] of the pitfalls of self-representation by a high-level defendant, especially one as talented at the art of *defense de rupture* or a "rupture defense" as Vojislav Šešelj.[37] The courtroom mayhem could have been anticipated, given that Šešelj had made his attitude towards the Tribunal abundantly clear when he turned himself in, "With their stupid charges against me they have come up against the greatest living Serb legal mind. I shall blast them to pieces."[38] The accused was unfailingly boorish, constantly playing to his supporters back in Serbia and seizing any opportunity to make a mockery of the courtroom. He became enraged when technical faults suspended the Tribunal's internet service,[39] and was inclined to expressions of pathos, "I am alone in the universe, in the cosmos."[40]

In his cross-examination of prosecution witnesses, Šešelj was often abusive and bullying: he regularly questioned their intelligence,[41] called them liars,[42] and accused them of being agents or plants of the Croatian intelligence service.[43] As Judge Mandiaye Niang commented

---

[35] Marko Milanović, quoted in, "In Releasing Seselj, ICTY Solves One Problem – But Creates Many Others." Daisy Sindelar, 20 November 2014. Radio Free Europe. www.globalsecurity.org/military/library/news/2014/11/mil-141120-rferl02.htm

[36] Amply documented and analyzed by Gideon Boas (2007).

[37] "Defense de rupture" is a term coined by the flamboyant French criminal defense attorney Jacques Vergès, and refers to an anarchic style that upends the conventions of the criminal courtroom. See "Khmer Rouge Genocide Tribunal Stumbles as French Defense Lawyer Demands New Translation." Claire Duffett. www.law.com International News Section 10 December 2008. www.law.com/jsp/law/international/LawArticleFriendlyIntl.jsp?id=1202426601165

[38] "Vojislav Šešelj: Fallen Leader of Great Serbia." Manja Ristic. *Balkan Transitional Justice*. 15 March 2012. www.balkaninsight.com/en/article/vojislav-seselj-fallen-leader-of-the-great-serbia

[39] T.2045, 12 December 2007.   [40] T.10584, 9 October 2008.   [41] T.2148, 12 December 2007.

[42] T.2164, 13 December 2007.

[43] "Besmirching the Witness," *Sense Tribunal*, 15 October 2008. www.sense-agency.com/icty/besmirching-the-witness.29.html?cat_id=1&news_id=10977

in his separate opinion, "The Accused spared no one. He bullied and ridiculed witnesses well beyond any acceptable level of tolerance, even for a vigorous cross-examination. He was not always admonished. And when he was, he frequently turned a deaf ear to the Chamber's injunctions. He did what he pleased."[44]

There were rare moments when Šešelj was almost cooperative, correcting the factual errors of the prosecution in an avuncular fashion.[45] Sometimes, Šešelj's asides were even quite witty. At the climax of the trial, as the lead prosecutor introduced members of his team, Šešelj raised an objection before they even began the substance of their closing arguments. When the judge inquired as to his grounds, he protested that five prosecutors are too few "because they're unable to speak reasonably for – and make sense for longer than an hour."[46]

However, Šešelj was not just any ordinarily irascible self-representing defendant. The accused regularly scorned courtroom procedure and ventured into a terrain that was truly dark and venomous. Šešelj browbeat and threatened the prosecuting attorney Christina Dahl to the point where she appealed to the presiding judge for his protection, on the grounds that she felt like a battered woman.[47] Šešelj misused the platform of the Tribunal to engage in vicious outbursts against Croats, Muslims and Albanians and to envisage violence against Albanians as Kosovo gained independence from Serbia, "Now, we are going to have big flows of blood, rivers of blood on account of Albanians. If they take Kosovo away from us now, blood is going to flow in streams, for hundreds of centuries."[48]

With a defendant this disorderly, the situation needed a presiding judge in firm control of his or her courtroom. No observer has ever described Presiding Judge Jean-Claude Antonetti in such terms, and many have evaluated his performance harshly, with legal analyst Marko Milanović writing, "The trial itself has truly devolved into a travesty, with the presiding judge in particular showing an incredible lack of ability to manage the self-representing Šešelj."[49] Judge Antonetti sat silently during the defendant's violent outbursts, and appeared unable

---

[44] Šešelj TC, Individual Statement of Judge Mandiaye Niang, §7.

[45] For instance, Šešelj reminded the OTP that Milan Panić was Prime Minister of the Federal Republic of Yugoslavia, not Minister of the Interior (T.10422 8 October 2008).

[46] T.17114, 5 March 2012.   [47] T.2143, 12 December 2007.

[48] T.2133, 12 December 2007. Kosovo gained independence from Serbia the following year, 2008.

[49] Marko Milanovic. "ICTY Trial Chamber Suspends Seselj Trial." EJIL: Talk! Blog of the European International Law Journal. 11 February 2009. www.ejiltalk.org/icty-trial-chamber-sus pends-seselj-trial/

Figure 4.1 Vojislav Šešelj during his ICTY trial
Credit: *Courtesy of the UN International Criminal Tribunal for the Former Yugoslavia*

or unwilling to rein in the excesses of the defendant. At times, Antonetti adopted a faintly chastising tone, but regularly permitted Šešelj to disrupt the proceedings at will. Several legal commentators observed that the defendant essentially ran his own trial.[50]

Judge Antonetti's shortcomings went beyond mere passivity, and he was inclined to join in when Šešelj flouted procedure and interrupted prosecution eyewitnesses during their examination-in-chief. The judge was almost as eccentric and colorful as the accused himself. He was prone to vainglorious admiration at the sharpness of his own critical faculties, as when he declared that "nothing escapes me"[51] because "I have a good memory, and I record everything in my brain,"[52] and when he compared his efforts to discover the truth to the Greek philosopher

---

[50] See Zahar (2008:241) and Sluiter (2007:529).   [51] T.10440, 8 October 2008.
[52] T.10347, 7 October 2008.

Diogenes of Sinope: "just like Diogenes, I'm trying to – with my lantern, I'm trying to find explanations."[53]

Judge Antonetti's deportment was more than just a question of personality, as his manner crystallized the clash of legal cultures in the international criminal courtroom. Antonetti, a French judge from the inquisitorial tradition, apparently could not accept the common-law-inspired adversarial structure of the ICTY courtroom. The presiding judge balked at the idea that the prosecutor serves as the motor of the trial and he continually elbowed the prosecution aside like an investigating magistrate or inquisitorial *judge d'instruction*, seizing control of the prosecution's examination of its own witnesses. At other times, he adopted the role of defense counsel and inappropriately

Figure 4.2 ICTY Judge Jean-Claude Antonetti
Credit: Courtesy of the UN International Criminal Tribunal for the Former Yugoslavia

[53] T.10569, 9 October 2008. Diogenes walked around holding a lantern during the day claiming to be looking for an honest man.

advanced exculpatory arguments in the middle of the prosecution's examination-in-chief of key fact witnesses.[54]

Between the extraordinary length of the trial, the disruptions of the defendant, the removal of one judge for bias and a dereliction of duty on the part of the presiding judge, it is more than likely that the case would have been ruled a mistrial in many municipal jurisdictions. At the very least, the procedural irregularities in the trial ought to concern anyone who prefers trials that adhere to established procedure and due process. Having said that, the case is still an instructive one, since it illustrates how international prosecutors construct a case against a political leader for instigating his followers to persecute civilians from another social group. It underscores the special challenges of such an undertaking, and offers lessons of both a legal and theoretical kind.

4.4 THE PROSECUTION CASE AGAINST VOJISLAV ŠEŠELJ

> "Some people need no encouragement to go out and commit crimes, some need only a little encouragement, but most people require a lot of encouragement, and propaganda does this." ICTY Senior Trial Attorney Mathias Marcussen[55]

Put simply, the essence of the prosecution case against Vojislav Šešelj, was that he "was a fanatic propagandist contributing to an illegal enterprise,"[56] who instigated material perpetrators to commit crimes in four principal ways: by using denigrating language towards non-Serbs in press and public speeches, by travelling to the frontlines to encourage Serb forces, by dispatching members of his political party to spread a message of revenge and ethnic cleansing and by failing to act against soldiers and irregular fighters who called themselves Šešeljevci, or Šešelj's Men, as they persecuted non-Serbs in a widespread and systematic fashion.[57] How did the prosecution seek to prove their case beyond a reasonable doubt that Šešelj's speeches instigated others and thereby made a "substantial contribution" to the commission of crimes?[58]

This section concentrates on the heart of the instigation case against the accused – his speech at Hrtkovci on 6 May 1992. In the investigations

---

[54] See T.10419, 8 October 2008.   [55] Author interview, 2013.   [56] T.17136, 5 March 2012.
[57] Prosecution's Closing Brief (2012, §589).
[58] The Prosecution's Closing Brief (2012, §590) reminds us that the causal threshold of instigation is "substantial contribution."

phase, and as the trial got underway, the prosecution provided the court with damning evidence from insider witnesses – individuals close to Šešelj and his organization – that might have persuaded a trier of fact. In their written statements, four insider witnesses who were local Serb leaders and Šešeljevci, provided information about the relationship between the accused and the group undertaking criminal acts, including the structure and character of his ultra-nationalist organization. Prosecuting attorney Lisa Biersay described the character of their evidence in this way:

> We had insiders who talked about how powerful he [Vojislav Šešelj] was. How they looked up to him like he was a god. How his influence is evidenced by his popularity and the number of volunteers he was able to recruit, and the number of people who identified their group by using his name – the Šešeljevci.[59]

The prosecution team laid the foundations for their case regarding the accused's authority and operational responsibility for war crimes and crimes against humanity by calling two expert witnesses to speak about the unique character and structure of the Chetnik movement that the accused presided over, as head of the Serbian Radical Party (SRS) and Serbian Chetnik Movement (SCP). Balkans historian Yves Tomić spoke about how the Chetnik movement was, from its initial formation, an essentially military enterprise that mobilized irregular guerrilla volunteers in the Second World War and in the 1991–5 war in the former Yugoslavia.[60]

Belgian Defense Ministry military intelligence analyst Reynaud Theunens indicated that in the 1991–5 armed conflict SRS volunteers, while attached to different units on the battlefield, would wear their own Chetnik insignia and receive instructions through the parallel command structure of the Serbian Radical Party.[61] According to Theunens, Serbian Radical Party (SRS) "Vojvodas" like Šešelj were considered military superiors who commanded respect and devotion from their followers, over whom they exercised authority.[62] During the 1991–5 armed conflict, the SRS created a "War Staff" in Belgrade that coordinated activities, issuing instructions to commanders in the field who then sent reports back up the chain of command.[63] Furthermore, the Serbian Radical Party War Staff also possessed the authority to appoint and dismiss Chetnik commanders attached to various units.[64] The accused admitted receiving

---

[59] Author interview, 2014.   [60] T.2869, 2875, 3038–9.   [61] T.3748, 19 February 2008.
[62] T.3826, 19 February 2008.   [63] T.3733, 19 February 2008.   [64] T.3875, 20 February 2008.

regular and exhaustive reports from Šešeljevci in the battlefield,[65] and the expert witness referred to evidence of orders issued personally by the accused to field commanders.[66]

Prosecution expert Theunens painted a clear picture of the accused's position of leadership and authority in the SRS party structure. This vertical politico-military party structure, from the SRS "War Staff" down to the Chetnik insignia-wearing volunteers, constituted a parallel chain of authority that equaled the Yugoslav National Army or Bosnian Serb Army. At the same time, the Šešeljevci were distributed across many units and many were integrated into a formal military structure in which the accused had no official rank, title or authority. This explains why the prosecutors emphasized the accused's "ideological and moral authority"[67] over the Šešeljevci, rather than forms of authority that were more directly and formally sanctioned. This could also explain why prosecutors portrayed the accused's authority in such convoluted, equivocal and possibly self-contradictory language; for instance, Mr. Marcussen stated in his closing arguments, "This quasi-military politician exercised his authority and influence over each and every aspect related to the volunteers, even though he did not have operational command over them."[68]

The prosecution team also sought testimony from insiders, former high-ranking Šešeljevci, to corroborate the theory advanced by the experts. Insiders who once revered Šešelj turned against their "Duke." Now middle aged, often unemployed and debilitated by war injuries, many felt used and abandoned by their leadership. However, this cornerstone of the prosecution's case disintegrated over the course of the trial. All seven insiders, to a man, later withdrew their testimony and refused to testify in The Hague, or recanted or partially recanted on the stand.[69]

In an interview given after the trial, Judge Flavia Lattanzi spoke about the intimidation of insider witnesses: "Of course, I cannot reveal the contents of our discussion. I can, however, guarantee, that denials were the result of threats and intimidation. It is clear even if you read the minutes of the hearings. These people were scared, they were petrified before Šešelj. Šešelj's gaze was all it took. I constantly looked at the witnesses, and then at Šešelj, who cross-examined. Some had the courage to testify, despite everything. Others did not."[70]

---

[65] Prosecution's Closing Brief (2012, §144, §533).   [66] T.3657–8, 14 February 2008.
[67] Prosecution's Closing Brief (2012, §593).   [68] T.17187, 6 March 2012.
[69] Prosecution's Closing Brief (2012, §§656–70).   [70] Rossini (2016).

Some witnesses made allegations of ethics violations against the prosecution during their testimony, allegations that were investigated by a Tribunal-appointed inquiry and found to be baseless. The prosecution counter-alleged that "The recantations were the product of an organized campaign to deter witnesses from testifying truthfully."[71] In January 2015, the ICTY issued arrest warrants against two defense lawyers and an associate of Šešelj, charging them with contempt of court because they threatened and intimidated two prosecution witnesses and offered them bribes.[72]

One insider, Zoran Rankić, retracted his earlier signed statement and switched to testify for the defense. Rankić, former deputy head of Vojislav Šešelj's Serbian Radical Party War Staff, ceased to cooperate with the prosecution and became a defense witness in 2007, citing excessive pressure on him and his family from prosecutors. Under cross examination, another picture emerged, and prosecutors alleged that when they met with Rankić in 2006 to finalize a second statement, he reported that a group from Belgrade had warned him "not to play with your life," a statement Rankić denied on the stand. The witness did admit, however, that his family had received a bomb threat by telephone and that he had requested to be relocated to Sweden for the safety of his family.[73] Prosecutors continued to refer to the insider testimony as plausible statements of fact even after their repudiation, but their credibility and probative value was severely downgraded.

Insider witness testimony has been a boon to prosecutors at international tribunals, insofar as insiders provide a behind-the-scenes account of the accused's acts, but these witnesses also bring their own problems. They may have mixed motives for testifying, including blaming others to evade culpability for their own actions. While the early cases at international criminal tribunals had few insiders, more have been called to testify in the last ten years. At first, they were received relatively uncritically (even jubilantly) by international judges, but over time, international judges became more searching in their questioning and evaluating of insiders. The ICTR Appeals Chamber in Muvunyi, for instance, cast doubt on the credibility of one insider

[71] T.17148, 5 March 2012.
[72] "ICTY unveils arrest warrants for three involved in Seselj trial." Ashley Hogan. 4 December 2015. Jurist.org http://jurist.org/paperchase/2015/12/icty-publicly-announces-charges-and-arrest-warrants-for-three-involved-in-seselj-trial.php#
[73] T. 15987. 12 May, 2010. "Šešelj Trial Hears Why Witness Switched Sides." Julia Hawes. Institute for War and Peace Reporting, 18 May 2010. http://iwpr.net/print/report-news/seselj-trial-hears-why-witness-switched-sides

witness on the grounds that he might have been motivated to amplify the role of the accused in order to diminish his own responsibility.[74] Even though there is no unblemished source of witness testimony, the prosecution case in a speech crimes trial is usually more persuasive with insiders than without them.

The recanting of prosecution witnesses is a feature of all types of international criminal tribunal cases, yet the phenomenon does seem more endemic in speech crimes cases, in part because the accused are often high-level politicians with continued government backing and a zealous following. At the International Criminal Court in the Ruto–Sang case relating to ethnic violence during the 2007 Kenyan elections, the Court ordered nine prosecution witnesses to testify after they stopped communicating with the prosecution or recanted their statements.[75] Compelling the recalcitrant witnesses to testify against their will via a video link from Nairobi was ultimately counterproductive. As one witness after another defected to the defense, prosecutors scrambled to petition the court to declare a succession of witnesses as hostile witnesses,[76] a designation that allows the prosecution to cross-examine and challenge the witness on any contradictions between their court testimony and their prior statement.[77]

In the Ruto–Sang trial at the ICC, prosecutors alleged that the witnesses recanted their earlier testimony only after the prosecution's witness list was disclosed to the defense and the witnesses were approached and bribed by persons aligned with the defendant.[78] Issues also arose involving defense witnesses, and in January 2015, Meshak Yebei, a defense witness in Ruto–Sang who had been under the court's protection, was found murdered in Nandi County in Kenya. The press release of the Office of the Prosecutor indicated that it held "information indicating that Mr. Yebei was deeply implicated in the

---

[74] Muvunyi AC §§129–31.

[75] For instance, "Decision on Prosecution Request for Issuance of a Summons for Witness 727 of 17 February 2015." Ruto and Sang (ICC-01/09-01/11), 17 February 2015 at §37–8. "Witness Testifies about Fundraising Event He Said Did Not Take Place." Tom Maliti, International Justice Monitor, 16 September 2014.

[76] "A hostile witness is a witness who is not desirous of telling the truth to the court at the instance of the calling party" declared the ICC judge in Ruto–Sang, "Trial Chamber Declares Witness 743 a Hostile Prosecution Witness." Tom Maliti. International Justice Monitor. 20 January 2015.

[77] Trial Hearing (ICC-01/09-01/11), 25 September 2014. Witnesses 495, 516, 604 and 637. See "Witness 516 is Declared a Hostile Prosecution Witness." Tom Maliti. International Justice Monitor, 25 September 2014.

[78] Trial Hearing (ICC-01/09-01/11), 9 September 2014, at 70–71. See "Prosecutor Asks Witness Whether He Fears Implicating Ruto or Sang." Tom Maliti, International Justice Monitor, 10 September 2014.

scheme to corrupt Prosecution witnesses in the case against Mr. Ruto and Mr. Sang."[79]

Amid swirling allegations and counter-allegations of bribery, intimidation and murder, trials at international criminal tribunals share many of the attributes of major organized crime cases in domestic settings,[80] especially when the accused is a national political leader.[81] Unlike national governments, however, international criminal tribunals have significantly less security presence on the ground to enforce special protective measures for witnesses, and the Registrar of the International Criminal Court, Herman von Hebel, aptly described the court's protection program as "vulnerable."[82] Their reliance on recalcitrant national states for search, seizure, arrest and protection of witnesses has long been the Achilles' heel of international justice institutions.

After the defection of its insider witnesses, the prosecution in Šešelj was forced to turn to the second-best source of testimony – victim or bystander testimony – and it called six fact witnesses for the Hrtkovci part of the indictment. Five were Croats who quit the village after Šešelj's election rally: Katica Paulić,[83] Franjo Baričević,[84] and three protected witnesses.[85] Their testimony was accompanied by the report and testimony of an expert witness, demographer Ewa Tabeau, who documented the radical demographic shifts in the towns and villages of Vojvodina where Šešelj had given his speeches. The victim testimony was quite powerful and compelling in its own right. Katica Paulić was present at the election rally on 6 May 1992, and she offered her interpretation of Šešelj's speech to the courtroom: "You can't survive here. Get out of here, save your skin and that of your family, any way you know how. The message was that we Croats and Hungarians had to get out of that village."[86] She fled the village

---

[79] Statement of the Office of the Prosecutor regarding the reported abduction and murder of Mr. Meshak Yebei. 9 January 2015.
[80] And, in particular, "RICO" cases in the United States: Racketeer Influenced and Corrupt Organizations Act, enacted by section 901(a) of the Organized Crime Control Act of 1970.
[81] "Congolese Politician is Found Guilty of Tampering." Marlise Simons, New York Times, 20 October 2016.
[82] "Witness Protection and Outreach Cited as Areas in Need of Improvement." Taegin Reisman. 25 July 2014. International Justice Monitor. www.ijmonitor.org/2014/07/witness-protection-and-outreach-cited-as-areas-in-need-of-improvement/?utm_source=International±Justice±Monitor&utm_campaign=5c15eeffd7-kenya-monitor-rss&utm_medium=email&utm_term=0_f42ffeffb9-5c15eeffd7-49388625. Last accessed 13 January 2015.
[83] T.11909, 19 November 2008.   [84] T.10626, 15 October 2008.
[85] VS-061, VS-067 and VS-1134.
[86] T.11909-11910. Testimony included in the Prosecution's Closing Brief (2012, §508).

when Serb refugees simply moved into her house and informed her that she must leave.[87]

The most gripping testimony came from Aleksa Ejić, a farmer who had been born and raised in Hrtkovci.[88] Ejić is an ethnic Serb who was active in Serbian nationalist politics, and in 1992 he was a member of the Serbian Renewal Party (SPO) which shared the intense nationalist ideology of Šešelj's Serbian Radical Party.[89] During the war, he joined the paramilitary Serbian Guard and fought with Serb units in Bosnia and Herzegovina. In the Hrtkovci context, Ejić was neither a victim nor a perpetrator, but a prominent local political actor without an ethno-nationalist axe to grind against Serbs. Ejić described how Serbs had always been the minority in Hrtkovci, only constituting ten percent of the total, with Croats and Hungarians holding an overwhelming majority.

This changed in 1991 as Serb refugees, fleeing persecution in Croatia and Bosnia, began to cross the border. At first there were only a few hundred, who were spontaneously welcomed and cared for by the whole community. The refugees were housed on a farm in accommodation usually reserved for seasonal laborers, but as their numbers swelled, they began to enter vacant houses whose owners were away working in other European countries. By 1992, there were over a thousand refugees and the resettlement process became less orderly, as refugees began to invade the homes of non-Serbs by force after Šešelj's election rally of 6 May.[90]

Aleksa Ejić described the men who accompanied Šešelj that day. They wore the black uniforms of Chetniks in the Second World War and sported pistols and army daggers. He reported that every hundred meters a man stood vigil with an automatic weapon. Their objective, for Ejić, was "to create fear."[91] At the rally, Šešelj gave his speech to an audience of about three hundred, most of whom were Serb refugees not originally from the village of Hrtkovci. According to Ejić, the displaced and relocated were Šešelj's main constituency, not the longstanding Serb villagers of Hrtkovci who had coexisted with their Croat and Hungarian neighbors for decades:

> I believe that actually this was a message to them to the effect of, "Judge things for yourself and you know what you should do. You've been

---

[87] Prosecution's Closing Brief (2012, §517).   [88] Beginning at T10328, 7 October 2008.
[89] For a while the parties were allies, but over time became bitterly opposed.
[90] T.10328, 7 October 2008.   [91] T.10335, 7 October 2008.

expelled. You have nowhere to go, whereas Croats and Hungarians are living here. Carry out an exchange with them." That was my understanding of . . . these words, and that is what I took away with me from the rally.[92]

In effect, Šešelj was providing Serb refugees, who were themselves the victims of recent persecution in Croatia, with the authorization for a property grab, and they responded enthusiastically. Šešelj's speech was greeted with applause and calls and chants of "Ustasha Out!" and "This is Serbia!"[93] Aleksa Ejić recounted how after Šešelj spoke, a certain Mr. Zilić who was a Serb refugee from Croatia, took the microphone and read out the names of prominent Croats in the village, saying they were not loyal to Serbia and had no place in Hrtkovci.[94] At this crucial point in Ejić's testimony, Vojislav Šešelj interrupted the witness, flouting standard procedure:

> The people that are mentioned here were the people that went to [Croatian President Franjo] Tudjman's army to fight against the Serbian people. That was the essence of this speech, not just mentioning all Croats residing in this village.[95]

Presiding Judge Jean-Claude Antonetti not only allowed the challenge, but posed it himself to the witness, asking if the Croats named had left the village to fight in the Croatian National Guard. The judge then took over the cross-examination of the witness, while the Italian prosecuting attorney, Mr. Calogero Ferrara, abjectly stood by. The witness disputed Šešelj's rebuttal, pointing out that wealthy and prominent Croats were named because they were the first to be dispossessed of their property: "the point was to intimidate and to make the population start with the exchanges."[96]

Standard court procedure was only reinstated when Judge Flavia Lattanzi, in the guise of defending Judge Antonetti, adroitly stepped in to chastise the defendant for his "unacceptable behavior" in lecturing the court and telling the presiding judge what to do.[97] Nonplussed, Šešelj was satisfied with his latitude for maneuver, and declared to Judge Antonetti later on during the examination of witness Ejić,

---

[92] T.10355, 7 October 2008.
[93] Ejić, T.10343. This was confirmed by witness Baričević at T.10621.
[94] T.10335, 7 October 2008.   [95] T.10348, 7 October 2008.   [96] T.10347, 7 October 2008.
[97] T.10351, 7 October 2014.

> I have to confess to you right now that there is a danger that you will become more popular than me in Serbia, because you have exhibited a high level of tolerance in these proceedings.[98]

The prosecution rested its case after over 577 trial hours, 99 witnesses (six of whom were experts) and 1399 evidence exhibits.[99] Procedurally, after the prosecution rests its case, the defense can request a "Decision on Motion for Judgment of Acquittal" under Rule 98 *bis* of the ICTY and ICTR Rules of Procedure and Evidence. Also known as an "interim judgment," this decision delivers the judges' assessment regarding which charges are unsubstantiated and can be dismissed, and which counts are substantiated with enough evidence that a reasonable trier of fact might (but only might) convict the accused. Note that the 98 *bis* procedure employs a lower standard to review the evidence than the final Trial Chamber judgment, and provides a mechanism to dismiss those charges for which the prosecution has failed to present sufficient evidence.

On 4 May 2011, the three judges handed down their Rule 98 *bis* decision, or interim judgment. The majority opinion, Judge Antonetti dissenting, found that the evidence met the low threshold that a reasonable trier of fact could find guilt based on the evidence presented for all nine counts of the indictment. The majority opinion emphasized the defendant's speech outside the Croatian town of Vukovar in 1991 where Šešelj told a rally on the eve of a Serb offensive against the town that "not one Ustasha must leave Vukovar alive."[100]

Antonetti's dissent countered that there was "not sufficient evidence to establish a nexus" between Šešelj and the instigation of crimes, "For example, what words uttered [by Šešelj] led to brutal and inhumane living conditions? ... What are the reasons [for these conditions]? The words uttered by the accused or some other reason."[101] Antonetti opined that the prosecution did not enter sufficient evidence into the trial to demonstrate that the accused was part of a JCE.[102] His grounds were that the accused did not share a common purpose with other members of the JCE such as Slobodan Milošević since he campaigned for a nationalist Greater Serbia,

---

[98] T.10481, 8 October 2008.   [99] *Šešelj* TC Annex 2, Procedural Background, §4.
[100] "Šešelj Trial Cleared for Defence Phase." Institute for War and Peace Reporting. Rachel Irwin. 6 May 2011. http://iwpr.net/report-news/seselj-trial-cleared-defence-phase
[101] "Šešelj Trial Cleared for Defence Phase." Institute for War and Peace Reporting. Rachel Irwin. 6 May 2011. http://iwpr.net/report-news/seselj-trial-cleared-defence-phase
[102] T. 16988 5 May 2011.

whereas Milošević desired a federal Yugoslavia in which Serbs domi-nated the political institutions.[103] These were two radically different political visions and the accused repeated clashed with leaders such as Yugoslav President Slobodan Milošević and Bosnian Serb politician Radovan Karadžić.

Antonetti's dismissal of JCE was consistent with his dissenting opinions in previous ICTY cases such as *Prlić et al.* and *Tolomir*. In his dissenting opinion in *Prlić*, Antonetti wrote that it was "unneces-sary to create an 'umbrella' form of responsibility" such as JCE, which was not established in the ICTY Statute.[104] In particular, Antonetti's dissenting opinion in *Prlić et al.* energetically rejected the third category of JCE "does not validly exist and must be discarded."[105] In his dissent-ing opinion in the *Tolomir* Appeals Chamber judgment, Antonetti stated that the *Tadić* Appeals Chamber erred in finding that JCE existed in customary international law[106] and that it was "not necessary to create this notion" which was the product of an "academic contest" along ICTY judges to create a new doctrine in international law.[107] Furthermore, added Antonetti, the application of JCE at the ICTY and other inter-national tribunals has resulted in "many violations of the rights of the accused, in particular those linked to the presumption of innocence and a fair trial."[108] Given these profound objections, JCE was simply not a criminal concept that Judge Antonetti was going to endorse in the Šešelj case. Of course, whether a judge should be presiding over a criminal trial when he is unwilling to apply the prevailing case law of the tribunal is another question.

Although it dismissed JCE, Antonetti's majority opinion in the Rule 98 *bis* decision retained other charges in the indictment. Both the majority and dissenting opinions indicated their preference for instiga-tion as the mode of liability most appropriate to describe the actions of the accused. Instigation is more challenging to prove in that it requires a higher standard of "substantial contribution" rather than the "sig-nificant contribution" required by JCE, and instigation implies a more direct nexus between speech acts and criminal acts.

---

[103] T. 16956 *et passim*, 5 May 2011.
[104] *Prlić et al.* TC "Separate and Partially Dissenting Opinion of Presiding Judge Jean-Claude Antonetti," p. 182.
[105] *Prlić et al.* TC "Separate and Partially Dissenting Opinion of Presiding Judge Jean-Claude Antonetti," p. 173.
[106] *Tolomir* AC "Separate and Partially Dissenting Opinion of Judge Antonetti" 14 July 2015, p. 102.
[107] *Ibid.*, p. 104.   [108] *Ibid.*

In my reading of events, the judges preferred the more demanding mode of liability because they were uncomfortable with convicting an accused based almost entirely on what he said in public. The Šešelj trial was precedent-setting in its reliance on evidence of speech acts rather than other material contributions, and the judges wanted to set the bar high in requiring proof of the direct form of causation entailed in instigation. After this interim ruling, the prosecution team refocused on tightening up the causation elements of their case for instigation. From then on, prosecutors redirected their energies to the charges of instigation and hate speech and the more stringent task of connecting the defendant's speeches to specific crimes.

Intriguingly, the prosecution did not completely abandon JCE, and still invoked it when the evidence for instigation and direct causation was not very compelling. As lead prosecutor Mathias Marcussen told me in an interview, "The ICTY Office of the Prosecutor considered JCE to be the mode of liability that most accurately described the full scope of Vojislav Šešelj's responsibility."[109] JCE as a mode of liability has been tremendously popular with international prosecutors because it is more expansive in scope and less demanding in its burden of proof of causation. It permits relatively loose and weak assertions of cause and effect, effectively lowering the bar of causation in a way that is similar to the charge of conspiracy in US criminal law.[110]

For instance, while making the case for JCE, prosecution attorney Biersay referred to press conferences that Šešelj gave, and then she notes that "around the same time," non-Serbs were being murdered and tortured at various locales.[111] In passages like this one, the prosecution strayed from the charge of instigation to invoke JCE and support a more indirect type of cause and effect. After the interim judgment, the prosecution team turned to JCE when constructing the accused's role as a propagandist who recruited fighters who committed crimes. This was the basis of his "significant contribution" to the JCE of persecution and ethnic cleansing, "he filled his Serb forces with his hateful propaganda, which they took with them to the front lines. His ability to offer a fighting force was a significant contribution to the common purpose

---

[109] Author interview, 2015.
[110] See, for example, T.17180-2, 6 March 2012. This also can be seen in the Prosecution's Closing Brief, where the argumentation and evidence presented for JCE is more formless and indirect than for instigation.
[111] T.17181, 5 March 2012.

of the JCE and it was a substantial contribution to the commission of the charged crimes."[112]

In the final stages of the trial, the prosecution largely abandoned the charge of "ordering." Despite the efforts to establish his authority in the early parts of the case through the testimony of military expert witness Reynaud Theunens,[113] prosecutors presented little or no evidence of superior responsibility in the latter stages of their case. Perhaps they lacked confidence in their ability to show that Šešelj exercised effective control over the Šešeljevci. Instigating, as we have seen in Chapter 3, does not require a relationship of authority or for the instigator to exercise effective control. Quietly and without ceremony, the charge of ordering faded away in the prosecution case against Šešelj, and the Prosecution's Closing Brief (2012) does not accuse the defendant of issuing any specific order for a particular crime. By the end of the trial, the last viable charge left standing, then, was instigating crimes against humanity.

4.5 CLOSING ARGUMENTS

> He [Šešelj] used his political and moral authority to encourage and instigate groups and individuals within the Serb Forces, including Šešeljevci, through his persecutory propaganda.
>
> Prosecution's Closing Brief (2012, §2).

On 5 March 2012, the prosecution presented its final closing arguments and sought to convince the bench of the causal nexus between the accused's speeches and resulting acts of persecution. The team was led by Mathias Marcussen, a Danish trial attorney who was widely seen at the Tribunal as a "safe pair of hands." The Šešelj case was his first appearance in the international trial chamber, as his prior experience had been in the appellate division of the ICTR.

Marcussen made the best of a case in disarray. He opened the prosecution arguments with Vojislav Šešelj's threat made on 5 March 1992, exactly twenty years earlier to the date, that if Bosnia declared independence, there would be "rivers of blood on Bosnia and Herzegovina's soil."[114] A month or so later, the senior prosecuting attorney pointed

---

[112] T. 17182, 6 March 2012.
[113] The testimony of Reynaud Theunens regarding the authority exercised by the accused can be found at T.3815-3886, 19–20 February 2008.
[114] T.17115, 5 March 2012.

out, the town of Zvornik was attacked by irregular Serb forces, including Šešeljevci. Non-Serb men were separated from the women and children who were expelled from the town. Eighty-eight Croat and Muslim men were then executed by firing squads. The prosecution line of argumentation asserted a clear connection between Šešelj's speech in one part of Serbia, and violent actions committed in another region by Serb paramilitaries, some of whom were his avowed followers.

Indeed, this was the template for the prosecution team's final arguments in the trial and the accompanying Prosecution's Closing Brief (2012). The evidence for each "crime base," be it Hrtkovci, Vukovar or Zvornik, was organized according to the same narrative structure and arc. The prosecution would start with a speech by Šešelj, and then proceed to show the awful events that subsequently transpired and assert that these events were the direct consequences of the speech. Each Šešelj speech represented the final link in a chain of causation that culminated in the target crime. There may have been other factors and other preparations might have existed, but it was the speech that directly triggered the crimes against humanity, according to prosecutors. To prove instigation, the prosecution adopted a robust, direct causal argument in which speech acts, then crimes, marched in lock step. The prosecution theory of the case could be summed up in five words: Šešelj speaks, then atrocities occur. And in only three words: chronology proves causation.

Given the slim evidentiary proof for direct instigation, legal causation was demonstrated through a chronological ordering of the facts, as is apparent in the prosecution's narration of the Hrtkovci situation by American prosecuting attorney Lisa Biersay. She recounted how Šešelj's infamous "hate speech" was delivered on 6 May, the Serbian national holiday of St. George's Day, the most popular and celebrated patron saint day in the Serb Orthodox calendar. The accused and his Chetnik entourage wearing black Second World War uniforms roared into the village, blaring Chetnik music. They posted men armed with automatic rifles on street corners, the prosecution alleged, all with the objective of creating an intimidating atmosphere for Croat villagers.[115]

Biersay described the content and meaning of the speech, and then claimed that "Immediately after his speech, many Croats began

---

[115] T.17299–17302, 6 March 2012.

preparing to leave Hrtkovci, showing they felt denigrated and threatened, just as the accused intended."[116] Directly following Šešelj's 6 May speech, said Biersay, Croats were harassed and threatened. Hand grenades were thrown into Croat homes, dogs were killed, and Croats received bomb threats over the telephone.[117] Evidence of the exodus of the Croat population was found in the register of the Catholic Church, which showed a spike in requests for birth and marriage certificates, as Croats gathered their identity documents in preparation for emigrating to Croatia. According to the Prosecution's Closing Brief, Hrtkovci's Croat population, about forty percent of the village, declined by seventy-six percent in 1992.[118] The prosecution was not able to be very precise about the actual numbers that were displaced from the village, and could only estimate a range of between 700–800 persons.[119] By August 1992, Serbs were a majority in the village for the first time in recent history, and the leadership changed the name to Srbislavci or, "Glorifier of Serbs."[120]

That the prosecution sought to demonstrate a causal connection between the threatening speech and the atrocities through their temporal proximity is explicitly acknowledged in the Prosecution's Closing Brief (2012, 521–2):

> In fact, a strong causal inference is raised by the temporal connection between Šešelj's speech and the departure of a large number of Croats from Hrtkovci. This mass departure is evidenced by the dramatic increase in the number of requests for marriage and christening certificates from the Catholic Church in Hrtkovci in May 1992 ... In light of the inflammatory content of Šešelj's 6 May 1992 speech and how rapidly news of its content spread through Hrtkovci, the logical inference from these figures is that a number of Croats made the decision to leave Hrtkovci, and did in fact leave, as a result of Šešelj's speech.

The relevance of temporal proximity for showing causation was reinforced in my interviews with prosecutors involved with the Šešelj trial. Speaking with ICTY Senior Trial Attorney Hildegard Uertz-Retzlaff, it became apparent that prosecutors planned to prove causation through a chronological ordering of events, starting from the earliest phases of the investigations, "I was in charge of the initial investigation in the Šešelj case and together with my team drew up the indictment and the opening statement of the prosecution. We emphasized where he said

[116] T.17304, 6 March 2012.   [117] T.17310, 6 March 2012.
[118] Prosecution's Closing Brief (2012, §520).   [119] Ibid., §523.   [120] Ibid., §515.

something and what happened next, like his speech in Vukovar or his speech in Hrtkovci. We believed there was a clear connection between these speeches and crimes."[121]

When asked, "What convinced you that the speech at Hrtkovci caused the crimes against Croats?" Uertz-Retzlaff responded, "Šešelj comes into this area with a lot of tension and says 'Let's get rid of the Croats.' And the Croats hear this and start to leave the area and the Serbs in positions of power start a persecution campaign against Croats, it starts immediately afterwards." "Is the speech a proximate cause?" I asked. "It's a trigger for the audience to remove Croats, speeches can be triggers of violence," she replied.

How do judges evaluate the prosecution's *modus operandi* of asserting causation via chronology? When asked how he might determine a link between a speech and criminal acts, Judge Frederik Harhoff, who served on the bench in *Šešelj*, replied, "Sometimes there is a clear link to an upcoming conflict or link, like the taking of Vukovar. If a powerful leader says to a mob or group of armed commanders 'It is of vital importance to take Vukovar' and the next day Vukovar is taken, then there is a nexus." I then asked, "How do you know that the speech was the main trigger of violence and not another factor?" and he replied, "You don't." Harhoff then acknowledged that temporal contiguity was not enough in itself to show causation.

My interviews with judges and prosecuting attorneys revealed that the view that "chronology shows causation" is widespread in international criminal tribunals. When I asked one ICTY judge what evidence he would look for in deciding a case where the defendant was charged with instigating crimes against humanity, he replied,

> I'd want to know where the speaker spoke and what happened next. If he spoke in a town and violence occurred the next day, then that would be strong evidence of causation. If, however, violence didn't occur there, but occurred some weeks or months later, or in another place, then that would be less convincing.[122]

The prosecution supplemented their "causality through chronology" theory with other efforts at rhetorical persuasion, repeating Šešelj's words as a refrain throughout the trial, and using video footage to provide a visceral visual element. Throughout their closing arguments Marcussen, Biersay and other members of the prosecution team

---

[121] Author interview, October, 2013.   [122] Author interview, 2013.

repeated the defendant's pronouncement that "words can be a very dangerous weapon. Sometimes they pound like a howitzer."[123] Other moments in the prosecution's summing up served as a powerful finale in an exhausting trial. Marcussen's understated delivery of the following words might even have had more impact than if they had been spoken by a more theatrical attorney:

> The accused ... engaged in a vicious and relentless propaganda campaign against non-Serbs, including Croatians and Muslims as well as Kosovar Albanians. He claimed that Serbs had an historic right to the territory of Greater Serbia. He denigrated and dehumanized non-Serbs. He equated Croatians to Ustasha fascists who had committed crimes against Serbs and Bosnian Muslims to Ottoman Turks that he said had subjugated Serbs for hundreds of years. He claimed Serbs were under an imminent threat of genocide at the hands of Croats and enslavement by Muslims. He repeatedly raised the specter of crimes against Serbs during the Second World War and he called for blind revenge in which rivers of blood would flow.[124]

The emotional highpoint of the prosecution's closing arguments came when the court viewed a video clip of Šešelj giving a speech at a Serb Orthodox religious celebration on 6 May 1991 in the presence of Bosnian Serb leader Radovan Karadžić. He whipped up the crowd into a nationalist frenzy, saying, "Our western enemies are attempting to carry out a new genocide against the Serbian people. Brothers and sister Serbs, it is our duty to stop it and we are sending this message to our enemies: not only shall we avenge the present victims, but we shall avenge the previous ones too, when they dared to put the Ustasha knife under the Serbian throat again."[125] Šešelj then pressed upon an exceptionally sensitive and provocative subject at that time, referring to "the resistance in Borovo Selo." He was recalling an incident in Borovo Selo, Croatia that had occurred only four days earlier, in which Serb paramilitaries (who the prosecution alleged were "Šešeljevci") ambushed and killed twelve Croat police officers.[126] For many observers, this incident represented the beginning of the violent disintegration of Yugoslavia, when the point of no return was passed. The crowd drowned out the speaker at that point, chanting, "Revenge! Revenge! Revenge!"[127]

---

[123] T.17159, 5 March, 2012.   [124] T.17122, 5 March 2012.   [125] T.17164, 5 March 2012.
[126] The ambush and killing of Croat police officers in Borovo Selo in May 1991 is discussed in the Prosecution's Closing Brief (2012, §88).
[127] T.17165, 5 March 2012.

While the video carried a strong emotional charge, it conveyed little evidence of probative value. After showing the film, the trial attorney moved to speak about deployment of Šešeljevci to Croatia, but he made no claim about the connection of any specific speech to any subsequent crimes. Indeed, it is hard to see the relevance of the speech to the charge of instigation since it followed the murder of Croat police officers at Borovo Selo. The prosecution does not inform the court where the speech was given, or define what its relationship was to the events at Borovo Selo, or anywhere else. Therefore, we could conclude that the film is less proof of causation than it is a poignant and rhetorical attempt at persuasion.

The footage could be construed as an illustration of the accused's power over his audience, and his willingness to condone war atrocities that were only a few days old, in which case the film might be germane to the charge of aiding and abetting, but the prosecution never makes this entirely clear.[128] In the Prosecution's Closing Brief (2012), prosecutors did, however, decide to conjure the image of the accused before crowds of supporters thus:

> The Trial Chamber has viewed videos of crowds responding to Šešelj's charismatic and inflammatory propaganda. Šešelj used all available media resources – television, radio, newspapers and monthly periodicals (including the SRS newspapers *Velika Srbija* and *Zapadna Srbija*) and personal appearances to disseminate denigrating, hateful and violent speech about non-Serbs. He inspired and instigated violence through his use of brutal, vulgar language and boasting about acts of vandalism and violence committed by him and those members of the Serb forces who perpetrated the crimes charged in the indictment.[129]

In summing up, the prosecution claimed that across all the crime bases in the indictment, Šešelj's Men, the Šešeljevci, had killed at least 905 Croats and Bosniaks, tortured and raped numerous civilians, deported tens of thousands of non-Serbs, and destroyed religious monuments. Senior Trial Attorney Marcussen appealed to the judges to impose a sentence of twenty-eight years, adding that, since the accused paraded his lack of remorse as a badge of honor,[130] there were no mitigating factors.

---

[128] On the dramatic use of film at the International Military Tribunal at Nuremberg, see Lawrence Douglas (1995).

[129] Prosecution's Closing Brief (2012, §594).

[130] "I am being tried for atrocious war crimes that I allegedly committed through hate speech as I preached my nationalist ideology of which I am proud." Vojislav Šešelj, "Vojislav Šešelj: Fallen Leader of Great Serbia." Manja Ristic. *Balkan Transitional Justice*. 15 March 2012. www .balkaninsight.com/en/article/vojislav-seselj-fallen-leader-of-the-great-serbia

4.6   THE TRIAL CHAMBER JUDGMENT IN ŠEŠELJ

Evaluating the 2016 trial chamber judgment that acquitted the defendant Vojislav Šešelj of nine counts of crimes against humanity and war crimes is a balancing act. As noted, the Šešelj trial was characterized by procedural irregularities and a prosecution case that struggled with insider witnesses and ended up relying on circumstantial evidence. At the same time, the Trial Chamber judgment made contentious and questionable findings of both fact and law. As we saw at the ICTR, international speech crimes trials can produce controversial judgments, and the outcry over the Šešelj judgment is likely to rival that of *Nahimana*.

The judgment commenced in the customary manner, placing both intention and causation at the heart of the trial chamber's inquiries into instigation: "For a Chamber to be able to find that instigation to commit crimes existed, it must establish that there was a physical element, or *actus reus*, for the acts constituting instigation, which must have contributed substantially to the commission of the crimes, and that there was a mental element, or *mens rea*, showing the intention of the instigator to cause the commission of the crimes."[131] The judgment did not set the bar of causation for instigating particularly high; that is, at the level of *sine qua non*. Instead it only required the speech constitute a factor contributing to the commission of the crime: "It is not necessary to prove that the crime would not have been perpetrated without the involvement of the accused, it is sufficient to demonstrate that the instigation was a factor contributing to the conduct of another person committing the crime."[132]

The trial chamber majority, Judge Antonetti dissenting, found that the intentionality element was fulfilled in three speeches given by Šešelj's speeches that clearly constituted calls for the expulsion and forcible transfer of Croats: the speech at Hrtkovci on 6 of May 1992,[133] and two speeches given in the Serbian Parliament on 1 and 7 April 1992.[134] These elements of the judgment could have created a firm foundation for a conviction, since the accused expressed the requisite intentionality for instigating, and the threshold of causation applied in the judgment only requires that his speeches be a factor contributing to the actual deportation of non-Serbs.

According to the majority, what was lacking in the prosecution's case was proof beyond a reasonable doubt that there was "an undeniable

---

[131] *Šešelj* TC §294.   [132] *Šešelj* TC §298.   [133] *Ibid.*, §333.   [134] *Ibid.*, §335.

nexus between the conflict in Croatia and in BiH and the situation in Vojvodina."[135] The documented attacks on Croats in Hrtkovci were not connected to the armed conflict elsewhere in the country and did not in themselves constitute a widespread or systematic attack on a civilian population.[136] The majority interpreted the evidence of attacks on Croats as pointing towards "acts driven by essentially domestic motives, private in nature, whose focus was the acquisition of housing, which the Serbs did not have due to their refugee status."[137] In sum, Šešelj did incite deportations but his words were not causally connected to the attacks on non-Serbs, which were privately organized, driven by material gain rather than ethnic animus, and not part of a widespread campaign of persecution.

The majority rejected the testimony of demography expert Ewa Tabeau and Witness VS-061 that there was a connection between the accused's words and the departure of Croats from Hrtkovci.[138] The prosecution team had commissioned expert witness Tabeau to write a report indicating that Croats had fled villages such as Hrtkovci in great numbers after being subjected to Šešelj's speeches and a widespread and systematic campaign of harassment and intimidation. The trial chamber criticized the "weakness" of Tabeau's expert report because it covered the entire year of 1992 rather than the period immediately following 6 May 1992, and because the report did not identify the actual causal mechanisms involved in the departure of Croats.[139]

The trial chamber, having rejected the assertion that the accused's speeches triggered crimes against humanity, could still have affirmed hate speech as a form of persecution (and an inchoate crime, *pace Nahimana*). After all, the trial chamber had found that Šešelj's speech at Hrtkovic contained the requisite intentionality. Yet it abjured this finding as well, declaring that "The mere use of an abusive or defamatory term is not sufficient to demonstrate persecution."[140] Such abusive speech by the accused was aimed not at the commission of crimes, rather the legitimate mobilizing and rallying of troops during wartime.

Without a doubt, the recantation of insiders played a significant role in the bench's dismissal of the prosecution case. In its closing brief,[141] the prosecution made the best argument still available to it that the testimonial recantations of these witnesses should not be rejected by

---

[135] *Ibid.*, §194. [136] *Ibid.*, §195. [137] *Ibid.*, §196. [138] *Ibid.*, §195. [139] *Ibid.*, §333.
[140] *Ibid.*, §283. [141] Prosecution's Closing Brief (2012, §§651–70).

the Trial Chamber, and it furnished corroborating evidence to bolster many aspects of the insider witnesses' preliminary statements. And while the insider statements were formally accepted into evidence by the Trial Chamber, their probative value was grievously harmed by the spate of recantations, and this is the ultimate explanation for the failure of the prosecution's case. The trial chamber judgment addressed the issue of recanting witnesses briefly at the outset,[142] and at the end of the judgment in Annex 2 "Procedural Background."[143] However, its statements were anodyne and unrevealing, indicating that judges may exercise direction on whether to give weight to the initial statements of witnesses. In an interview given a few days after the trial chamber's judgment, Judge Flavia Lattanzi, the dissenting judge in Šešelj, confirmed that the written statements of witnesses against the accused were not considered.[144] The chamber only considered their testimony on the stand, at which point many withdrew their statements after being subjected to bribery and/or intimidation by the accused or his associates.

The fiercest criticism leveled at the Šešelj trial chamber judgment came from Judge Lattanzi, who opened her dissent with an extraordinary repudiation: "In fact, unusually for a dissenting opinion, I disagree with the majority of the Chamber on almost everything: the description of the context, the use of the evidence, the flawed or, at best, cursory analysis of the evidence, the disregard for the jurisprudence, and the conclusions."[145] Leaving aside Hrtkovci and Vojvodina, "which was a more delicate and complex issue," Lattanzi strenuously objected to the finding that there was no widespread or systematic attack on a civilian population, pointing out that "for Croatia and Bosnia and Herzegovina there are many verdicts based on the same facts and the same evidence which confirmed the existence of a widespread or systematic attack."[146] Judge Lattanzi stated her opinion that "no trier of fact could reasonably find, in the light of the evidence admitted to the record, that there was no widespread or systematic attack against the Croatian and Muslim civilian population of Croatia and BiH, during the period covered by the Indictment."[147]

Judge Lattanzi's critique of the majority does have some basis, especially given that the Šešelj judgment repudiated the factual findings of prior ICTY cases. In ignoring compelling evidence about a widespread

---

[142] *Ibid.*, §24–7.   [143] *Ibid.*, §44–54.   [144] Rossini (2016).
[145] *Šešelj* TC, Partially Dissenting Opinion of Judge Flavia Lattanzi – Amended Version, Volume 3, IT-03-67-T31, March 2016, §1.
[146] Rossini (2016).   [147] *Ibid.*, §39.

Figure 4.3 Serbian nationalist politician Vojislav Šešelj addresses supporters during an anti-government rally in Belgrade on 15 November 2014
Credit: Andrej Isakovic/AFP/Getty Images

and systematic attack on a civilian population, the majority view exhibited a seemingly conscious desire to construe the evidence in a way favorable to the accused. The preferences of the majority revealed themselves in an astonishing line that inexplicably construes the deportations in Vojvodina as some kind of humanitarian operation: "the buses which were chartered in this context were not forced to transfer operations of population, but rather acts of humanitarian assistance to noncombatants who fled areas where they no longer felt safe."[148] Judge Lattanzi refrained from mentioning this line in her dissenting opinion, but showed her exasperation in an interview, "We arrived to such a point where it was stated that buses chartered by Serb forces to get people to leave were acts of humanitarian assistance ... This is really unheard of. I can't say anything more ..."

The trial chamber judgment contains other incomprehensible interpretations, for instance when it construes Seselj's statement on a megaphone to troops that "Not one *Ustasha* will be allowed to leave Vukovar alive" as a call for Croats under arms to surrender.[149] The trial chamber

[148] *Šešelj* TC §193.   [149] *Ibid.*, §318.

majority grasped at the remote possibility that "the speeches were made in a context of conflict and were aimed at reinforcing the morale of the troops on the Accused's side, rather than being an appeal to them to show no mercy."[150] If a politician thundering "none shall leave alive!" to troops before battle does not constitute a criminal declaration that no quarter will be given, then it is unclear what would.[151]

Judge Lattanzi, in an interview only a few days after the trial chamber verdict, provided damning insights into the thinking of the majority, disclosing that "efforts were made to reduce the evidence to nothing, to make the exam[ination] of the evidence meaningless. This attitude destroyed the process from the ground up ... From my point of view, this ruling amounts to nothing ... in the sense that it is done so poorly, both in fact and law, that it is a nullity."[152] The Italian judge concluded her dissenting opinion thus: "with this Judgement we have been thrown back centuries into the past, to a period in human history when we used to say – and it was the Romans who used to say this to justify their bloody conquests and the assassinations of their political enemies during civil wars: *Silent enim leges inter arma.*"[153]

As a final coda, prosecutors at the ICTY have appealed the trial chamber judgment and the ICTY has pursued contempt charges against individuals who pressured prosecution witnesses to sign fabricated statements that "contained false allegations against the Prosecution and misrepresented the role and responsibilities of Vojislav Šešelj during the war."[154] This book goes to press without the benefit of the appeals chamber ruling in *Šešelj*, so it's not possible to know the final verdict on the charges against the accused. My expectation is that many elements of the trial chamber judgment will be reversed on appeal. If the acquittal on all counts stands, then the trial will be consigned to the dustbin of legal history and become invisible in law reviews and international criminal law textbooks. Even if that transpires, the Šešelj case still merits scrutiny, as it offers a paradigmatic instance of the practical and theoretical rigors of proving direct causation in speech crimes cases.

---

[150] *Ibid.*, §318.

[151] Declaring that no quarter will be given is listed as a war crime in the ICC Statute at Article 8 (2)(b)(xii).

[152] Rossini (2016).

[153] *Šešelj* TC, Partially Dissenting Opinion of Judge Flavia Lattanzi – Amended Version, Volume 3, IT-03-67-T31, March 2016, §150.

[154] *Jojić, Ostojić and Radeta* TC "Order Lifting Confidentiality of Order in Lieu of Indictment and Arrest Warrants," §13.

4.7 REFLECTIONS ON LAW, SCIENCE AND CAUSATION

> It would be a mistake to assume that science and law are answering the
> same questions when asked to determine causation.
>
> *National Research Council (2002:23)*

In domestic and international criminal law, the ideal evidence to prove
instigation comes from material perpetrators providing unimpeachable
testimony that but for the speech of the accused, the result crimes in
question would not have occurred. When asked, what would constitute
the clearest evidence of causation, prosecutors invariably replied "the
testimony of an insider," and they gave illustrative examples of ideal
testimony such as; "I heard his words and I would die for him and do
anything he says,"[155] and, "he was an authority figure who commanded
my behavior. I heard his words and I acted."[156] Insiders gave evidence
very close to this ideal for other crime sites such as the Vukovar front.
Šešelj confidantes such as Zoran Rankić and Goran Stoparić described
how Šešelj was a "sort of god" who held great moral sway over his
followers and successfully incited them through declarations such as
"Not a single Ustaša should leave Vukovar alive."[157]

The prosecution lacked "smoking gun" testimony from perpetrators
in Hrtkovci, and therefore it could not document the mechanisms of
mobilization that translated a shared criminal intent into action.
Circumstantial evidence has the potential to persuade the court, but
it is more susceptible to the defense rejoinder that the defendant's
speeches were all symbolic performance: *sturm und drang* with no actual
consequences. For the Hrtkovci crime base, prosecutors called victims
who told the court about an atmosphere of fear and intimidation that
included hand grenades being thrown into people's homes and dogs
being killed. Yet victims possessed no direct knowledge about the network that coordinated the offences, nor knowledge about the role of the
accused in the planning and execution of atrocities. Lacking evidence
that would demonstrate cause-in-fact, the prosecution turned to anecdotal, secondary evidence that might satisfy a criterion of "legal"
causation. In their theory, prosecutors connected the speech acts of
the accused to the crimes by their temporal contiguity to prohibited
acts of persecution and deportation.

---

[155] Author interview, 2013.
[156] ICTY Senior Trial Attorney Dan Saxon, Author interview, October 2013.
[157] Prosecution's Closing Brief, 2012, §161–5).

In formulating their strategy, prosecutors were aware of the "contemporaneous" criterion advanced in earlier ICTR cases of direct and public incitement to commit genocide. To remind the reader of the discussion in Chapter 2, the Appeals Chamber in *Nahimana* and Trial Chamber in *Bikindi* found that the defendants could only be held liable for speeches, publications and broadcasts issued at or very near the time of the genocide.[158] In ICTR jurisprudence, speech acts before the start of the genocide on 6 April 1994 could not be considered causally connected to the genocide or the program of persecution of the Tutsi minority. The three defendants in *Nahimana* were acquitted by the Appeals Chamber of incitement to commit genocide and instigating persecution of Tutsis for their speech acts before 6 April 1994, but were held responsible for speech acts after that date when the genocide of the Tutsi was underway. The ICTR cases also suffered because they lacked testimony from physical perpetrators that they had been directly instigated to commit violations by the words or broadcasts of the accused.[159] The ICTR judgments conveyed the message that temporal proximity is paramount in evaluating whether speech acts constitute an inchoate crime or a mode of liability for a crime against humanity.

This stands in contrast to the Nuremberg judgment against Julius Streicher, which held the defendant responsible for crimes against humanity, despite the hiatus between Streicher's publications and the Nazi's systematic program to exterminate the Jews. The ICTR's chronological approach concurs with the prosecution's case theory in *Šešelj*. Here it is worth noting that before he came to the ICTY, Mathias Marcussen, the senior attorney for the prosecution in *Šešelj*, previously worked in the ICTR's appeals division on incitement to commit genocide cases such as *Akayesu, Kambanda*, and *Nahimana*.

Lacking insiders, demonstrating the direct nexus required for the charge of instigation was a steep hill for the prosecution to climb. What of other modes of liability? The prosecution favored JCE as the type of criminal responsibility that most accurately described Šešelj's participation in the crimes, primarily in his role as a recruiter for paramilitary units committing atrocities. However, the judges disfavored JCE in their interim Rule 98 *bis* decision. Ordering,

---

[158] *Nahimana* AC at §993–4 and §1012–4, *Bikindi* TC at §417–26. Gordon (2010:623) deserves credit for coining the term used here: "In effect, the Tribunal impliedly incorporated a contemporaneousness criterion-the offensive words must have been uttered at or near the time of the contextual violence that renders them genocidal."

[159] Zahar (2005:37–8, 41).

as we saw, was largely abandoned because of the indeterminacy of Šešelj's official position. That left accomplice liability and the charge of "aiding and abetting in the planning, preparation or execution" of crimes against humanity and war crimes. Based upon the evidence presented to the courtroom, aiding and abetting is the mode of liability most appropriate for describing the role of the accused. Shared intent is not formally required for complicity (although of course it helps). The accused evidently shared the intent of the material actors to commit the crimes, applauding and condoning crimes that had been recently committed (such as the Borovo Selo killings), and encouraging his followers to commit new crimes in furtherance of an overarching political strategy, carving a Greater Serbia out of the collapse of Yugoslavia. Given that the judgment did not confirm instigation, future cases against political leaders like Šešelj might benefit from a more cautious strategy that favors accomplice liability over direct forms of criminal responsibility.

The most common misstep of the prosecution at international tribunals (as in domestic trials) is the failure to disclose key evidence to the defense in a timely manner. The second most common prosecutorial blunder is overreach. Over-indicting occurs for justifiable reasons: prosecutors understandably feel an obligation to victims to reach for the highest charge carrying the maximum sentence. They also want to include all the lesser charges, just in case the more demanding modes of liability are not met. Yet in adopting a kitchen-sink strategy, they create insurmountable complications and divert energy and resources into unattainable goals. Accomplice liability is not only an attainable goal that satisfies a pragmatic strategic imperative; it is, according to what we know from the social science of inciting speech, the most accurate legal description of what propagandists like Šešelj actually do during an armed conflict. The argument for accomplice liability in speech crimes cases is developed in more detail in the final chapter.

For now, it is worth briefly addressing some of the wider issues raised by the prosecution's efforts to establish the *actus reus* elements of instigating crimes against humanity. We could start with the question; does chronology constitute sufficient proof of causation? Alas it does not, and *post hoc ergo propter hoc* ("after this, therefore, because of this") is considered a logical fallacy in philosophy and jurisprudence alike. The idea was famously discredited by the Scottish Enlightenment philosopher David Hume, whose position was rearticulated by Hart and Honoré (1985) as, "not all events which follow each other in invariable sequence are causally related." Any analysis of a sequence of events must assess whether other intervening factors could have ruptured the apparent connection between them.

Applying Humean skepticism to the issue in question in Šešelj, it is possible that in Hrtkovci in May 1992, there were many factors that induced Croats to flee the village apart from the speech by Šešelj. These might include, *inter alia*, the outbreak of armed conflict between two conventional armies, television and radio broadcasts from Belgrade about the conflict, the influx of one thousand Serb refugees into the village, and the activities of local Serb nationalists who hosted Šešelj's visit. How do we measure Šešelj's contribution to the exodus of Croats, compared with these other factors?

Judge Antonetti, ever alive to possible exculpatory evidence, was asking the right questions during his dissenting opinion in the Rule 98 *bis* decision, "what words uttered [by Šešelj] led to brutal and inhumane living conditions? . . . What are the reasons [for these conditions]? The words uttered by the accused or some other reason."[160] The prosecution never argued that the May 1992 speech constituted a but-for cause of the forcible transfer of non-Serbs, and that their expulsion would not have happened without Šešelj's election rally and speech. There were one thousand Serb refugees with nowhere to go in the village, prowling around the homes of local Croats. Even before the rally, displaced persons were breaking into the empty homes of Croats working abroad. The thrust of the prosecution's case was that Šešelj's words *hastened* the displacement of non-Serbs and this is one reason why temporality assumed such a central role in the prosecution case for causation.[161]

What is striking is how there are no well-articulated and accepted tests in international criminal law for determining whether a connection between two acts or events is the result of correlation, causation, or mere coincidence in time. In science generally, the chronological juxtaposition of two events is insufficient to establish a causal nexus unless accompanied by other tests. In social science, demonstrating causation would necessitate a large sample study that controlled for other factors. Social researchers normally refrain from strong claims for causation based on one speech, or even three speeches. Instead, a well-designed study would require an aggregate of approximately fifty

---

[160] "Seselj Trial Cleared for Defence Phase." Institute for War and Peace Reporting. Rachel Irwin. 6 May 2011. http://iwpr.net/report-news/seselj-trial-cleared-defence-phase

[161] Accelerating a harmful outcome is, in US criminal law, a legitimate argument for material causation: see *Oxendine v. State* 528 A.2d 870 (Del. 1987).

speeches and reliable documentary evidence on their aftereffects within a defined range and period of time, in order to determine whether there was a statistically significant relationship between words and crimes and, if so, whether this relationship warranted the attribution of causation rather than mere correlation.

It might be countered that prosecutors (or, indeed, defense counsel) could not conduct such a study, given the unstable conditions of war and the resulting paucity of reliable evidence. However, the prosecution commissioned demographer Ewa Tabeau to support their claim that in 1992 the Croat population collapsed in the region of Vojvodina as non-Serb minorities were driven out.[162] In addition to comprehensive population data from election rolls, national censuses, and municipal registers, the prosecution also possessed transcripts of over 400 speeches that Šešelj gave during the 1990s. There is no reason why it could not have designed and conducted a study to test the assertion that Šešelj's speeches led to greater violence or changes in the demographic composition of a geographical area. Controlling for other relevant factors, such a study could have provided a general indication as to the statistical relationship (or not) between the speeches and subsequent crimes against humanity and war crimes, as the prosecution repeatedly claimed.

Similar studies have been conducted by social researchers in other contexts such as Rwanda, where political scientist Scott Straus (2006, 2007) and economist David Yanagizawa-Drott (2014) have investigated the relationship between radio broadcasts and participation in the genocide against Tutsis in 1994. Without assuming that social research would provide the smoking gun of causation (and indeed, it may well prove exculpatory), it might have a number of benefits for a criminal trial, including complementing the other forms of knowledge in the courtroom, and concentrating the court's attention on the material cause elements of causation that are prior to proximate and legal causation. It could also encourage prosecutors to be more precise about their claims regarding the effects of speeches. We saw how in their closing arguments, prosecutors referred to the defendant's speech in one month in 1991, and drew a direct causal link to violence in the next month in the town of Zvornik, in another part of the country.

Law's epistemology in the criminal courtroom, and its propensity to generalize based on a few scarce examples, mitigates against a systematic and rigorous approach to causation. The structure of prosecution

---

[162] See Tabeau and Bijak (2005) for information on Tabeau's sources and methodology.

cases at international tribunals seldom identifies a general pattern in a region based upon a large sample.[163] Instead it reviews a few incidents in meticulous detail. In Šešelj, there were just three: Hrtkovci, Vukovar and Zvornik. To prove its case beyond a reasonable doubt in each crime base, the prosecution needed unimpeachable witnesses able to testify in the trial chamber. In an adversarial trial process, this is a laborious and time-consuming exercise, requiring several days of examination-in-chief and cross-examination for each witness.

This rigor, while necessary for the standards of a criminal court, results in a detrimental reduction of the sample size in mass crimes. In Šešelj, a main issue at stake in the testimony of fact witnesses was, "what did the intended audience understand by the words of the accused?" At a rally with three hundred participants and onlookers, how does the court determine with great certainty the intention of the speaker and the reception of such a large audience? In the crime bases of Zvornik and Hrtkovci, the two sites where Šešelj's speeches allegedly instigated persecution and deportation, prosecutors relied upon a remarkably small number of fact witnesses. For Zvornik, the prosecution called only six witnesses to give testimony on the deportation of hundreds of non-Serbs and the murder of eighty-eight persons.[164] As we have just seen, at Hrtkovci, six fact witnesses testified about the forcible transfer of seven to eight hundred non-Serbs.[165] This pattern can also be found in other, similar international trials. In Akayesu, the prosecution convinced the court based on six fact witnesses that the one to two hundred persons at the meeting at Gishyeshye during the early hours of 19 April 1994, understood Akayesu's calls to eliminate "the accomplices of the RPF" to mean all Tutsis.[166] Expert witness Mathias Ruzindana (2012:157) writes, "Obviously, not everyone among the more than 100 people who attended the meeting was called to testify in this case."

Prosecutors could conceivably call more fact witnesses, but judges often impose severe constraints on the prosecution case during the pretrial phase. Judges frequently demand that prosecutors reduce their indictments by an arbitrary figure such as twenty percent. Trials at international criminal courts are notoriously vast and cumbersome,

---

[163] There are a few exceptions, such as the compendious Amended Indictment "Bosnia and Herzegovina" of 22 November 2002 against former Yugoslav President Slobodan Milošević which alleged killings, illegal detentions and forcible transfers of a civilian population in 17, 24 and 45 municipalities respectively.

[164] Prosecution's closing arguments, T.17248.

[165] Counted in the Prosecution's Closing Brief (2012, §509).

[166] Akayesu TC §361. The judgment reviews the six fact witnesses at §§333–8.

often encompassing hundreds of crimes committed in a wide region over a period of months and years. This is one reason why they regularly last four to five years, and in extreme circumstances can drag on for over a decade as in the Šešelj trial.

After the UN Security Council sounded the alarm at the pace of the trials, the "managerial judging" model introduced by the ICTY President Claude Jorda in 2000 granted judges the enhanced powers they conventionally enjoy in the inquisitorial system.[167] The sharp blade of judicial case management radically pared down the number of the crime bases and witnesses in virtually all prosecution indictments at the ICTY, ICTR and ICC after 2000. In the pretrial phase, the Šešelj Trial Chamber removed five entire crime bases from the indictment altogether[168] and trimmed the witness list by twenty percent, reducing it from 131 to 105.[169] Ultimately, only eighty-one prosecution witnesses were called.[170]

The advent of a model of judicial case management often meant that international prosecutors are compelled to generalize from insufficient evidence. Given these constraints, several prosecutors interviewed for this book indicated that they would feel that they had a solid case if they could call two to three credible eyewitnesses per crime scene. If the criminal liability of the defendant hinges on the meaning and content of his or her words and the understanding of the audience, an international court could arrive at a conclusion based on only a handful of fact witnesses.

In social science, this approach would be considered flimsy and anecdotal. Any research claiming to have determined the meaning of a speaker's words beyond a reasonable doubt based on interviews with two to three members of a crowd of three hundred would likely face a negative evaluation in the peer-review process, and yet international

---

[167] On the managerial judging model and the shift from adversarial to inquisitorial forms of case management, see Mundis (2001) and Langer (2005).

[168] Western Slavonia, Brčko, Bijelina, Bosanski Šamac and Boračko Jezero.

[169] Prosecution's Submission of Revised Final Witness List With Confidential Annex A, Case No. IT-03-67-PT, 29 March, 2007, §1, 3–4. The prosecution requested special protective measures for at least a third of the witnesses.

[170] This created a variety of legal and logistical problems for prosecutors. First, in order to meet the gravity threshold required by international law, the prosecution has to show that the crimes against humanity constituted a widespread and systematic attack on a civilian population. Second, the prosecution must show a pattern to the occurrence of the crimes that can only be explained by the existence of a single policy or plan (with the accused at the epicenter) to conduct a campaign of persecution or genocide.

courts could conceivably convict defendants on the basis of small and unrepresentative samples.

Ironically, while international criminal courts are accustomed to adjudicating cases on the basis of a small and unrepresentative sample, the stakes are higher in law than in social science, and so is the threshold of proof. The reasonable doubt standard lies well above any claim of certainty found in the social sciences and the physical sciences too. If we recall that reasonable doubt is a qualitative, not quantitative, standard then it is worth observing that qualitative social scientists seldom claim that one social fact directly causes another. If they do, they generally only do so in a general sense that recognizes multiple causation. Biomedical science in randomized clinical trials and quantitative social science can identify causation using certain criteria and tests, but their statistical methods and definitions of proof are quite unlike those of law, and they eschew the category of beyond reasonable doubt.[171]

These comments point towards a deeper chasm between law's ways of knowing and other approaches to knowledge, as noted by scholars such as Shklar (1986), Jasanoff (1995) and Monahan and Walker (2010), as well as legal practitioners, including one US judge who commented to a high-level panel on science in the courtroom that law and science are "about as different as they can be."[172] Science is interested in the nomothetic; classes of events and generalizations based upon wider patterns that explain those patterns. Science seeks to identify causation to explain categories or types of events which regularly, frequently occur, rather than events which are exceptional, rare or unusual. Some branches of science (e.g., epidemiology) can embrace composite or multifactorial notions of causation, rather than the criminal law's linear chain of cause and effect. When applied to social life, science is generally concerned with populations rather than single individuals.

By contrast, as Hart and Honoré (1985:9) write, the lawyer is "primarily concerned to make causal statements about particulars, to establish that on some particular occasion some particular occurrence was the effect or consequence of some other particular occurrence." Law, and especially criminal law, erects a shrine to the idiographic, the

---

[171] In social science, claiming a causal relationship between two variables requires a test of statistical significance, usually accompanied by disclosures on the margin of error, the difficulties of sampling and any possible issues of measurement bias in the research design. This approach to causation results, at least in part, from the process of peer review which is quite different from the test for causation found in criminal law, despite the appellate review structure of most court systems.

[172] National Research Council (2002:22).

idiosyncratic event. The individual case with all its particularities may serve as the basis of a new legal precedent that transforms the entire body of law on a topic. Findings of causation need not be based upon a pattern of regularly observed events. Indeed, such findings may be built upon an unusual, even bizarre, concurrence of factors that has never transpired before, and may never transpire again. For example, in a murder case, the criminal law asks, "what was the proximate and necessary cause of this individual person's death on this unique occasion?" Science asks, "what are the necessary and sufficient conditions to cause the death of a human being on most occasions?"

In Chapter 3, we saw how causation at international criminal tribunals had largely been overtaken by policy considerations, but even determining cause and effect relationships according to cause-in-fact principles does not truly proceed according to scientific precepts and methods. The standard but-for test for cause-in-fact constructs a singular hypothetical and counter-factual statement of the type "If event A had not happened, then bad outcome B would not have happened." In law, then, cause-in-fact is always hypothetical and non-realist, and we might recall that cause-in-fact is considered the granite bedrock of causation before we even arrive at the castles-in-the-air conception of legal cause or proximate cause.

Causal statements in the law are "not verifiable or falsifiable in any straightforward way," according to Hart and Honoré (1985:101).[173] What matters above all else for the criminal court is not verifiable causation or explanation according to scientific methods, but the attribution of guilt with a level of certainty not found in any other field of human endeavor. Despite its penchant for particularity and idiosyncrasy, and despite its unverifiable test for material cause, criminal law projects a remarkable level of certainty, as Hart and Honoré (1985:47) confirm, "what we want is *certainty*, not explanatory force." And this certainty is comparatively final. The verdict of a lower court may be overturned on appeal, but once the appeals court has ruled, that is that, in the absence of any fresh evidence. Science is a relatively more open system of knowledge, and there is the possibility of revision over

---

[173] On innovative legal theories of causation, see the NESS (necessary element of a set of sufficient conditions) approach expounded by Richard Wright (1985:1782), who draws from the earlier standpoint of Hart and Honoré (1985:112) that "a particular condition was a cause of (condition contributing to) a specific consequence if and only if it was a necessary element of a set of antecedent actual conditions that was sufficient for the occurrence of the consequence." Stewart (2012a:1205–6) recommends theories of adequate causation in German law that inspired Hart and Honoré.

time. Newtonian physics held from the 1680s to early 1900s, and then it was overturned. While the law and sentencing standards for theft may change over time, the individual executed in Isaac Newton's London in 1680 for stealing half a loaf of bread remains executed.

Criminal law, while it uses logical reasoning and evidence, does not employ scientific principles of reasoning or methods of evaluating evidence. It is therefore a form of non-scientific rationalism. It proceeds by a formal logic, but the rules of logic are wholly internal to legal epistemology. The law uses evidence to make determinations, but its evidence would be insufficient in other branches of human knowledge. Returning to our case study, chronology does not prove causation, and half a dozen victim/bystander witnesses do not prove the broadly held view (if any exists) of a listening audience. Arguing that this is so is mere prosecutorial rhetoric, which complicates matters when evaluating a case that hinges on the damaging implications of rhetoric.

To be clear, I do not wish to set up science as an objective, rarified yardstick of knowledge that is free of contingency or error. Science is the most powerful and rigorous method developed to comprehend our world, yet because it is a human creation, scientists recognize that its findings are imperfect and open to revision. It is science's embrace of imperfection and openness, whilst still engaging in a rigorous pursuit of relations of cause and effect, that could inform the law more than it does at present. Also, criminal law might learn something from the social science of hate speech which recently has produced unexpected and counterintuitive findings, as we will see in Chapter 7.

CHAPTER FIVE

METAPHORS, AGENCY AND MENTAL CAUSATION IN SPEECH CRIMES TRIALS

5.1 INTRODUCTION

> Much contemporary writing on causation in the law is a literature of revolt against an older conception of the character of those issues which courts discuss and decide in causal terminology so often with an accompanying cloud of metaphors.
>
> Hart and Honoré (1985:88)

For a criminal court to determine in a specific trial whether a speech act of the accused caused subsequent criminal acts entails a general legal theory of the causal nexus between speech and behavior. The theory of speech commonly utilized in international criminal law mistakenly comprehends the connection between speech acts and material crimes according to the regular laws of physical causation. Prosecutors and judges in international speech crimes trials regularly describe speech acts as if they were material objects, using metaphors of fire, poison, weapons and viral contagion. This chapter examines the metaphorical models of causation commonly used in international speech crimes trials, and proposes in their place a plain-language template that sets out the necessary sequence of mental and physical causation.

In embarking on this exercise, it is evident that there is something distinctive about speech crimes cases compared with other categories such as war crimes. Stated simply, speech crimes cases are metaphor-rich environments. Judges and prosecutors alike frequently resort to colorful expressions to describe the effects of words, and they do so more often than in trials where the speech element is absent or minimal.

There are various reasons why legal actors engage in verbal flights of fancy when adjudicating cases of incitement and instigation. One possible explanation is that judges turn to metaphors when they wish to generate and legitimate new legal norms, an activity that legal commentators have termed "expressivism"[1] in the law. Direct and public incitement to commit genocide and instigating crimes against humanity are crimes with little extant case law in a relatively new and emergent area of international law, and judges and prosecutors turn to analogy to articulate evolving international norms and to extend the jurisdictional reach of contemporary international courts.

Yet this is not the whole story, and a fuller understanding necessitates delving more deeply into what metaphorical language actually does in a court judgment. Metaphors are not merely a hollow rhetorical move or moralizing window dressing for the more substantial legal arguments. Drawing on the writings of philosopher Donald Davidson (2001), I contend that the significance of metaphors in law is not their meaning but their use. The main question is not "what do metaphors of speech really mean?" but rather "what do judges and prosecutors accomplish by using metaphors?" The answer lies in the acute difficulties that courts have in proving mental causation beyond a reasonable doubt, especially when there is a dearth of evidence about the subjective state of mind of the material perpetrators. Speech crimes such as instigating crimes against humanity imply direct mental causation, and mental states are notoriously impenetrable, as illustrated in the Šešelj trial. Moreover, the independent and voluntaristic agency of the listener, except in instances where there is force, fraud or coercion, constitutes an intervening cause that interrupts the sequence of causation connecting the speaker to the crime.

Metaphors allow judges to resolve both sets of problems by reconfiguring words as material objects with physical relations of cause and effect. This judicial sophistry is especially perilous in the setting of speech crimes where defendants are being tried for their use of metaphorical language; for instance, Hassan Ngeze's 1993 article in the newspaper *Kangura* titled "A Cockroach (Inyenzi) Cannot Bring Forth a Butterfly."[2] For due process to

---

[1] In law, expressivism serves to legitimate new laws and shift social norms in a certain direction, and one that is generally progressive according to commentators such as Anderson and Pildes (2000), Drumbl (2007) and Sunstein (1995). See Meijers and Glashuis (2013) on expressivism in the Karadžić trial at the ICTY.

[2] *Nahimana* TC §179.

prevail, international criminal law's mode of causation needs to be replaced by a more accurate and transparent account of mental causation.

5.2 METAPHORICAL LANGUAGE IN SPEECH CRIMES CASES

In reviewing the legal documents in the speech crimes trials conducted thus far at international tribunals, from the indictments to the interim decisions to the final appeals judgments, one is immediately struck by the frequency, color and vividness of the figurative language used by legal actors. Adjudicating criminal cases where the defendant's public oratory is an ultimate issue in the trial elicits soaring rhetoric from judges and prosecutors. Three documents in the principal speech crimes trials in the history of international law stand out: the 1946 *Streicher* judgment handed down by the International Military Tribunal at Nuremberg, the 2003 Trial Chamber judgment in *Nahimana* at the ICTR, and the Prosecution's Closing Brief and Arguments submitted in 2012 in *Šešelj* at the ICTY. The metaphors in these documents are consistent across all the texts, even though they were written in different epochs and even though judges wrote two of the documents and prosecutors wrote the third.

Overall, the three documents contain twenty-five metaphors describing the character or consequences of the speech of a defendant who was charged with crimes against humanity (Streicher), or direct and public incitement to commit genocide (Nahimana) or instigating crimes against humanity (Šešelj). This is counting metaphors of the "Juliet is the sun" type that, following Aristotle's understanding of metaphor, "consists in giving the thing a name that belongs to something else."[3] Also included were analogies of the "Juliet is like the sun" type and expressive adjectives such as "inflammatory" speech that drew on metaphors appearing elsewhere in the text.[4]

Far and away the most prevalent causal metaphors conjured up images of fire and conflagration (fifteen occurrences), followed by

---

[3] Aristotle (2001/1941:21). Aristotle's formulation continues to be the basis for modern understandings of metaphor, including that of Lakoff and Johnson (1980:5) who write that "the essence of metaphor is understanding and experiencing one kind of thing in terms of another."

[4] Berger (2013:164) illustrates the linguistic difference between metaphors and analogies by writing that "Juliet is the sun" is a metaphor, "Juliet is like the sun" is an analogy.

references to weapons and arms (five). Metaphors of poison (two) and viruses that infected the minds of listeners (two) were also common. Finally, there were times when the judges or prosecutors were truly carried away and mixed their metaphors (two). Two examples illustrate each category:

Images of Fire and Conflagration

"Šešelj's hate speeches were like oil to the flame of ever increasing ethnic strife."[5]

"(Radio Télévision Libre des Mille Collines, or RTLM) spread petrol throughout the country little by little, so that one day it would be able to set fire to the whole country."[6]

Speech as a Weapon

"Šešelj understood the power of his propaganda: 'Words can be a very dangerous weapon. Sometimes they pound like a howitzer.'"[7]

"RTLM was Nahimana's weapon of choice, which he used to instigate the killing of Tutsi civilians."[8]

Poisonous Words

"He [Ngeze] poisoned the minds of his readers, and by words and deeds caused the death of thousands of innocent civilians."[9]

"The ethnic hatred that permeates *Kangura* had the effect of poison, as evidenced by the testimony of the witnesses."[10]

Propaganda as a Virus

"He [Streicher] infected the German mind with the virus of anti-Semitism."[11]

"The virulent writings of Kangura."[12]

Mixed Metaphors

"(RTLM) spread petrol throughout the country little by little, so that one day it would be able to set fire to the whole country. This is the poison described in the Streicher judgment."[13]

"The accused poisoned and pounded non-Serbs and Serbs with his campaign of hatred."[14]

---

[5] Prosecution's Closing Brief in *Šešelj*, §561.   [6] *Nahimana* TC §1078.
[7] Prosecution's Closing Brief in *Šešelj*, §591.   [8] *Nahimana* TC §974.
[9] *Nahimana* TC §1101.   [10] *Nahimana* TC §243.
[11] *Streicher* Judgment, International Military Tribunal.   [12] *Nahimana* TC §1073.
[13] *Nahimana* TC §1078.
[14] Prosecution's Closing Arguments in *Šešelj*, T17149. This phrase was not expressly used in the written closing brief but was part of the oral presentation of that Brief, so I have included it.

Documents in speech crimes trials seem to contain more metaphors than other kinds of cases. To verify this, I undertook a comparison with the category of war crimes, which are the oldest and most well-established set of offenses in international law.[15] I selected trial chamber judgments from what are commonly thought of as the three most fundamental war crimes cases at the international tribunals that matched the sample from Nuremberg (*Goering*), the ICTR (*Bagosora*) and the ICTY (*Perišić*).[16] An initial review encountered no metaphors in the Goering judgment, six possible examples in the Bagosora trial chamber document and one potential incidence in the Perišić judgment. Twenty-five examples from the speech crimes trials versus a maximum of seven from the war crimes cases already gives an indication of the greater frequency of causal metaphors in speech cases.

A more careful review of the examples of metaphors in the war crimes documents justifies adjusting the numbers downwards. In the one *Perišić* example, the judges are not actually using a metaphor themselves, but are quoting the figurative speech of a witness.[17] In *Bagosora*, five of the six examples are simply quotations of the inciting speech acts of the accused and Rwandan radio broadcasts, or else they relate to the crime of conspiracy. Including solely the content related to war crimes in *Bagosora*, we are left with the one example below, and even that could reasonably be considered an illustration of figurative speech rather than metaphor *per se*:

> In launching this attack, the RPF consciously made a strategic and carefully planned first step that would eventually lead to a violent seizure of power, leading to a full-blown ethnic conflagration in Rwanda.[18]

Comparing one (rather anemic) metaphor from our review of three war crimes documents, with twenty-five vibrant and causal metaphors from the speech crimes cases, confirms the initial impression that legal actors

---

[15] See William Schabas (2007:65) on the antiquity of war crimes.

[16] Hermann Goering was Commander-in-Chief of the Luftwaffe in Nazi Germany. Théoneste Bagosora was chief of staff in the Ministry of Defence of the Rwandan government during the genocide, and the main defendant in the ICTR "Military I" case. Momčilo Perišić was Chief of the General Staff of the Yugoslav Army during the 1991–5 armed conflict. In order to compare like with like, the selection of war crimes documents ought to have included the prosecution's closing brief in the Perišić case, but the brief was unavailable from the ICTY Registry. I therefore used the trial chamber judgment, which incorporated key elements from the prosecution's arguments and cited the Prosecution's Closing Brief ninety-one times, although it did not always replicate the exact language.

[17] "Sacirbey testified that the goal of these sanctions was to have the FRY put a halt to all actions that continued to 'fuel the conflict,' including sending troops to BiH." *Perišić* TC §1341.

[18] *Bagosora* TC §196.

have more frequent recourse to causal metaphors in speech crimes cases than other kinds of cases. They invoke metaphors of fire and conflagration most frequently, and here it would be remiss to overlook a renowned domestic corollary in US legal history. In a decision reviewing the enforcement of the 1918 Amendment to the Espionage Act of 1917, US Supreme Court Justice Oliver Wendell Holmes suggested that a pamphlet comparing military conscription in the First World War to slavery was analogous to "falsely shouting fire in a theatre and causing a panic."[19] The Court dismissed the grounds of the appeal based upon First Amendment principles and upheld a ten-year sentence for the leaflet's authors, Socialist Party activists Charles Schenck and Elizabeth Baer. The analogy between fire and inciting speech has proved irresistible to both municipal and international jurists over the last one hundred years and has become a governing model of incitement. It is valuable to consider why this might be so, and try to understand what legal actors are trying to achieve with metaphorical speech.

5.3   WHEN JULIET IS STORMY: LAW'S AMBIVALENCE TOWARDS METAPHORS

> [A] judicial opinion has no business to be literature. The idol must be ugly... The deliverance that is to be accepted without demur or hesitation must have a certain high austerity which frowns at winning graces.
> *Benjamin Cardozo (1931:3)*

As the above quote from US Supreme Court Justice Cardozo illustrates, the legal professional has generally handled figurative speech in judicial decisions with a great degree of caution. In John Searle's (1994) words, metaphors are "indirect speech acts." Jurists conventionally exhibit a preference for straightforward language containing clear propositional content that can be confirmed or rebutted by the evidence. According to one strand of legal opinion, metaphors are positively distorting and therefore cannot serve as the proper basis of legal reasoning.[20] A skepticism towards analogy and metaphor also prevails in international law, and the principle of legality militates against *analogia legis*, or the use of analogy to extend the reach of a criminal rule into areas where there is no established precedent.[21] The prohibition on *analogia legis* is widely

---

[19] *Schenck v. United States*, 250 US 616 (1919). Holmes reversed his view in the same year in *Abrams v. United States*, 250 US 616 (1919).
[20] Winter (1989:1162).   [21] Cassese and Gaeta (2013:33).

recognized and, in modern international criminal law, enshrined in Article 22(2) of the ICC Statute "The definition of a crime shall be strictly construed and shall not be extended by analogy. In case of ambiguity, the definition shall be interpreted in favor of the persons being investigated, prosecuted or convicted."

Likewise, US law domestic law harbors a deep-seated resistance to metaphorical language, and not only among the ranks of doctrinal literalists. In one of the most often-cited law review articles ever written in the United States, legal realist scholar Felix Cohen (1935:821) sought to puncture the grandiloquence of jurisprudence and reorient the law towards a greater concern for empirical social facts and the "social forces which mold the law and the social ideals by which the law is to be judged" (p. 812). For Cohen, metaphorical language was aligned with formalism and doctrinal reasoning, which he thought needed to be replaced with an empirical realism based on social facts and legislative policies.

Cohen famously excoriated the reasoning of the US Supreme Court in the case of the Susquehanna Coal Company which was chartered by the State of Pennsylvania but was sued in New York.[22] The corporation objected that it could not be sued in New York, even though it regularly conducted business there, because it was headquartered and established elsewhere. Cohen condemned the Court's use of metaphor and analogy in determining the factual question "where is a corporation?" because figurative speech interfered with a rational and scientific deliberation on the facts of the case. He assailed the US Supreme Court's inquiries into whether a corporation was like a person. Even though a corporation is a legal fiction that is artificially created, "this does not give us the right to hypostatize, to 'thingify,' the corporation, and to assume that it travels about from State to State as mortal men travel . . . [or to] approach a legal problem in these essentially supernatural terms" (p. 811). For Cohen, the turn to metaphors and legal metaphysics to solve essentially factual problems are nothing more than "transcendental nonsense" (p. 812).

Exasperated, Cohen (1935:821) asks rhetorically, "How are we going to substitute a realistic, rational, scientific account of legal happenings for the classical theological jurisprudence of concepts?" Cohen's references to "supernatural terms" and "theological" jurisprudence is germane to our analysis of causal metaphors in international speech crimes documents. International court judges and prosecutors employ

---

[22] *Tauza v. Susquehanna Coal Company* 220 N.Y. 259, 115 N.E. 915 (1917).

metaphors of speech that are inspired, consciously or unconsciously, by longstanding images in the Judeo-Christian religious tradition. One short passage of the Bible contains three of the five categories of metaphor found in ICTR case law:

> And the tongue is a fire, a world of iniquity. The tongue is so set among our members that it defiles the whole body and sets on fire the course of nature; and it is set on fire by hell . . . But no man can tame the tongue. It is an unruly evil, full of deadly poison [James (3:6–8)].

Legal philosophy, perhaps under the influence of Plato's notorious invective against poetry and rhetoric in *Republic*, has largely embraced Cohen's trenchant critique.[23] In *Causation in the Law*, Hart and Honoré (1985:30–3) comment that the concept of legal causation has generated a plethora of metaphors that misrepresent the facts of a case. Specifically, they note that causal metaphors often speak of active forces as having "potency" or "coming to rest," even when it is apparent that the cause in question does not imply action or movement. The fixation with metaphors of movement and force has obscured the degree to which negative conditions or omissions might also serve as causes, and Hart and Honoré (1985:31) consider the example of a railway signalman who fails to move a lever, thus causing a train to crash.

A hardened stance against metaphor can even be found in unexpected places such as literary criticism and in Susan Sontag's (1991:91) self-avowed "polemic against metaphors of illness." For Sontag (1991: 5–9), the lurid metaphors of tuberculosis, cancer and AIDS emanate from ignorance, dread and a desire to conceal, and her riposte was that "illness is not a metaphor, and that the most truthful way of regarding illness . . . is one most purified of, most resistant to, metaphoric thinking" (p. 3). More unequivocal still is Sontag's damning contention that by deterring sufferers from seeking proper medical treatment, "The metaphors and myths . . . kill" (p. 99).

The most far-reaching recent philosophical critique of metaphorical language, however, is provided by Donald Davidson (2001:244) whose position was famously expressed in his aphorism, "Metaphor is the dreamwork of language." For Davidson, metaphors call much to our attention, but they are generally not propositional in character (p. 262). The meaning of metaphors lie in the literal interpretation of

---

[23] Plato (1993:362) cautions against the effects of poetry on morality and rational political discourse.

the words, and nothing more. Understanding them doesn't require any special linguistic conventions other than those that govern ordinary meaning. Metaphors have no extended meanings, and what you see is what you see (p. 247). There is nothing more to say, since paraphrasing a metaphor does not usually enhance what the metaphor itself accomplishes (p. 245). As to truth and falsity, all similes are all true, but in a trivial sense, "because everything is like everything, and in endless ways" (p. 253). Conversely, like irony, metaphors are usually false in the ordinary semantic sense: Juliet is not the sun and the adult Tolstoy was not an infant, moralizing or otherwise.[24] In fact, argues Davidson, if we didn't instinctively understand *a priori* that metaphors are false, then the following Woody Allen joke would not work: "The trial, which took place over the following weeks, was like a circus, although there was some difficulty getting the elephants into the courtroom" (p. 257). Davidson's central claim is that "what distinguishes metaphor is not meaning but use – in this it is like assertion, hinting, lying, promising or criticizing" (p. 258). Davidson's observation that the significance of metaphors lies in their use, not their formal propositional meaning, is central to my thesis.

For most of the twentieth century, the dominant stance towards metaphorical language on the part of practicing attorneys and legal scholars was one of ambivalence and skepticism. On the one hand, jurists are aware that their opinions must persuade others, (including the public), but on the other, metaphors are not propositional enough in their content to convey meaning transparently. A judicial decision that lacks any embellishments whatsoever misses a fleeting opportunity to sway the reader at an emotional level and thereby to convince them of the validity of the judges' reasoning. Figurative speech is sometimes considered acceptable as garnishing that brings the material to life, and even Felix Cohen conceded that "myths may impress the imagination and memory where more exact discourse would leave minds cold" (*Ibid.*, 812). Benjamin Cardozo (1931:9) wrote, in his inimitably vivid style, "The opinion will need persuasive force, or the impressive virtue of sincerity and fire, or the mnemonic power of alliteration and antithesis, or the terseness and tang of the proverb and the maxim. Neglect the help of these allies, and it may never win its way." Yet Cardozo (1926:61) also harbored doubts about common legal metaphors such as "piercing the corporate veil." He counseled in his New York Court of

---

[24] In his essay, Davidson (p. 247) quotes a critic who once called Tolstoy "a great moralizing infant."

Appeal decision in *Berkey*, "Metaphors in law are to be narrowly watched, for starting as devices to liberate thought, they often end up by enslaving it."[25]

All this changed with the publication of George Lakoff and Mark Johnson's (1980) *Metaphors We Live By*, which transformed modern thinking about metaphorical language across the humanities, social sciences and the law. The authors made unbounded claims about the role of metaphor in human thought and behavior: "[M]etaphor is pervasive in everyday life, not just in language but in thought and action. Our ordinary conceptual system, in terms of which we both think and act, is fundamentally metaphorical in nature" (p. 3). Nearly thirty years later, Lakoff (2009:27) continues to extend the scope of his theory of metaphor, drawing on new developments in neuroscience to advance a "neural theory of metaphor" that consists of an integrated system in the human brain that "will dominate your thought, your understanding of the world, and your actions."

After Lakoff and Johnson, metaphor became widely accepted as a legitimate linguistic device.[26] No longer considered marginal, metaphorical language became widely embraced by legal academics, even if practitioners going about their daily practice continued to remain circumspect. Steven Winter's (1989:1114) article, written at the height of "metaphor fever" in legal scholarship, channeled Lakoff and Johnson's theory to call attention to the "ubiquity and necessity of metaphor in human thought" and assert that "metaphor is inevitable in legal analysis because it is central to human rationality" (p. 1166). For Winter, metaphorical language performs the essential function of promoting a more "realistic"[27] conception of law, leading to a more durable and consequential conception of the rights of citizens. Greater equality in society would be achieved not by expunging legal metaphors altogether, but by replacing old, dead metaphors with new ones that advanced an inclusive political agenda based upon an experiential and embodied conception of the law.[28]

---

[25] *Berkey v. Third Ave. Ry. Co.* 244 N.Y. 84, 94, 155 N.E. 58, p. 61 (1926).

[26] Sontag (1991:91) moderated her views in the eleven years between writing *Illness as Metaphor* (1978) and *Aids and its Metaphors* (1989), granting in the end that "Of course, one cannot think without metaphors" (1991:91). She couldn't help qualifying her concession with the caveat; "but that does not mean that there aren't some metaphors we might well abstain from or try to retire" such as military metaphors of treating AIDS.

[27] By "realistic," Winter seems to mean "informed by legal realism," a theory of law that grants more weight to social context, convention and contestation in law, rather than to legal doctrine, narrowly conceived.

[28] See Winter (1989:1130, 1227, 1237).

To this day, some scholars continue to applaud the use of metaphors in legal practice. For instance, Linda Berger (2013:193–4) encourages lawyers to employ metaphors when encountering new information and situations, and to draw upon existing cognitive schemas to render new subject matter more accessible. However, the modern moment is quite distinctive from the era of Cohen and Cardozo, and metaphorical thinking is now a topic that is studied empirically by psychologists. Intriguingly, their studies support a diverse range of views on metaphor. Behavioral experiments show that metaphorical utterances that draw an analogy between people and animals ("John is a shark") convey a wider range of meanings than mere literal statements ("He is scary"), thus suggesting, contra Davidson, that metaphors do in fact have extended meanings.[29] Conversely, psychological research has also challenged Lakoff and Johnson's theory that metaphor is *the* essential feature of human thought. When a familiar source domain of meaning is mapped into a novel target domain, a range of cognitive models govern how new meaning is made, and metaphorical thinking is only one of a range of options.[30]

In concluding this review, it is worth noting that even though metaphorical language might be unavoidable, and even constitute a central feature of human thought, this does not make it desirable in legal judgments. Objections of both a legal and factual kind may still be justified. Even referring to judicial turns of phrase considered earlier as "metaphors" might be to dignify them unduly. In many instances, they are just clichés and like all clichés, they are indicative of lazy and abstruse thinking. For two of the leading legal philosophers of the twentieth century, metaphorical phrases in judicial opinions are "empty of guidance for the court."[31] Even proponents of metaphorical language in the law such as Berger (2013:175) acknowledge the indeterminacy and elasticity of meaning in metaphors: "The author of a metaphor is able to advance positions without being held to them. When you use a metaphor, the listener usually understands that you have said one thing but that you likely have meant another."

Advancing positions without being held to them is appropriate in an academic seminar but it is troubling in a criminal courtroom. If we recognize that metaphorical statements are indirect statements whose status is indeterminate, then this has implications for due process of law. To ensure fair and predictable procedure, legal judgments must consist of propositions of a definite kind, in which the judges' meaning

---

[29] Kao et al. (2014:3).   [30] Camp (2006:160).   [31] Hart and Honoré (1985:97).

is plain and forthright and most importantly, can be subjected to further judicial review. Metaphorical language may compromise a defendant's right to challenge their conviction on appeal, since metaphors do not operate at the level of the verifiable or falsifiable. Metaphors cannot be satisfactorily challenged by standard propositional assertions or falsified by empirical evidence. They can only be replaced by another more persuasive metaphor. One can imagine the predicament of defense counsel being compelled to argue on appeal thus: "Your honor, my client's words were not like a weapon, instead they were like mere acorns falling on the heads of listeners: that is, painful but not lethal." I illustrate this point lightly, but with a serious intention, since in criminal law, the stakes can be very high, as Benjamin Cardozo (1931:100) acknowledged, "A metaphor ... is to say the least, a shifting test whereby to measure degrees of guilt that means the difference between life and death."

Figurative language that says one thing but means another is not the ideal medium of communication in which to adjudicate crimes of genocide, war crimes and crimes against humanity, and to send a convicted defendant to jail for the rest of their lives. Some judges at international criminal tribunals agree with this view, as one made clear when asked for his view on the ICTR incitement judgments, "I am opposed to emotional language. It is too individualistic and as a lawyer we should not be carried away by our emotions. Imprecise language seldom clarifies."[32] Rhetoric is perhaps an inescapable element of legal reasoning, but insofar as rhetorical flourishes cannot be subjected to evaluation, then they can be empty, misrepresentative and potentially damaging in a criminal trial. In their appeal to everyday expressions and common sense, metaphors invite the listener to understand an abstract and complex concept or event by reference to a superficial gloss of the qualities of a familiar object. Metaphors naturalize an assertion about a complex event, but of course common sense can be misleading, and the qualities of the abstract idea may not map commonsensically onto the ordinary object.[33] If courts are to determine whether certain speech acts have subsequent causal consequences, then we require as precise an account as possible of that causal relationship, or at least an account that is more exacting than Biblical images of poison, fire and conflagration.

[32] Author interview, 2015.
[33] See Rosenfeld (2011) for a lively and critical genealogy of the idea of common sense in the politics and law of America and Europe in the seventeenth and eighteenth centuries.

5.4   METAPHORS AND COGNITIVE SCHEMAS

> [Metaphors] provide a kind of lens or lattice ... through which we view
> the relevant phenomena.
>
> Donald Davidson (2001:260)

We need not determine once and for all the question of whether metaphors
are generative of new and beneficial meanings, or distorting and to be
eschewed in legal reasoning. The aim here is to explain the function of
metaphors in speech crimes law, that is, what they accomplish. The
indictments and judgments issued by international tribunals are not only
a set of propositions to be understood according to the meanings they
convey. Additionally, they are classic illustrations of Austin's performative
utterances that do things. If the accused is found to be innocent, then the
judgment, which is usually delivered in the presence of the defendant, is
the speech act that grants his or her freedom. If guilty, then the judgment
itself sentences the accused to a period of incarceration. Judgments may
also perform broader functions, such as morally denouncing international
crimes, legitimating the legal authority of international tribunals and
consolidating their international jurisdiction vis-à-vis nation-states.

The approach adopted here is inspired by Davidson's (2001:245)
aphorism that "metaphor belongs exclusively to the domain of use.
It is something brought off by the imaginative employment of words."
Metaphor's domain of use implies what Austin (1962:98) called its
illocutionary aspect (see Chapter 2). As Cardozo (1931:9) noted above,
the utility of a metaphor lies in its "persuasive force" and it is worth
asking what judges or prosecutors accomplish when they harness the
illocutionary potential of a metaphor.

This chapter opened with the observation that metaphorical language
is a common feature of speech crimes trials and is less prevalent in settled
areas of law, and therefore we can surmise that one of its functions is to
establish a new and emergent area of international criminal law. Cardozo
(1931:17) was cognizant of the fact that the "use of the maxim or the
proverb ... is characteristic of legal systems in early stages of development." Metaphors legitimate legal precedents by couching them in the
comfortable, familiar terms of the ordinary and routine. They ground
a new, problematic or complex legal idea in a beguiling appeal to everyday experience, a practice that Cardozo heartily endorsed:

> The precept may be doubtful in the beginning. How impossible to fight
> against it when the judge brings it down to earth and makes it walk the

ground ... The rule that is rooted in identities or analogies of customary belief and practice is felt and rightly felt to be rooted in reality.

(pp. 18–19)

Flouting the injunction against *analogia legis*, metaphorical language employs analogy to extend the boundary of law into new and uncharted territories. In so doing, it harnesses the illocutionary force of the imaginative expression to legitimate a new rule or interpretation, and to extend the sovereignty of the court to adjudicate in unsettled legal domains. As one might recall, before the *Akayesu* and *Nahimana* judgments at the ICTR, no one knew what a conviction for direct and public incitement to commit genocide looked like or what the "direct" element meant, or how a court could determine special intent to commit genocide by examining a speech act.

Additionally, and more importantly, metaphors objectify mental states and "thingify" abstractions and invisible relations.[34] Metaphorical language promulgates a schema of perception, and can establish an entirely new cognitive template for apprehending a legal issue such as protected speech. A classic example in modern US constitutional law that redefined the boundary between protected and unprotected speech was US Supreme Court Justice Oliver Wendell Holmes' "marketplace of ideas" metaphor, articulated shortly after the First World War. US law did not always grant broad protections to free speech. During the period from the Revolution until after the end of the First World War, it was quite censorious of certain forms of political speech, and suppressed sedition and profane and abusive language about the US government and its flag and armed forces.

The modern conception of freedom of speech in the United States did not emerge until 1919 and two successive US Supreme Court decisions, first *Schenck* and then *Abrams*. In *Schenck*, as we saw earlier, Oliver Wendell Holmes compared political hyperbole against military conscription with shouting "fire!" and causing panic in a crowded theater. Holmes reversed his views later that year in *Abrams* and applied the now famous marketplace of ideas model.[35] This contributed to the repeal of the Sedition Act in 1920 and represented a watershed moment in US constitutional law. By applying the

---

[34] To use Cohen's (1935:811) expression.

[35] Warburton (2009:25) cites John Stuart Mill's defense of free speech as the forerunner to the marketplace model. Bosmajian (1992:67) reviews the various and sundry critiques of the marketplace of ideas metaphor.

normative assumptions of unfettered trade and commerce to political speech, Holmes laid the foundations for the modern understanding of the First Amendment that would prevail for the rest of the twentieth century. *Abrams v. United States* upheld the 1918 Amendment to the Espionage Act of 1917, and criminalized speech that incited resistance to the war effort and urged the curtailment of production of necessary materials for the war against Germany.

Justice Holmes notoriously dissented because, "the ultimate good desired is better reached by free trade in ideas – that the best test of truth is the power of the thought to get itself accepted in the competition of the market."[36] Holmes' free trade metaphor, still invoked today, objectifies ideas and speech and transforms them into commercial products and commodities that are bought and sold freely in the marketplace. The marketplace metaphor construes speech acts as items that can be exchanged on a voluntary basis, with each buyer and seller entering freely into an arrangement that seeks maximum gain. Ideas and speech require no regulation, since in a free market people will buy the good ideas, and bad ideas will remain on the shelf, unsold. Let the market decide, counseled Justice Holmes, rather than the legal establishment, the legislature, or worse, the inherently thin-skinned executive branch. Holmes' model has been subjected to extensive criticism because "it leads us to perceive ideas as commodities to be bargained for, things to be bought and sold to those who will pay the highest price. But it is questionable that speech, the expression of ideas, should be metaphorized into a consumer item."[37]

Similarly, metaphorical language at international criminal tribunals generates a new, idealized cognitive model that erroneously resolves central problems in mental causation in international criminal law. A mental schema that construes words as things classifies and organizes complex social phenomena, but as with most metaphorical language, it is constructed upon frameworks that operate in ordinary language and thought. As with the marketplace of ideas, metaphors in international speech crimes cases convert the desires, beliefs and especially intentions of speakers and their audience into the kind of physical objects that make up the material-object world, transforming interpersonal social relations into material-object world relations.

Configuring mental causation as physical causation allows judges and prosecutors to envisage a mechanical relationship between the

---

[36] *Abrams v. United States* 250 US 616 (1919), at 630 (Holmes' J. dissenting).
[37] Bosmajian (1993:61).

mental states of actors and between mental states and observed behavior. When courts perceive the relationship between speech and intentionality as analogous to guns, poison, fire and viruses that are governed by physical laws of cause and effect, they align speech and intentionality with the criminal law's billiard ball model of causation. Yet this analogy is built on a false premise. Unlike humans, physical objects like guns, fire and poison do not contain inner subjectivity or agency.[38] They are merely objects knocked this way and that by forces acting externally upon them.

As we saw in the Šešelj trial, crimes such as instigating, co-perpetrating or ordering crimes against humanity require proof of mental causation, and the metaphors of speech prevalent in these trials are an inadequate response to the special problems attendant to demonstrating mental causation beyond a reasonable doubt. When legal actors seek to circumvent these complications by subsuming mental causation under a theory of material causation, they elide the fundamental distinction between physical causation and mental causation. Whereas mental causation necessarily involves human subjectivity and psychological states, the properties of physical objects are mind-independent.

In positing a distinction between mental and physical causation, I do not mean to imply that mental states are not physical. Mental states are physical in the sense that they occur in the neurological processes of the brain. However, we should not lose sight of the fact that mental states are constituted by intentions, beliefs and desires, and that the causal relationship between speaker A's intention and listener B's intention is of a qualitatively different order than the causal relationship between material-object A that collides with material-object B. Briefly, this is because material objects are not reflexive agents capable of rationality and intentionality, and humans are.

Legal theorists of causation Hart and Honoré (1985:52) have highlighted the "*radical* differences which separate 'He induced me to do it' from 'His blow caused the victim's death'" (emphasis in original). They counsel against the temptation to assimilate mental causation and the attendant relationships between human actors under what they call "ordinary cases of causal connection," by which they mean material,

[38] By "agency" I refer to intentionality and a minimum capacity to take preliminary steps towards the fulfillment of the intention. Searle (2001:95–6) sees agency and the self as interchangeable and identifies the following feature of an agent: she is conscious, persists through time, operates with reasons, and is capable of deciding, initiating and carrying out actions and is responsible for at least some of her behavior.

physical causation. They conclude that it is misleading to say that one person has caused another to act in cases where "one person merely advised, or tempted, or requested another to act" (p. 52). We can only speak of one person causing another to act when the instigated act is not wholly voluntary, for instance when the person is threatened, coerced, instructed by authority or misled by false statements. (p. 52).

Even enthusiastic advocates of metaphorical language such as Lakoff and Johnson (1980:71) accept the distinction between physical causation and mental causation: "In physical causation the agent and patient are events, a physical law takes the place of plan, goal, and motor activity, and all of the peculiarly human aspects are factored out." John Searle (1983:115) has formulated a distinction between "agent causation" (for agents who possess intentionality) and "event causation" (for the rest of the universe), all the while reminding us that ultimately there is only one kind of causation and that is "efficient causation" that entails some things making other things happen. The causal relations in agent causation between intentional social actors are a subcategory of efficient causation, yet they are special in many respects, especially insofar as they may not instantiate a universal causal regularity (p. 135).[39] Searle reserves a prominent role for the volition of agents and he reminds us of the indeterminacy of agents' actions.

It is worth considering in more detail those "peculiarly human aspects" that Lakoff and Johnson refer to above. Mental causation is not peculiarly human, but it is peculiarly hard to see and measure.[40] This is not because mental causation is mysterious, illusory or impossible to verify. It is one element of the wider category of intentionality, understood as a condition of the mind in which mental states are oriented towards altering circumstances in the world.[41] With respect to speech acts, the conditions of satisfaction are achieved by the successful transfer of intentional mental states between persons, such that A and B come to share the same intention, when before the speech act in question only A possessed

---

[39] Searle (1983:117–119) develops a complex argument with respect to "agent" causation that claims that the agent need not endorse any universal law to explain the cause of his behavior. Physical causation, on the other hand, does imply universal laws of causation between material objects.

[40] Mental causation in non-humans is evident when I ask my Schnauzer, Pepper Pot, to bring me her squeaky toy, and she retrieves it faithfully. She is also an agent with her own volition, evidenced by the fact that she sometimes prefers to hide under the bed and keep her toy for herself.

[41] This gloss follows John Searle's (1998:64–5) definition of intentionality as "that feature of the mind by which mental states are directed at, or are about or of, or refer to, or aim at, states of affairs in the world." On mental causation, see Searle (1983:112–40).

the intention. As an illustration, when I ask a server in a restaurant to bring me a bowl of soup, my intention expressed in a speech act causally forms an intention in her that she did not have before I made my request. My request was therefore the reason for her bringing me a bowl of soup. Simply conceived, this is mental causation. Aristotle (2004:89) succinctly summarized mental causation in *Rhetoric* thus: "The use of persuasive speech is to lead to decisions."

In physical causation, for my physical act to be causally related to the harm or injury, it would have to be determined, say, that my placing compound 1080 rat poison in the soup of my enemy while having lunch was the cause of his early demise, as opposed to his heart condition, or his lunchtime habit of drinking and eating excessively whilst simultaneously smoking a cigarette and talking a load of old twaddle. Physical events usually leave visible evidence that can verify assertions of proximate cause, such as traces of compound 1080 on the soup bowl or in the body of my enemy that are detected during a postmortem examination. This type of material evidence is impossible to come by in mental causation, as it resides in layers of intentionality, subjectivity and mental states that are, even in the era of functional Magnetic Resonance Imaging (fMRI), invisible to other people.

As yet, there is no independent verification of an agent's subjective intentions that is external to the mind of the agent. In the absence of a plausible statement from the agent regarding his or her state of mind, criminal courts usually infer intent on the basis of words, actions and circumstances.[42] These challenges are not unique to the adjudication of crimes involving speech acts, but pertain to the *mens rea* requirement of criminal law more generally. Fact-finders always face the task of deciding whether the mental state of the accused corresponded to the actual outcome and whether the two are close enough to warrant the imposition of criminal liability.

The usual complications that a domestic criminal court faces in ascertaining *mens rea* are compounded in the international tribunal setting when a collectivity of persons coalesces to commit systematic and widespread mass crimes over an extended period. In the international trials considered in this book, a conviction for instigating or joint criminal enterprise (JCE) rests on demonstrating that one mind (the accused's) had causal effects on the minds of others (the material perpetrators) and there existed, however fleetingly, a collective

---

[42] See Dressler and Garvey (2012:155) on inferring intent in criminal law.

intentionality in which a plurality of actors shared the same desire, belief and intention to commit mass crimes.[43] Metaphors of fire, poison, virus and weapons give the illusory impression of making visible that which is normally invisible; namely the shared desires, beliefs and intentions of an assortment of actors that together constitute the reason why their actions were directed towards a single goal or set of goals.

Metaphors make tangible and plain the *mens rea* element of the prosecution case, which would otherwise be circumstantial if it were only known through the evidence presented on the defendant's words and behavior. They do so, however, in a way that is misleading and rests on a defective psychology, since human desires, beliefs and intentions are not like fire, poison or viruses in their properties or interactions or causal effects. Metaphors are therefore more than showy rhetoric that expresses moral values. They also advance an idealized cognitive model that fills in the evidential gaps in the sequence of causation. They smooth over inconsistencies and make the fragments of evidence for mental causation seem to cohere.

Predrag Dojčinović (2014:4), a linguist in the ICTY's Office of the Prosecutor, accurately notes that "metaphors ... figures of speech, or tropes, only indicate an evidentiary and logical vacuum in legal analysis and deliberations." In filling logical and evidentiary gaps, figurative speech bypasses the agency of the listener and neglects possible inter-vening causes. Rather than recognizing an audience as intentional rational actors who exercise voluntary choices, causal metaphors turn humans into automatons. Physical metaphors of causation eradicate listeners as legally responsible agents,[44] and with them a troublesome feature in the sequence of mental causation that could interfere with the judicial conclusion that the accused caused the death of thousands through his words alone (as declared in *Nahimana*).

5.5 THE SEQUENCE OF MENTAL AND PHYSICAL CAUSATION IN SPEECH CRIMES

What international tribunals require is a clearly articulated model of causation in speech acts that does not invoke misleading metaphors

---

[43] John Searle (1995:85) defines collective intentionality thus: "Collective intentionality exists both in the form of cooperative behavior and in consciously shared attitudes such as shared desires, beliefs and intentions."

[44] Morse (2007:7) defines legally responsible agents as "people who have the general capacity to grasp and be guided by good reason in particular legal contexts. For example, they must be generally capable of properly using the rules as premises in practical reasoning."

to gloss over the problem of mental causation or fill in the gaps in the prosecution's evidence. This section proposes such a model.

In adjudicating charges of instigation, ordering and co-perpetrating, courts assess the mental effects of what John Searle (1998:149–50) termed "directives," which include orders, commands, and requests, all of which are based on desires and constitute expressions of intentionality. When an individual is charged with instigating crimes against humanity, the prosecution must show that the accused provided a reason for the material perpetrator to commit a criminal act and that her words set in motion a succession of events that culminated in the commission of the crime.[45]

What that progression consists of when a defendant is charged with instigating, inducing, soliciting, ordering or co-perpetrating an international crime requires setting out as unambiguously and plainly as possible. The whole sequence of causation, from an incipient desire to a direct intention to the conditions of satisfaction of an intention (that is, the completed crime), integrates both mental causation and physical causation, or what Searle (1983:115) terms agent causation and event causation. The sequence's initial stages originate at the level of agent causation, and its latter phases encompass event causation, and the direction of causation is mind→world. A causal sequence could be posed as a series of questions that a criminal court must answer, as below:

[Mental/Agent Causation]
1. Did the speaker possess the desire to commit a crime?
2. Did the speaker develop the intention to commit a crime?
3. Did the speaker's utterances urge another person to commit a crime?
4. Did the listener understand the speaker's utterances as encouragement to commit a crime?
5. Did the listener accept the reason communicated by the instigator?
6. Did the speaker's utterances constitute the reason for the criminal actions of the listener?
7. Was the listener's intention to act criminally formed after hearing the speaker's inducement?

[Physical/Event Causation]
8. Did the listener initiate physical steps to commit the crime that was intended by the speaker?
9. Did the listener's physical actions rise to the level of the execution of the crime?
10. Was the crime completed by the listener?

Figure 5.1 The Sequence of Causation from Intention to Action

---

[45] Timmermann and Schabas (2013:171).

Desires logically precede intentions, and Searle (1983:3) distinguishes between desires, which may not be directed towards a goal, and intentions, which are. He also (1983:84–5) distinguishes between intentions that are formed prior to action (stages 1–2) and "intentions in action" that are constitutive of action and provide the directive element of action (stage 3 onwards). Intentions and intentions in action are "causally self-referential" in that the intentional states themselves (desire, intention, encouragement) stand in a causal relationship to one another and to the rest of their conditions of satisfaction.[46]

Searle's philosophical template of the relationship between mind and language maps straightforwardly onto the criminal law of speech. Stated in legal terms, for a court to justifiably assign liability to the speaker for ordering, instigating or co-perpetrating a crime, all the questions in the causal sequence above must be answered in the affirmative. For instigation to have occurred, it must be evident that the material perpetrator committed the crime because he or she formulated a reason as a consequence of the speaker's performative utterance. While s/he may have held the desire to commit a crime before the moment of the illocutionary speech act, his or her intention to commit the crime was only fully formed and integrated into his or her intention in action after the illocutionary speech act.

In such a scenario, we could say that the criminal intention (*mens rea*) that the speaker expressed in his speech act secured the necessary conditions of satisfaction and became a collective criminal intention that was shared between at least two actors. If the answer to any of the mental causation questions (nos. 1–7) is negative, then the causal connection between intention and action is broken and the desires and intentions of the speaker are not causally connected to the acts of others. If the sequence of mental causation is interrupted, then causal liability cannot be attributed to the speaker. However, the speaker could still conceivably be held responsible for inchoate crimes like inciting genocide or hate speech as a form of persecution, crimes which do not require mental causation, only proof of the speaker's criminal intentionality expressed in an illocutionary speech act

---

[46] Searle (1983:85) uses the example of perceptual experiences and memories which "stand in causal relations to the rest of their conditions of satisfaction."

(nos. 1–3)[47] The speaker may also be liable as an aider and abettor, as some forms of complicity do not require proof of a causal nexus to the crime.[48]

When considering the array of categories of criminal liability in international law, it is apparent that identifying the sequence of causation in speech crimes is more straightforward in some modes of criminal liability (such as ordering) than others (such as instigating and inducing). In evaluating whether the accused is guilty of ordering crimes against humanity, the series of questions above could be answered in part by reference to the structure of command and control that governs the relationship between a superior officer and a subordinate. The hierarchical structure of a military organization or quasi-military political party like the Nazi party does most of the work required for mental causation. Once it is shown that the order was successfully formulated, delivered, understood and obeyed, one need not elaborate on the mental states of the subordinates much further. This line of argumentation does not imply that an illegal order is justified, only that when an order is given from a military superior to a subordinate the efficacy of mental causation can be assumed, because the formal and structural nature of the relationship furnishes the necessary and sufficient conditions of uptake. An order is an order, and failure to comply with a superior's order is a criminal offense in all militaries. In some, disobeying an order on the battlefield may be punished (whether legally or illegally) by immediate punishment, including execution.[49] When an order is issued and obeyed, the causal relationship between the intentions of the superior and the intentions in action of the subordinates is evident for all to see.

Instigating, or prompting another to commit an offence, requires no such political or military structure and can apply to individuals who are not in a hierarchical relationship and who have no immediate or prior relationship. Proving mental causation in instigation

---

[47] The ICTY and ICTR statutes did not criminalize attempt. The ICC Statue includes attempt at Article 25.3(b) "In accordance with this Statute, a person shall be criminally responsible and liable for punishment for a crime within the jurisdiction of the Court if that person: (b) Orders, solicits or induces the commission of such a crime which in fact occurs or is attempted."

[48] For instance, omissions and acts committed after the crime is completed, such as covering up evidence of the crime. See *Blaškić* AC §48 on causation and complicity. See *Mrkšić et al.*, AC §§131–5 on omissions as a form of aiding and abetting.

[49] As an example, see the infamous ICTY case of Dražen Erdemović who was threatened with immediate death by firing squad by a superior officer if he did not execute captured prisoners at Srebrenica in 1995. The Trial Chamber in *Erdemović* accepted his account as a mitigating factor in sentencing him (§14).

cases immediately confronts the obstacle of the agency and volition of the listener, who in a normal situation (that is, not incapacitated or under duress) retains the capacity to veto the attempt at persuasion and to refrain from acting in accordance with the speaker's desires.[50]

Unlike the issuing of an order in a military organization, instigating is more dependent on (and therefore more vulnerable to) the agency of the actors, and it allows for certain gaps in the series of agent causation, gaps which are filled by the listener's capacity for active decision-making. The standard view in criminal law is that these gaps constitute a break in the chain of causation and the listener's voluntary decision-making represents an intervening factor, as articulated by Glanville Williams (1989:392) in his classic article *"Finis* for *Novus Actus?"*:

> I may suggest reasons to you for doing something; I may urge you to do it, tell you it will pay you to do it, tell you it is your duty to do it. My efforts may perhaps make it very much more likely that you will do it. But they do not cause you to do it, in the sense in which one causes a kettle of water to boil by putting it on the stove. Your volitional act is regarded (within the doctrine of responsibility) as setting a new "chain of causation" going, irrespective of what has happened before.

Speech act theory gives us an accurate model for thinking about agent causation, and leads us to a better understanding of its inherently "gappy" nature. As we saw in Chapter 2, Austin (1962:112–3) distinguished between the locutionary (or semantic), illocutionary (or persuasive) and perlocutionary (or consequential) aspects of a performative utterance, and he insisted on there being a discontinuity between an illocutionary act and its consequences. The locutionary and illocutionary dimensions of a performative utterance (nos. 1–3) are under the control of speaker, and after their performance there is a "regular, natural break in the chain" which is followed by perlocutions or consequences (nos. 4–10). Perlocutions following a speech act are no longer controlled by the speaker, and as John Searle (1998:190) observed, in most speech acts, "the perlocutionary effects on the hearer are in large part up to the hearer." Some perlocutionary effects, such as convincing the listener of the reasons to commit a criminal act (nos.

---

[50] In psychology, agency refers to the capacity to do, or intend to do, something, and in the law it is a necessary element of moral and criminal responsibility (see Gray and Wegner 2012).

4–7), may occur almost simultaneously with the illocutionary act. Yet specifically *criminal* perlocutions (nos. 8–10) must logically occur after an illocution, because the listener not only has to intend to undertake the criminal act, but she then must embark upon the enterprise of undertaking it.

In the breach between locutions and illocutions on the one hand and perlocutions on the other, many things can happen. At least two types of situations can arise after stage 3, one of which relies on the volition of the listener, and the other does not. In the first, the listener consciously interprets the speaker's words and adopts a disposition towards them. The listener exerts voluntary control over all her subsequent actions, unless she is mentally incapacitated or under duress. In the second scenario, other intervening causes may present themselves. An intervening cause in the context of this discussion is a separate act or omission that breaks the direct connection between the speaker's words and the listener's acts.

The context may change in various ways after the performative utterance: another speaker with a different intentionality might speak, which we could describe as an intervening intention. A weapon might be put in the hand of the listener by another actor who is not the speaker. A weapon might be taken away from the listener by a bystander. Members of the audience might be attacked by an opposing group. Each of these events fundamentally alters the conditions of causation and the causal effects of the speaker's words, and with them her criminal liability for the consequences of her words. The gap between each step in the causal series allows indeterminacy to flourish and separate intervening causes to crop up, and these new causes can undermine the relationship between the speaker, the listener and the crime.

It is possible to hear and not understand, it is possible to understand and not be convinced, it is possible to be convinced and decide not to act, it is possible to decide to act but then fail to act, and it is possible to initiate an act but then abandon it. In this context of indeterminacy, causal metaphors are more than superficial grandiloquence, or glorified "transcendental nonsense." In international criminal tribunal judgments on speech crimes, they function to gloss over and conceal the critical causation problems outlined above. In short, they constitute judicial sophistry. By filling in the gaps in the evidence of mental causation and peddling false analogies that advance a mechanistic view of relations between agents, the benefits of causal metaphors only accrue to one party in a so-called "propaganda trial" – the prosecution. Perhaps this is one reason why we seldom, if ever, see defense counsel uttering them in speech crimes trials.[51]

5.6 AGENCY, INTERVENING CAUSES AND MULTIPLE CAUSATION

> We are agents.
>
> Stephen J. Morse (2004:64)

This concluding section reviews the social science and neuroscience literature to evaluate its implications for the legal and normative arguments on the autonomy of agents and mental causation. Some scientists subscribe to an essentially volition-free model of mental causation. Many evolutionary psychologists claim that our behavior is so determined by biological processes that the idea of free will is simply an illusion.[52] It is indeed the case that recent advances in psychology and neuroscience make a maximalist version of autonomous agency and intentionality increasingly hard to maintain. Studies by psychologists such as Benjamin Libet (1999:47) demonstrate that volition can be initiated unconsciously, and that our brains make decisions about intentional actions several hundred milliseconds before we are even consciously aware of the intention to act. Persuasive speech acts may therefore convince the listener to commit to act even before she is aware of her desires and intentions.

Yet it is still possible to accept that human consciousness is inextricably part of the biological brain's computational machinery and that our choices are never utterly free without arriving at the conclusion that humans are automatons, political pawns, or, in one influential neuroscientist's view, "biochemical puppets."[53] While there is little doubt that human behavior is to some degree determined, there

---

[51] In my review of the cross-examination and closing arguments of defense counsel in the international speech crimes trials included in this book, I did not find one incidence of metaphorical language.

[52] Wegner (2002) has taken this view. For a summary of the views of evolutionary psychologists on free will see Workman and Reader (2014:257–8). For a review of the idea of free will in neuroscience and criminal law, and an emphasis on indeterminacy see Gazzaniga and Steven (2004).

[53] A hubristic expression coined by popular neuroscientist Sam Harris. In a similar vein, evolutionary biologist Jerry Cohn writes "So it is with all of our . . . choices: not one of them results from a free and conscious decision on our part. There is no freedom of choice, no free will [both cited in Nahmias (2015:78)]."

remains a great deal of indeterminism within both social systems and individual psychology, and that indeterminism allows for alternative possibilities and therefore voluntary conscious agency.

Despite the vaunted claim that neuroscience has eradicated the concept of free will, in fact psychological studies safeguard a role for conscious intentionality. Even Benjamin Libet (1999:47), the neuroscientist who has perhaps done most to dispute the concept of autonomous agency, finds that the human subjects in his experiments can "veto" an act in the instant that lies between the awareness of an intention to act and the performance of the intended motor act. This conscious function can still control outcomes and, as Morse (2004:58) recognizes, conscious intentionality is not incapacitated and still does causal work. Additional psychological studies have pinpointed the part of the brain (the fronto-median cortex) associated with the exercise of a conscious veto power.[54]

In social psychology, persuasion research starts with the premise that listeners are autonomous agents who may or may not be persuaded by a speaker. Indeed, the findings of persuasion research and political communication studies presented in Chapter 7 convincingly demonstrate that listeners are often not persuaded for a variety of reasons related to their personality type, the conditions in which they hear a message, the credibility of the speaker and the content of the message. They may of course be influenced by persuasive speech, but they bear responsibility for their subsequent acts, unless they are coerced. Because of this, a consequence of social science persuasion research is that individuals can be justifiably held legally and morally responsible for their actions, as social psychologist Richard Perloff (2010:33) explains lucidly:

> Persuasion assumes without question that people have free choice – that they can do other than what the persuader suggests. This has an important consequence. It means that people are responsible for the decisions they make in response to persuasive messages. Naturally people can't foresee every possible consequence of choices that they make. They cannot be held accountable for outcomes that could not reasonably have been foreseen. But one of the essential aspects of life is choice – necessarily based on incomplete, and sometimes inaccurate, information. Provided that individuals have freedom of choice, a foundation of persuasion, they are responsible for the decisions they make.

[54] See the neuroscience experiments of Brass and Haggard (2007:9141–5).

172

Additionally, there is a normative argument to be made for agency. Retaining a role for human volition is both empirically justifiable and normatively desirable, as the entire system of western criminal justice relies on the proposition that persons are minimally rational agents who can be held responsible for their actions unless there is evidence of incapacity, an absence of volition or duress. The official position of criminal law since the first known legal code, the Code of Ur-Nammu (c. 2100–2050 BC), holds that conscious, intentional, rational and uncompelled agents may be held responsible for their actions.[55] For good reasons, modern criminal justice shows no sign of abandoning the concept of individual responsibility anytime soon.[56] As Stephen Morse (2004:52–3) explains:

> The capacity for intentional movement and thoughts – the capacity for agency – is a central aspect of personhood and is integral to what it means to be a responsible person. We act because we intend. Responsibility judgments depend on the mental states that produce and accompany our bodily movements ... Law and morality as action-guiding normative systems of rules are useless, and perhaps incoherent, unless one accepts this view of personhood.

Criminal law, with some support from psychology, relies upon a theory of human agency and volition to undergird its underlying conception of responsibility. Of course, the view that each of us is a potentially rational agent responsible for our voluntary conscious actions does not require that persons always behave according to a universal yard-stick of rationality. This is criminal law, after all. It only means, following both Morse (2007:6) and Searle (1983:1) that persons can act for conscious and intentional reasons, based on a minimal rationality that corresponds to the rules and norms of their society.

In contrast to the metaphors of causation expounded by judges and prosecutors in international courts, listeners can evaluate the locutionary and illocutionary aspects of a political speech or broadcast in accordance with their decision-making powers and cognitive capacity. At a minimum, the listener processes the speaker's message in a way that implies ownership and therefore legal responsibility for his or her subsequent actions. Unless the listener is deceived or under duress, then

---

[55] Morse (2007:19).
[56] See Ashworth (2009:23 *et passim*) on the concept of "individual autonomy" in criminal law that maintains that each individual is responsible for his or her own actions.

she exercises voluntary choice and owns her subsequent acts and is responsible for them.

If we are to retain this agency-based conception of speech acts, then we must reject the mechanistic and simplistic clichés commonly used by judges and prosecutors in cases of incitement and instigation. This was certainly the view of the ICTY Trial Chamber that adjudicated the case against Predrag Banović, a low-ranking guard at the Keraterm camp near the town of Prejidor in 1992, during the Bosnian armed conflict. Banović pleaded guilty to participating in acts of persecution as a crime against humanity that included murder, beatings and maintaining non-Serb prisoners in inhumane conditions at the camp. However, his defense counsel argued in mitigation of his sentence because; "his participation in these crimes should be put into the broader context of the aggressive wartime propaganda that was prevalent in the whole territory, particularly in the Prijedor area and the Keraterm camp. As a young, uneducated and immature person, the Accused succumbed to the propaganda."[57] In support of lessening the sentence, the defense submitted an expert report from a clinical psychologist that claimed that because of his low level of education, emotional immaturity, and poor impulse control, he was easily swayed by propaganda that fomented a collective hysteria among Bosnian Serbs.[58]

The Trial Chamber rejected the view that Banović was an unfortunate hostage of the wartime media, and maintained instead that he made a series of voluntary choices to commit serial crimes that included murdering seven prisoners. The judgment held the accused fully and criminally responsible for his actions.[59] Even though he was exposed to Serb wartime propaganda that incited hatred of non-Serbs and urged extreme measures against the "enemy," Banović's agency represented a *novus actus interveniens*, or new intervening act, that broke the sequence of causation, and recommenced it again, starting with Banović's own intentional acts and decisions.[60]

The view advanced above is consistent not only with the tenets of criminal law, but also with the findings of social science studies on the role of an inciting media during hostilities regarding the ability of listeners to reject the media's calls to violence. As reviewed in Chapter 2, Mironko's interviews with convicted perpetrators in the

---

[57] *Banović* TC §44.   [58] *Banović* TC §77–8.
[59] *Banović* TC §81. See Timmermann (2015:259–60) for a discussion of the Banović case.
[60] The Trial Chamber noted that Banović was not under duress when he committed his crimes at §81.

Rwandan genocide showed that many rural Rwandans were skeptical of RTLM broadcasts which they saw as intended for a largely urban audience who held distinctive interests and priorities. Interviews by Straus with Hutu *genocidaires* indicated the extent to which peer-to-peer interactions shaped the ways in which Rwandan actors processed the broadcasts. Both Straus and Mironko are critical of the ICTR's neglect of perpetrators' views and the tribunal's tendency to see *genocidaires* as mindless puppets of Hutu Power propaganda.

Christopher Browning's (1998) *Ordinary Men*, an historical account of the murderous campaign in Poland of Reserve Battalion 101 during the Second World War, famously rejected the thesis that the Holocaust was the logical result of anti-Semitism engendered by Nazi propaganda. German soldiers were not willing executioners of one single mind: "perpetrators not only had the capacity to choose but exercised that choice in various ways that covered the spectrum from enthusiastic participation, through dutiful, nominal or regretful compliance, to differing degrees of evasion." Browning (1998:74–5) estimated that ten to twenty percent of those German soldiers assigned to firing squads at the Józefów massacre asked to be released from their duties and his research found that "some refused to kill and others stopped killing."

These findings on the behavior of soldiers during wartime have been reinforced and extended by social science research elsewhere, including in the Balkans. Cultural anthropologist Jordan Kiper (2015) conducted fieldwork with war veterans in Serbia, and his findings paint a fascinating and complex picture of wartime media. Kiper conducted ethnographic interviews with Serbian war veterans and concluded that combatants who were subjected to a media campaign of enmity towards non-Serbs were not simply hapless pawns.

Intriguingly, Serbian war veterans in Kiper's study presented themselves less as passive consumers of wartime propaganda and more as active producers and originators of (often inaccurate) news stories. War veterans recalled that they themselves created stories about the conflict on the frontline. These narratives then circulated among the soldiers, and were picked up by journalists who reported them as fact in the national news. Nationalist political leaders often seized upon the most extreme stories and repeated them, with embellishments, in their speeches. Some frontline stories were based on what soldiers had immediately witnessed, and others were obviously fabricated, such as the story that Croatian doctors were scavenging Serbian corpses to harvest their organs for profit (Kiper 2015:2).

Of course, memories may fade or become altered over time, but veterans explicitly told Kiper that they were not incited to more intense violence by media broadcasts for a host of reasons. The news was blocked on the frontline, and soldiers were not allowed access to newspapers, radios or television (p. 10). They did, however, recognize the media's role in recruiting new volunteers to join up and fight for the Serb cause (p. 10). Veterans generated narratives to bridge the cognitive dissonance they experienced in an armed conflict in which many victims were civilians. As Kiper concludes (p. 15) "Soldiers in campaigns involving heavy fighting or collective violence were not automatons but rather conscious human beings forced to come to terms with, and justify, their violent acts." Understanding how wartime propaganda can function as an *ex post facto* rationalization for mass atrocities corresponds with what we know about the Rwandan genocide, where many genocidal speeches and broadcasts came after the genocidal attacks on Tutsis, and therefore constituted acts of complicity after the fact. Here, wartime propaganda is less a trigger of violent events than it is a retroactive justification for them.

In the light of this evidence, war crimes analyst Nenad Fišer (2012:34, 53) justifiably questions the "top-down" model of propaganda for war that is prevalent in international criminal courts and advocates a more "bottom-up" perspective that focuses on the subject's receptivity to certain messages. Fišer also calls for more empirical and psychological studies of the media preceding and during armed conflict that test the receptivity of its target audience (pp. 55–6). Kiper's ethnographic research with Serb war veterans similarly undermines a legal view of causation that draws a straight line from immoderate politicians down to their political followers who embark on collective violence. Kiper notes that "In the Serbian case, war propaganda did not motivate collective violence but rather the two shared a cyclical relationship that was not linear, as recent speech-crime trials purport" (p. 2).

Kiper's informants provide an image of the wartime media in Serbia that does not support the view that there was a straightforward causal nexus between official incitement and specific war crimes. If the top-down, linear model of propaganda does not accurately reflect what is happening on the ground, then that complicates the formal model of causation proposed in Figure 5.1, which starts with the speaker's desires and intentions and proceeds to the intentions of the listener, and then ends with the commission of the crime. What if, as Jordan Kiper's research with Serb war veterans suggests, the listener is a combatant who also provides some of the content of the media, and who is co-constructing the wartime narrative of the nationalist political leader? If we are to model inciting speech in the media accurately, we need to start thinking in terms of systems of multiple, interdependent and reciprocal causes, rather than singular causal sequences. This requires a revision of the model in Figure 5.1 to add an arrow from stage 10 back up to number 1 again to represent the positive feedback loop between inciters and material perpetrators that sometimes develops.

When secondary causal effects themselves exert an influence on preceding causes, we can say that there exists a feedback loop. The concept of a system of circular and reinforcing causation has been widely recognized in institutional economics since the writings of Swedish economist Gunnar Myrdal.[61] According to Myrdal (1978:774), circular causation implies that if one condition changes, then others will similarly change in response. The secondary changes will themselves cause further effects, including on the primary causal stimulus that initiated the sequence in the first place. At this point, there ceases to be a fundamental or originating cause within the social process, and the interdependent causal factors operate as an integrated system that moves in a certain direction in a cycle that can be virtuous or vicious.

In his influential account of US race relations in *American Dilemma*, Myrdal (1944: Appendix 3) coined the concept "cumulative circular causation" to analyze racism in the United States, and to explain how racial prejudice and poverty reinforce one another and have a cumulative effect. Myrdal's (1957:13) concept of circular causation not only explains how variables interact with and reinforce one another, but also how the system gathers increasing momentum in certain circumstances: "Because of such circular causation a social process tends to become cumulative and often to gather speed at an accelerating rate."

Incorporating ideas of multiple causation and circular causation into our theory of speech acts has several implications for international criminal law. For starters, it describes in a less opaque language what international judges are grasping for when they allude to lurid metaphors of fire and contagion to describe the effects of denigrating and inciting speech during armed conflict and genocide. Second, a complex theory of causation has definite repercussions for assigning liability.

---

[61] Myrdal was apparently not the first to use the idea of circular causation, and Berger and Elsner (2007:529) recount how his institutional economics were influenced by previous writers, including the early twentieth century sociologist Thorstein Veblen.

Compared with a conventional linear, unidirectional vector of causation, a reciprocal series of interactions likely reduces the liability of the speaker and elevates the liability of the material perpetrator, since the latter is a co-producer of the intentionality required for any collective criminal enterprise. It also steers international tribunals away from modes of liability that require direct causation such as instigation, and towards those that allow multiple and indirect causation, or no clear sequence of causation at all, such as complicity. I work through the implications of these social science models of causation for international criminal law in Chapter 8.

CHAPTER SIX

SOCIAL RESEARCH IN INTERNATIONAL SPEECH CRIMES TRIALS

[L]aw has a love–hate relationship with expert witnesses. They are often helpful, and sometimes indispensable ... Experts are needed, but they are not always to be trusted."

Julie Seaman (2008:828)

The courts ... often insist that the causal questions which they have to face must be determined on commonsense principles.

H. L. A. Hart and Anthony Honoré (1985:26)

6.1 INTRODUCTION

This chapter evaluates the role and effectiveness of expert witnesses called by the prosecution in speech crimes trials at international criminal tribunals. Expert witness testimony has been a salient feature of international criminal trials generally, and experts are called more frequently than in the domestic criminal setting. Their presence is even more pronounced in "propaganda" trials. When the defendant is charged with instigating war crimes, crimes against humanity or inciting genocide, understanding the local resonance of speech acts can determine the ultimate issue in a trial.

This is particularly demanding in the international context since it requires a grasp of local languages and the cultural context of their usage in order to determine what utterances meant (what Austin calls the locutionary aspect), what the utterances encouraged the listener to do (or the illocutionary aspect), and what consequences of the speech acts were (or perlocutionary aspect). Grasping these dimensions requires an expert in language and wartime media, particularly in the eyes of the prosecution, which calls twice as many experts as the defense.

International criminal trials often feature several expert witnesses from both the prosecution and defense who testify on a range of issues; including, *inter alia*, the standard protocols followed by forensic scientists when exhuming cadavers, the financial transactions of political leaders, and the conventional command structure of a military organization. Even if we recognize that experts are called in virtually all international criminal trials, it is important not to overestimate their influence. Expert evidence is considered by judges, in the vast majority of instances, as secondary to the "material evidence," understood as authenticated documentary evidence of physical acts. Defendants are seldom, if ever, convicted solely on the basis of expert testimony, despite the fact that experts can play a major role in tilting the judges towards the case theory of one party.[1] As the International Criminal Court Pre-Trial Chamber in *Gbagbo* stated unambiguously, material evidence and firsthand eyewitness testimony is paramount:

> As a general matter, it is preferable to have as much forensic and other material evidence as possible. Such evidence should be duly authenticated and have clear and unbroken chains of custody. Whenever testimonial evidence is offered, it should, to the extent possible, be based on first-hand and personal observations of witnesses.[2]

With regard to expert evidence, judges have expressed their predilection for scientific expertise on a number of occasions. The statistical data that I assembled on over 480 incidences of expertise at the ICTY bears this out. Judges are doing what they say they are doing when evaluating experts. However, there is one notable exception and that is the treatment of social researchers in speech crimes trials, which stands out as an intriguing special case. It seems that judges reject evidence from quantitative social scientists in propaganda trials more frequently than from qualitative language experts. This runs contrary to the general pattern in which scientific methods have more probative value. Scientific evidence on speech is not as highly valued as

---

[1] Perhaps the best-known example of an expert having a major influence on the outcome trial is the Krstić trial at the ICTY, when a forensic team showed that Srebrenica victims had not been killed in combat as the defense asserted, but had been captured and summarily executed with their hands bound by ligatures.

[2] *Gbagbo* Confirmation of Charges Decision, 3 June 2013, §§26–27.

scientific studies of ballistics that are presented in a run-of-the-mill war crimes trial.

In order to understand this anomaly, I explore two case studies: one of a language expert at the ICTR and the other of a political sociologist at the ICTY. There are several possible explanations for why the evidence of the language expert was embraced by the court and the sociologist's testimony was spurned. It appears that judges accept language experts since they perform the role of an enhanced translator and do not challenge the status hierarchy of the courtroom. Judges have disqualified quantitative social science experts on the effects of political communication because they believe that the law has all the tools it needs to comprehend speech. Ordinary reasoning and common sense are deemed sufficient to determine the meaning of a speech act.

6.2 EXPERTS IN THE INTERNATIONAL CRIMINAL COURTROOM

An expert is defined in Rule 94*bis* of the ICTY's Rules of Procedure and Evidence as, "a person who by virtue of some specialized knowledge, skill or training can assist the trier of fact to understand or determine an issue in dispute."[3] The admissibility of expert evidence at the ICTY and ICTR is also governed by Rule 89 of the Rules of Procedure and Evidence, which states: "A Chamber may admit any relevant evidence which it deems to have probative value [89(C)]," with the only grounds for exclusion being, "if its probative value is substantially outweighed by the need to ensure a fair trial [Rule 89(D)]." A body of case law upholds and refines these admissibility rules, such as the ICTY decision in *Blaškić* that "barring exceptions, all relevant evidence is admissible, including hearsay evidence."[4] Further, for an expert report to be admissible in evidence, it must meet the "minimum standard of reliability"[5] and the

---

[3] ICTY Rules of Procedure and Evidence (2015). This was affirmed in the case law in *Strugar* Decision on the Defence Motions to Oppose Admission of Prosecution Expert Reports Pursuant to Rule 94*bis*, 1 April 2004, p. 4.

[4] *Prosecutor v. Blaškić.* Decision on the Standing Objection of the Defense to the Admission of Hearsay with No Inquiry as to its Reliability. IT-95-14-T, 21 January 1998. §§10–12. More recent case law upholding Rule 89C can be found in the Trial Chamber judgments in *Halilović* (§14) and *Blagojević and Jokić* (§20). The International Criminal Court's Rules of Procedure and Evidence do not include a well-defined statement on the admissibility of witness evidence, expert or otherwise, as can be found in the ICTY/ICTR Rules.

[5] UNICRI (2001:104, §22) citing *Prosecutor v. Stanislav Galić,* "Decision on the Prosecution Motion for Reconsideration of the Admission of the Expert Report of Professor Radinajoj" Case No. IT-98-29-T, §9.

content of the report must fall within the accepted area of expertise of the witness.[6]

Beyond that, very little guidance is given to international judges about how to evaluate expert reports or testimony.[7] There is, for instance, no admissibility rule that approximates Rule 702 of the US Federal Rules of Evidence which explicitly addresses the principles and methods of expert testimony:

> If scientific, technical, or other specialized knowledge will assist the trier of fact to understand the evidence or to determine a fact in issue, a witness qualified as an expert by knowledge, skill, experience, training, or education, may testify thereto in the form of an opinion or otherwise, if (1) the testimony is based upon sufficient facts or data, (2) the testimony is the product of reliable principles and methods, and (3) the witness has applied the principles and methods reliably to the facts of the case.

Since experts represent approximately ten percent of all witnesses called before the ICTY,[8] it is worth examining in more detail the types of expert evidence most likely to persuade international judges. In the US domestic setting, the US Supreme Court has explicitly stated its preference for expert testimony based on the reasoning and methodology of positivist science.[9] The few official statements by international criminal courts on the topic also state a preference for scientific methods, which they see as an indicator of objectivity and neutrality, whether the expert appears for the prosecution or the defense:

> In assessing the testimony of expert witnesses, the Chamber considered factors such as the established competence of the particular witness in his or her field of expertise, the methodology used, the extent to which the expert's findings were consistent with other evidence in the case and the general reliability of the expert's evidence. On this last point, the

---

[6] *Prosecutor v. Milan Lukić and Sredoje Lukić*, "Decision on Second Prosecution Motion for the Admission of Evidence Pursuant to Rule 92*bis* (Two Expert Witnesses)" Case No. IT-98–32/1-T, 23 July 2008, §15.

[7] Article 69, which governs evidence in the ICC Statute, does not mention experts. The Statute makes passing reference to experts in other articles such as Article 93(1)(b,e) and 93(2) on forms of state cooperation. Regulation 44 on Experts of the Regulations of the Court indicates that the court shall create a list of experts and allows the experts to be called by the Chamber. No guidance is given, however, on the criteria for evaluating expert reports and testimony.

[8] This percentage is based upon 473 documented experts out of a total of 4600 witnesses at the ICTY, as reported in *ICTY-Facts and Figures* (ICTY Communications Service, April 2015).

[9] *Daubert v. Merrell Dow Pharmaceuticals, Inc.*, 113 S. Ct. 2786 (1993).

Chamber considered scientific evidence to be objective, even if the expert was appointed by only one party or by the Court.[10]

As yet, however, there has been no empirical verification of whether the stated preferences of international judges are actually borne out in practice. Observers have highlighted the contribution of experts to certain precedent-setting international cases,[11] and social researchers have considered the objectives of the legal parties when they integrate expert testimony into their cases. For instance, socio-cultural anthropologists have analyzed expert testimony on local cultural practices and historical debates in trials heard at the ICC,[12] the Special Court for Sierra Leone[13] and at the ICTY and ICTR.[14]

However, to my knowledge there has not been any comprehensive assessment, statistical or otherwise, of the overall significance of expert testimony using a reasonably large sample. To fill this gap, I developed a database of expert testimony based on a comprehensive list created by the Association of Defense Counsel of the ICTY of 473 experts that had appeared in cases at the ICTY for both the prosecution and defense over a twenty-year period (1993–2013).

The list included the 473 experts' educational background and area(s) of expertise, as well as the specific cases in which they participated.[15] To enable comparisons between the myriad types of expertise, I grouped experts under nine category headings:[16]

- Document Authentication and Verification
- Engineering
- Forensics
- Finance
- Law and Human Rights
- Medicine
- Military, Police and Intelligence
- Social Research, Humanities and Balkans Area Studies
- Weapons and Ballistics

---

[10] *Ngudjolo* TC §60.
[11] See Klinkner (2008) on the major role played by forensic science expertise in the Krstić case at the ICTY.
[12] Clarke (2009:87) and Wilson (2011:192–215).   [13] Anders (2011; 2014) and Kelsall (2009).
[14] Eltringham (2013), Swigart (2015), Wilson (2011:170–91).
[15] Some of the 473 individual experts had more than one area of expertise and in these cases, one area was chosen as the primary area of expertise. In a few instances where both areas were equally important, both were counted, leading to a total of 481 separate incidences of expertise.
[16] See Appendix 2 for details on the subcategories included in each type.

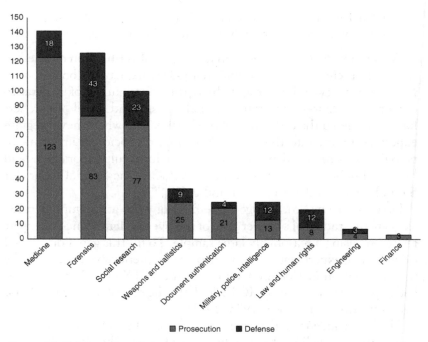

Figure 6.1 Total number of experts by category

Given the judges' stated proclivities, my hypothesis was that scientific experts would be called and cited more frequently than humanist or qualitative experts, and that judges would favor "material object" science (e.g., medicine, forensic science and ballistics) over social research. I did not presume that expertise in the international courtroom would be any more or less valued overall than in the domestic criminal justice setting.

The data analysis proved both informative and unexpected. Confirming the hypothesis, scientific experts were called more frequently than non-scientists, by a factor of almost two to one (308 to 173), and "material object" science experts outnumbered social researchers by a factor of more than three (333 to 100). But that is where the successful prediction ends. All types of experts were cited on average nearly eighteen times in trial chamber judgments, a startling endorsement of expert testimony in international courts when compared with domestic settings.[17]

The top three types of experts in ICTY trials are medical experts with 141 appearances, forensic scientists (126), and social researchers (100). The prosecution relies much more on expert testimony than the defense, calling 357 (74%) experts to the defense's 124 (26%). At the ICTY, prosecution teams summoned medical experts (123), forensic scientists (83), and social researchers (77) most frequently and indeed, the prosecution called experts more regularly in every category, with only a few exceptions. Defense counsel relied most on forensic scientists (43), social researchers (23) and medical experts (18) and they commissioned legal and human rights experts more often than prosecutors.

The distribution of expertise at the international level contrasts with the US criminal justice context: one prominent study by Groscup et al. (2002:345–6) of nearly 700 criminal cases found that the most frequent topic of expert testimony concerned police procedures. In domestic courts, law enforcement agents are called to testify as "technical experts" most often of any category, followed by medical experts, scientific experts (including chemists, biologists and behavioral social scientists) and then, finally, business experts. The collective nature of the widespread crimes adjudicated at international tribunals necessitates a different profile of expertise.

In absolute terms, prosecution witnesses were cited by the ICTY nearly twice as many times as defense witnesses (5523 to 2804). However, the underlying numbers tell a more complex story, in that defense experts enjoy a significantly higher average citation rate; twenty-three citations per expert per judgment compared with sixteen per expert for the prosecution.[18] With greater funds at its disposal, prosecution teams could afford to call more expert witnesses but, in practice, judges were more likely to be persuaded by defense experts. Again, these results stand in contrast to domestic criminal trials in the United States. In criminal cases in US federal district courts, two–thirds of prosecution challenges to defense experts are successful,

---

[17] Moran (2010:535) concludes that social science evidence represents mere "window dressing" in US constitutional disputes on race. She observes that most social science evidence is introduced in cases before the Supreme Court through amicus curiae briefs, but only three percent of amicus briefs were cited by the Court between 1946 and 1995 (*Ibid.*, p. 534, citing Kearney and Merrill 2000:759–60).

[18] The standard errors are 5.08 for the defense expert citation mean and 2.33 for the prosecution.

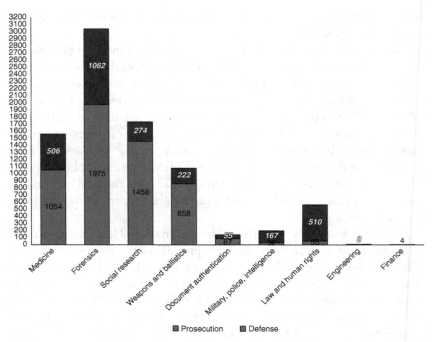

Figure 6.2 Number of expert citations by category

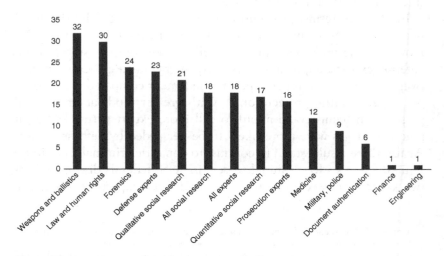

Figure 6.3 Average rate of citation per category of expert

whereas government experts are excluded less than ten percent of the time.[19]

While there is no perfect way to evaluate the significance of an expert witness, a standard method in socio-legal scholarship is to count the number of times that an expert witness is cited in a final trial chamber judgment.[20] The average rate of citation per judgment of each category of expert provides a sense of what types of expertise international judges perceive as dispositive, that is, brings about a determination of fact. Weapons and ballistics experts have the highest citation rate at 31.8 per expert, followed by legal and human rights experts (29.7) and forensic scientists (24.5). Intriguingly, social researchers (18.2) achieved a much higher citation rate than medical experts (11.7), the most numerous category of all experts. Social researchers also exerted more influence on the outcome than military and police experts (8.7). At the bottom of the scale were document verification experts (5.7), financial experts (1.3) and engineers (1.1).

The relative prominence of social researchers in international trials – they are the third most numerous category of expert and their testimony is more likely to be accepted than engineers or the police – demands further scrutiny. To ascertain what types of social research are most valued by judges, I divided the social research category into quantitative (economics, political science, demography, and statistics) and qualitative methods (anthropology, cultural heritage, history, Balkans and Eastern European specialists, media, phonetics, political experts and sociology).[21] Given that the parties called scientists more often, and judges preferred science both formally and in practice, I predicted that quantitative social scientists would fare better in the courtroom than qualitative social researchers. Data analysis, however, confounded my prediction. Surprisingly, judges accorded qualitative social research more probative value, citing it nearly twice as often as quantitative expertise (1133 to 593). Comparatively, qualitative social researchers also

---

[19] Saks and Faigman (2005:121).

[20] Kearney and Merrill (2000:811) measure the influence of social scientists on the US Supreme Court by counting the number of times they are cited in judgments. Of course, an expert can be cited and then dismissed in a judgment, so citation could be negatively correlated to influence. My review of a sample of expert citations found that international judgments cited experts more often when they find the expert's evidence to be dispositive.

[21] Recognizing that these categories overlap. For example, some political scientists use qualitative methods and some historians and sociologists use quantitative ones. I handled this by distributing individual scholars across groups based upon their stated methods preferences.

maintained a significantly higher citation rate (21) than quantitative scholarship (17).[22]

As a general observation, experts are quite well received in the international criminal courtroom, and judges especially value defense experts and those experts who use scientific methods. Within the category of science, though, there are variations: ballistics experts had the most influence on judicial decisions of any type of expertise. Judicial review of social research runs counter to the general trend in favor of scientific approaches, and here qualitative studies are more likely to be dispositive than quantitative ones.

We need to be mindful of this overall picture when assessing the influence of experts in speech crimes trials. My review of the main propaganda trials at the ICTY and ICTR confirms the overall trend in favor of qualitative experts. In speech crimes trials, judges appear more resistant to quantitative and statistical expertise and more open to linguists and cultural experts who offer an informed opinion on the locutions and illocutions of the accused. Since there are not enough speech crimes trials to demonstrate this statistically, my investigation adopts a more qualitative approach and examines the role of experts in the most definitive speech crimes trials at international criminal tribunals: *Akayesu*, *Nahimana* (at the ICTR) and *Šešelj* (at the ICTY).

Judges are, as is apparent in the first case study at the ICTR, open to evidence from a language expert who provided testimony on the locutionary and illocutionary aspects of a language, Kinyarwanda, that the judges do not speak. Experts who adopt interpretive approaches to language are, I argue, more easily integrated into criminal court's own epistemic framework for determining the facts of the case. Judges are more likely to accept qualitative expertise regarding the meaning of utterances since it represents an enhanced translation service that fits comfortably into the already existing epistemology and status hierarchy of the courtroom.

The second case study at the ICTY shows a different picture, in which judges were circumspect and even hostile when experts used quantitative methods to identify the content of a political leader's discourse and the mechanisms through which his performative utterances prompted violence. Even though judges are well disposed towards quantitative and

---

[22] I have not found data that would allow comparisons with social research in domestic criminal jurisdictions. In the US, however, there is a literature on the role of social researchers in specific criminal trials. See Jenkins and Kroll-Smith (1996) on sociologists and Shuy (2005) on sociolinguists.

scientific methods in the arenas of ballistics and forensics, they do not seem to fully grasp the methods and theories of social research on persuasion and political communication, and seldom trust that they are accurate, neutral and objective. Quantitative analysis of political discourse diverges from the law's own rationalist (but non-scientific) epistemological framework, which, recalling the earlier discussion of causation and beyond reasonable doubt, determines the facts of the case according to ordinary common sense reasoning. Furthermore, allowing quantitative researchers to determine the consequences of speech acts may be considered by judges as trampling judicial prerogative. In the second case study, judges reacted with resistance and skepticism when instructed by a quantitative social scientist, who they deemed to have usurped their sovereign decision-making powers as the triers of fact. As Henry Maine (1982/1861:396) observed long ago, the sovereign authority to judge and punish has been at the heart of criminal justice for centuries: "The theory of criminal justice ... ended in the doctrine that the chastisement of crimes belonged in a special manner to the Sovereign as representative and mandatary of his people."

Even though scientific expertise is generally preferred in international criminal courts, my quantitative analysis shows that social science evidence bucks the general trend. Understanding why this is so requires a qualitative inquiry into the strategies and motivations of the legal actors in international criminal trials, so as to grasp the ideas, concepts and assumptions behind the raw numbers.

6.3 AN ENHANCED TRANSLATION SERVICE: LANGUAGE EXPERTISE AT THE INTERNATIONAL TRIBUNAL FOR RWANDA

> Up to the early 1960s, the word *Inyenzi* meant "cockroach." In the early 1960s, this word acquired another meaning ... it broadened to include the mainly Tutsi rebels who were attacking the country ... When the *Inkotanyi* attacked the country in 1990, this second meaning was reactivated. For Hutu extremists, the word came to be generalized to Tutsis as an ethnic group.
>
> Mathias Ruzindana (2012:155)

In the first case study, the report and the courtroom testimony of a sociolinguist testifying for the prosecution were well received by the Trial Chamber and cited extensively by the judges in convicting the accused.

The first defendant tried before the ICTR was Jean-Paul Akayesu, a town mayor accused of the international crime of direct and public incitement to commit genocide on the basis of his public speeches in 1994. Akayesu's guilt or innocence on the charge of incitement hinged on the larger question of whether the mass killing of Tutsi minority group members resulted from an orchestrated state policy to exterminate Tutsis as a protected group as such, or whether the killing was secondary to the core objective of the Hutu-dominated regime to defeat the invading Rwandan Patriot Front (RPF) army, whose soldiers and supporters were predominantly of Tutsi origin. Specifically, Akayesu openly encouraged his followers to exterminate the "*Inkotanyi*" (lit. "warriors") and "*Inyenzi*," and the judges were compelled to parse the locutionary and illocutionary aspects of these Kinyarwanda terms, which could either constitute calls to eliminate illegitimate civilian targets (innocent Tutsis) or lawful military ones (RPF soldiers/combatants).

The panel of three international judges confronted a number of obstacles as they evaluated the content, meaning and intentions of Akayesu's speeches. None of the judges spoke the local African languages or came to the Tribunal with a deep and abiding knowledge of the history and culture of the African Great Lakes region. They were open, at least early on, to instruction by an expert on the meanings of Kinyarwanda terms and their socio-cultural context. As a practical matter, they faced intractable translation difficulties as they were working in English and reviewing documents translated from Kinyarwanda to French to English.[23] In the courtroom, they cross-examined Rwandan witnesses in translation from English to French to Kinyarwanda, with an occasional Swahili step added between French and Kinyarwanda, and then back through the entire progression again. These circumlocutions of translation both compounded the monotony of courtroom procedure and undermined the integrity of eyewitness testimony.

In the first ICTR trials, one translation issue immediately arose: how should translators render Kinyarwanda terms whose meaning was disputed by the prosecution and defense? It was decided that the translators providing simultaneous courtroom translation would articulate key terms in the original Kinyarwanda, and leave it up to the opposing parties to interpret them. Moreover, the judges encountered a noticeable reticence on the part of many ordinary Rwandan eyewitnesses to answer

---

[23] Swigart (2015) carefully documents the translation challenges at the ICTR and other international courts operating in Africa.

direct questions such as "What does *Inyenzi* mean?"[24] Rwandans were frequently overawed by the international courtroom, and asking such direct questions in Rwandan society is conventionally considered rude and somewhat childish.[25] Finally, the judges had to determine whether or not Akayesu's speech acts constituted a direct call to his followers to embark upon the genocide of Tutsis as a group, but there were few if any explicit appeals by the accused Jean-Paul Akayesu to exterminate Tutsis. Like many political leaders in ethno-nationalist armed conflicts, the accused had avoided explicitly genocidal speech. Exhortations whose meaning was sufficiently veiled or coded might escape liability for the international crime of "direct and public incitement to commit genocide."

Enter Dr. Mathias Ruzindana, a linguist at the National University of Rwanda who was called by the prosecution to submit a report and testify as an expert witness.[26] Ruzindana (2012:146) started with the premise that "law cannot do without linguistics," and his report set about explaining the basic meaning of Kinyarwanda terms used by the accused. He emphasized that their meaning depended on context and how the meaning of ordinary words was transformed during and after the 1994 genocide (pp. 156–62). Even though these Kinyarwanda terms conveyed an ominous message in certain circumstances, Ruzindana was careful to point out that each of the terms also carried an inoffensive meaning. "*Gukora*," for instance, means literally "to work," but during the genocide became a euphemism for "to kill or massacre the Tutsi."[27] In the prosecution's theory, *Inkotanyi* literally meant "warriors," but for Hutu extremists, it came to denote the RPF Army and eventually Tutsis in general, because the majority of RPF combatants were Tutsis. Similarly, terms like *Inyenzi* (lit., "cockroach"), *Umwanzi* ("enemy") and *Icyitso* ("accomplice") by extension denoted Tutsis as a group.

This was Mathias Ruzindana's first time in a criminal courtroom and he reflected on the experience of testifying as an expert witness:

> Lawyers do not reason the way we do. They have a case to win, and they try to corner the expert. The expert is standing between two opposing sides. The opposing party asks you trick questions. When the defense got

[24] Swigart (2015:584) also remarks on the "circuitousness of witness responses" at the ICTR.

[25] Ruzindana (2012:147) notes that cross examination was "irritating for ordinary non-educated Rwandans who, also out of ignorance of court practices, regularly find the type of questions asked 'stupid' or 'irrelevant.'" Combs (2010:79 *et passim*) details these cultural divergences at the ICTR in painstaking detail.

[26] Expert witness testimony may be called by a party and challenged by the opposing party under Rule 94*bis* of the ICTR's Rules of Procedure and Evidence.

[27] Ruzindana (1998:22).

the impression that I had made a vital point, they asked a question to make me angry, to show bias. These questions are meant to test you, not to test your evidence ... On the other hand, the prosecution wanted me to be categorical at times and give a certain answer that I might not be sure about. As an expert, it's important to not express what you don't believe to be true ... at times the prosecution found this disappointing.[28]

The Tribunal convicted Jean-Paul Akayesu of direct and public incitement to commit genocide, in large part on the evidence from Ruzindana's testimony and that of a few key eyewitnesses.[29] The judgment cited Ruzindana fourteen times and acknowledged that in assessing the locutionary dimensions of the accused's use of Kinyarwanda terms, "The Chamber has relied substantially on the testimony of Dr. Mathias Ruzindana, an expert witness on linguistics, for its understanding of these terms" (§146). The chamber affirmed his opinion that ordinary Rwandans are not always direct in answering questions about linguistic expressions and therefore Kinyarwanda terms have to be "decoded" by an expert "in order to be understood correctly" (§156).[30] The Trial Chamber concluded in its "factual findings" section that "On the basis of consistent evidence heard throughout the trial and the information provided by Dr. Ruzindana, appearing as an expert witness on linguistic issues, the Chamber is satisfied beyond a reasonable doubt that the population construed the Accused's call as a call to kill the Tutsi" and that "there was a causal link between the statement of the Accused at the 19 April 1994 gathering and the ensuing widespread killings at Taba" (§§361–2).

Akayesu's defense counsel appealed the decision, objecting to the Trial Chamber's reliance on Ruzindana's testimony, but the Appeals Chamber affirmed the expert's evidence and the accused's conviction for incitement. Ruzindana's interpretations of Kinyarwanda terms were later consolidated in a number of successive judgments by the Tribunal.[31] After *Akayesu*, it became an "adjudicative fact" or a "fact of common knowledge"[32] not subject to reasonable dispute at the

---

[28] Author interview, 2015.   [29] See *Akayesu* TC §§338–44 for key witness testimony.

[30] Combs (2010:99) sees it as "vital" for international criminal trials to hear experts such as Ruzindana who can explain local cultural norms to judges and thereby assist them in assessing witness credibility.

[31] Ruzindana's interpretation of the meaning of *Inkotanyi–Inyenzi* reappear in successive ICTR decisions, including; *Niyitegeka* TC §273, *Kayishema and Ruzindana* TC §293, *Bagilishema* TC §207 and *Karera* TC §449.

[32] Rule 94 of the ICTR Rules of Procedure and Evidence state that "A Trial Chamber shall not require proof of facts of common knowledge but shall take judicial notice thereof."

Tribunal that "in the minds of Hutu hardliners, the words *Inyenzi*, *Inkotanyi*, *enemy* and *accomplice* were closely associated with the Tutsi ethnic group."[33]

Despite this overwhelming triumph of interpretation for the Office of the Prosecutor, Ruzindana expressed some discomfort at the way his report and testimony were simplified and instrumentalized by prosecutors:

> The prosecutors were mainly interested in the use of the words as they related to proving the charges. The prosecution needed to show that words like *Inkotanyi* and *Inyenzi* meant Tutsis, but those words could also mean other things in other contexts. For instance, *Inkotanyi* could also mean the RPF Army. This causes confusion. The words are ambiguous, and we need to understand how the words were understood in their context.[34]

To avoid oversimplification, Dr. Ruzindana (2012:156–7) recommends that each trial chamber judgment illustrate exactly how it arrived at its interpretation of key terms by providing a thorough account of the context in which they were uttered. While he felt that the judgment in *Akayesu* did this, not every ICTR judgment was as punctilious in detailing the social or cultural indicia that informed its interpretation of individual speech acts. He indicated in our interview that "overgeneralization can be found in some of the judgments" and he wrote that some of the trials "adopted a simplistic approach."[35]

Subsequently, Ruzindana's interpretations were central to the prosecution case in the most important speech crimes trial in the history of the ICTR; the "Media Trial" (hereafter *Nahimana*) against three defendants Ferdinand Nahimana, Jean-Bosco Barayagwiza and Hassan Ngeze who were owners of Radio Télévision des Milles Collines (RTLM) and the Hutu Power newspaper, *Kangura*. The *Nahimana* prosecution team brought Ruzindana in again as its language expert, and by this time he was an ICTR staff member in the language section of the Registry. His testimony was complemented by another prosecution expert, Dr. Alison Des Forges, who was at the time a senior adviser for Human Rights Watch and who held a doctorate in African History from Yale University.[36] Ruzindana was somewhat overshadowed by Des Forges[37] and yet he still contributed appreciably to the prosecution's theory that calls on the radio to exterminate the *Inkotanyi* and *Inyenzi*

---

[33] Ruzindana (2012:153).   [34] Author interview, 2015.

[35] Author interview and Ruzindana (2012:146).

[36] Ruzindana testified over six days between 19–28 March and 9–10 July 2002.

[37] In the judgment, Ruzindana was cited only five times compared with Des Forges' ninety-three.

constituted a genocidal incitement to eradicate Tutsis as a group (Ruzindana 2012:153, 258). His expert report contained dispositive evidence to this effect, insofar as it contained transcripts of RTLM broadcasts that patently equated *Inkotanyi* and *Inyenzi* with Tutsis.[38] The court also heard from prosecution eyewitnesses who understood the disputed terms as direct calls to exterminate Tutsis as a group.[39]

Ruzindana (2012:145) labelled RTLM and *Kangura* as "hate media" that played a central role in triggering the Rwandan genocide. This assertion of a causal relationship between speech acts and misdeeds was reinforced by Des Forges, who told the Trial Chamber how during the genocide Rwandans were begging her to "stop RTLM."[40] Ruzindana (2012:15) maintains that "The TC [Trial Chamber] relied mainly on expert witnesses' opinion" in assessing the meaning of publications and broadcasts. His claim is borne out in the judgment in passages such as:

> "While the extent of causation by RTLM broadcasts in these killings may have varied somewhat ... the Chamber finds that a causal connection has been established by the evidence, noting the widespread perception of this link among witnesses, best represented by all the urgent telephone calls Des Forges received at the time from the people in Rwanda, desperately seeking to 'stop that radio.'"[41]

Trials (such as those at the ICTR) in the adversarial tradition of Anglo-American law regularly become a war of experts, in part because the parties select those experts who are most likely to advance their particular case theory:

> In the courtroom, the goal is not a consensus truth but a definitive decision. Although there may be a consensus in the scientific community about a particular question, this consensus is unlikely to appear in the courtroom. Instead opposing attorneys search out experts from the tails of the bell-shaped curve.
>
> (National Research Council 2002:16).

The Media Trial was no exception. The defense aimed to rebut Ruzindana's inferences through their own expert witness, Roger Shuy,

---

[38] See *Nahimana* TC §351–8.

[39] An indication of the import of these terms can be found in the fact that the *Nahimana* Trial Chamber refers to the terms *Inyenzi*, *Inkotanyi*, *enemy* and *accomplice* 179, 228, 179 and 31 times respectively in the final judgment.

[40] *Nahimana* TC §458. Des Forges (1999) wrote her own compelling account of the Rwandan genocide and the role of the radio in inciting genocide.

[41] *Nahimana* TC §482.

Emeritus Professor of Linguistics at Georgetown University. Shuy is a battle-hardened expert witness who has appeared in over fifty US criminal and civil trials. He has regularly been called by the defense in criminal cases to challenge and rebut incriminating language evidence recorded in undercover police operations.[42] His stock-in-trade is sewing doubt by seizing on the ambiguity of utterances, and his contribution to the defense case seems to be: "words don't always mean what you think they mean."

Dr. Shuy (2003:12) excoriated the prosecution expert's methods and conclusions, saying that Ruzindana provided no linguistic evidence whatsoever regarding the extended meaning of terms such as *Inkotanyi* and *Inyenzi*. All the Kinyarwanda terms in dispute had multiple meanings, according to the defense expert. Whereas Ruzindana interpreted a term like *Inyenzi* (lit., "cockroach") to denote the Tutsi, it was, according to Shuy, "also very capable of meaning the army or the RPF" (p. 26), who were called cockroaches because the insurgents were seen only at night. Defense expert Shuy criticized the qualitative methods and theories employed in Mathias Ruzindana's report, contending that they exhibited a flawed and inadequate view of linguistics (pp. 2–6).

First, Shuy alleged that they lacked any basis in discourse analysis of a delineated sample, and failed to use standard statistical methods and sociolinguistic data analysis procedures (p. 34). Ruzindana's claim that media owners were extremists planning genocide was not proven by his sociolinguistic research, nor could it ever be, since according to Shuy (2003:3), "Content, including political content, is not the realm of the socio-linguist." The prosecution expert had erroneously ventured outside the disciplinary confines of linguistics, because, "there is no way that linguistics can lead a scholar to reach into the minds of a writer to determine such motives or intentions" (p. 12).

Dr. Shuy concluded that Ruzindana's claims were based less on the methods and theories of socio-linguistics than they were on a highly selective reading of texts and broadcasts, the case theory of the prosecution, and his personal opinions about the speech acts of the accused as a native Kinyarwanda speaker who had observed the mass killing firsthand. Roger Shuy censured Ruzindana for what he saw as the prosecution expert's inappropriate and biased references to "the Hutu extremist press," "Hutu hate media," and the three accused as "genocide planners" who he termed "racist" and "killers" (p. 9). Shuy claimed that the mantle

---

[42] Shuy (1993:xxi) and Shuy (2005).

of sociolinguistics was merely a subterfuge for Ruzindana's personal opinions (pp. 9–11). When interviewed, Ruzindana conceded Shuy's point about drawing too heavily from his own experiences during the genocide:

> It's very hard to be neutral when you have experienced events before your eyes. There was a time in the courtroom testimony when I recalled to a situation where a speaker in a crowd referred to a child as an "*Inkotanyi*." How could a child be an *Inkotanyi*, in the sense of "an RPF soldier?" On reflection, I shouldn't have relied on that prior personal experience.[43]

The performance of an expert witness can be assessed on whether their views are cited in the final criminal court judgment, and by this standard, Ruzindana prevailed in the battle of the experts. His interpretations swayed the judges' decisions on the meaning of the radio broadcasts disseminated by the three defendants. The Media Trial judgment cited Ruzindana significantly less than the Trial Chamber did in *Akayesu* (five times versus fourteen times in the earlier case), but the defense expert's substantive contributions on, for instance, the meaning of *Inyenzi* or *Inkotanyi*, are not referenced at all.

Whether Shuy was justified in his views regarding the unknowability of the defendants' intentions and the uncertainty surrounding their speech acts, Ruzindana's testimony on the locutions and illocutions of the defendants did seem to be informed largely by his being a native Kinyarwanda speaker, and his contextual knowledge of Rwandan culture and the genocide itself, rather than socio-linguistics, discourse analysis and statistical methods per se. What Shuy perceived to be a flaw however, may ironically have granted Ruzindana an advantage in the international criminal courtroom by conforming to the standards of the courtroom and rendering his testimony accessible to judges. For his part, Ruzindana was consciously aware of the need to present his findings in a style appropriate to the criminal courtroom and he astutely tailored his evidence to suit the legal setting:

> In socio-linguistics, meaning arises from the context of usage and you don't always need a scientific justification. The judges were reassured when we said that a word's meaning varied according to context. That's something that everyone understands. I know the language very well as a linguistics lecturer and an educated Rwandan, and that built credibility. We looked at the context of each speech and asked the simple

---

[43] Author interview, 2015.

question, "Taking into account the conditions in which the speech act occurred, what would the average Rwandan listener have understood by the words?" We avoided making it too complicated and using social science jargon. The end users were lawyers, after all.[44]

Ruzindana's forthright strategy was effective insofar as his testimony proved convincing to the judges, and crucially, did not imperil judicial sovereignty in the courtroom. Judges, as we will see in more detail in a later section, comprehend the meaning of performative utterances by situating them in their local context of usage, rather than through the prism of a technical discipline such as socio-linguistics. When the meaning of allegedly inciting utterances is contested, they typically settle the matter by asking the simple question, "what would the average listener understand by the utterances?" Anthropologists and socio-linguists regularly ask this question as well, but they complement their answer with ethnographic observation, and analysis, including the contemporary historical and social science literature on the culture concerned.[45]

When offered a translation of a language they do not know, judges insist on remaining the ultimate arbiters of the effects of the speech acts. International judges' position of authority is not endangered by a local expert witness such as Ruzindana, who essentially perform the role of a specialized, elite translator for the court. Translators are a perennial feature of international tribunals and judges know how to evaluate their contributions. Judicial preeminence is threatened by social science experts who analyze speech acts using methods that depart from the prism of ordinary language.

International courts seem to find it harder to accept a quantitative analysis of language and behavior than an interpretive and contextual approach, since the latter comports with legal epistemology. Additionally, it has the advantage of preserving intact the status hierarchy of the courtroom. Even though experts on language are formally allowed to pronounce upon the ultimate issue in the trial, if they do so in a way that is perceived as a challenge to the authority of the court, they are unlikely to fare well.

---

[44] Author interview, 2015.
[45] In the case of *Elonis v. United States*, 13–983 US (2015), the United States Supreme Court asks whether it is enough to show that a "reasonable person" would regard rap lyrics written by Anthony Douglas Elonis as threatening.

These observations about the relative value in the courtroom of inter-pretative and contextual evidence from experts are not peculiar to the ICTR or the Akayesu and Nahimana cases, and can be found in other international courts. In dismissing the case against Mathieu Ngudjolo of Ituri Province in the eastern region of the Democratic Republic of the Congo, the Trial Chamber of the International Criminal Court chided the prosecutor for not bringing in more expert witnesses to provide information on notions of hierarchy and obedience in family relationships and the position of fetish-priests in Ituri.[46] According to the trial chamber, prosecutors had neglected the socio-cultural framework and should have discussed it at the beginning of their case.[47]

6.4 JUDICIAL GATEKEEPING AND THE PROPAGANDA EXPERT

> Now, these texts were extremely straightforward. There's nothing very subtle about nationalist discourse. You know, we're not translating the poetry of Baudelaire . . . "amputate Croatia" is really what it says. I mean, it's very vivid, it's clear. There's no subtle double meaning to it.
>
> Anthony Oberschall, ICTY Šešelj Transcript T. 1967–8,
> 11 December 2007.

It is instructive to contrast Dr. Ruzindana's expert testimony with an example where an expert was largely rejected by the Trial Chamber. A negative case comes from the trial at the ICTY of Vojislav Šešelj, the Serb nationalist politician charged with nine counts of war crimes and crimes against humanity committed between 1991–3 during the conflict in the former Yugoslavia.

The Šešelj trial is similar to the ICTR trials just considered insofar as all the defendants were public figures charged based on public speeches they gave in the context of armed conflict, ethnic cleansing and genocide. Yet the legal issue at stake in the Šešelj trial was unlike the Rwandan cases. Šešelj's guilt or innocence hinged less on the locutionary and illocution-ary aspects of his public speeches which were more direct (and lurid) than those of Akayesu or the RTLM broadcasters, than on the consequences or perlocutionary aspects of his utterances. The ultimate issue in the Šešelj trial was, did the defendant's speeches motivate his followers to murder, torture, sexually assault and deport Croats and Bosnian Muslims? Was

---

[46] *Ngudjolo* TC §122.   [47] *Ngudjolo* TC §123.

there a discernible causal nexus between his utterances and atrocities committed during armed conflict?

Enter Sociology Professor Anthony Oberschall of the University of North Carolina-Chapel Hill, who was called by the prosecution as an expert witness. Oberschall is an eminent sociologist of social movements in Germany and Europe and he came to the Tribunal having written numerous articles on conflict in the former Yugoslavia. The prosecution provided Dr. Oberschall with 242 texts of the accused's public speeches, articles and interviews that appeared on television, radio and in newspapers between 1991–4, the period of the indictment.[48] Oberschall studied the texts using content analysis, a quantitative social research method in which the researcher creates a coding framework made up of specific key terms and phrases and then counts the frequency with which they appear. Oberschall spoke of his mandate from the prosecution team:

> We got 242 texts and conducted the content analysis. He [Vojislav Šešelj] used the same phrases again and again ... they [the prosecution team] not only wanted me to characterize his discourse, but also decide the impact on people listening, and not only the impact of the negative stereotypes but also of the threats. He constantly talked about the threat from Croats and Albanians and how we [the Serbs] are victims in history and will be again. That was the dominant finding I had- this threat discourse in Šešelj's speech.[49]

His expert report, *Vojislav Šešelj's Nationalist Propaganda*, conveyed his findings, which are summarized in the report's subtitle, "How mass media propaganda impacts on ordinary people's acceptance and participation in collective violence, and how Seselj's nationalist propaganda promoted and justified coercion and violence by the Serbs against non-Serbs." The expert reviewed the scholarly literature on nationalism, collective violence, and mass communication, and indicated that he subscribed to the "ordinary men" thesis of collective violence associated with historian of Nazi Germany Christopher Browning (1998) in which average, unexceptional citizens are brought by social structures and political ideologies to participate in, or at least sanction, mass atrocities.[50] Even though a majority of citizens usually do not actively

---

[48] Oberschall (2006:3–4). The expert report was revised and published as a scholarly chapter in Oberschall (2012).

[49] Author interview, 2013.

[50] Browning (1998:167) is influenced by psychologist Ervin Staub and approvingly cites Staub's view that "Evil that arises out of ordinary thinking and is committed by ordinary people is the norm, not the exception."

Figure 6.4 Prosecution expert witness Anthony Oberschall during his testimony in the Šešelj trial, 2007
Credit: Courtesy of Mirko Klarin and Sense *Tribunal-Sense News Agency*

take part in the widespread and systematic crimes themselves, they are often aware of them and condone them.

As Oberschall expressed it in an interview, "Ordinary people may not participate in the killings, but they vote people into power and tolerate their crimes."[51] Oberschall's report cited a large-scale survey conducted across Yugoslavia in 1990 in which an overwhelming majority of respondents favored a supra-national "Yugoslav" identity, and eighty-five percent of respondents described ethnic relations in their neighborhood as "good" or "satisfactory" (p. 14). This changed only after a sustained campaign of hate propaganda pursued by political leaders on all sides who amplified threats and fomented violent actions against other groups (p. 7). The threat discourse of the accused replaced the peacetime cognitive frame of ethnic and national relations with

[51] Author interview, 2013.

a "crisis frame" that repeatedly conjured up the grim history of the Balkans in the first half of the twentieth century (p. 15).

Oberschall's (2006:18) central finding was that in ninety-nine speeches, Šešelj notified Serbs that they were faced with an imminent and existential threat. This crisis mentality created a public demand among Serbs for action and, combined with the message (repeated twenty-seven times in the texts) that Serbs are not responsible for any retaliatory acts, morally justified collective violence against non-Serbs (pp. 18–21), as this passage of classic nationalist *Sturm und Drang* illustrates:

> We will defend Serbian lands as long as we breathe … [against the] poisonous snake, that's the Croats … This is the third time that poisonous snake has headed for us, and for the third time bit us on the heart. Now we need to smash its head so it never bites anyone again … The Serbian revenge will come very soon, the Serbian revenge is already starting.

Before the courtroom proceedings got underway, the ICTY Trial Chamber rejected Anthony Oberschall's expert report and status as an expert on two grounds.[52] First, while they acknowledged that the professor is a senior academic with many sociological publications, including on collective violence in the former Yugoslavia, they found that his expertise was not specific enough to the case at hand. He was not an expert on the mass media in Serbia and the nationalist propaganda of the accused. The judges noted that he worked through a translator (p. 5). Further, the judges found fault in Oberschall's citation of eighty-seven books and articles on nationalism, propaganda and violence. The expert had not written these publications himself, and the judges construed this as a sign that he did not have sufficient expertise in the subject (p. 6).

The criterion of inadmissible hearsay is more commonly found in US courts[53] and by this measure, virtually every peer-reviewed social science journal article would be disqualified in an international criminal trial. The exclusion from evidence of an expert report at the ICTY is, "very rare" according to one United Nations study which cited only three incidences, all of them involving prosecution experts.[54]

---

[52] *The Prosecutor v. Vojislav Šešelj.* "Decision on Anthony Oberschall's Status as an Expert." 30 November 2007. Case No. IT-03-67-T. This decision was followed by "Decision Regarding the Admission of Evidence Presented During the Testimony of Anthony Oberschall," *Šešelj* (IT-03-67-T), Trial Chamber, 24 January, 2008.
[53] On experts and hearsay, see Seaman (2008).   [54] UNICRI (2011:105, §31–3).

The disqualification of experts is not unprecedented in the US domestic setting. In 2011, forty-three percent of experts in criminal and civil cases were disqualified in whole or part, although prosecution experts tend to be excluded much less frequently than defense experts.[55]

What came next, however, was surprising. Despite their ruling that Oberschall was not fit to testify pursuant to Rule 94*bis* of the Rules, the judges nevertheless admitted his report "for practical reasons,"[56] and allowed him to testify as a prosecution witness. It is unclear on what terms he was to testify, given that courtroom witnesses must either be an expert or a "fact witness" who was present at the crime scene, and Oberschall fit neither category. Even though he was permitted to testify, the judicial ruling had critical consequences for the prosecution case, since it meant that Oberschall could not pronounce upon the ultimate legal issue or make inferences regarding the guilt or innocence of the accused.

The prosecution plowed ahead regardless, and called Oberschall as one of the first prosecution witnesses. His testimony proved something of a spectacle. The defendant Vojislav Šešelj, who was representing himself in the trial, furiously objected to Oberschall's very presence in the courtroom.[57] Presiding Judge Jean-Claude Antonetti allowed Oberschall to proceed, but reminded him pointedly that whether his evidence was accepted by the judges depended upon his performance on the stand.[58] Oberschall remained levelheaded given the hostile reception. He calmly noted that the social research methods he had used were well established and widely accepted. He described how scholars have analyzed the techniques of persuasion in ethno-nationalist propaganda, including stereotyping, labelling, generalization and misinformation.[59] Oberschall defended the academic practice of citing prior scholarship on a topic, explaining that sociological knowledge builds over time, as each individual researcher builds upon the work of others. Shrewdly, he drew an analogy between incremental academic practices and the case law method in common law jurisdictions.[60]

Despite his efforts to proceed carefully during his examination-in-chief, Oberschall was in the hands of prosecutors who were bent on simplifying and sharpening his testimony against the accused.

---

[55] The figures on exclusion are from Price Waterhouse Coopers's 2011 review (2011:6). See DeCoux (2007:132–3) and Risinger (2000:109–10) on the relative treatment of prosecution and defense experts.

[56] T.16968, 5 May 2011.   [57] T.1950, 11 December, 2007.   [58] T.1958, 11 December, 2007.

[59] T.1973, 11 December, 2007.   [60] T.1969, 11 December, 2007.

Prosecutors emphasized how speech acts directly triggered criminal acts, prompting Oberschall to make an outsized claim about the action component of mass persuasion:

DAHL: How does propaganda work?
OBERSCHALL: Propaganda is a technique of persuasion that is based upon
                emotional appeals. . . . Through negative stereotyping,
                through generalizations, appeals to victimhood, creating
                a sense of threat, you create a demand for action, including
                violent action.[61]

The expert reiterated the link between the language of the accused and violent acts throughout his court testimony, "The crucial part of the propaganda that sets in motion actions is actually the threat speech," a sentence that was highlighted in the Prosecution Closing Brief in the Šešelj trial.[62] Oberschall proceeded to characterize the vivid and violent images in the accused's speech, including his calls for the "amputation of Croatia" to recover what Serb nationalists considered Serb lands and his recurrent threats that "rivers of blood will flow."[63] Overall, Oberschall's testimony was an unyielding condemnation of the accused, connecting his speeches to the commission of war crimes and crimes against humanity.

The defendant Vojislav Šešelj opened his cross examination by making light of his violent imagery and indicating that such imagery is a vital (and therefore routine) part of Serb nationalist narratives.

ŠEŠELJ: Mr. Oberschall, you do not know Serbian literature and Serb
                heroic epics that are full of passages about blood flowing, but
                it's about blood flowing in war. Two armies clash on the
                battlefield and blood flows in rivers. We have a whole cycle of
                these Serb popular epics that talk about that. It's one thing to
                talk about blood flowing in rivers, and it's another thing to say,
                "Go on. Kill Bosnian or Croat civilians."[64]
OBERSCHALL: Well, that's what you say. But if you look at, actually, the
                military events, both in the Croatian and the Bosnian war,
                most of the blood that was flowing was not that of soldiers but
                of civilians.[65]

After a few barbed exchanges, the cross-examination descended into rancor, as Šešelj questioned Oberschall's intelligence and credibility.[66]

---

[61] T.2054, 12 December 2007.   [62] T.2114, 12 December, 2007.
[63] T.2075, 12 December, 2007.   [64] T.2126, 12 December 2007.
[65] T.2126, 12 December 2007.   [66] T.2093, T.2148, 12 December 2007.

Noting that Oberschall's first university degree in 1958 was in physics, Šešelj ambushed him with irrelevant mathematical puzzles he had prepared in advance.[67] Šešelj asked questions he did not really want answered, cutting off the witness mid-sentence and criticizing him for wasting time.[68] Presiding Judge Antonetti did nothing to shield the witness from this browbeating, offering instead the shrugging apology, "this is the adversarial procedure."[69] After a duration, the Italian Judge Flavia Lattanzi intervened to rein in the defendant and proscribe any questions outside of the purview of the indictment.[70] In moments such as this, the tension between Judge Lattanzi and Presiding Judge Antonetti was palpable.

Overall, the bench of three judges seemed nonplussed by the social science expertise on offer, and they struggled to apply it to the task of adjudicating the charges against the accused of ordering, aiding and abetting and instigating crimes against humanity and war crimes and participating in a joint criminal enterprise (JCE). They expressed uncertainty about whether the social research methods and analyses truly constituted science, and therefore could establish stable facts or whether they represented mere opinion. Rule 95 of the ICTY Rules of Procedure and Evidence on the exclusion of certain evidence seemed to drive their inquiry:

> No evidence shall be admissible if obtained by methods which cast substantial doubt on its reliability or if its admission is antithetical to, and would seriously damage, the integrity of the proceedings.

Concretely, they expressed their concern that the keywords for the coding used in the content analysis derived from the scholarly literature on nationalism.[71] The judges indicated their desire for a wholly scientific set of methods not besmirched by personal opinion, with Judge Harhoff requesting that the judges be "reassured that in your own understanding, you did not include any qualitative assessments in your report. You're basing this on a purely quantitative method that does not apply qualitative techniques."[72] Oberschall admitted that the coding process involved qualitative assessments and that, for example, his coding of instances expressing a sense of Serb victimhood relied on his qualitative evaluation of the text. Additionally, Judge Harhoff expressed his concern that content analysis as a method did not seem

---

[67] T.2100–2, 12 December 2007.   [68] T.2185, 13 December 2007.
[69] T.2103, 12 December 2007.   [70] T.2095, 12 December 2007.
[71] T.2210, 13 December, 2007.   [72] T.2226–7, 13 December 2007.

to be able to incorporate the context of the speech acts, for example where and when they were published or broadcast, nor assess the degree of persuasiveness and influence of the speech acts.

In reply, Oberschall pleaded for understanding regarding the limits of social science inquiry, "it's not possible to do this kind of experimental work in a natural historical setting."[73] In reflecting on his performance, Oberschall indicated that the chasm between legal and social science approaches to knowledge revolved around their different approaches to causation: "No matter how I explained my methods to them, I was never going to convince the judges that my social science approach could help them. Judges are interested in a specific causal sequence that leads to a specific crime."[74]

Judge Antonetti also objected on freedom of speech grounds, and challenged the prosecution witness indignantly, observing that politicians everywhere meet prospective voters, shake hands and give speeches in which "their words are basically the same as the ones we have just heard ... I do not want to be a victim of any kind of propaganda either."[75]

The judges balked at the idea that one could separate out the accused's contribution to the violence from all the other voices espousing nationalist rhetoric on television and the radio.[76] Oberschall acknowledged the validity of this line of judicial inquiry:

> Judge Antonetti asked a good question, saying 'I can think of many prominent actors in Serbia saying similar things.' But Šešelj played that card more than others, even though his speech was similar to many others at the same time. The question is, can you connect the speech of one person to the crimes? That person alone and not the others? No. It's the ensemble that does it. For propaganda to be effective, you don't need to influence 100% of the population, if 45–50% vote you into power, that's enough. In the judges' way of thinking, if it's not 100%, then it's not a cause.[77]

Oberschall's comments here offer insight into the "lost in translation" elements of his court appearance, which result partly from the diverse understandings of causation held by lawyers and social researchers. For the defendant to be found guilty in a criminal court, the judges must be persuaded that there was an "invariable sequence" of causation, in which the accused's act or acts at the end of the sequence caused the

[73] T.2214 13 December 2007. [74] Author interview, 2013. [75] T.2063, 12 December 2007.
[76] T.2071, 12 December, 2007. [77] Author interview, 2013.

criminal act.[78] As discussed in Chapter 3, this is the "proximate cause" that incurs criminal liability. Proximate cause differs from the much greater number of material or "real" causes.[79]

Social scientists have observed that in a chaotic wartime setting, typically there are multiple actors acting semi-independently of one another, and any one event is the product of a complex set of causes and enabling conditions.[80] When crimes emerge from a tangled web of causation, it is an arduous undertaking to unravel causation in the precise and exacting manner that would allow the assigning of criminal liability to specific individuals.[81] Social scientists acting as experts seldom pinpoint a proximate cause to which guilt can be attributed in their reports and testimony, but instead offer insights into material cause or "cause-in-fact" by identifying the range of enabling conditions that contributed to the commission of the crime.

Social researchers studying political speech generally address conditions that are positioned much earlier in the sequence of causation than proximate cause. Judges may in theory be interested in the multiplicity of conditions relevant to understanding cause-in-fact, but they have an immediate task at hand, which is to determine specific legal causation beyond all reasonable doubt. This involves winnowing down the complex multiplicity of conditions and causes to a manageable and discernible sequence of causation and then deciding whether the accused committed an act that constitutes a proximate cause. Oberschall was critical of this narrow legal view and he made the case for social science accounts of the general conditions created by the media:

> What they [the judges] didn't understand was, why does a majority of voters put people in power who then control the media and arm the military and make all those specific crimes possible? That's the relevance of the broader context and climate. If voters didn't put them in power,

---

[78] On cause in terms of an invariable sequence, see Hart and Honoré (1985:22).

[79] On proximate cause and causation in the law more generally, see Hart and Honoré (1985:86) and Moore (2009:83–4).

[80] I understand enabling conditions as background factors that contribute to a result. They may be a necessary condition of that result, but are not sufficient and they do not themselves constitute independent and proximate causes of an event. A conventional example is a plane that crashes because of a malfunctioning component, where the component is the cause of the accident and gravity is an enabling condition. Philosopher David Lewis (1973:556) disagrees with this distinction and counts even minimal background conditions as causes equal to the precipitating act.

[81] A literature critical of assigning individual responsibility for war crimes has emerged in the anthropology of international justice institutions. See, for example, Clarke (2009:55) and Kelsall (2009:255).

then the larger political events – the unwillingness to compromise, the civil war and the violence, may not have happened. That's where I come in with propaganda studies.[82]

In the courtroom, the judges seemed unreceptive to Oberschall's evidence and their reluctance was apparent in the Trial Chamber judgment. The judgment summarized Oberschall's report accurately, stating that its main contribution was to distinguish propaganda from routine political communication.[83] However, the judgment found fault with Oberschall's method, stating that it relied on speeches for which the dates and sources were not provided.[84] The judges applied a contemporaneity criterion akin to that established in the ICTR jurisprudence on incitement and excluded all speeches outside the period of the indictment.[85]

The judgment then went on to interpret the content and consequences of the speeches to refute Oberschall's interpretations. The accused's speeches, it maintained, constituted electoral speeches and speeches supporting the war effort.[86] Even the most controversial speeches, such as Šešelj's deleterious call to troops to not let one *"Ustasha"* leave Vukovar alive, were deemed to be a call for Croat soldiers to surrender rather than a call for no quarter to be given.[87] The entire corpus of the speeches of the accused represented a critique of the official policies of the Serbian government of the time, and the espousing of "an alternative political program that was never implemented."[88]

The judgment's most telling statement on the prosecution expert's analysis of the accused's speeches held that "the Prosecution has not succeeded in assessing their impact, and the work of Witness Oberschall does not seem to assist greatly. At the end of his testimony he admitted, in reply to a question from Judge Harhoff, that it was almost impossible to establish the impact of these speeches."[89] Oberschall's report fell, then, at the hurdle of proving causation, as did the prosecution case as a whole.

Judge Mandiaye Niang, the Senegalese judge brought into the trial after the removal of Judge Harhoff, issued a separate opinion in which he found it "difficult to comprehend" the exclusion of Oberschall as an expert witness.[90] Judge Niang called this outcome "legally unsound and untenable" and went on to note the inconsistency that "the Judges forgot their previous ruling and constantly referred to Oberschall as an

---

[82] Author interview, 2013.   [83] *Šešelj* TC §298.   [84] *Ibid.*, §340.   [85] *Ibid.*, §301.
[86] *Ibid.*, §303.   [87] *Ibid.*, §314.   [88] *Ibid.*, §338.   [89] *Ibid.*, §338.
[90] Individual Statement of Judge Mandiaye Niang, *Šešelj* TC §18.

expert witness."[91] Judge Niang confirmed the damaging corollary of rejecting Oberschall's standing as an expert, "By denying him the status of an expert witness against the view of the Accused, the Chamber left no room for Oberschall to be heard. He was simply dismissed."[92]

While Judge Niang is correct that Oberschall's expertise was eventually set aside, it would be mistaken to infer that international judges are inherently hostile to social research since the citation data presented earlier showed otherwise. Judges did not reject social research *per se*, but balked at quantitative analyses of the content and consequences of the accused's speech acts.

6.5 PROSECUTORS AND DEFENSE ATTORNEYS ON SOCIAL RESEARCHERS

All experts have the same role in an international criminal trial – to advance the case theory of the party who has called them. While some may strive for neutrality, they are only involved in the legal process to further the goals of one side in the adversarial process, as was apparent in the courtroom examination of both Dr. Ruzindana and Dr. Oberschall. We must not labor under any illusions: experts enter a process in which the parameters of their participation have already been set for them by the legal actors. The international criminal courtroom is quite unlike the university seminar and the central objective is not knowledge for knowledge's sake. Experts are an adjunct, a secondary accessory to the prosecutor's or defense attorney's case, as one ICC Senior Trial Attorney acknowledged in rather colorful terms, "Ours is an exercise in marketing, to persuade, to convince the judges that the facts assembled match the charges. I'm a prosecutor, and when I smell blood, I go for it. That's my job."[93]

The prosecution calls a social researcher for one reason only – to buttress the prosecution's theory of the case, and this has been a general feature of other speech crimes trials at the ICTY, not only the Šešelj trial. For instance, in the trial of Slobodan Milošević, the prosecution team led by Sir Geoffrey Nice contracted Professor Renaud de la Brosse (2003) to analyze political communication in Serbia during the armed conflict. Geoffrey Nice asked the expert how "propaganda directly leads to atrocities"[94] and about the "link between national rhetoric and the

---

[91] Individual Statement, §19. [92] *Ibid.*, §18. [93] Author interview, 2015.
[94] T. 20720, 19 May 2003.

commission of fearful atrocities." In both the Milošević and Šešelj trials, the prosecution represented the effects of the accused's speech acts as conforming to a linear, unidirectional model of causation to establish "smoking gun" material evidence that could convict the defendant.

The prosecution's direct causation theory not only misapprehends how political communication functions, it repeatedly misfires with judges. In the cross-examination of Professor de la Brosse in *Milošević*, Judge Robinson objected to the "categorical, unequivocal way" in which the effects of political speech had been framed by the prosecution, and he indicated his preference for a statement that propaganda could "likely lead to atrocities."[95] Stated so categorically, the prosecution's claim could not be substantiated, Judge Robinson concluded. Judges may become indignant when prosecutors make unqualified claims about the causal effects of speech, but they also seem perplexed when social researchers cited a body of academic literature and commented on social patterns, macro-causation and enabling background factors. One reason that quantitative social research does not fare so well in the international criminal courtroom is that it does not conform to criminal law's direct nexus requirement, and yet when prosecutors attempt to make it conform, the judges frequently perceive the prosecution's claims to be overblown and unsubstantiated.

To fully understand the reception of experts in speech crimes trials, we need to delve further into the underlying assumptions, attitudes and motivating principles of prosecutors, defense counsel and the judges. A survey I conducted in 2009 provides an indication of the relative standing of "propaganda experts" in the overall hierarchy of expertise. The survey asked roughly equal numbers of prosecutors and defense attorneys at the ICTY to assess the value of expert witness testimony on different contextual or background topics.[96] Sixty-nine percent of respondents thought that ICTY expert witnesses had provided important information on "the authority structures of political parties" and sixty-six percent valued the information provided on "regional or municipal histories." Yet when respondents were asked whether experts had provided important information on "the hidden meanings of political leader's speeches and statements" at the ICTY, the approval rating plummeted to forty-one percent, the lowest value for the range of survey questions on

[95] T. 20784, 19 May, 2003.
[96] The 2009 survey included sixty-nine respondents and had a margin of error of twelve percent. There was an approximate parity in responses between defense counsel and staff from the Office of the Prosecutor. For more information, see Wilson (2011:227–30).

this topic. There seems to be something especially unconvincing to legal actors at the ICTY about expert evidence in speech crimes trials.

Since the discussion compares two prosecution expert witnesses, we will start with the prosecution side. The two examples just considered illustrate how prosecutors incorporate social research into their case theory and as we saw earlier, prosecutors call over twice as many social scientists as defense counsel. Eleven out of eleven attorneys in the Office of the Prosecutor interviewed in this study expressed a willingness to include social research if that evidence assists them in convicting the accused.

ICTY Senior Trial Attorney Hildegard Uertz-Retzlaff expressed confidence in both social researchers and judges' willingness to accept their opinions: "The expert will explain what a phrase or speech will trigger in an audience. They show the effects of propaganda. They have the expertise to say whether the words will influence the listeners in the way it's intended to." "Are the judges persuaded?" I asked. She replied, "Yes, I think so ... Look at the Nazis and Goebbels – the German population tolerated the crimes because of Nazi propaganda. Why would Serbs not protect their Croat neighbors? This is the result of propaganda. Only a small group of armed men commit the crimes, but they need all the others to keep silent and not protest."[97]

ICTY Senior Trial Attorney Dan Saxon favored using experts but was motivated more by caution: "Not everyone is sensitive to the effects of propaganda, including highly educated judges. It depends on the culture you're from or your personality. How a speech in the former Yugoslavia or Rwanda comes across will vary. Particular words, when translated, may sound benign, unless you look at the local resonance of those words. As a prosecutor, I don't want to assume that the judges are going to get it. I would want it explained how hate speech worked."[98]

Lisa Biersay, a prosecuting attorney in Šešelj also indicated the importance of highlighting the underlying mechanisms through which hate speech has social effects:

> The view of the prosecution team was that he [Oberschall] was able to present to the Trial Chamber a rational approach to speech, to remove it from the emotional and break it down and identify those elements that made the accused speeches such effective propaganda ... especially the idea that propaganda creates a threat response and brings people together to remove that threat.[99]

---

[97] Author interview, 2013. [98] Author interview, 2013. [99] Author interview, 2014.

While all prosecutors interviewed indicated that the expertise of social researchers is desirable, it is also important to acknowledge that speech crimes trials in international criminal tribunals are quite new, and therefore the appearance of social researchers as experts is somewhat novel. There is little in the way of established precedent, and some prosecutors felt they were in uncharted waters, as ICTY prosecutor Mathias Marcussen indicated,

> We all have our intuitions, but a propaganda expert, through empirical work that has gained wide acceptance, can show the mechanisms through which propaganda influences and mobilizes ... that might complement the facts of the case.[100]

Finally, lest the reader get the wrong impression that prosecutors are motivated only by lofty and noble goals, most prosecutors interviewed also cited instrumental reasons for calling social researchers in propaganda trials, such as introducing video and documentary evidence into the record. It is a common practice to tender evidence of speeches in written or video form during expert testimony, asking the expert to comment on the significance of each document or piece of video footage. One ICTY prosecutor observed pragmatically, "We tender a huge amount of evidence on speeches through our experts."[101] In these instances, the medium often matters less to prosecutors than the material evidence that is presented.

The attitude of defense attorneys working on cases at international criminal tribunals is forthrightly negative towards experts testifying about inciting speech. No member of a defense counsel team interviewed for this book thought such experts could be intrinsically useful. A majority indicated that they would not reach for an expert on their own merits, and would only do so to counter the prosecution team's expert. As with Roger Shuy's report, sometimes the sole rationale of the defense expert is to undermine the credibility of the prosecution expert report, rather than advance any independent findings. Since experts of equal credibility tend to nullify one another, this can favor the defense, which is bent on refuting as much of the prosecution case as it can, rather than necessarily constructing an independent case theory. For this reason, one Belgrade-based defense attorney told me, "The best way to use an expert is to neutralize the prosecution's expert."[102]

---

[100] Author interview, 2013.   [101] Author interview, 2013.   [102] Author interview, 2013.

As part of this research project, I convened a focus group of three defense attorneys with extensive experience at the ICTY and Cambodia Tribunal in trials that involve conflict based on race, ethnicity and religion. The question, "If you were an international trial judge in a speech crimes case, would you call a social researcher as an expert witness?" prompted an animated exchange between focus group participants A, B and C:

A: Me, personally? No. I have very little faith in experts. Most are myopic and this is not an area in which I need expert testimony to be perfectly honest with you . . . we're talking about things that are part of the human condition, and they're bred in the bone and it needs to be understood that we each carry a set of prejudices and any politician is going to figure out a way of keeping those prejudices alive in order to get elected.

B: But you would agree as a judge that the parties would have some kind of cultural expert or historian . . .

C: Yeah, that I would do.

B: to speak about the context of what these words mean, because maybe historically, culturally, the political situation . . .

C: Yeah, politically . . .

A: I do want to know about the political situation of the area I am dealing with, but I don't want someone necessarily to tell me what is offensive.

B: But you do want, okay, how would the objective listener, what would they derive from this particular message?

A: If I understand the history of the nation, then I'll understand that. If I am dealing with a certain part of the world and they use the word "Turk," then I understand it has significance in the same way that you can go through all the pejorative terms used for ethnic and racial groups.

C: I would have a historical expert for sure, and an expert on language.

It is worth noting how Participant A emphasizes that hate speech can draw on hostility that is a universal attribute of the human condition, and also assert that such speech needs to be understood historically. The image of the "objective listener" raised by Participant B invokes the longstanding criminal court convention of determining reasonable provocation with reference to a legal fiction, namely the "reasonable man." [103] The arc of the focus group conversation is also

---

[103] In *Regina v. Smith*, 4 AER 289 (2000), Lord Hoffman wrote: "My Lords, the concept of the "reasonable man" has never been more than a way of explaining the law to a jury; an anthropomorphic image to convey to them, with a suitable degree of vividness, the legal principle that even under provocation, people must conform to an objective standard of behaviour which society is entitled to expect" (§11).

interesting in that it began with a generalized antipathy to social researchers, but then shifted to an acceptance of enhanced language interpretation. This maps onto the case studies in this chapter and offers a window into the rejection of Oberschall's and the acceptance of Ruzindana's expert testimony.[104] However, to understand the separate impacts of the two experts more fully, we need to enquire further into the thinking of international judges, the ultimate arbiters of fact and law.

6.6   COMMON SENSE AND JUDICIAL GATEKEEPING

> Judges are asked to serve a "gatekeeping" role in deciding whether the expert testimony is sufficiently reliable to be presented at trial. In doing so, judges, few of whom have technical training, are asked to exercise a degree of expertise themselves in grappling with cause-and-effect issues on which scientific experts themselves may disagree. Of equal concern are the differences in language and culture between science and law that are heightened in the courtroom.
>
> National Research Council (2002:4)

> As a frame of thought, and a species of it, common sense is as totalizing as any other: no religion is more dogmatic, no science more ambitious, no philosophy more general.
>
> Clifford Geertz (1983:84)

In one conversation I had with an international prosecutor, the attorney ruminated that calling a social researcher to speak about the mechanisms of inciting speech might be considered a little adventurous as a strategy. Why would commissioning an expert on incitement be "adventurous," given the plethora of experts appearing in international trials on a multiplicity of substantive topics, from forensics to forgeries to finance? I inquired with four judges at the ICC, ICTR and ICTY whether a social researcher could assist the court in determining the charges against a defendant in a speech crimes trial. Two fulsomely endorsed this category of expertise. Judge Frederik Harhoff, who served on the Šešelj case, replied,

> Experts can offer a checklist of the basic elements of inciting speech and help us to analyze a speech to determine whether it is hate speech. It is

---

[104] None of the defense counsel focus group participants were parties to the trials of Akayesu, Nahimana et al. or Šešelj.

not easy to determine causality, since the psychological implications in the audience are so rich and multifaceted, so putting up a checklist makes a lot of sense, even if it cannot offer final proof of a hate speech. That way, we can consider all the aspects that are active to determine whether incitement to violence occurred and arrive at our conclusions holistically.[105]

The two judges who responded negatively emphasized their role as the decision-makers and gatekeepers of the courtroom. An ICTY judge stated that "It remains a judicial decision whether a speech had an impact beyond a reasonable doubt . . . judges shouldn't adopt the conclusions of experts and should decide cases on the basis of legal reasons. Judges have to be very careful."[106] Judge Schomburg reiterated this point, "I am hesitant about so called expert witnesses. Each party can buy their own expert. No, this is the genuine task of the judge to interpret the words in a situation, not the expert. It's a hard task for a judge but it is part and parcel of our job. You can't outsource it simply by asking a so-called expert. He doesn't know any better."[107] He added that the main target audience for judicial decisions are . . . other judges, "In the end we are the trier of fact. We have to arrive at our conclusions and then we have to write them in a reasonable way and then they have to be accepted by the Appeals Chamber."[108]

In making sense of how social research is received in the international criminal courtroom, we need to focus closely on the degree to which judges jealously guard their preeminence as the "trier of fact." This is a deeply ingrained premise in western criminal law, and we can go back to the philosophers of ancient Greece such as Aristotle (2004:4) for assertions of the unassailable pre-eminence of judges in a criminal trial: "Questions as to whether something has happened or has not happened, will be or will not be, is or is not, must of necessity be left to the judge."

Even though modern international criminal tribunals are a little over twenty years old, disputes in the criminal courtroom over the meaning and consequences of speech acts are time-honored. Since the invention of the printing press, judges have adjudicated cases in which the defendant is charged with circulating opinions in the mass

[105] Author interview, 2013. [106] Author interview, 2013. [107] Author interview, 2014.
[108] Author interview, 2014.

media that constitute libel, sedition, incitement or which simply represent views that are not in good odor with the political establishment.[109]

Courts have expressed ambivalence towards non-legal expertise since the late eighteenth century when, as a result of the Enlightenment, the first experts began to appear in European courts.[110] Modern criminal courts usually propose a balancing act, in which science is permitted in the courtroom, but does not challenge the authority of the court, and the sovereignty to decide the case remains with the judge or jury. For instance, in a US case that engaged with the medical profession to formulate a viable test for insanity in criminal cases, the judge opined that,

> Any legal standard ... must reflect the underlying principles of substantive law and community values while comporting with the realities of scientific understanding ... Finally the definition must preserve to the trier of facts, be it judge or jury, its full authority to render a final decision.[111]

The social science of political speech occupies an uncomfortable space in this balancing act, because the "realities of scientific understanding" as represented by Oberschall's content analysis can seem incommensurable with conventional ways of construing the meaning of speech acts, as articulated by Mathias Ruzindana. Criminal courts in the United States and at international criminal tribunals determine meaning according to the same standard of proof that asks, "What would a reasonable person understand by the speech acts?" Deference to the view of the "reasonable man" or "ordinary man" is a central tenet of Anglo-American legal theory, as Hart and Honoré (1985:91) attest: "the criteria for deciding such questions were not inventions of the law but were to be found outside the law in what was assumed, rightly or wrongly, to be part of the ordinary man's stock of general notions."

---

[109] See, for example, the instructions given in 1749 by Thomas Marland, Lord Chief Justice of His Majesty's Court of King's Bench to the grand jury of Dublin in a case involving sedition and libel of the King [Lamoine (1992:345–51)]. Marland's charge includes observations that might elicit mirth in modern readers such as "Nothing can preserve the Liberty of the Press, but an effectual Restraint of the Licentiousness of Printing."

[110] *Folkes v. Chadd* (1782) is widely seen as the earliest precedent establishing the admissibility of scientific expert evidence in English law.

[111] Dressler and Garvey (2012:599) citing *State v. Johnson*, Supreme Court of Rhode Island, 1979. 121 R.I. 254, 399 A.2d 469.

A similar reliance on ordinary, commonsense reasoning at international tribunals was apparent in the prior discussion of the reasonable doubt standard.

Anthropologists, historians and sociologists have found that beneath appeals to common sense operate highly normative assumptions that conventionally reinforce the social and cultural status quo.[112] There is something unassailable about invocations of common sense, as Geertz (1983:75) observed: "Religion rests its case on revelation, science on method, ideology on moral passion; but common sense rests its on the assertion that it is not a case at all, just life in a nutshell. The world is its authority." In *Common Sense*, intellectual historian Sophia Rosenfeld (2011:15), concludes that entreaties to common sense are "almost always polemical; statements about consensus and certainty used to particular, partisan and destabilizing effect." One of their effects, notes Rosenfeld (p. 6) is patently to exclude from political and legal decision-making experts, intellectuals, scientists and other "peddlers of dangerous nonsense."

Applying these insights directly to the operation of courts, Kahan et al. (2009:842) have advanced a powerful critique of the hubris of judges who invoke commonsense when deciding questions of fact, because "our perceptions of fact are pervasively shaped by our commitments to shared but contested views of individual virtue and social justice." That is, individuals habitually perceive the same event in radically different ways based upon their social position and prior preferences and attitudes, a stance that is readily accepted by most researchers on knowledge and perception. Cognition, rather than being pure and unadulterated, is invariably motivated by entrenched values and experiences. It is also vulnerable to suggestion, therefore an over-reliance on ordinary reasoning and an unwavering faith in the reliability of sensory perceptions can lead to what Kahan calls "cognitive illiberalism" in the courtroom (p. 843).

On occasion, US courts and legislators have accepted the findings of studies regarding the unreliability of sensory perceptions persuasive and they have sought to integrate empirical social science into the standards and procedures of criminal trials. *State v. Henderson* addressed a widespread problem in US criminal law: the degree to which mistaken eyewitness identifications have led to false convictions.[113] After

---

[112] See Bourdieu (1984, 2000) and Geertz (1983:73).
[113] *State v. Henderson*, 27 A.3d 872 (N.J. 2011). Harvard Law Review (2012:1514-21)

reviewing more than 200 scientific studies and consulting seven experts on identification, the Supreme Court of New Jersey openly acknowledged the fragile nature of human memory, the unreliability of eyewitness testimony in cross-racial identification, and the degree to which police lineup procedures were "impermissibly suggestive" (§998). State criminal courts were from that point onwards mandated to explicitly inform juries about the factors affecting the reliability of eyewitness identification.

In contemporary international criminal trials, complex contestations over meaning are usually decided by reference to ordinary reasoning, not any special theory or technical language derived from social science, be it socio-linguistics or sociological content analysis. That this convention holds in international law became plain in my interview with an ICTY judge, who pronounced on the relevance of experts in speech crimes trials thus:

> It depends on the type of expert. A ballistics expert may tell me about the type of gun used in a case. The problem with speech is that its effects are difficult to measure, they are not visible. If I hit a table with a hammer it leaves a mark ... Speech evidence is also different from ballistics evidence because the latter is not part of my experience but speech is part of common human experience ... I'm not saying that expert evidence on speeches cannot assist, but that the distance between speech and common experience is less than with ballistics. A criminal law theorist told me: forget about psychology, you interpret what you see. Use your ordinary human experience. It's a legal evidentiary concept. My common human experience hardly counts when it comes to ballistics.[114]

The judge is not alone in emphasizing common experience and ordinary reasoning in fathoming the consequences of utterances and determining whether they constituted a causal factor in the criminal act. The most important work in legal philosophy of the twentieth century, Hart and Honoré's (1985) *Causation in the Law* observes repeatedly that causation is decided on the basis of ordinary human experience and common understandings rather than any technical or scientific basis. They note, for instance, that the generalizations needed to defend causal statements are largely "truisms derived from common experience" (p. 15). As the judge notes above, there are times when the court must consult an expert on ballistics or forensics. However, speech

---

[114] Author interview, 2013.

is not seen as a topic that requires external expertise. This largely explains the differential treatment of a social science expert of propaganda and incitement, compared with an expert in ballistics or forensic anthropology.

Underlying the treatment of Anthony Oberschall in the courtroom is an entrenched judicial view that speech is an issue that the judges fully understand. The Šešelj trial is part of an enduring pattern, and it was not the first time that the ICTY Trial Chamber disqualified an expert who utilized sociological content analysis to comprehend the public speeches of the accused. A similar incident occurred in the 2003 trial of Bosnian Serb political leader Radoslav Brđanin. As Presiding Judge Carmel Agius ruled the prosecution's expert report inadmissible, his indignation at the usurpation of his role was palpable:

> Expert evidence should be evidence on a particular matter on which the Tribunal needs expertise. But the Tribunal does not need expertise to understand or to look at a particular newspaper cutting or a particular video recording or a particular transmission or the transcript of a speech. We don't need an expert. We will reach the decision ourselves when we read those transcripts and for an expert to come here and try to influence us basing herself or himself on the supposed expertise, influencing us that according to expert there is no way we could look at those documents but in an incriminating manner is an abuse of the process. An expert should not – an expert should never involve himself or herself in deciding a matter which the Tribunal has to decide.[115]

Moreover, this tendency to disqualify experts on hate speech and inciting speech is not confined to international criminal trials. In his review of the recent jurisprudence on hate speech at the European Court of Human Rights in Strasbourg, Belavusau (2014:268) cannot discover any consistent standard of proof used by the Court to evaluate expertise from socio-linguists, psychologists and political scientists in deciding these cases. This has allowed the Court to engage in "a somewhat ad hoc instrumentalization of expert testimony" (p. 268) in hate speech cases, foregrounding some experts and neglecting others. The ECtHR has not yet furnished an official clarification of its criteria for evaluating expert evidence in hate speech cases, leaving the impression that the Court is "methodologically confused" (p. 268). Lest we

---

[115] T.17980, 23 June 2003.

form the misguided impression that international courts are uniquely bewildered on how to handle expert evidence, we might observe here that many social science studies of US criminal and civil courts have found that judges struggle to apply the US Supreme Court's four criteria laid out in *Daubert* for evaluating scientific evidence, and especially the criteria of falsifiability, peer review and error rate.[116]

The widespread methodological confusion regarding expertise in speech crimes cases is not the end of the story, however. My interviews with judges elicited a pattern of responses that was remarkably like those that surfaced in the focus group with the defense attorneys. An initial vehement denial of relevance of the social research on the media was later leavened by an acceptance of enhanced translation and interpretation from a language expert. For example, when asked whether expert testimony from a language expert could assist the court to understand the context and meaning of utterances, Judge Schomburg replied:

> Here you are going in a different direction and I would agree because we underestimated the problem of translation at the ICTR where people testified in Kinyarwanda and then it was often translated into Swahili before going through French and finally to English. By then it's very hard to know what the witness said. A language expert can analyze the words in an appropriate way and not simply rely on the translator. Here to be on the safe side, it would be better for the judges to call an expert, not to interpret what an alleged perpetrator said, but to understand what exactly the perpetrator said. Judges are not sensitive enough to the problems of translation and precise wording when it comes to hate speech and calls to genocide. If the words are hiding the true meaning, for instance, in Rwanda they called others to "Do your work" then we may need the assistance of additional experts and an interpreter.[117]

As with the defense attorneys in the focus group, here is a judge who is willing to accept a language expert to help the court, after having earlier rejected the idea of an expert on inciting speech. Prosecutors and defense attorneys are accustomed to what they see as the fickle proclivities of judges, and they learn to adjust their strategies according to the signals from the bench during a trial. Attorneys often express the view that judges do not always know what information they require to

---

[116] Gatowski (2001:444–7) and Groscup et al. (2002:364–5).   [117] Author interview, 2014.

decide a case, and the parties must push and probe to ascertain what will be efficacious. We saw a moment ago how the presiding judge in *Brđanin* scorned the notion that the bench required any instruction from a prosecution expert on the meaning of the accused's public speeches on radio and television. On the same day, the prosecution brought a fact witness on the media, protected witness BT94 from Banja Luka, who had kept a diary during the period of the indictment of the speeches of the accused and the violent events that followed. At first, the presiding judge was dismissive of the value of the witness in an opening statement that bordered on the contemptuous, and he granted the prosecution only an hour to lead the witness. Yet after hearing his testimony and cross examining the witness, the judges were drawn into his account and they became intrigued, so much so that they called him back later as a court appointed witness for a lengthy testimony over two days.[118] Perhaps if the fact witness had been called first, the judges might have been more open to the quantitative social science expert on political communication.

This episode is something of a vindication of the adversarial process in international criminal tribunals.[119] Prosecutors remain optimistic about the probative value of expert testimony in speech crimes trials and keep calling social researchers. One prosecutor from the ICTY Matthew Gillett told me, "Yes, judges do use common sense to figure things out and they could benefit from a psychological explanation of speech that was made clear for the lay person." I followed up by asking, "What would judges want from such an expert?" He replied, "That the expert knows their subject, that they're unbiased towards the defendant and that they are willing to change their mind on the basis of new evidence."[120]

6.7 THE EVER-ELUSIVE HOLISTIC APPROACH TO SPEECH

Statistical analysis confirms that overall, international criminal court judges prefer expert witnesses who employ scientific approaches, except in the subcategory of social research, where they prefer qualitative expertise. In speech crimes trials, judges prefer interpretative

---

[118] T.24655–T. 24661.
[119] At least at the two ad hoc tribunals, the ICTR and ICTY. The ICC has more of a continental-style judicial case management system.
[120] Author interview, 2013.

approaches to language and cultural meaning over quantitative, statistical analyses. Judges are open to assistance from experts who discern the local meaning and force of the accused's utterances, i.e., their locutionary and illocutionary aspects, but they are resistant to instruction from quantitative social scientists on the effects or perlocutions of utterances, an arena that they regard as their own special, protected domain.

Judges consider themselves experts on human behavior and they allow social research only in an area in which they are willing to concede their own ignorance (e.g., Kinyarwanda). Speech itself, however, is not one of these areas. Indeed, for judges to accept that they may require assistance in comprehending speech acts and their consequences would undermine the entire adjudicative enterprise. Once they are summarily translated, speech acts are decoded using the one intellectual resource all judges have in abundance, ordinary reason. Common sense does double duty, both as an authoritative cognitive frame and as a bulwark against expertise, since, as Clifford Geertz (1983:91) observes, "its tone is anti-expert, if not anti-intellectual." In fact, both social science research and ordinary reasoning are needed in a criminal trial which hinges on the meaning and effects of speech acts. This chapter, and indeed this whole book, represents a call to greater cognitive liberalism and methodological pluralism in the international criminal courtroom.

Here, it is worth considering again "The Sequence of Causation from Intention to Action" (Figure 5.1) proposed in Chapter 5. The causal sequence begins with the intentions of the speaker (steps 1–2), proceeds through his or her performative utterances and their meanings (step 3), reviews the potential range of meanings for the listener (4–5) and then considers the intentions (6–7) and actions of the listener (8–10). To comprehend the full gamut of a speech act, a court needs to hear from both a Ruzindana and an Oberschall; the former to identify the specific and contextual meaning of the performative utterance and what it was encouraging others to do (steps 1–3), and the latter to inform the court about the mechanisms through which speech acts could be connected (albeit at an aggregate and probabilistic level) to consequences (steps 3–5). Other social researchers can provide evidence for mental and physical causation (steps 6–10), for instance by documenting when and where the speech acts of the accused took place and ascertaining whether there was any identifiable correlation with violence.

To my knowledge, no international trial has benefitted from both types of experts: the interpretative and the scientific. Perhaps given the openness of the bench in *Brđanin* to new evidence on the role of the media during the armed conflict, we might remain sanguine that judges might one day be willing to hear testimony from all quarters equally; from fact witnesses, cultural experts, enhanced translators and quantitative researchers of political speech.

CHAPTER SEVEN

THE SOCIAL SCIENCE OF INCITING SPEECH AND PERSUASION

7.1 INTRODUCTION

In both international criminal courts and legal scholarship, there has been a worrying reliance on untested assumptions about inciting speech acts. To summarize from previous chapters, prosecution arguments regularly ascribe a directly causal role to speech acts. In ascertaining whether a speech act triggered criminal behavior, prosecutors and judges often assume that political speech works straightforwardly, even mechanistically, upon a receptive audience and they frame mental causation in colorful metaphors of infectious viruses or loaded weapons. Furthermore, in a number of landmark cases, international criminal judgments have asserted that some types of inciting speech are more egregious than others; for instance, dehumanizing language is generally held to be the most harmful form of inciting speech.

It is worth asking how legal actors arrive at their understandings of the effects of inciting speech. The causal models of speech prevalent at international criminal tribunals are largely anecdotal and the product of commonsense reasoning that becomes consolidated as material fact as the case law progresses. Individual judges may develop an expertise on inciting speech as a result of their involvement in cases with a speech element, and in speech crimes trials judges have been receptive to expert witness evidence from some strands of (mostly qualitative and linguistic) social science. Yet, as we saw in the last chapter, the responsiveness of judges to expert opinion is influenced by longstanding reservations about quantitative social science in the courtroom. It is also motivated by a deep-seated impulse to defend the judges' status as the triers of fact.

In this context, legal commentator Susan Benesch (2012) has proposed a checklist to guide international legal actors as they assess the likelihood that a speech act will prompt, or has already prompted, international crimes. Benesch's criteria represent a valuable contribution, and they might be further improved by consulting social science research on persuasive speech and by subjecting them to empirical evaluation. This is necessary because many of the models of speech found in both international law and legal scholarship are either profoundly inaccurate or in need of major revision.

At this relatively preliminary stage in the international law of speech crimes, it is worth acknowledging that our ability to understand the effects of speech through intuition and *a priori* reasoning alone is actually quite limited. Many recent findings in persuasion research and communication theory are counterintuitive, or at least not immediately obvious, even to seasoned political and legal observers. Speech acts influence listeners in ways that are, in part, unconscious and that operate at a deep level of affect. The effects of political speech are multiple, complex and contradictory, and are embedded in both individual psychology and a multi-causal political and historical context. This all means that the consequences of certain forms of inciting political communication are extremely hard to predict in advance, and to reconstruct after the fact.

This chapter reviews the current state of the social science of persuasion and inciting speech, gleaning its most relevant insights on political communication during armed conflict and genocide. It also presents new and original empirical research on the topic using actual material evidence from one of the key speech crimes trials at an international tribunal. Social research cannot determine with absolute certainty the concrete effects of a particular speech act uttered in the context of widespread and systematic violations. However, social research can identify the felicity conditions of a performative utterance; that is, the conditions most likely to enable the uptake of a speech act.

Social science research deals with probabilities and aggregate societal and psychological patterns rather than specific outcomes. Knowing more about the felicity conditions of inciting speech has policy implications for atrocities prevention and for adjudicating inchoate crimes (e.g., incitement to genocide and hate speech as a form of persecution).

If we have a sense of which types of speech acts are most likely to elevate the risk of violence in a particular context, then this could assist international criminal courts in concentrating on those that are most deserving of a penal response. With respect to completed crimes, social research on speech could also aid an international court in evaluating the likelihood that a speech act materially contributed to the commission of an offense in international law.

7.2 ETHOS, PATHOS AND LOGOS: THE SOCIAL SCIENCE OF PERSUASIVE SPEECH

Over the last two decades, social research on political communication and persuasion has provided compelling evidence about the types of speech that are most persuasive and the conditions that facilitate persuasion. At the same time, this is not a process of discovering iron-cast laws.

Social scientists responding to the rise of the mass media such as Harold Lasswell (1927) often overstated the power of the means of mass communication, making extravagant claims about the ability of the media to convince the public of practically any opinion. In its early days, mass communication research once relied on untested folk models such as the "hypodermic needle" metaphor of speech, in which the virus of hatred was injected into the public mind, but these were rejected in favor of less directly causal models that emphasize ego involvement or consistency with previous attitudes.[1]

Social science has moved away from a single mechanistic model of direct effects to an appreciation of causal complexity and the variety of interacting factors that influence the consequences of a speech act. While it still persists in international criminal law, a single all-encompassing framework for understanding speech acts is generally considered simplistic in persuasion research. Nonetheless, it is possible to distill the salient aspects of recent research on political communication and persuasion, and to make qualified generalizations about inciting speech in the context of social conflict.

The rigorous and systematic study of persuasive speech begins with Aristotle's *Rhetoric*, a remarkable philosophical treatise that remains salient today even though it was written over two thousand years ago. In the 4th Century BC, Aristotle (2004) was reacting to Plato's famous invective

[1] See Jowett and O'Donnell (2012:168) on the hypodermic needle theory of propaganda.

225

against poetry, rhetoric and persuasion. In *The Republic*, Plato denounced rhetorical methods as the basis for philosophical sophistry and political demagoguery, whereas Aristotle accepted that political, ceremonial and legal speech is inherently imbued with sentiment and moral character, the aim of which is to move and persuade the listener. Techniques of persuasion are employed on all sides of a question and whether or not the rhetoric is beneficial depends on the ends to which it is directed, rather than the mere fact of its existence.

Aristotle (2004:7) valued empirical observation over deductive reasoning and he identified the distinguishing characteristics of rhetoric, noting that whether or not a speech will persuade depends on three principal qualities: *ethos, pathos* and *logos*. *Ethos* refers to the "personal character of the speaker," his or her status, authority and credibility: "his character may almost be the most effective means of persuasion he possesses."[2] *Pathos* denotes the frame of mind of the audience and whether listeners are inclined to emotions such as anger, shame, envy, indignation, pity and fear. Aristotle observed how persuasive speakers have the ability to intuit the angry state of mind of the populace. They know who the general public conventionally gets angry with, and for what reasons, and they adeptly direct the angry crowd towards thoughts of vengeance (p. 60–1). Aristotle (2004:64) presciently reflected,

> Clearly the orator will have to speak so as to bring his hearers into a frame of mind that will dispose them to anger, and to represent his adversaries as open to such charges and possessed of such qualities as do make people angry.

The types of proof (or apparent proof) that are conventionally accepted in a knowledge community are the *logos* of the speaker's message, and in ancient Greece these encompassed, *inter alia*, inductive reasoning, historical illustrations, hypothetical examples, and syllogisms or false syllogisms. Finally, Aristotle (2004:119 *et passim*) emphasized the style and manner of expression, including the prevalence of metaphors and colloquial or elevated speech. Aristotle did not identify one particular style of speech as the most appealing, but recommended adopting the language that is most appropriate to the occasion and the emotional state of the audience:

---

[2] Aristotle (2004:7).

Your language will be appropriate if it expresses emotion and character, and if it corresponds to its subject. "Correspondence to subject" means that we must neither speak casually about weighty matters, nor solemnly about trivial ones; nor must we add ornamental epithets to common-place nouns, or the effect will be comic ... as in phrases as absurd as "O queenly fig-tree" (p. 129).

If the outline in Aristotle's *Rhetoric* seems like a rudimentary version of Benesch's matrix for evaluating speech crimes (presented in Chapter 2), that is because it represents the ur-framework that has inspired all subsequent models of persuasive speech. While *Rhetoric* is a remarkable treatise that still merits reading, Aristotle did not have access to empirical social research, and the modern social science of mass communication and popular persuasion did not emerge until the twentieth century. It arose out of the desire to comprehend the unprecedented mobilization of the European population during the First World War and the dramatic rise of new modes of mass communication such as the radio and television.[3] The publication of *Propaganda* in 1928 by Edward Bernays, the nephew of Sigmund Freud, looms large here. In a comparison that was considered radical at the time, Bernays equates politicians' speeches on weighty matters of public concern with advertisements for a bar of Ivory Soap, insofar as business marketing strategies and electioneering share the same methods of mass distribution and emotional manipulation (p. 112).

The modern social science literature on persuasion both confirms and qualifies Aristotle's insights into the speaker's attributes (*ethos*), the emotional state of the audience (*pathos*) and the accepted modes of reasoning and expression in a society (*logos*). A number of studies from the Milgram (1974) experiments onwards confirm a pervasive and deep obedience to authority figures (even those with malign intent), a criterion at the top of Benesch's checklist.[4] In the Milgram experiments conducted at Yale University in the 1960s, otherwise normal and empathetic individuals ("teachers") were willing to administer what they believed to be severe and dangerous electrical shocks to middle-aged "learners" (who feigned severe pain on being "shocked"). For decades, psychologists asked, "Would people still obey today?" Psychologist Jerry Burger (2009) replicated Milgram's results in 2009,

---

[3] Jowett and O'Donnell (2012:49) note that the term "propaganda" does not become part of common usage until after World War I.

[4] Burger (2009), Kelman (1973) and Milgram (1974).

finding that nearly three quarters of participants delivered shocks of 150 volts as instructed, thus (rather dispiritingly) answering the question in the affirmative.

Whereas authority is associated with the individual's formal position in a social hierarchy, credibility derives from an array of personal qualities, such as: expertise in a subject, reliability, dynamism and extroversion, perceived goodwill towards the audience and trustworthiness. Perloff (2010:166) defines credibility as "a psychological or interpersonal communication construct." A public figure may possess authority but lack credibility, and vice versa, or she can possess both. To a certain extent, recognized experts on a topic often possess the necessary credibility to sway opinion, and this is why attorneys frequently call them in criminal trials or civil litigation.[5]

Even if they lack expertise, communicators who are perceived to possess authenticity, honesty and trustworthiness may be persuasive, particularly ones who express strong skepticism towards established authority figures.[6] Charisma is closely related to the notion of credibility. Charismatic leaders who have a commanding physical presence, and who are given to forceful oratory that invokes the longstanding myths of a people, can ascend quickly to public prominence in circumstances of instability and uncertainty. Political constituencies can be quite superficial, and the more physically attractive a candidate is, the more likely they are to be considered superior public speakers.[7] When we consider the array of charismatic politicians in the twentieth century, from Hitler to Kennedy to Mandela, it is apparent that there are numerous and varying expressions of charisma that can advance a wide range of political platforms.

In addition to their personal attributes, the content of a political leader's speech acts may have a strong bearing on his or her capacity to persuade. Intriguingly, fear messages elicit complex and unpredictable responses. Humans do not react predictably like Pavlov's dogs to fear stimuli. In fact, it can be quite difficult to frighten the public, as government health officials have repeatedly discovered. Many individuals embrace a "myth of invincibility" where they think that undesirable health outcomes like lung cancer, heart disease or contracting HIV will only happen to others, and not to themselves.[8]

---

[5] Fiske and Dupree (2014). [6] See Fiske and Durante (2014) and Perloff (2010:166–7).
[7] See Dion et al. (1972) and Feingold (1992).
[8] Richard Perloff (2010:196–202) provides an excellent account of the variable impact of fear messages.

Even if a person is genuinely frightened by a message, a shift in attitude may not translate into an observable behavioral change, since attitudinal changes do not straightforwardly correspond to behavioral changes,[9] and because, in some instances, the individual may be paralyzed by fear or not know how exactly to respond. Arousing fear is not in itself sufficient to prompt action because a cognitive as well as an affective element is required. There is a consensus in the social science literature that cognitive and affective dimensions are equally significant in persuasion.[10] Fear seems to be effective as a motivating factor in behavioral change only when there is an identifiable path of action that allows the listener to deflect the threat or remove the source of the fear. Similarly, guilt is a complex emotion and its effectiveness depends on whether it is consistent with prior moral principles and is accompanied by particular motivations (giving rise to "consistency theory" in persuasion research).[11]

The efficacy of persuasive speech is further complicated by the fact that distinct personality types react in varying ways to the same message. Individuals with high self-esteem are not easily swayed by attempts to persuade them of a belief they do not already hold. Individuals with low self-esteem are not inherently more suggestible either, but for different reasons, because they are less likely to cognitively process the message in the manner intended by the speaker.[12] Studies indicate that individuals with moderate self-esteem are the most vulnerable to persuasive communication, but this group is so large and heterogeneous as to be analytically useless. This all undermines our ability to make any meaningful generalizations about the type of personality most susceptible to persuasion.[13] Relatedly, there is a correlation between intelligence and openness to influence, but again, the relationship between the two is too complex to allow precise generalizations. Nor does the persuasion literature support the idea that there are marked sex differences in "persuadability."

Aristotle's attention to rhetoric has been vindicated by studies that show that intense and vivid language, of the kind commonly found during the armed conflicts considered in this book, may have particularly strong effects. Speeches full of graphic metaphors may produce greater attitudinal changes than plainer communications.[14] Repetition and exaggeration can be convincing, which is why they are so often

---

[9] Fazio (1990). [10] Fiske and Dupree (2014:4). [11] O'Keefe (2002:340).
[12] Petty and Wegener (1998). [13] Rhodes and Wood (1992). [14] Sopory and Dillard (2002).

found in political communication.[15] The verbal speed of a speaker, however, has variable effects. Fast speakers may be considered more credible in contexts where the audience has a low ego involvement (understood as low personal investment) in a topic.[16] Slower speakers are often seen as possessing more goodwill and empathy towards their audience, and the perceived warmth of the speaker can be an indicator of their trustworthiness.[17] What does seem to function well in most scenarios is what persuasion researchers call "powerful speech:" concise, strong, direct communications delivered without hesitations ("uhm"), hedges ("kinda") or qualifications.[18]

Social psychology can provide valuable insights into the dynamics of persuasion in one-on-one encounters, but struggles to engage fully with the historical and political dimensions of political speech and therefore needs to be complemented by other disciplinary studies. Certain factors transcend the binary relationship between speaker and listener and exert an external influence on that relationship. For instance, all regimes at war, and not just the authoritarian kind, attempt to regulate media sources and control the amount and quality of information to the public. Social research has documented how some governments achieved a monopoly on the sources of communication, with deleterious consequences. For instance, Jowett and O'Donnell (2012:46) observe how, during the early 1990s, the governments of both Croatia and Serbia seized control of the radio, television and newspapers in their countries and released biased and distorted messages that exacerbated national tensions. The ICTY *Tadić* Trial Chamber judgment correctly cited this monopoly on the media as an aggravating factor in the armed conflict.[19]

A monopoly on the media matters because individuals are sensitive to the circumstances in which inciting speech occurs. As they cognitively process their leaders' exhortations to hatred and/or violence and decide whether to act, they will often weigh the likely consequences of their actions, even if unconsciously. In most countries, there are moral and/or legal injunctions against interpersonal violence generally, and

[15] Kaid (2004:28). See Jowett and O'Donnell (2012:265, 303) on exaggeration.
[16] Smith and Shaffer (1995).   [17] Fiske et al. (2002).   [18] Perloff (2010:211–12).
[19] *Tadić* TC states: "The premier of Serbia, Slobodan Milošević, had for some years not only exercised a high degree of personal power in Serbia but had also established a very effective control of the Serbian media and it, together with the media in Serb-dominated areas of Bosnia and Herzegovina, was very effectively directed towards stirring up Serb nationalist feelings and converting an apparently friendly atmosphere as between Muslims, Croats and Serbs in Bosnia and Herzegovina into one of fear, distrust and mutual hostility" (§83).

assaulting members of other ethnical or religious groups more specifically. If all they hear in the media are denigrating speech and exhortations of violence from authority figures, they may conclude that the usual strictures have been lifted and that now such behavior will go unpunished.

Economists have ventured into this terrain and constructed models of the influence of hate speech on behavior, with thought-provoking results. Dharmapala and McAdams (2005:94) cite sources indicating that there are as many as 50,000 hate crimes a year in the United States.[20] Drawing on "esteem theory" in the economics of social norms, they hypothesize that individuals who actually commit hate crimes are motivated by the desire to win widespread acclaim from a network of (often distant) sympathizers to whom they are connected via social media. In what they call a "stranger esteem" model, they assert that "publicizing the identity of the hate crime perpetrator ... allows the perpetrator to achieve the fame he desires" (p. 110). Raising the costs of hate speech through private or government regulation and sanctions, they argue, tends to reduce the prevalence of hate crimes (p. 98). In particular, their work supports a policy of suppressing public expressions of approval of the murder of members of particular ethnic, religious, racial or national minority groups (p. 130). One conclusion of this economic model is that the context of public discourse can shape the felicity conditions (or uptake) of hate speech at the individual level.

One of the most trenchant studies of the contextual factors influencing audience uptake comes from Scott Straus (2006, 2007) who analyzed the relationship between hate radio and violence in the Rwanda genocide of 1994. Straus's study tackles causation head on, finding that radio was relevant to the genocide, particularly as a tool of communication between Hutu Power elites, but fell far short of causing the genocide. Straus (2007:610) starts by appraising the strong claims made by the ICTR about the effects of radio fomenting genocide. He laments the paucity of political communication research in the Tribunal's deliberations, and in particular its neglect of factors such as the timing, content, frequency and exposure of radio broadcasts. The Tribunal's mechanistic model of causation, Straus concludes, is at odds with four decades of political communication research.

---

[20] A figure that is probably underreported, given that in 2014–15, there were 52,528 hate crimes recorded by the police in England and Wales (Corcoran, Lader and Smith, 2015), which have a combined population that is approximately one fifth that of the United States.

The strength of Straus's research design lies in its interdisciplinary methods that combined 200 qualitative perpetrator interviews with a quantitative and statistical analysis of the relationship between broadcasts and actual violence in 1994. Triangulating the evidence paints a very different picture to the one espoused by ICTR judges in *Nahimana*. Straus (2007:626) found that less than 10 percent of the Rwandan population owned a radio, and a majority (60 percent) of perpetrators did not listen to RTLM. Interviewees cited factors other than the radio to explain their participation in the genocide, including face-to-face solicitation from an authority figure and groups of men who went door to door, coercing their neighbors and kin into joining them at the barricades. One might reasonably counter that perpetrators are not consciously aware of their own motivations, and here Straus's statistical analysis undermines the theory that RTLM mechanically caused the genocide.

Straus identified significant gaps in RTLM's broadcast range (pp. 616–17), and little to no correlation between the broadcast range and the onset of genocide in different locales (pp. 618–19). Violence started in areas with no RTLM coverage at the same time or even before areas with coverage. Crucially, most of the genocidal violence had already occurred before the most explicit calls to genocide were made on the radio (pp. 623–5). He concludes that, while the radio had "conditional media effects" and a marginal impact on popular violence, the radio cannot account for the Rwandan genocide in the way that the Tribunal's "simplistic models of political behavior" claim (p. 611).

A comprehensive understanding of violent political communication obliges us to augment social psychology with anthropological, historical and sociological analyses of intergroup relations and the role of history and culture in conflict. It is readily apparent that in all of the contexts considered in this book – for instance, in the 1990s armed conflict in the Balkans, the genocide in Rwanda and the inter-ethnic violence during the Kenyan elections of 2007 – politicians tapped into historical narratives and mythologies that anchored their communications in a preexisting animus (whether real or conjured). As Jowett and O'Donnell (2012:34) indicate:

> People are reluctant to change; thus, to convince them to do so, the persuader has to relate the change to something in which the persuadee already believes. This is called an *anchor* because it is already accepted by the persuadee and will be used to tie down new attitudes or behaviors [emphasis in original].

The speeches of Serb nationalists such as Radovan Karadžić were filled with references to God, Serb mythology and the historical destiny of Serbs to live in a unified state of their own.[21] Hutu Power extremists in Rwanda revived the "Hamitic myth" found in colonial racial ideology that portrayed Tutsis as a distinct race of foreigners who invaded Rwanda from Ethiopia and North Africa.[22] According to ICC prosecutors, Kenyan Vice-President William Ruto resuscitated colonial narratives in the 2007 elections to vilify the Kikuyu ethnic group and encourage his Kalenjin followers to commit violent attacks and drive Kikuyus and other ethnic groups out of the Eldoret and Nandi Hills areas.[23] In each of these cases, the language and mythology that is effective in rousing supporters is specific to that situation, and we must be attuned to the fact of cultural variation.

Just as each setting has its own salient historical narratives, the other factors we have identified as relevant features of persuasive speech may vary from place to place. For example, Perloff observes (2010:169) that perceptions of the credibility of the speaker vary in the United States and Japan, and what constitutes credibility will likely vary in other places as well. At present, we just do not know how much cultural variation there is in the factors shaping persuasion, as systematic research has not been done on the topic by social psychologists, who as a discipline are overly reliant on studies involving western university students. Anthropological and historical studies of the collective and cultural nature of communication are less explicit and categorical in their findings than social psychology. While they can elucidate the cultural underpinnings of political communication during group conflict, they often avoid identifying clear variables and making definitive causal conclusions. At present, our understanding of the role and effectiveness of mythological narratives and the degree of cultural variation in the content and consequences of inciting speech is relatively rudimentary.

In summary, a number of salient themes emerge from our review of the social science of inciting speech. First, and perhaps most importantly, social scientists no longer maintain that "Propaganda offers ready-made opinions for the unthinking herd,"[24] and they do not

---

[21] See Donia (2015:184–6) and Surdukowski (2005).
[22] On the Hamitic thesis, see the anthropological accounts of Eltringham (2004, 2006) and Taylor (1999:80–1).
[23] See the ICC Information Sheet on the case against William Ruto at www.icc-cpi.int/iccdocs/PIDS/publications/RutoKosgeySangEng.pdf
[24] Quote attributed to E.D. Martin, cited in Jowett and O'Donnell (2012:168).

generally conceptualize speech as a direct Pavlovian stimulus of behavior. In fact, the effects of a speech act are varied and often contradictory, and dependent on a large number of psychological and contextual factors, thus militating against the criminal law's imperative to isolate a simple causal sequence. For this reason, social science models of inciting speech look nothing like the obsolete metaphors and paradigms found in the international criminal court setting. Second, inciting speech connects individual psychology with culture, society and history to such an extent that a variety of social science disciplines are required for a full understanding of the effects of speech acts. No one social science theory or method has a monopoly on understanding inciting speech and each can present valid information on one aspect of the problem. As yet, insights from both social psychology and more contextual analyses in economics, political science and anthropology have yet to be satisfactorily integrated. A genuinely interdisciplinary and cross-cultural study of inciting speech is therefore still in its initial stages.

7.3 THE DISTINCTIVE EFFECTS OF DIFFERENT KINDS OF POLITICAL SPEECH

Currently, international criminal courts are deciding speech crimes cases without the full benefit of social scientific understandings of speech. Their judgments on incitement and instigation of crimes rely upon a theory of speech and behavior that is largely untested by relevant social science research. The Tribunals' judgments contain a number of questionable assumptions about human psychology and behavior, and, in particular, assumptions about how inciting speech acts directly cause subsequent international crimes. There seem to be two operating psychological assumptions in the judges' language. First, judges have required that inciting speech directly motivate violent behavior, as when the ICTR's *Akayesu* trial chamber judgment demanded "proof of a possible causal link" between the defendant's exhortations to his Hutu followers and the ensuing genocide of Tutsis.

Second, the jurisprudence of international criminal trials frequently maintains that dehumanizing language is the most egregious form of hate speech, as during the Rwandan genocide when Tutsis were labeled *inyensi*, or "cockroaches," by Hutu extremists (Van Schaack and Slye, 2010). This view has its origins in the Nuremberg trials, and especially in the verdict against Julius Streicher that noted that his articles in the pro-Nazi publication *Der Stürmer* "termed the Jew as a germ and a pest, not a human being, but 'a parasite, an enemy, an evildoer, a disseminator of diseases who must be destroyed in the interest of mankind'" (Van Schaack and Slye, 2010:883). Historian John Dower (1986:3–15), writing about the conduct of war in the Pacific during the Second World War, famously opined, "The Dehumanization of the Other contributed immeasurably to the psychological distancing that facilitated killing." The most prominent legal philosopher today arguing for the legal regulation of hate speech, Jeremy Waldron (2012:66), has emphasized language that characterizes members of other racial groups as "bestial or subhuman." This view of the deleterious effects of dehumanizing language is so widespread that we could call it the "standard model" of hate speech.

Assumptions about dehumanizing speech, however, are not securely grounded in testimonial evidence from fact witnesses and expert witnesses at international tribunals. As we saw in the Šešelj trial, prosecutors struggled to find insider witnesses who would testify at the ICTY that they were instigated to commit crimes by the words of the accused, and this pattern has been replicated at the ICC and ICTR.[25] Nor have the courts been particularly receptive to certain types of expert witness evidence, including those who describe the concrete mechanisms by which speech can motivate action. Linguists, historians and a sociologist have appeared as experts for the prosecution in speech crimes trials, yet to my knowledge no social psychologist has testified on inciting speech at an international criminal tribunal. At present, international courts function in a vacuum of social psychological theory and evidence. As a result, judges rely on unproven assumptions about the effects of different kinds of hate speech, as well as misleading and unscientific metaphors of fire and poison, as we saw in Chapters 2 and 5.

The few studies by anthropologists, political scientists and economists that have investigated the specific role of hate speech and dehumanizing language in mass violence have thus far produced contrasting results.[26] These mixed findings call for other social science approaches such as behavioral science to understand the phenomenon of inciting speech. Much like international legal actors, social psychologists have

---

[25] At the ICC, one could cite the cases of *Mbarushimana* and *Ruto and Sang*. This observation has also been made by Zahar (2005:41) for the ICTR.

[26] See Straus (2007), Mironko (2007) and Yanagizawa-Drott (2014).

long theorized that dehumanizing speech is the main contributor to genocidal violence.[27] However, this long-standing and thus far undisputed theory has yet to be evaluated empirically. There is a pressing need, therefore, to test whether inciting speech has the causal properties often attributed to it by the courts and social psychologists and, if so, what psychological mechanisms might be functioning; and secondly, whether different types of speeches have distinct psychological effects.

Seeking greater understanding of these topics, I designed an empirical study with a team of researchers that included anthropologist Jordan Kiper and psychologists Lasana Harris and Christine Lillie.[28] The study started by coding 242 public statements of Serb nationalist politician Vojislav Šešelj, based on the categories used in the original analysis conducted by Dr. Anthony Oberschall (2006) as part of his expert report for the Office of the Prosecutor in Šešelj. The materials Oberschall identified are from between 1990 and 1994, and included the defendant Šešelj's writings, speeches, radio and television broadcasts, and newspaper and magazine interviews, ranging from one sentence to two paragraphs in length, selected from 44 volumes of Šešelj's authored texts and materials provided by the ICTY. Building upon the coding framework used in Anthony Oberschall's expert report in Šešelj, the study coded the speeches into eight subcategories: calls for revenge, extreme nationalist sentiments, negatively stereotyping other groups, dehumanizing language, demands for justice, references to past atrocities, references to the victimization of one's own group, and warnings of a direct threat to the in-group.[29] Figure 7.1 shows the number of overall references to each category in the 242 speeches. Many of the speeches contain multiple themes.

The most common message in Vojislav Šešelj's speeches identified a direct and immediate threat against Serbs. This effort to instill fear in a Serb audience was followed by reminders of past atrocities against Serbs and a portrayal of Serbs as victims of widespread historical cruelties. Intriguingly, dehumanizing language of the kind identified by international courts and legal observers as the most injurious type of

---

[27] Harris and Fiske, 2006; Harris and Fiske, 2011. On the propensity of dehumanizing language to lower empathy for the outgroup see Goff et al. (2008). On dehumanization generally in social psychology, see Haslam (2006).

[28] The full results of this study are available as Lillie, Knapp, Harris and Wilson (2015).

[29] Four researchers independently coded the speeches and reached consensus on which speeches to include in each category.

Category	Frequency
Direct threat	99
Past Atrocities	47
Victimization	40
Negative out-group stereotypes	40
Nationalism	29
Dehumanization	21
Revenge	21
Justice Systems	18
Political References	2

Figure 7.1 Frequency of themes in Šešelj's speeches

speech was only one-fifth as frequent as fear/direct threat messages. Speeches that called for acts of revenge for past atrocities were expressed at the same frequency as dehumanizing language. Finally, it appears that Šešelj was not particularly reliant on Serb Orthodox images, as his religious references are fairly minimal.

Based on the coding, we created composite speeches representative of each category, using excerpts from the original speeches. Additionally, we created a control speech describing the weather in the two countries. Only the names of the countries were altered, such that Serbia was replaced with "East Margolia" and Croatia became "West Margolia." Abbreviated examples of the composite speeches can be found in Appendix 3 of this book. 408 subjects participated in an online survey through Amazon's MTurk crowd sourcing web service.[30] The sample consisted of US citizens, 58 percent women, and the average age range was 30–39. The majority of the participants self-identified as middle-income level, politically moderate, and moderately religious. Participants were randomly assigned to the different conditions.[31] The survey opened with a series of standard personality questionnaires used in social psychology, including the scales for Authoritarianism,[32] Belief in a Just World,[33] Disgust Sensitivity[34] and

---

[30] 394 participants were included in the final analysis as 14 participants either failed to complete the survey or were not able to correctly name one of the countries after reading the speech.

[31] The entire survey lasted roughly 15 minutes and the participants were reimbursed for their time.

[32] Robinson, Shaver and Wrightsman (1991:546–7). [33] Collins (1974).

[34] Haidt, McCauley and Rozin (1994). The Disgust Scale was subsequently modified by Olatunji et al. (2007).

Economic System Justification.[35] After completing the personality questionnaires, participants read either one of the nine thematic speeches or the control speech.

Just prior to reading the speech the participants were given the context of rising tension between the countries of East Margolia and West Margolia, and told that they were reading a speech from the leader of East Margolia. Hereinafter the countries are referred to as the "in-group" (East Margolia, a.k.a. Serbia) and the "out-group" (West Margolia, a.k.a. Croatia). We devised in-group and out-group as the speeches referred to the East Margolians as "us" and "we," creating in-group identification, and the West Margolians as "they" or "them," creating the out-group. After reading the speech, participants answered demographic questions about their age, gender, religion, socio-economic status, political affiliation and the amount of time they usually spend engaging with violent video games.

Participants answered questions to test their willingness to morally justify violence, their empathy for the in-group and out-group and their perception of the degree to which the actions of the in-group or the out-group were intentional.[36] The moral justification questions consisted of seven items such as: (1) Do you think that force is necessary to resolve certain problems? (2) Do you think violence can be justified? (3) Do you think people can commit violent acts for good moral reasons? The empathy questions asked: (1) To what extent do you think you could understand the East/ West Margolian's point of view? (2) To what extent do you think you felt the emotions that the East/ West Margolians felt? (3) How likely would you have been to behave similarly to the East/ West Margolians? The perception of intentionality factor consisted of two questions: (1) How intentional are the acts of the East/ West Margolians? (2) How morally responsible are the East/ West Margolians for their behavior?

---

[35] Also known as System Justification, testing the proposition that "If people work hard, they almost always get what they want." See Jost and Thompson (2000).

[36] A principle components analysis used a varimax rotation; the Kaiser–Meyer–Olkin measure of sampling adequacy was .754, and Bartlett's test of sphericity was significant ($\chi 2$ (136) = 2801.073, p < .000). The survey questions loaded onto four unique factors, all of which had primary loadings over .5 and explained 64% of the total variance. The factors were moral justification of violence (explaining 22.62% of the variance), empathy for the in-group (explaining 13.79% of the variance), empathy for the out-group (explaining 13.65% of the variance) and perception of intent (explaining 13.36% of the variance). The intent factor was divided into perception of intent for the in-group and perception of intent for the out-group, based on previous research demonstrating that people perceive intentions differently for themselves and their in-group as compared to out-groups (Kruger and Gilovich, 2004).

In the analysis, we created composite variables that indicated overall positive and negative attitudes towards the in-group and out-group by combining the empathy and intentionality factors.[37] The empathy factor reflects a more affective and emotional response, while perception of intentionality speaks to a more cognitive response. Specifically, perceiving a lack of intentionality on the part of the out-group suggests that participants view members of the out-group as not having intelligible mental experiences, and that they perceive the out-group only on a group level and not as individuals. Thus, in-group positive attitudes are consistent with higher levels of empathy and a greater perception of group intentionality, and out-group negative attitudes imply lower levels of empathy and a lower perception of intentionality.

7.4 FINDINGS ON THE PSYCHOLOGICAL EFFECTS OF SPEECH: US POPULATION

The personality and demographic variables were correlated with the five survey factors, as well as overall positive attitudes towards the in-group and overall negative attitudes towards the out-group.[38] A table showing personality correlations for the US population is provided in Appendix 4.1.

A propensity to morally justify violence positively correlated with political conservatism, a greater amount of time engaging with violent media, and male gender, and it negatively correlated with belief in a just world. Increased empathy for the in-group correlated with authoritarianism, belief in a just world, disgust sensitivity and economic system justification. Empathy for the out-group correlated with greater engagement in violent media, economic system justification and belief

---

[37] Empathy and intent were correlated for the in-group, r (395) = .228, p = .000, but not for the out-group, r (394) = .039, p = .437, suggesting that the factors are distinct only with respect to attitudes towards the out-group.

[38] Linear models explored the main effects of the conditions, while controlling for all of the demographic and personality variables. When controlling for all of these variables, moral justification of violence had a significant overall model, F (19, 340) = 6.003, p < .000, adj. R^2 = .209. Empathy for the out-group also had a significant overall model, F (19, 346) = 2.682, p < .000, adj. R^2 = .081, as well as empathy for the in-group, F (19, 345) = 2.792 p < .000, adj. R^2 = .086. Perception of the intent for the out-group had a significant overall model, F (19, 344) = 1.945, p = .001, adj. R^2 = .047, and perception of intent for the in-group also had an overall significant model, F (19, 345) = 2.310, p = .002, adj. R^2 = .064. General negative attitudes towards the out-group had a significant overall model, F (19, 344) = 1.804, p = .021, adj. R^2 = .040, and overall positive attitudes towards the in-group also had an overall significant model, F (19, 344) = 2.549, p < .000, adj. R^2 = .075. Therefore, the results were not driven by the measured personality or demographic variables.

239

in a just world and with gender. Increased perception of intent for the in-group correlated with religiosity. There were no significant correlations with perception of intent for the out-group. Overall positive attitudes towards the in-group correlated with economic system justification, disgust sensitivity and religiosity. Overall negative attitudes towards the out-group negatively correlated with system justification, belief in a just world and time engaging with violent media.

A series of linear regressions determined the relative predictive power of the different speeches. The only significant predictor for a propensity to morally justify violence were speeches that reference past atrocities. Calls for revenge were marginally significant.[39] Increased empathy for the in-group was significantly predicted by speeches that reference revenge, nationalism, and direct threat.[40] Decreased empathy for the out-group was significantly predicted by speeches that reference dehumanization, justice systems, revenge, direct threat, past atrocities, victimization and negative stereotypes.[41] Perception of in-group intent was significantly predicted by speeches that reference negative stereotypes, nationalism, dehumanization, justice systems and revenge.[42]

Perception of out-group intent was significantly predicted by speeches that reference dehumanization, a direct threat, justice, past atrocities and negative stereotypes.[43] Overall positive attitudes towards the in-group (increased empathy and increased perception of intent) were significantly predicted by the nationalism, revenge, negative stereotypes, dehumanization and justice speeches.[44] However, overall negative attitudes towards the out-group (decreased levels of empathy and decreased perception of intent) were only significantly predicted by the revenge speech.[45]

This study demonstrates that reading the actual speeches of a defendant charged at an international criminal tribunal has certain identifiable effects on a US population: lowering their propensity to empathize with the out-group, increasing empathy with the in-group, changing how they impute intentionality to the in-group and out-group, influencing overall positive and negative attitudes towards the different groups, and enhancing their willingness to morally justify

---

[39] $R^2 = .033$, $F (9, 389) = 1.458$, $p = .162$. Past atrocities were significant at .021 and revenge at .052.
[40] $R^2 = .042$, $F (9, 395) = 1.889$, $p = .052$.   [41] $R^2 = .074$, $F (9, 396) = 3.443$, $p = .000$.
[42] $R^2 = .061$, $F (9, 395) = 2.764$, $p = .004$.   [43] $R^2 = .050$, $F (9, 393) = 2.230$, $p = .020$.
[44] $R^2 = .054$. $F (9, 394) = 2.420$, $p = .011$.   [45] $R^2 = .022$, $F (9, 393) = .943$, $p = .487$.

violence. Not all categories of speech had the same kinds of effects on people's attitudes, however. Revenge language and references to past atrocities emerged as the types of speech with the most significant impact across all areas measured, thus challenging the established view in many circles that dehumanizing speech is the most damaging form of hate speech.

7.5 FINDINGS ON THE PSYCHOLOGICAL EFFECTS OF SPEECH: SERBIAN POPULATION

After translating the survey into Serbian, I led a team that included Jordan Kiper, Serbian translator Biljana Belamarić Wilsey and Drs. Aleksander Bošković and Bojan Todosijević of the Institute of Social Sciences in Belgrade that administered the survey with a Serbian population in 2015.[46] The statistical analysis conducted by Jordan Kiper started by correlating personality and demographic variables with the five survey factors as well as overall attitudes towards the in-group and out-group. A table illustrating all personality correlations for the Serbian population is provided in Appendix 4.2.

Similarly to the US sample, moral justifications of violence positively correlated with greater amounts of time engaging in violent media. Unlike the US sample, however, political conservativism and belief in a just world did not have a significant influence on responses to the questions for Serbs. Instead, higher economic standing and intense nationalist beliefs were strongly correlated with a willingness to morally justify violence, while older age and being male negatively correlated with such a justification. For Serbs, increased empathy for the in-group correlated very strongly with nationalism, authoritarianism, belief in a just world and, unlike the US sample, religiosity. Empathy for the out-group did not significantly correlate with any personality or

---

[46] The survey included the same format and questions as the survey with the US population, but we added additional questions on nationalism, self-esteem and whether the participant was from a rural area, a small town or a large city. We excluded questions from the original US survey relating to beliefs in systems of justice and propensity for disgust. As with the US survey, a principle components analysis was undertaken using a varimax rotation; the Kaiser–Meyer–Olkin measure of sampling adequacy was .754 and Bartlett's test of sphericity was significant (X2 (190) = 3436.55, p < 0.000). Survey questions for the Serbian population loaded onto five factors, all of which had primary loadings over 0.5 and explained 64.44% of the total variance. The factors were moral justification of violence (explaining 24.23%), empathy for the in-group (explaining 13.66%), empathy for the out-group (explaining 10.72%), perception of intent for the in-group (explaining 9.47%), and perception of intent for the out-group (explaining 6.36%).

demographic variables. Increased perception of the intent for the in-group varied significantly from the US sample. While only religiosity correlated for US participants, Serbian participants' perception of intent for the in-group correlated with authoritarianism, higher economic standing, being male and engaging violent media, and negatively correlated with religiosity and nationalism.

Whereas US participants showed no significant correlations with their perception of intent for the out-group, Serb participants' perceptions of the intentions of the out-group correlated with self-esteem, higher economic standing and being male, and negatively correlated with engaging in violent media, political conservativism and religiosity. Overall positive attitudes towards the in-group correlated with nationalism, authoritarianism and self-esteem; and, unlike the US sample, overall positive attitudes towards the in-group did not correlate with religiosity.

Overall negative attitudes towards the out-group were similar to the US sample insofar as they correlated with belief in a just world and political conservativism. Uniquely to the Serb sample, coming from a rural area or village correlated with negative attitude towards the out-group. Additionally, Serb participants differed from the US participants insofar as attitudes towards the out-group positively correlated with being male and having higher income. In sum, the personality and demographic characteristics of US and Serbian populations showed both similar and different attitudes to inter-group relations. While there are some similar correlations, the variations suggest that we should carefully evaluate claims that there are universal personality or demographic attributes that predispose persons towards certain attitudes towards one's own group and other groups.

As with the US sample, we conducted a series of linear regressions to determine the relative predictive power of the different speeches.[47] Beginning with moral justifications of violence, like the US sample, the overall model was not significant, and for the Serbian sample, no predictors were significant, including calls for revenge and references to past atrocities. This is one of the main differences between the US and Serb populations: the US participants were more willing to morally justify violence after reading speeches that called for revenge or referred

---

[47] As with the US study, we constructed linear models to explore the effects of the different speeches for the Serbian speeches, while controlling for demographic and personality variables. The Serbian results were not driven by measured personality or demographic variables, consistent with the US survey.

to past atrocities. With the Serb population, none of the speeches caused participants to countenance violence.

The effects on attitudes towards the in-group and out-group were more similar for the US and Serb populations. For the Serb sample, increased empathy for the in-group was significantly predicted by speeches that reference victimization, revenge, nationalism, dehumanization and justice.[48] Speeches that referenced victimization and revenge were especially strong in evoking in-group empathy. Decreased empathy for the out-group was significantly predicted only by speeches that reference revenge.[49] Perception of in-group intent was significantly predicted by speeches that reference dehumanization, revenge, direct threat, religion, nationalism and justice.[50] Perception of out-group intent was significantly predicted by every kind of speech; that is, speeches that reference revenge, dehumanization, victimization, nationalism, justice, direct threat, past atrocities, religion and negative stereotypes.[51] Taken with the strong correlations for out-group intent, these results suggest that Serbs, compared to US participants, already see groups as having a great deal of intentionality in their actions, which is heightened by the aforementioned propagandistic speeches.

Speeches invoking revenge and nationalism led to an increase of the perception of the intentionality of the outgroup. We divided the intent variable into its original two components and analyzed them separately for the Serbian sample. The first question (how intentional are the acts of the West Margolians?) was significantly predicted by revenge, dehumanization, victimization, past atrocities, nationalism, religion, direct threat and negative stereotypes.[52] The second question (how morally responsible are the West Margolians for their behavior?) was predicted by speeches referencing dehumanization, revenge, nationalism, direct threat and justice.[53] Overall positive attitudes towards the in-group (increased empathy and increased perception of intent) were significantly predicted by revenge, victimization, dehumanization, nationalism, direct threat, past atrocities, religion and justice.[54] Overall negative attitudes towards the out-group (decreased levels of empathy and decreased perception of intent) were significantly predicted by

---

[48] $R^2 = .095$, F $(9, 389) = 4.527$, p $= .000$. [49] $R^2 = .051$, F $(9, 389) = 2.313$, p $= .015$
[50] $R^2 = .045$, F $(9, 389) = 2.039$, p $= .034$ [51] $R^2 = .098$, F $(9, 389) = 4.675$, p $= .000$
[52] $R^2 = .091$, F $(9, 389) = 4.308$, p $= .000$. [53] $R^2 = .044$, F $(9, 389) = 1.994$, p $= .039$.
[54] $R^2 = .044$, F $(9, 389) = 1.994$, p $= .039$.

nationalism, religion, dehumanization, victimization, revenge, past atrocities and direct threat.[55]

In conclusion, as with the US sample, the results for a Serb population demonstrate that reading the actual propaganda speeches of a defendant charged at an international criminal tribunal has certain identifiable effects on readers: lowering their propensity to empathize with the out-group, increasing empathy with the in-group, affecting propensity to impute intentionality to the in-group and out-group, and influencing overall positive and negative attitudes towards the different groups. As with the US sample, not all categories of speech had the same kinds of effects on people's attitudes in Serbia. Once again, revenge language emerged as one of the most significant kinds of speech in various areas measured. Dehumanizing language was also consistently significant, as well as victimization language and nationalism.

Unlike the US sample, though, these speech categories appear to cluster together in their effects on Serbs, suggesting that politicians' speeches are unlikely to affect all populations in the same way. Where US participants are especially sensitive to speeches that referenced revenge, Serb participants are less influenced by revenge but appeared sensitive to dehumanizing languages, references to victimization and nationalistic speeches. Given the surge of nationalism during the armed conflict in Serbia in the 1990s, it is not surprising to see the influence of these additional speeches.

7.6 REVENGE SPEECH, CULTURE AND INDIRECT CAUSATION

Revenge language and references to past atrocities powerfully reinforce collective identity and internal solidarity, thus adding a fresh component to existing theories of inciting speech. Not only did revenge speeches marginally increase the willingness of US participants to morally justify violence, but it also consolidated in-group identity, surprisingly to the same extent as highly nationalistic rhetoric. References to past atrocities, essentially revenge speech without a call for violence, had a statistically significant effect on the propensity of the US population to justify violence. With both US and Serb populations, revenge speech exhibits multiple and mutually reinforcing properties that shape attitudes across a number of key areas.

[55] $R^2 = .046$, F (9, 389) = 2.087, p = .030.

By integrating aspects of increasing internal solidarity, lowering empathy and enhancing justifications of violence, we begin to see how revenge speech might have an outsized role in the commission of international crimes. However, the persuasion literature reminds us that attitudinal changes do not always lead to behavioral changes. Any theory that claims that revenge has a greater impact on listeners' actions than, say, dehumanizing language, requires additional evidence that revenge combines affect and cognition and identifies a clear path of action that can be taken by the listener.

These findings stand in contrast to the accepted view in both international law and social psychology that dehumanizing language has the most deleterious impact on armed conflict and genocide. Rather, our study suggests that, across two quite distant societies, revenge speech has the most powerful effects overall, and references to past atrocities (which are conceptually related to revenge speech) enhance moral justifications for violence. Several current theories potentially explain the widespread ethic of revenge in human societies. Revenge acts as a group-level signaling that particular offences and unfair behavior will be censured and punished, and revenge sends a signal that similar future acts will also be punished, thereby setting the standard of acceptable behavior.[56]

There is increasing evidence that punishment is not simply a negative attribute contributing to conflict, but is also an essential part of the evolution of cooperation in human societies.[57] In public goods games, Fehr and Gachter (2002) found that cooperation increases dramatically when individuals can punish freeloaders and cheaters. Further, in a neuroscientific study, De Quervain et al. (2004) found that thinking about revenge results in increased activity in the part of the brain – the caudate nucleus – which is known to process rewards, suggesting that persons punishing defectors and norm violators experience a pleasurable psychological payoff.

While the Serbian population was less influenced by calls for revenge, many of the other speeches did have significant effects that enhanced in-group solidarity and decreased empathy for the out-group. These findings on how speeches bolster internal solidarity have implications for the debate about why ordinary people commit mass atrocities. Historian

---

[56] McCullough et al. (2010).

[57] Ostrom (1990) argues that punishment systems are a necessary element of all societies. And then, of course, there is the tit-for-tat model of Axelrod (1984:85) that explains how cooperation and punishment for defection are self-reinforcing.

Christopher Browning (1998), in his landmark study *Ordinary Men*, found that the SS's anti-Semitic ideological indoctrination of Reserve Police Battalion 101 was not enough to explain the crimes they committed against a civilian population during the Second World War. Browning (1998:184) maintains that the reliance in the literature on racism and anti-Semitism in Nazi Germany implies a one-dimensional model of mass communication, in which the men of Reserve Police Battalion 101 are "deprived ... of the capacity for independent thought."[58] For Browning, an additional element is required to explain why ordinary German men would commit murder and other atrocities against Jews. Mass orchestrated killing is a social activity, and for a member of a police or military unit to avoid participating was considered disloyal to his peers, a violation of group norms and an abandonment of one's rightful duties to do the "dirty work." Thus, Browning (1998:184–6) highlights a constellation of factors gravitating around conformity, "the bonds of comradeship" and in-group solidarity, and identifies these as the salient motivators to murder, rather than antipathy to the out-group.

Our two surveys provide insights into the effects of a politician's speeches, but qualifications are also in order. This study did not evaluate the credibility or authority of the speaker or the effects of repetition and the frequency and duration of speech. Nor were we able to ascertain the effects on the two sample populations of the interactions between types of speeches. The studies did not take place with populations experiencing armed conflict in their countries. In real world settings, listeners would be exposed to a variety of categories of speech (and likely additional categories not included in our study), potentially simultaneously and over a longer duration. Speeches might reinforce one another in ways that increase positive attitudes towards the in-group and negative attitudes towards the out-group and enhance moral justifications for violence.

The social science of inciting speech is still relatively nascent, and many more studies need to be conducted, especially outside western societies. We saw how the US and Serb populations differed in important respects, and other questions remain, such as, what is the cross-cultural salience of our research: would the speeches have the same effects in

---

[58] Browning states that (1998:178) "a look at the actual materials used to indoctrinate Reserve Police Battalion 101 raises serious doubts about the adequacy of SS indoctrination as an explanation for the men becoming killers."

Syria, South Africa and Singapore? How do the effects of speeches vary according to the existence or not of an armed conflict between groups? With more comparative data, we could ascertain whether there is wide variation in the impact of different types of inciting speech in different locales. And finally, the most ambitious and far-reaching point at issue is: is revenge speech a universal human phenomenon with similar effects everywhere?[59]

Social research on persuasion and political communication is highly relevant to the adjudication of international speech crimes. Denigrating and inciting language have identifiable and measurable effects upon an audience, predisposing them towards certain attitudes and beliefs. However, we must exercise caution. Many factors – both psychological and contextual – are at work simultaneously when a speaker incites an audience to commit an offence against members of the out-group. Therefore, legal models might acknowledge this causal complexity when determining whether a particular speech act contributed to a set of conditions jointly sufficient to result in a crime, and which mode of liability (e.g., instigating, ordering, aiding and abetting) is most applicable to the circumstances. As Straus (2007:611) concludes, our grasp of the effects of inciting speech in any particular instance must allow for "causal complexity to help explain what was a very complex and multi-dimensional outcome." The next chapter draws out the implications for international courts of social research on persuasion and inciting speech.

---

[59] For Jacoby (1983), revenge or *lex talionis* is a universal attribute of human societies.

CHAPTER EIGHT

A NEW MODEL FOR PREVENTING AND PUNISHING INTERNATIONAL SPEECH CRIMES

8.1   INTRODUCTION

This final chapter engages in a synthesis of the international criminal law and social research of inciting speech. The proposal advanced here is that prosecutors, in the first instance, ought to consider charging two inchoate crimes – direct and public incitement to genocide or hate speech as a form of persecution – as preventative measures. Inchoate crimes are advantageous since the offence is the conduct itself and proof of causation is not an element of the crime. The central utility of criminalizing particularly dangerous utterances lies in prevention, yet this function has been overlooked by international tribunals, which thus far have issued indictments only after mass atrocities have already occurred.

If the moment for prevention has elapsed, then international prosecutors ought to consider two modes of liability for completed crimes; ordering and aiding and abetting. Ordering is relevant to a hierarchical relationship between a superior and subordinate, usually within a military structure of command and control that (mostly) resolves the agent causation problems commonly encountered in prosecuting instigation. Aiding and abetting either implies no causation at all, or only minimal causation, and does not require mental causation since the accomplice need not share the intent of the principal committing the crime. Other modes of liability such as inducing/instigating or soliciting or co-perpetrating entail a high threshold of direct causation and standard of intentionality and are therefore to be used sparingly. Social research on persuasion and political communication can contribute in several ways to the legal process, including parsing the local meanings of coded speech and identifying the types of speech and conditions that raise the relative risk of a violent attack on a civilian population.

8.2 INCHOATE SPEECH CRIMES AND THE PROMISE OF PREVENTION

Mass atrocities seldom take local or international observers utterly by surprise. In most instances, there are early warning signs that include political rhetoric from leaders that encourages or condones violence, discriminatory attacks on civilians, the arming of the population and their organizing into militias and so on.[1] Power's (2002) *Problem from Hell* is a grim chronology of the failure of the United States to take reasonable steps to thwart genocides in the twentieth century, even though it is generally acknowledged that some genocides (e.g., Rwanda) could have been forestalled by the strategic deployment of a relatively small contingent of well-trained troops.[2]

In such circumstances, international prosecutors seeking to avert a widespread or systematic attack on a civilian population may indict speakers for inchoate crimes rather than consummated, or completed crimes. As discussed in Chapter 2, the two inchoate speech crimes available to international prosecutors are direct and public incitement to commit genocide and hate speech as a form of persecution (a crime against humanity).[3] Charging vocal agitators with inchoate speech crimes rather than modes of liability for completed crimes (such as "instigating" and "inducing") could be justified on two grounds. Inchoate crimes do not require proof of causation and therefore have one less element to fulfill. In practice, the successful prosecution of speech crimes under "causal" theories of liability involves just the kind of evidence, namely insider testimony about direct causation, that international prosecutors often struggle to acquire and then retain. Convicting the accused of instigating crimes against humanity demands evidence of

---

[1] The idea of creating an early warning system to prevent genocide and mass atrocities goes back at least to Kuper (1985:219).
[2] Caplan (2007:29).
[3] In international criminal law, hate speech as a form of persecution may also be a completed crime once the offence is committed against the victims. However, even in in these instances, there may be no need to demonstrate further causal effects (or perlocutions) of the hate speech act, making the conduct the crime, as is conventionally the case with inchoate crimes.

mental causation and thus, credible testimony from co-perpetrators. Yet, as is apparent in *Šešelj* and in *Ruto and Sang*, international courts often do not adequately protect insider witnesses from bribery, intimidation and harassment by zealous supporters of the accused.[4]

Without their own police force or powers of arrest, and with only weak witness protection programs, international courts do not possess the coercive power of many national criminal justice systems. They lack the resources to investigate and indict a criminal enterprise with the same thoroughness as a national attorney-general and compel plea bargains from both major and minor criminal actors. Not that such outcomes are impossible, and a few high-ranking figures such as Rwandan Prime Minister Kambanda have cooperated with international tribunals. However, these defectors were less numerous than expected, because international prosecutors had fewer levers than their national counterparts to obtain compliance from the associates of high-ranking military and political leaders.

The second, and perhaps more significant, reason to prefer inchoate speech crimes involves preventing mass atrocities before they occur. As we saw in Chapter 2, the drafters of the 1948 UN Genocide Convention included the separate crime of direct and public incitement to commit genocide as a means of preventing future genocides.[5] For this reason, inciting genocide may be prosecuted even if genocide does not take place. Even though several genocides occurred between the late 1940s and 1990s, the inchoate crime of inciting genocide went unprosecuted for fifty years. Only in 1998 after the murder of nearly 1 million people in the Rwandan genocide was the first individual, Jean-Paul Akayesu, convicted of inciting genocide at the ICTR.

In part because of the failure to prevent genocide in Rwanda and Bosnia-Herzegovina, governments and international agencies have launched various initiatives to bolster the atrocities prevention mechanisms of the international system. Already in existence were the Chapter VII powers contained in the Charter of the United Nations that permit the Security Council to assemble a military response to threats to international peace and security.[6] The deadlocked UN Security Council, however, often proved unable or unwilling to respond adequately to deteriorating security situations. In the aftermath of the NATO bombing

---

[4] *Šešelj* TC §46; *Ruto and Sang* TC §§37–8. [5] Schabas (2009:319–24, 520).
[6] Charter of the United Nations, Chapter VII, see articles 42–51, www.un.org/en/sections/un-charter/chapter-vii/ Accessed 16 March 2016.

in 1999 to prevent widespread Serb military attacks on civilians in Kosovo, it was apparent that a new doctrine and framework of prevention was needed.[7] "The Responsibility to Protect" doctrine, arising out of an initiative of the Canadian government, legitimized military intervention on humanitarian grounds to prevent genocide and other atrocities, even potentially without the authorization of the UN Security Council.[8]

In addition to its ethical concern with saving civilian lives, the Responsibility to Protect Report makes a compelling economic case for prevention, citing estimates that the international community spent approximately $200 billion on conflict management in the 1990s in Bosnia and Herzegovina, Somalia, Rwanda, Haiti, the Persian Gulf, Cambodia and El Salvador, and could have saved $130 billion of that amount if it had mounted more effective preventive measures.[9] The Responsibility to Protect, and a concern to globalize risk management more generally, quickly gained traction at the United Nations where it has become official policy. The UN Secretary General has issued a report on implementing the Responsibility to Protect doctrine[10] and created a Special Adviser to the Secretary-General on the Prevention of Genocide and a Special Adviser on the Responsibility to Protect.[11]

Alongside these international developments, national efforts also sought to integrate prevention doctrines into foreign policy. In 2012, President Barack Obama announced a new program to prevent atrocities in Presidential Study Directive 10, which declared that "preventing mass atrocities and genocide is a core national security interest and a core moral responsibility of the United States of America." President Obama approved a review of the US government's capabilities in this regard, including the establishing of an "Atrocities Prevention Board," a new mechanism chaired at the National Security Council. The original documents related to this initiative, however, did not include any references to hate speech, incitement or government propaganda.

By 2016, however, the President and White House staff no longer even mentioned the Board, which seems to have become a casualty of the Obama Administration's policy in Syria. The US State Department

---

[7] Independent International Commission on Kosovo (2000).
[8] International Commission on Intervention and State Sovereignty (2002).
[9] International Commission on Intervention and State Sovereignty (2002:20). The figures are drawn from the report of the Carnegie Commission on Preventing Deadly Conflict.
[10] UN Secretary General (2009).
[11] Further, in 2015, the Human Rights Council adopted a resolution (HRC/RES/28/34) on the Prevention of Genocide that refers to incitement at §2 and hate speech targeting protected groups at §15.

continued to claim in 2016 that the Board had shaped its assessment of atrocity risks in other countries where early warning signs exist, such as Burma, Nigeria, the Central African Republic and Iraq.[12] The State Department has not specifically indicated how its atrocity prevention policies have been modified, however.

The promising international atrocities prevention framework that emerged in the 1999–2002 years is presently in tatters, a casualty of the United States' invasion of Iraq in 2003 and the subsequent political turmoil in the Middle East. Military intervention to save the lives of civilians under sustained attack from governments or non-state actors still does not count with widespread domestic or international support. In this context, international tribunals could play an enhanced role. One potential avenue of prevention could involve the Chief Prosecutor of the International Criminal Court issuing indictments against political leaders engaging in inciting speech before a dangerous situation spirals out of control.[13] The ICC Chief Prosecutor has the power to intervene preventatively even before she arrives at the stage of issuing indictments. In February 2015, a day before her visit to Nigeria, ICC Chief Prosecutor Fatou Bensouda issued a press release ahead of the Nigerian state elections warning that "any person who incites or engages in acts of violence by ordering, requesting, encouraging or contributing in any other manner to the commission of crimes ... is liable to prosecution either by Nigerian Courts or by ICC."[14] As an African (Bensouda is from The Gambia and studied law in Nigeria), the current Chief Prosecutor is especially well positioned to play such a precautionary and stabilizing role in African countries.

Such targeted prosecutorial actions could be most effective in the early stages of political instability, before a confrontation deteriorates into full-blown armed conflict. Here, ICC prosecutors may be more

---

[12] A claim made on the US State Department website at www.state.gov/j/atrocitiesprevention, accessed 16 March 2016.

[13] Even though the ICC is a permanent court with jurisdiction over crimes of all world states that sign and ratify the Rome Statute of 1998, the Chief Prosecutor exercises discretion over what cases to pursue, and given the size of the Court relative to the number of violations of international law, the majority of international crimes will go unprosecuted. Under most conditions, and especially where full-scale armed conflict is ongoing, speech acts are generally considered of lower gravity than actual commission of genocide and widespread or systematic war crimes or crimes against humanity. This is why the early, preventative issuing of indictments for speech crimes might constitute their best utility.

[14] Press Release, International Criminal Court Office of the Prosecutor, "Statement of the Prosecutor of the International Criminal Court, Fatou Bensouda, ahead of the general and state elections in Nigeria," 2 February 2015.

effective if they charge inchoate crimes (hate speech or incitement to genocide, depending on their relevance) and focus on the content and illocutionary force of a call to violence, rather than on any perlocutions or consequences. At the outset, it would make sense to target the most egregious statements by authority figures, public proclamations that unambiguously communicate the intention to incite mass atrocities. An indictment is more likely to be confirmed by the ICC's Pre-Trial Chamber if it cites utterances that go beyond denigrating language and expressions of hatred and openly appeal for imminent violence. Threatening to kill or injure another person, terroristic threats and calls to imminent public violence and disorder are crimes in virtually every national jurisdiction, and even in free-speech strongholds such as the United States.[15]

Achieving the preventative potential of international criminal justice will necessitate reforming and clarifying the international law of speech crimes and ensuring that the flawed ICTR jurisprudence on direct and public incitement to commit genocide does not crystallize into settled law. The legal principle of *stare decisis* could conceivably exert a strong inertia effect on future trials for inciting genocide, with negative effects. Given that all of the ICTR incitement cases have now been heard on appeal, that option to overturn the jurisprudence is now foreclosed, but other possible avenues are still open.

The disarray in the international law of incitement to genocide sprang from the International Law Commission's 1996 Draft Code for war crimes and crimes against humanity. Therefore, it falls to the ILC to reaffirm that incitement to genocide: 1. Is an inchoate crime in which the conduct is the crime and proof of intention does not rest upon causation; and 2. Can transpire before a genocide is actually underway, thus nullifying the ICTR's condition in *Nahimana* and *Bikindi* that genocidal speech be contemporaneous with an actual genocide.[16] These clarifications of law, while representing a repudiation of recent doctrine, would hardly represent a blow to the reputation of the International Law Commission and over time, might even enhance its authority, especially if we recall that historically,

---

[15] US Model Penal Code §211.1. However, it should be noted that words are generally not sufficient to satisfy the material element of threatened battery assault and they must be accompanied by threatening gestures. In addition, the threat of physical harm must be unambiguous and immediate. See *Clark v. Commonwealth*, 676 S.E.2d 332 (2009).

[16] *Nahimana* AC §636, 754; *Bikindi* TC §255, 421. See also Gordon (2010:262) for a critical commentary on the contemporaneity criterion.

international criminal law has been constructed upon a patchwork of international conventions, judgments and guidelines generated by a variety of national and international bodies.

Turning now to the ICC, the Rome Statute's framing of inchoate speech crimes also gives cause for concern for reasons set out in Chapter 2. To summarize: in Article 25(3)(e), the status of direct and public incitement to commit genocide appears to have been downgraded from a separate, standalone crime to a mode of liability for the completed underlying crime of genocide. One interpretation of Article 25(3)(e)'s prefatory "In respect of the crime of genocide," could be that inciting genocide may only be charged after genocide has actually occurred. Formulating inciting genocide as a completed crime obviously defeats the prevention element of the United Nations Convention on the Prevention and Punishment of Genocide.

The inclusion of incitement to genocide along with types of responsibility for completed crimes in Article 25 apparently resulted from an oversight on the part of the drafters of the Rome Statute. In his careful study of the drafting of the incitement to genocide provision in the Rome Statute, Davies (2009:266) concluded that "no attention seems to have been paid during that (drafting) process to the conceptual and practical differences between treating incitement to genocide as a separate crime and treating it as a mode of criminal participation." Davies (2009:270) recommends moving direct and public incitement to commit genocide from Article 25(3)(e) to Articles 5 (listing the crimes under the jurisdiction of the Court) and 6 (defining the crime of genocide) of the Rome Statute. This amendment to the Statute would establish incitement to genocide as a distinct, inchoate crime and preclude the requirement to prove causation in future incitement cases at the ICC.

Additionally, there is a need to ensure that the early jurisprudence of the ICC on incitement to commit genocide does not reiterate the unwarranted contemporaneous requirement of ICTR judgments, which was neither included nor envisaged in the UN Genocide Convention. Timely prevention also necessitates a proper interpretation of those aspects of Article 6 (genocide) of the ICC's *Elements of Crimes* that could be interpreted as supporting the ICTR's contemporaneous criterion, especially the stipulation that any prohibited conduct take place "in the context of a manifest pattern of similar conduct directed against that group." The *Elements of Crimes* explains that the term "in the context of" could include "initial acts in an emerging pattern," which clears up some of the confusion.

Yet this still allows the possibility that calls to genocide that are not uttered in an advanced enough context of genocidal attacks might be discounted, precisely when an indictment could be most effective as a preventative measure. Taking an example from the Rwandan genocide, this could mean that Hassan Ngeze, a co-defendant of Nahimana in the Media Trial, could escape liability for publishing *Kangura*, a Hutu Power newsletter that was infamous for the cover of its 1991 issue (i.e., three years before the genocide began in April 1994) that posed the question "Which weapons are we going to use to beat the cockroaches for good?" next to the image of a machete.

In all likelihood, the crime of inciting genocide will only apply to a small number of extreme instances and will therefore exclude many other types of speech that are currently prohibited in some municipal criminal jurisdictions. Article 130.1 ("Incitement to Hatred") of the German Criminal Code, for instance, creates a criminal sanction against "Whosoever, in a manner capable of disturbing the public peace, incites hatred against a national, racial, religious group or a group defined by their ethnic origins." Much inciting speech by political leaders falls short of advocating genocide or extermination and yet still could represent a consequential form of participation in the persecution of a protected group.

At present, there is not a coherent and established framework in international criminal law that prohibits hate speech as an inchoate crime. As we saw in the introduction, two United Nations Conventions contain a prohibition on hate speech. The International Convention on the Elimination of Discrimination of All Forms of Racial Discrimination at Article 4(a) considers an offence: "all dissemination of ideas based on racial superiority or hatred, incitement to racial discrimination, as well as all acts of violence or incitement to such acts against any race or group of persons of another colour or ethnic origin." Article 20(2) of the International Covenant on Civil and Political Rights (1966) maintains that "Any advocacy of national, racial or religious hatred that constitutes incitement to discrimination, hostility or violence shall be prohibited by law." International human rights conventions do not speak in unison on this matter, and the European Convention on Human Rights makes no reference to hate speech or propaganda and instead enshrines freedom of expression at Article 10.

The case law at international criminal tribunals declaring that hate speech is an inchoate crime is remarkably meager and equivocal. At present, there only exists one precedent from the *Nahimana* Trial Chamber that hate speech targeting a population on discriminatory grounds fulfills the crime of persecution (a crime against humanity) under Article 3(h) of the ICTR Statute.[17] Crucially, *Nahimana* unambiguously defined hate speech as an inchoate crime in which "there need not be a call to action in communications that constitute persecution. For the same reason, there need be no link between persecution and acts of violence."[18] That is, persecution as a crime against humanity could be committed even in instances where the hate speech did not directly call for violence and where a causal connection to subsequent violence was not present.

The *Nahimana* Appeals Chamber decision upheld the finding that hate speech uttered after 6 April 1994 and in the context of a widespread and systematic attack against the Tutsi themselves constituted acts of persecution.[19] As with direct and public incitement to commit genocide, the Appeals Chamber in *Nahimana* insisted that the hate speech in question be contemporaneous with the atrocities committed. Unlike the argument for inciting genocide, however, this contextual element of hate speech is valid and justifiable because the elements of scale and a prevailing context of widespread or systematic attacks have always been part of the definition of crimes against humanity, which must occur in the context of "a widespread or systematic attack directed against any civilian population."[20]

Therefore it makes sense that hate speech can only be charged when an attack on a civilian population is ongoing and has attained a significant scale. This blunts the preventative power of hate speech as an inchoate crime, but does not utterly invalidate it, as it would still be possible to indict a speaker for persecution in the early stages of a widespread campaign against a civilian population. As I have argued, a contemporaneity requirement should not apply to inciting genocide for reasons of scale and gravity: scale is not an element of genocide as it is with crimes against humanity; and the underlying crime of genocide

[17] *Nahimana* TC §1072.   [18] *Nahimana* TC §1073.

[19] *Nahimana* AC §995. Judge Meron manifestly disagreed, as is self-evident in the subheading in his dissent that read, "Mere Hate Speech Is Not Criminal" (§5–8).

[20] Article 7.1 of the Rome Statute of the ICC states that "For the purpose of this Statute, 'crime against humanity' means any of the following acts when committed as part of a widespread or systematic attack directed against any civilian population, with knowledge of the attack," and then it goes on to list the *actus reus* elements.

is of greater gravity than persecution and therefore more deserving of vigorously preventative measures.

Beyond *Nahimana*, there is not much else in international criminal law to support a prohibition on hate speech as a form of persecution, and the trial chamber in *Šešelj* dismissed the notion that incitement to hatred even constitutes a crime in international law.[21] Timmermann (2015:261) makes a strong case for "incitement to hatred" as an international crime and her arguments are accurate and persuasive. Nevertheless, the view that hate speech can fulfill the international crime of persecution is aspirational, given the fact that the crime is not listed in the ICC Statute, and given the otherwise unfavorable language of the ICC Statute and the present state of ICC jurisprudence on speech crimes. At the ICC, persecution is a crime against humanity at Article 7(1)(h): "Persecution against any identifiable group or collectivity on political, racial, national, ethnic, cultural, religious, gender as defined in paragraph 3, or other grounds that are universally recognized as impermissible under international law, in connection with any act referred to in this paragraph or any crime within the jurisdiction of the Court," and Article 7(2)(g) defines persecution as "the intentional and severe deprivation of fundamental rights contrary to international law by reason of the identity of the group or collectivity."

Hate speech *per se* is not listed as such as an element of persecution in the Statute. It remains to be seen whether hate speech or discriminatory speech that encourages or condones violence against a protected group will be interpreted by the Court as an "intentional and severe deprivation of fundamental rights contrary to international law." At first glance, the terms "severe" and "fundamental" would seem to militate against a more capacious interpretation that would apply to the kind of deprivation of rights of a beleaguered minority group that could ensue from political speech. Furthermore, practically, given how highly regulated and rule-bound the ICC has proved to be, it is unlikely that ICC prosecutors would be allowed by a Pre-Trial Chamber to charge a defendant for a crime not manifestly listed in the Statute. Therefore, amending Article 7 of the Rome Statute to include hate speech as a form of persecution as a crime against humanity (i.e., in the context of a widespread or systematic attack on a civilian population) remains a priority.

Finally, the ICC Statute contemplates two, and possibly even three, new inchoate crimes for speech acts, although they have yet to be

---

[21] *Šešelj* TC §289, citing *Kordić and Čerkez*.

fully adjudicated so we can only speculate on their interpretation. Article 25(3)(b) of the ICC Statute indicates that "a person shall be criminally responsible and liable for punishment for a crime within the jurisdiction of the Court if that person: orders, solicits or induces the commission of such a crime which in fact occurs or is attempted," and Article 25(3)(d) "In any other way contributes to the commission or attempted commission of such a crime by a group of persons acting with a common purpose. Such contribution shall be intentional."[22] Kenyan radio broadcaster Joshua Sang was charged under 25(3)(d) for allegedly encouraging the followers of Vice-President William Ruto to commit ethnic-based atrocities during the 2007 presidential elections. In April 2016, a majority of the ICC Trial Chamber judges, Judge Fremr dissenting, terminated the *Ruto and Sang* trial and vacated three charges of crimes against humanity after the prosecution witnesses withdrew their testimony amidst allegations of witness interference and political intimidation.

Finally, the Statute criminalizes attempt at Article 25(3)(f), holding liable a person who "attempts to commit such a crime by taking action that commences its execution by means of a substantial step, but the crime does not occur because of circumstances independent of the person's intentions."[23] It is therefore conceivable that a speaker calling for others to commit crimes might be indicted before those crimes are committed under all or any of the provisions (b), (d) and (f) of Article 25(3) of the ICC Statute.

The provisions in Articles 25(b), (d) and (f) are not unambiguously articulated as inchoate crimes in which the crime is the conduct and is fully completed in the speech act itself. Instead they are modes of liability built around the concept of either the completion of the crime or the attempt to complete the crime. Even though "attempt" is commonly seen as an inchoate crime, it requires that an individual take a "substantial step"[24] towards committing the offence listed in

---

[22] Article 25(3)(d) goes on to require that the individual's contribution "shall either: (i) Be made with the aim of furthering the criminal activity or criminal purpose of the group, where such activity or purpose involves the commission of a crime within the jurisdiction of the Court; or (ii) Be made in the knowledge of the intention of the group to commit the crime."

[23] Article 25(3)(f) goes on to qualify thus: "However, a person who abandons the effort to commit the crime or otherwise prevents the completion of the crime shall not be liable for punishment under this Statute for the attempt to commit that crime if that person completely and voluntarily gave up the criminal purpose."

[24] The ICC Statute at Article 25(3)(f) holds criminally responsible an individual who "attempts to commit such a crime by taking action that commences its execution by means of a substantial step." This language echoes the US Model Penal Code's provision for attempt

the ICC Statute. In practice, the chances of holding an individual liable for inciting speech will be improved if there exists proof of a causal nexus between the speech act and the substantial step taken by a listener to commit a crime. This implies that the evidence advanced by the prosecution will look much like that presented for a completed crime "which in fact occurs," recalling the language of Article 25(3)(b). Therefore, proving that an order, inducement or solicitation brought about an attempted or completed crime will hinge on the perlocutionary dimension of the speech act. Once we are on the terrain of perlocutions, then we are well on our way to requiring causation, and we have at least one foot outside of the conceptual space of inchoate crimes.

It is worth noting here that the statutes of previous international criminal tribunals only included attempt as a form of liability in relation to the underlying crime of genocide.[25] It is fair to say that international tribunals have not been as dedicated to prosecuting attempted international crimes and inchoate crimes as much as completed crimes, on (quite reasonable) grounds of gravity. Cryer et al. (2014:380) note that the "ICTY prosecutor has shown an unwillingness to prosecute attempts to commit international crimes, preferring to conceptualize them under other headings of liability." Attempt is therefore the poor stepsister of completion, and likely will only be applied in extremis, when no other charges for completed crimes are sustainable, but an international prosecutor, perhaps quixotically, still wishes to intervene in a deteriorating situation.

On closer examination then, the modes of liability listed in Article 25(3) in the ICC Statute that could portend inchoate crimes are not in fact a propitious avenue for indicting speakers for uncompleted offences. Nor was this the function envisaged by the drafters of the Statute according to Cryer et al. (2014:380), who maintain that the references to attempt were included in the ICC Statute not to cover solicitations or inducements, but to make up for the lack of a provision in Article 25(3) that refers to planning and preparation of war crimes, crimes against humanity and genocide.[26]

---

liability, which prohibits an act that constitutes a "substantial step" towards the completed offence at §5.01(1)(c).

[25] Listed in the ICTY Statute at Article 4(d) and in the ICTR Statute at 2(d).

[26] Planning and preparation are not included as modes of liability with respect to war crimes, crimes against humanity and genocide, but are included in the 2010 amendments on the crime of aggression at Article 8bis (1).

8.3   INCHOATE SPEECH CRIMES THROUGH THE LENS OF SOCIAL SCIENCE

The social science findings on political speech summarized in the previous chapter have many policy implications and legal applications, especially regarding the ever-elusive goal of preventing atrocities. As we saw with Dr. Mathias Ruzindana's appearance in two ICTR cases (*Akayesu* and *Nahimana*), social science testimony can have probative value when an accused is charged with inchoate speech crimes such as inciting genocide and hate speech as a form of persecution. In inchoate crimes, intentionality is the ultimate issue at stake and the subjective state of mind of the speaker is expressed in the locutionary (content and meaning) and illocutionary (exhortation) aspects of his or her utterances. In addition, expert testimony from social researchers can assist the court in various ways when a defendant is charged with complicity, a form of responsibility that either does not imply causation (e.g., for omissions or *ex post facto* acts of aiding and abetting), or only entails minimal causation.

Speech crimes trials often face the challenge of interpreting the locutionary and illocutionary aspects of indirect, ambiguous and veiled speech. Very few speakers, even the most ostensibly irresponsible of demagogues, openly and publicly appeal for the extermination of a protected group. As we have seen throughout this discussion, military figures, politicians and broadcasters are usually guarded and metaphorical in their speech. To an outsider, the meaning of their speech acts may be obscure, and may not openly display a malign intent. In Rwanda, leaders and broadcasters instructed their followers to "go to work" or "take up arms against the *Inyenzis* ("cockroaches"). In the former Yugoslavia, some ICTY defendants spoke of *"istraga poturice,"* a Serbian expression taken from the epic poem *The Mountain Wreath* (1847). *"Istraga"* can mean "the investigation" but also, in archaic usage, "the annihilation," of converts (*poturice*) to Islam.[27] Only a person familiar with *The Mountain Wreath* poem and its role as a founding literary expression of Serbian nationalism would know this. General Ratko Mladić, presently on trial for genocide of Muslims at Srebrenica, used the term *poturice* in a 1993 interview, at a time when his subordinates were actively deporting, torturing and murdering Bosnian Muslims:

[27] See Davis (1996:28, 146) on *The Mountain Wreath* and the role of religion and mythology in the Bosnian conflict.

> We all know who the Turks are. As a matter of fact, these Muslims are not even Turks, they are converts [original: *"poturice"*]. They have betrayed the Serb people and repressed them for 500 years. They are the worst scum – the Serb people who changed their religion. To change a religion – means to betray one's own people, to betray oneself.[28]

When presented with coded or culturally specific utterances like this, an international tribunal has the onerous task of ascertaining the intentionality of the accused at the time they gave a speech. What was the content and meaning of the accused's speech act, and to what degree was euphemistic language understood by their followers as a direct call for criminal acts (i.e., what was its illocutionary force)? There are times when the language of inciters is so culturally specific that it is largely unintelligible to outsiders. For instance, Dr. Ruzindana assisted the ICTR by explaining to the ICTR Trial Chamber how everyday Kinyarwanda phrases such as "go to work" came to have new meanings in the context of armed conflict and genocide between April and July, 1994. Professor Oberschall's content analysis pinpointed the locutionary dimensions of Vojislav Šešelj's speeches that claimed there was a direct existential threat to Serbs, and Oberschall detected their illocutionary force in Šešelj's call to act immediately to remove that threat.

Having argued in favor of an intentionality-based understanding of inchoate crimes that focuses on the express locutionary and illocutionary aspects of speech acts, it is nonetheless highly likely that international prosecutors will continue to base their decisions to charge incitement or hate speech on a risk assessment model. Risk assessment models are a feature of many modern criminal justice systems, having emerged in response to the dramatic increase in pretrial detentions and criticism that the bail system discriminated on the basis of race and economic status. In the United States, pretrial courts use actuarial risk assessments based upon the past behavior of individuals with similar characteristics to predict the likelihood that they will fail to appear at their trial and/or commit an offence in the period before their trial.[29] The Federal Pre-Trial Risk Assessment Instrument provides a risk score based upon a checklist containing ten risk factors such as the current charge against the defendant, prior pending charges, prior convictions,

---

[28] *Mladić* TC Exhibit P07719. The interview appeared in the Belgrade-based weekly NIN as, "I am Just a Soldier," interview with Jovan Janjić, on 25 June 1993.

[29] See Mayson (2016) and Monahan and Skeem (2016) for an evaluation of risk assessment models in US criminal law.

residence, employment, substance abuse, age and education.[30] The aim is to assist the court in distinguishing low-risk defendants from high-risk defendants and to provide judges with a rational basis for ordering preventative pretrial detention that precludes biases about the race, class or supposed citizenship status of the defendant.

When considering international speech crimes, a risk assessment model is unnecessary when the criminal intentionality is plainly expressed in the utterances of the speaker, as in the paradigmatic cases of Streicher ("The Jews in Russia must be killed. They must be exterminated root and branch"), Bikindi ("exterminate quickly") and Ngirabatware ("kill Tutsis"). The illocutionary force of the utterance is enough to warrant a penal consequence. However, a risk assessment instrument could provide valuable in hard cases where the speaker uses euphemistic language or makes denigrating and dehumanizing utterances but does not specifically call for violence (hate speech), or when the speech acts in question are uttered in the early stages of an armed conflict or widespread or systematic attack on a civilian population. In such scenarios, prosecutors at international tribunals and in national justice ministries are advised to follow a process of due diligence to ascertain the relative threat of a public figure's speech acts.

As criminal law theorists Ashworth and Zedner (2014:119) observe, "The premise that it is possible to assess risk accurately stands behind much preventative endeavor" and we can assume that a calculation of the probability that violence will ensue from a speaker's utterances will remain a significant factor in prosecutorial decision-making. In their study of risk assessment and the preventative role of criminal courts, Ashworth and Zedner (2014:119) accurately observe that "where there is doubt about the validity of risk assessment tools or the accuracy of their findings, much preventative endeavor becomes difficult to justify." This is the case presently at international tribunals. Risk evaluations by international prosecutors are subjective and impressionistic, and are often based upon incomplete and often conflicting reports about a mercurial political situation. Given that is the case, then the question arises; what risk assessment model could prosecutors employ that would indicate with more precision what types of speech acts uttered in what kind of conditions are most likely to precipitate imminent violent acts?

---

[30] Federal Pre-Trial Risk Assessment Instrument (PTRA), Version 2.0 1–4 (1 March 2010).

At least in part, the answer depends on the immediate situation on the ground, since every context is unique and merits a specific legal response. Having said this, social research addresses some of the most profound and demanding questions in the international law of speech crimes, especially with regards to the effects of distinct genres of speech on an audience. Generally, social scientists adopt a multi-factorial approach to the consequences of political communication, and recent research has identified many of the key factors in mass persuasion. Distilling the social science findings presented in Chapter 7, there are (at least) eleven recognized felicity conditions for the uptake of persuasive speech. The following checklist of risk factors is based on the current state of research on persuasion and political communication:

1. The speaker occupies an official position of authority.
2. The speaker is perceived as credible by his/her audience.
3. The speaker is perceived as charismatic by his/her audience.
4. The speaker is adept at summoning up pre-existing cultural symbols and narratives to cultivate historical grievances.[31]
5. The speaker makes dehumanizing references, refers to past atrocities and calls for revenge against the out-group.
6. The speaker uses intense language replete with vivid images, graphic metaphors and exaggerations.
7. His or her speech is experienced as "powerful" by an audience.
8. The message of the speaker is repeated across a variety of mass communication formats, from radio to television to Twitter.
9. The speaker wields a monopoly on the means of communication or can censor and suppress information.
10. The emotional state of the audience is affected by wider circumstances of insecurity and uncertainty.
11. His or her speech arouses fear by labelling a direct threat and then identifying a distinct and foreseeably violent course of action that can be taken by the audience to remove the source of that threat.

---

[31] *Karadžić* TC refers to how "the Accused and the Bosnian Serb leadership repeatedly referred to the historic grievances of the Serb people. The Chamber found that these speeches were used by the Accused and the Bosnian Serb leadership to remind the Bosnian Serb population about crimes committed against Serbs by Muslims and Croats and emphasised the need to ensure that they would not be repeated. The Chamber also found that these references were used as justification for renewing historical Bosnian Serb claims to land in BiH [Bosnia and Herzegovina] where they had once been a majority" (§2598).

Now for the caveats. This list is not exhaustive, and additional elements may be added as knowledge improves.[32] In themselves, none of these variables are causal in the sense of being an absolute prerequisite, nor do they always denote uptake on the part of the audience. Social science research alone cannot determine a trial chamber verdict: each individual case will be decided on the prevailing international criminal law, the specific evidential fact pattern and the merits of the arguments of each of the parties to the trial. Nonetheless, identifying the leading conditions most likely to persuade an audience can assist pretrial and trial chamber judges in assessing the gravity of the speech acts and the likelihood that international crimes against protected groups will ensue. Constructing a multifactorial matrix using the list above could guide prosecutors as they discharge their due diligence obligations under international law[33] and assess the gravity of a set of utterances by a politician or prominent public figure. The matrix could be quantified, with each factor above given a rating from 1–10 based upon a qualitative evaluation of each element in the matrix. Prosecutors could determine in advance that they will not indict until the average of the multiple factors reaches a certain percentage (e.g., eighty percent).

At the same time, I counsel humility in the construction of any probabilistic model of inciting speech used to forecast real-world events. These are not the experimental conditions of the laboratory. Statistical indicators are assembled by researchers making subjective decisions,[34] and, as Ashworth and Zedner (2014:119) caution, calculating risk is "a political construct defined by priorities of public policy, political climate, and changes in official views about the prevailing threats to public safety."

That said, the speech crimes model presented above represents an advance on the decision-making framework presently employed by international prosecutors, who tend to rely on vague and impressionistic

---

[32] For instance, Expectancy Value Theory predicts that audience behavior will be influenced by the expectation of future success and rewards (Fishbein 1967; Fishbein and Ajzen 1974; Wigfield and Eccles 2000). These expectations may include economic or material gain, and Kalyvas (2006:351) observes that during civil wars, average people often opportunistically take advantage of the vacuum of state authority to exact revenge as well as to appropriate their neighbor's assets.

[33] I refer here to the obligations of the 168 state parties to the International Covenant on Civil and Political Rights, which at Article 20 states: "1. Any propaganda for war shall be prohibited by law. 2. Any advocacy of national, racial or religious hatred that constitutes incitement to discrimination, hostility or violence shall be prohibited by law."

[34] See Merry et al. (2015) for an anthropological critique of global social indicators.

hunches about the effects of a speaker's words in a deteriorating security situation. The matrix has several advantages over the present set of established conventions at international criminal tribunals. Firstly, it quantifies and measures the conditions of uptake of inciting speech, a process that reduces (but does not eliminate) mere subjective opinion. Secondly, it grounds its indicators in peer-reviewed social science research on persuasion. It explicitly sets out its terms and criteria, permitting external review by defense attorneys and pretrial judges in international tribunals, as well as by social scientists studying denigrating and inciting speech. The aim of the matrix proposed here is to reduce the level of ambiguity and doubt about assessments of speech and risk: insofar as it achieves this aim, it represents an improvement on standard practice.

8.4 INFELICITOUS MODES OF LIABILITY FOR COMPLETED SPEECH CRIMES: CO-PERPETRATION, JCE, INSTIGATING/INDUCING AND SOLICITING

Regulating speech in accordance with the international legal framework of inchoate speech crimes is preferable to prosecuting completed crimes for reasons already provided at various points in the argument. Yet international prosecutors may have little choice but to charge speakers under one or more theories of liability for completed crimes, given the limited scope of existing inchoate speech crimes in international criminal law, and given that the international penal response to mass atrocities may only begin after a peace agreement is signed. These modes of liability in international criminal law featured in the causation discussion in Chapter 3, and the ones that are most relevant for speech acts are: perpetration/co-perpetration, instigating/inducing, ordering and aiding and abetting crimes against humanity and genocide, and disseminating propaganda as part of a joint criminal enterprise.[35]

In deciding which are the most appropriate for speech crimes in a context of crimes against humanity, genocide and/or war crimes, several questions arise. A pragmatic question frequently asked by international prosecutors is, which form of criminal responsibility is most likely to lead to a conviction? Additionally, we could ask which forms of

---

[35] For reasons of scope and to focus on distinct and well-defined modes of liability, I have not included in this discussion the residual form of responsibility listed in Article 25(3)(d) that holds liable an individual who "in any other way" contributes to the commission of an ICC crime.

liability most closely correspond to social science findings regarding how inciting speech operates in the context of political violence and armed conflict. And finally, the overall question guiding this book is, how can recent social science findings better inform trials at international tribunals?

The first matter to resolve is whether inciting speech acts can fulfill the highest form of criminal responsibility – that of perpetration or co-perpetration. Article 25(3)(a) of the ICC Statute holds criminally liable any person who commits a crime listed in the Statute, "whether as an individual, jointly with another or through another person, regardless of whether that other person is criminally responsible." In *Lubanga*, the Pre-Trial Chamber judges indicated that the *actus reus* element for co-perpetrating according to Article 25(3)(a) necessitates a "coordinated essential contribution made by each co-perpetrator resulting in the realisation of the objective elements of the crime" and this view was upheld in the Trial Chamber and Appeals Chamber judgments.[36]

A threshold of "essential contribution" for perpetration/co-perpetration implies *sine qua non* causation, where an act is a necessary and sufficient cause of the offence. Requiring that the prosecution prove that but for act A, offence B would not have happened is a very high bar of causality, and Judge Adrian Fulford strenuously argued in *Lubanga* that the Trial Chamber's test of essential contribution is "unrealistic and artificial,"[37] and "imposes an unnecessary and unfair burden on the prosecution."[38] Many non-speech physical acts will not attain this elevated degree of contribution. Given the skepticism about the efficacy of speech acts often found in criminal courts, most utterances will fall short of the threshold of constituting an essential (but-for) contribution to the commission of crimes. We can safely assume that the mode of liability of perpetration or co-perpetration included in Article 25(3)(a) of the ICC Statute will not be appropriate for most inciting speakers.

Turning to other modes of liability, joint criminal enterprise (JCE) is quite relevant for speech crimes because fulfilling its *actus reus* elements

---

[36] See *Lubanga* PTC "Decision on Confirmation of Charges Pre-Trial Chamber" (29 January 2007), §346, which sets out the elements of the crime of co-perpetration. *Lubanga* TC §1018, §§1271–2 and Lubanga AC §7 confirm the Pre-Trial Chamber's interpretation of essential contribution.

[37] *Lubanga* TC, Separate Opinion of Judge Adrian Fulford, §17.

[38] *Lubanga* TC, Fulford Opinion, §3.

depends less on evidence of direct causation of crimes and because with JCE, the participation of the accused can be only one element of a collectively orchestrated criminal enterprise. At the ICTY, several military and political actors were successfully prosecuted for making a significant contribution to a joint criminal enterprise by "disseminating propaganda" in the media.[39] Using JCE, international tribunals accurately construed the role of political leaders and propagandists who participated in a collective effort to commit widespread or systematic attacks on a civilian population such as forcible deportation from a territory. Such speakers significantly contributed to a JCE by encouraging others to participate in a common plan to commit crimes against humanity.

For instance, Milan Babić was the first President of the Republic of Serbian Krajina in 1991–2, a self-proclaimed (and now disbanded) Serbian state within Croatia, who "made ethnically based inflammatory speeches during public events and in the media that added to the atmosphere of fear and hatred amongst Serbs living in Croatia and convinced them that they could only be safe in a state of their own."[40] The accused's speeches represented compelling evidence of his participation in a joint criminal enterprise to commit crimes against humanity against Croats.[41] Another accused, Milan Gvero, Assistant Commander for Morale of the Bosnian Serb Army, was convicted of making a significant contribution to a joint criminal enterprise to forcibly remove women, children and elderly non-Serbs from Srebrenica and Žepa in July 1995 by prompting and disseminating false information, threats and propaganda (under Article 5(i) of the ICTY Statute):[42] "The Trial Chamber is of the view that Gvero, with his detailed knowledge of the strategic aim to remove the Bosnian Muslim population from the enclaves, made a significant contribution to the common purpose of the JCE through his efforts to delay and block international protective intervention."[43]

Most prominently, former Bosnian Serb President Radovan Karadžić was found guilty in 2016 of ten counts of genocide, war crimes and

---

[39] Milan Gvero (in *Popović et al.* TC) and Radovan Karadžić. [40] *Babić* TC §24(g).
[41] *Babić* TC §57.
[42] "The Trial Chamber is satisfied that by disseminating false information and issuing a serious threat, whether effective or not in the end, Gvero made a contribution to the JCE which by its nature cannot be classified as other than significant" (*Popović et al.* TC §1820). At §1826, *Popović* found Gvero guilty of "inhumane acts (forcible transfer) as a crime against humanity punishable under Article 5(i) of the Statute."
[43] *Popović* TC §1822. Milan Gvero died before the 2015 Appeals Chamber judgment.

crimes against humanity. His crimes included "disseminating propaganda" to Bosnian Serbs in an orchestrated effort to heighten their fear and hatred of non-Serbs. Karadžić's speeches and official propaganda made a significant contribution to an overarching JCE that had as its objective the permanent removal of Bosnian Muslims and Bosnian Croats from Bosnian Serb-claimed territory.[44] Appropriately, the Trial Chamber did not assert that Karadžić's speeches caused material perpetrators to commit crimes, but only expressed his intentionality to sew fear and hatred. That is, the tribunal laid emphasis on locutions and illocutions rather than perlocutions. Coming as they did from the office of the President, Karadžić's utterances extended a common purpose to persecute non-Serbs, and advanced the overall criminal program of creating an ethnically homogenous state:

> The Chamber finds that this rhetoric was used by the Accused to engender fear and hatred of Bosnian Muslims and Bosnian Croats and had the effect of exacerbating ethnic divisions and tensions in BiH [Bosnia and Herzegovina]. The Accused used fear and hatred to promote the historical territorial claims of the Bosnian Serbs and to garner support for the idea of creating a largely ethnically homogeneous Bosnian Serb state on this land ... The Chamber finds that these speeches and statements went beyond mere rhetoric and formed a core element in the policies and plans developed by the Accused and the Bosnian Serb leadership.[45]

The Trial Chamber referenced the speeches of the accused at several points in the judgment, and perhaps more than one might expect in a decision that dealt with much weightier crimes such as genocide. The judgment cited Karadžić's speeches because of the contribution they made to an overarching JCE by conjuring up historical grievances and promoting an ideology of ethnic separation. Propelled by an extreme nationalist ideology, the Bosnian Serb President, along with other members of the JCE, utilized the state institutions at his disposal to create an ethnically homogeneous territory under his control.[46] Such a common plan required a common ideology, and Karadžić proclaimed his plan in extreme nationalist speeches to both the masses and the elite. The Trial Chamber prudently did not refer to a causal nexus between specific words and specific criminal acts, but instead highlighted the way in which

---

[44] *Karadžić* TC §§3470–1. [45] *Karadžić* TC §§3486–7. [46] *Karadžić* TC §2598.

Figure 8.1 Radovan Karadžić at his initial appearance in court, 2008
Credit: Courtesy of the UN International Criminal Tribunal for the Former Yugoslavia

Karadžić's speeches created "a climate of impunity for criminal acts committed against non-Serbs."[47] By referring to a "climate of impunity," the Trial Chamber captured the macro-causal or conditioning effects of speech and demonstrated the relevance of joint criminal enterprise as a form of liability that included the contribution of incitement to a wider criminal common plan.

As a counterexample, there has also been one prominent acquittal of a politician for JCE, Vojislav Šešelj, who was accused of contributing to a JCE to forcibly displace a civilian population based on his speeches that recruited volunteers to the cause and incited them to deport and commit violent acts against non-Serbs. The Trial Chamber majority found that most of Šešelj's speeches merely aided the war effort, which was not in itself a crime. The majority found that even though some of the speeches did engender hatred and made explicit calls for the deportation of non-Serbs, the accused's exhortations were not uttered in a context of a widespread or systematic attack on a civilian

---

[47] *Karadžić* TC §3514.

population.[48] Since there was no pre-existing JCE to deport Croats in the Vojvodina region of northern Serbia, Šešelj's rhetoric could not have made a significant contribution to a JCE. However, given the eccentricity of the Trial Chamber judgment in *Šešelj* (on appeal at the time of writing), it would be imprudent to draw any general deductions from it regarding the applicability of JCE to speech crimes.

Overall, JCE as an enhanced form of complicity has its advantages as a theory of criminal liability. Sharing attributes with common law categories of conspiracy and aiding and abetting,[49] JCE is a broad net to ensnare those individuals who make contributions that do not rise to the level of *sine qua non*, but still participate in a criminal enterprise. International criminal law has been criticized for its emphasis on individual criminal responsibility,[50] and JCE represents international law's attempt to recognize the collective nature of criminality during armed conflict and state-sponsored genocide.

Despite its utility, JCE is now receding from view as the ICTY completes its last trials. Charged in the majority of indictments at the ICTY from the 1999 *Tadić* Appeals judgment onwards, JCE has only had a variable applicability at other international criminal tribunals. The concept had limited application at the ICTR, where it never achieved general legitimacy or widespread application, and was included in only sixteen percent of the indictments.[51] The various hybrid international tribunals each handled JCE differently. The Special Tribunal for Lebanon and the Special Court for Sierra Leone largely embraced JCE,[52] the Extraordinary Chambers in the Courts of Cambodia only applied it in part.[53]

When considering the future of JCE in international trials, it is essential to acknowledge that JCE was not included as a mode of liability in Article 25 (Individual Criminal Responsibility) of the

---

[48] *Šešelj* TC §195.

[49] See *Tadić* AC §229 on the distinction between JCE and aiding and abetting.

[50] Clarke (2009:55) argues that the idea of individual criminal responsibility is little more than a western liberalist notion that turns our attention away from structural causes of violence.

[51] Van Sliedregt (2012:143). See, for example, the discussion at the ICTR in *Kayishema and Ruzindana* AC at §§193–4 which upheld Ruzindana's conviction for JCE to commit genocide. Five other ICTR cases that applied JCE are: *Ntakuritimana, Karemera, Mpambara, Rwamakuba* and *Simba*.

[52] On 26 October 2009, the Appeals Chamber of the Special Court for Sierra Leone upheld the Trial Chamber convictions for Issa Sesay, Morris Kallon and Augustine Gbao for their participation in a joint criminal enterprise to commit war crimes and crimes against humanity under Article 6(1) and (3) of the Statute of the SCSL (*Sesay, Kallon and Gbao*, AC §§286–96).

[53] See "Decision on the Applicability of Joint Criminal Enterprise," Case File.: 002/19–09-2007/ ECCC/TC 12 September 2011.

ICC Statute, now the gold standard of international criminal law. The ICC replaced JCE with the theory of "co-perpetration" at Article 25(3)(a) to refer to the actions of two or more persons who devise a common plan to commit a crime listed in the Statute. As noted previously, a conviction for co-perpetration demands that each accused makes a "coordinated essential contribution."[54] The standard of essential, or *sine qua non*, causation is likely to rule out propagandists and speechifying politicians, since it is extraordinarily difficult to prove that the crime would not have been committed without the causal contribution of their performative utterances. The pre-eminence of the ICC Statute in international criminal law and the highly statutory and rule-bound nature of the ICC with its hierarchy of sources (The Statute, the Elements of Crimes and the Rules Procedure and Evidence) means that an ICC Pre-Trial Chamber is highly unlikely to confirm charges of JCE against an accused.[55]

Therefore, prosecutors might more profitably concentrate on other modes of liability for completed crimes listed in Article 25 of the Rome Statute. These are most likely to be applied in future indictments against individuals who encourage others to attack members of protected groups, namely: inducing/instigating, soliciting, ordering, and aiding and abetting.[56]

"Instigating" in the ICTR and ICTY Statutes and jurisprudence, and "inducing" (Article 25(3)(c) of the ICC Statute) are synonymous in international criminal law, and the two are generally seen as "interchangeable" by legal theorists such as Van Sliedregt (2012:108). Both share the same conceptual kernel that criminal liability is incurred when the accused prompts another person to commit an offence.[57] One of the enduring themes of this book is that direct causation is exceedingly hard to demonstrate beyond a reasonable doubt in cases where the accused is charged with instigating or inducing on the basis of his/her speech acts.

---

[54] *Lubanga* TC §923.

[55] See Van Sliedregt (2012:13) on the straightjacketed nature of the ICC, and the critiques of its "rigid code" that restricts judicial discretion and may contribute to the fragmentation of international criminal law.

[56] Inducing and ordering are listed under Article 25(3)(b): "In accordance with this Statute, a person shall be criminally responsible and liable for punishment for a crime within the jurisdiction of the Court if that person orders, solicits or induces the commission of such a crime which in fact occurs or is attempted," and Article 25(3)(c) holds a person responsible if that person "for the purpose of facilitating the commission of such a crime, aids, abets or otherwise assists in its commission or its attempted commission, including providing the means for its commission."

[57] *Kordić and Čerkez* AC §27; *Kvočka et al.* TC §252.

Exhibit A is the collapse of the prosecution cases against Mbarushimana, Ruto and Sang at the ICC and the acquittal of Šešelj for instigating crimes against humanity at the ICTY. As discussed in Chapter 2, even in *Nahimana* (or the Media Trial at the ICTR), the high-water mark of criminalizing speech crimes in international criminal law, the accused was acquitted of instigating genocide by the Appeals Chamber for lack of evidence that concretely and directly linked his specific speeches to specific offences. The conviction of Nahimana for the inchoate crime of inciting genocide, however, was upheld, showing how, even when the same fact pattern is presented to the court, the causation element can scupper the prosecution's case for instigation. At the ICC, all the signs indicate that it will maintain the direct causation element, and require that the instigator/inducer's speech acts have a "direct effect" on the commission or attempted commission of the crime.[58]

Another hurdle is the relatively prohibitive threshold of causation for instigating that demands that the speaker made a "substantial contribution" to the commission of a crime. This is a higher level of causation than required for JCE and other modes of liability such as aiding and abetting.[59] Additionally, social science research is seldom of great assistance in proving instigation, since it hardly ever supports a finding of direct causation beyond a reasonable doubt, and at the level of "substantial contribution" that is needed to convince the trier of fact. The scale of causation is partly at issue here. Social science research investigates the individual psychological effects of inciting speech (micro-causation), and the pervasive changes in societal or cultural conditions (macro-causation), but does not have as much to say about the middle ground of causation (a particular speaker at a certain election rally) that is the concern of an international criminal tribunal.

What kind of evidence of causation, then, might satisfy an international tribunal that an individual instigated another person to commit proscribed acts? As argued in Chapter 5, international courts need to move away from their reliance on colorful metaphors and instead delineate a clear chain of causation that commences with the criminal intention of the speaker, focuses on the illocutionary aspects of the utterances of the speaker, examines whether the listener hears,

---

[58] *Ntaganda* PTC Decision on the Confirmation of Charges, ICC-01/04–02/06, 9 June 2014, §153.
[59] Nevertheless, for instigating, it should be noted that the act of the accused "need not be a *conditio sine qua non*" of the commission of the crime (*Blaškić* TC §270).

understands and processes that intentionality as the speaker intended and whether that intentionality becomes the reason for criminal actions of the listener, and then establishes that the listener became a material perpetrator when he or she executed and completed the crime that the speaker intended.

Circumstantial evidence – that general offences were committed according to a particular pattern of activity and temporality after a specific speech act – does not seem to be enough to convince international judges who are often reticent to impinge on freedom of speech norms. Nor was the Trial Chamber convinced by the prosecution's argument in Šešelj that the accused's speeches hastened the deportation of Croats, even though accelerating an adverse result is an accepted test for causation in many domestic criminal jurisdictions.[60] International courts want to identify an inexorable chain of mental causation in which the speech act is a truly causal factor in a sequence that culminates in the offence. Social science expert evidence and testimony has thus far been of limited utility in proving the direct causation element required for instigation.

Followers of the speaker, or insiders, who can reliably testify about how they were motivated to action by the speaker represent the ideal evidence to prove instigation. It has not been challenging for the prosecution to identify those individuals, but retaining them in the trial is another matter. In Ruto and Sang and Šešelj, the prosecution started with a coterie of former devotees willing to give written depositions and testify in court about how they were moved to act violently by the speaker's exhortations. Over the course of the trial, however, insider witnesses have frequently succumbed to bribery and intimidation. As a logistical matter, international tribunals have not demonstrated that they possess the coercive institutional capacity to protect witnesses. In the absence of insiders, the prosecution must mount a circumstantial case that relies on the chronology of events to prove causality, and as we saw in Šešelj, a Trial Chamber can remain unconvinced by this case theory.

These perennial shortcomings do not justify, however, abandoning the categories of instigating and inducing altogether. Innovative social science methods could potentially offer dispositive evidence about the mental states of insiders and give substance to the mens rea elements of instigation. ICTY linguist Predrag Dojčinović (2012:71) agrees that the

---

[60] In US criminal law, see Oxendine v. State 528 A.2d 870 (Del. 1987).

273

existing evidential approach to inciting speech at international tribunals is inadequate. Drawing from recent studies in cognitive linguistics and the work of John Searle, Dojčinović develops a pioneering model in which some speakers who instigate have a unique and documentable "mental fingerprint" that demonstrates the link between the instigator and the instigated. The concept of a "mental fingerprint" denotes a distinctive phrase or expression that is devised and articulated by the accused and then spreads throughout the joint criminal enterprise.[61]

For instance, the Serb nationalist Vojislav Šešelj coined the ultranationalist term the "Karlobag–Ogulin–Karlovac–Virovitica (KOKV) line" to lay claim to highly contested Serb territory in Croatia.[62] This terminology was used solely by the accused and his followers (the "Šešeljevci") in the first instance. The Prosecution's Closing Brief in Šešelj quotes a drunken Serb paramilitary after the fall of Vukovar in 1991 referring to the KOKV line thus "War will be over when we have our limits – Karlobag, Karlovac, Ogulin, Virovitica. All place(s) where Serbian people live must be free, you know. We must clean up with the Croatians."[63] Dojčinović (2012:95) claims that documenting the transmission and circulation between a leader and his followers of a unique mental concept such as the KOKV line pinpoints the "evidentiary feedback loop" that connects the instigator and the instigated. This establishes the pattern of circular and reinforcing causation that institutional economists such as Myrdal identified decades ago when studying how social phenomena such as poverty and racism reinforced one another.

By this method, the mental state of the criminal agent could be cognitively "fingerprinted," providing evidence of mental causation and shared criminal intent in a joint criminal enterprise. Even though this evidence did not persuade the majority in the Šešelj judgment,[64] Nuremberg prosecutors adopted something akin to a "mental fingerprint" approach in the trial brief they prepared to argue for Julius Streicher's criminal liability, noting that "three speeches given by Streicher 'gave birth to the watchword which, 14 years later, was to become the official policy of the Nazi Government – the Annihilation

---

[61] Dojčinović (2012:95–6).   [62] Prosecution's Closing Brief, Šešelj, §§25–7.
[63] Prosecution's Closing Brief, Šešelj, §166.; Prosecution Exhibit No. P00057.
[64] Jugement, Šešelj (IT-03-67-T), La Chambre de Première Instance, 31 mars 2016. Judge Lattanzi, in her extensive dissenting opinion in Šešelj, found the prosecution's evidence of guilt compelling and dispositive.

of the Jews.' These speeches were: (1) in Nurnberg, 23 Nov. 1932, (2) in the Bavarian Diet, 20 Nov. 1924, and (3) in Nurnberg, 3 April 1925."[65] That is, Streicher invented the phrase "the Annihilation of the Jews," he broadcast it widely and it came to be an ideological cornerstone of the Nazi program to exterminate the Jews. Dojčinović's "mental fingerprint" analysis may establish proof of the unconscious effects and circulation of a politician's idiosyncratic speech patterns and terminology and could reinforce the often-unsteady testimony of insiders.

Establishing that the speaker's utterances contributed to the creation of a common criminal intentionality raises another impediment that has not been adequately dealt with by international criminal law, and that is the way that individual agency disrupts direct mental causation. Instigation does not require that the speaker enjoy a position of power and authority over the listener, and can command the listener's obedience. Thus, the speech act occurs in a context that may not result in uptake on the part of the listener. The speaker's perlocutions are therefore not like a series of billiard balls striking one another, since in the case of humans and instigating speakers, the individual components in the causal sequence have the capacity to think for themselves. When the speaker does not occupy a position of superior or command responsibility, the capacity for self-directed decision-making on the part of the listener means that mental causation is a highly complex phenomenon.

In such instances, criminal courts are disinclined to attribute responsibility to the speaker.[66] The expression "novus actus interveniens" in criminal law refers to how volitional acts of agents interrupt the chain of causation, introduce an intervening factor and activate a new sequence of causation.[67] Courts have found that principal ownership (and therefore criminal responsibility) resides with the listener, even in situations where the instigator has a psychological influence over the listener. As set out in Chapter 5, criminal law assumes that individuals are self-governing unless there is convincing evidence of physical compulsion, deceit or threat. The locus of decision-making resides within each of us, and self-governing individuals cannot evade punishment simply because they were persuaded by another person to commit an offence.

---

[65] Thomas J. Dodd, Trial Brief Concerning Streicher, 30 April 1946, University of Connecticut: Archives & Special Collections at the Thomas J. Dodd Research Center, http://archives.lib .uconn.edu/islandora/object/20002%3A1943#page/1/mode/2up.

[66] Hart and Honoré (1985:328–9) cite a case where an individual persuaded his mother to hang herself, but the criminal court held that he had not committed murder or attempted murder because there was no element of physical compulsion or threatening behavior.

[67] Williams (1989:391).

If the listener is not some way coerced or compelled, and the option exists to simply walk away and foreswear the crime being instigated/induced, then the decision to heed the listener is in large part their choice. Even if they are convinced by the speaker of the imperative to undertake a criminal act, they may still not decide to undertake it, including for selfish or immoral reasons, e.g., because the chances of being caught are too high. If they decide to commit an offence based on a criminal solicitation, then the responsibility for committing the offence is shared between the listener/actor and the instigator, according to the contextual circumstances in which the utterance took place. The principal perpetrator's choice to act constitutes an intervening cause that supplants and supersedes all previous causes.[68] The likely presence of intervening factors in most contexts of instigating/inducing represents a serious challenge to any prosecution team seeking to demonstrate that the instigator contributed to the offence at the level of direct causation needed to convict.

If we add to these concerns a profound lack of an international consensus on the prior question of whether the law ought to be regulating political speech in the first place, there are many inordinately high barriers to proving instigation at an international criminal tribunal. Thus, instigating and inducing should be charged as modes of liability very sparingly and under exacting circumstances. Such charges only make sense when the insider testimony is both overwhelmingly credible and compelling (i.e., where such evidence links specific speech acts causally to specific crimes) and when insider witnesses and their families can be protected from the inevitable onslaught of intimidation and pressure to recant their testimony.[69] That these propitious conditions will exist is likely to be the exception rather than the rule.

Finally, Article 25(3)(b) of the ICC Statute lists "soliciting" as an accessorial mode of liability alongside "inducing." In the United States, solicitation is an inchoate crime where the crime is the act itself of soliciting another person to commit a sufficiently grave offence (such as murder or grand larceny).[70] If soliciting were an inchoate crime at the ICC, then it could plausibly apply to speech acts that ask or entice others to commit an offence, regardless of whether they act upon the

---

[68] Moore (2009:229 *et passim*) opposes this view of intervening causes and instigation on philosophical grounds. His argument is elegant and persuasive, but I am also persuaded of the fact that, in practice, a majority of international criminal judges (and many domestic criminal judges) adopt the more conventional position outlined here regarding individual criminal responsibility, personal decision making and intervening causes.

[69] This implies that they and their families are no longer living in the countries concerned.

[70] Model Penal Code §5.02 Criminal Solicitation.

solicitation. Framed this way, soliciting would be a valuable way of closing the "accountability gap" between inciting genocide and hate speech as a form of persecution as a crime against humanity. Yet, alas, this is not the case at the ICC, since Article 25(3)(b) provides that the crime being solicited "in fact occurs or is attempted." International law scholars such as Jackson (2015:67) and Van Sliedregt (2012:107) view solicitation as a mode of liability for completed or attempted crimes that is equivalent to instigation and inducing, and therefore solicitation is not an inchoate crime. If this is the case, then "soliciting" suffers from the same shortcomings previously identified for instigation as a mode of liability.

8.5 FELICITOUS MODES OF LIABILITY FOR COMPLETED SPEECH CRIMES I: ORDERING

Many modes of liability in international criminal law do not straight-forwardly apply to speakers who promulgate hate speech or call for public violence. For a variety of reasons, joint criminal enterprise, instigating/inducing, and soliciting all have limited applicability. However, there are two forms of liability for completed crimes that are appropriate for speech crimes cases: ordering and complicity.

This assertion requires clarification as ICC case law has at times mistakenly combined the three modes of liability in Article 25(3)(b) in statements such as: "'ordering', 'soliciting' and 'inducing' in essence fall into a broader category of 'instigating' or 'prompting another person to commit a crime.'"[71] As we have just seen, soliciting, instigating and inducing do indeed share elements. However, ordering as a form of criminal responsibility possesses distinctive attributes that make it particularly germane to situations where the speaker and listener are in a superior–subordinate relationship.

Ordering as a mode of criminal responsibility is unique to international criminal law and can be traced back to the Nuremberg trials.[72] Ordering is distinctive in that it requires, at a minimum, a hierarchical relationship of authority between speaker and audience.[73] The

---

[71] ICC Pre-Trial Chamber I, "Decision on the Confirmation of Charges Against Laurent Gbagbo", 12 June 2014, ICC-02/11–01/11–656-Red, §243.
[72] Van Sliedregt (2012:105) supplies a useful history of ordering as a form of criminal responsibility in international criminal law.
[73] See *Blaškić* TC §474, §601 and *Gacumbitsi* AC §§181–2 on the relevance of authority in the concept of ordering. At the ICC, the Pre-Trial Chamber in *Ntaganda* confirmed that the person ordering must be in a position of authority [Decision on the Confirmation of Charges, §145].

International Law Commission's 1996 Draft Criminal Code states, "This principle of criminal responsibility applies to an individual who is in a position of authority and uses his authority to compel another individual to commit a crime."[74] The authority element was confirmed by the ICTY Appeals Chamber thus, "[T]he *actus reus* of ordering requires that a person in a position of authority instruct another to commit an offence." The authority to order may be *de facto* as well as *de jure*,[75] and a formal superior–subordinate relationship is not an element of the crime.

Subsequent jurisprudence has confirmed that it is sufficient that the accused possess the authority to order the commission of an offence.[76] Case law at the ICC has reinforced this interpretation: "the elements of 'ordering' overlap with those applicable to 'soliciting' and 'inducing,' with the exception of the requirement of a position of authority held by the person vis-à-vis the perpetrator(s) of the crime, which is particular to 'ordering' and is not a necessary element of 'soliciting' or 'inducing'."[77] Inducing, soliciting and instigating can refer to a speaker acting in a non-official capacity in a horizontal peer–peer relationship. At the ICC, instigators/solicitors/inducers need not have the authority to order the commission of an offence, nor stand in a superior–subordinate relationship with the material perpetrator. Unlike the superior officer who issues an order, the instigator/inducer must rely primarily on their personal skills of persuasion.

Construed thus, ordering as a mode of liability resolves some of the fundamental problems of intention and mental causation in speech crimes identified in Chapters 3 and 5. Notably, it addresses what Searle (1983:115) calls "agent causation" within a more structured and contained causal field.[78] In his groundbreaking paper "Causes and Conditions," philosopher John Mackie (1965:248–9) developed the term "causal field" to describe the conditions that surround, and may

---

See Jackson (2015:68) for a discussion of the relationship of authority between the person issuing the order and the principal perpetrator in international criminal law.

[74] International Law Commission (1996) *Draft Code of Crimes Against the Peace and Security of Mankind*, Article 2 ("Individual Responsibility"), *Commentary*, §8.

[75] *Boškoski and Tarčulovski* AC §160. *De facto* control is discussed at §163.

[76] *Brđanin* TC §270 and *Gacumbitsi* AC §182.

[77] ICC Pre-Trial Chamber II, "Decision on the Prosecutor's Application under Article 58", 13 July 2012, ICC-01/04–01/12–1-Red, §63; *Ibid.*, "Decision Pursuant to Article 61(7)(a) and (b) of the Rome Statute on the Charges of the Prosecutor Against Bosco Ntaganda", 9 June 2014, ICC-01/04–02/06–309, §145, §153.

[78] To remind the reader, agent causation occurs between agents who possess intentionality and is opposed to "event causation" in the material-object world.

contribute to or otherwise influence, singular causal events. Mackie gives the example of an individual who contracts flu at a time when there are influenza viruses circulating in a social environment. Here, the causal field refers to "human beings in conditions where influenza viruses are present."[79] Mackie's term can help us understand one element of the distinction the law makes between instigating and ordering. Instigating occurs in a weak causal field where the singular event is surrounded by only weakly contributing conditions, whereas ordering takes place in a strong causal field of institutional (often military) authority. The strong causal field that is usually present when an order is issued goes a significant way towards explaining whether and how mental causation occurs and therefore it usually resolves the *mens rea* element in any given trial.

International criminal law requires that an order issued by a superior have a "direct and substantial effect" on the commission of the offence.[80] When orders are issued by a commanding military officer, the mechanistic model of direct, singular and unmediated mental causation that criminal courts seek is often (although not always) fulfilled. First, the criminal intention is contained within the order itself, for instance, when a commanding officer declares that no quarter will be given.[81] When an order is issued, it is not a mystery how and why agent causation has occurred: the command structure of the military ensures that the intention of a commanding officer who issues an order will become the intention of the subordinate. In a strong causal field, it is assumed by a court that the actions of a military unit will conform to the intentions of the commanding officer, and, if not, then the commander must take punitive, disciplinary measures to restore order. For this reason, at the ICC, Article 28(a) concentrates criminal responsibility at the top of the chain of command:

> A military commander or person effectively acting as a military commander shall be criminally responsible for crimes within the jurisdiction of the Court committed by forces under his or her effective command and control, or effective authority and control as the case may be, as a result of his or her failure to exercise control properly over such forces.[82]

---

[79] Mackie (1965:249).   [80] *Kamuhanda* AC §75; *Milutinović* TC §88.

[81] At the ICC, Article 8 (2)(b)(xii) "War crime of denying quarter" has as its first element: "The perpetrator declared or ordered that there shall be no survivors."

[82] Also requiring that (i) That military commander or person either knew or, owing to the circumstances at the time, should have known that the forces were committing or about to commit such crimes; and (ii) That military commander or person failed to take all necessary

Military discipline and an ethos of obedience usually ensures that an order is complied with and the directness element is fulfilled, even if the order is unlawful.[83] As social science researchers Kelman (1973) and Milgram (1974) demonstrated, ordinary people typically feel obligated to obey a command from an authority figure, whether or not the order conforms with their personal preferences. The inherent "gappiness" of mental causation that bedevils instigating, inducing and soliciting, and creates uncertainty as to whether the speech act in question directly caused the offence (or whether there was an intervening factor), applies less to instances of ordering, since orders are issued in a strong causal field where the subordinate is generally unable to exercise autonomous moral choice. As Jackson (2015:68) affirms, "Ordering does not rest on persuasion but on command." As a result, the responsibility of lower-ranking soldiers for following an order is greatly diminished (although not entirely extinguished) in the strong causal field of military discipline, and primary responsibility for the crime resides with the speaker.

Formally, instigating does not require a hierarchical relationship of authority, but in practice the precedent-setting cases of instigating at the ICTY and ICTR have either been of military commanders (Blaškić, Čerkez) or political leaders who wield substantial military and political authority (Kordić, Gacumbitsi). That is, despite the formal properties set out earlier, international tribunals have tended to uphold the charge of instigation only in the strong causal field of military authority rather than the weak causal field of a radio presenter or demagogue who simply addresses a wider public over whom they exert little authority. In this way, instigation is less a mode of liability for propagandists than it is an adjunct mode of liability that reiterates the charge of ordering. Indeed, many defendants convicted of instigating at international tribunals are also convicted of ordering.

Compulsion, not autonomous agency, is at the core of a hierarchical structure of military command and control. Nowhere was this more evident than in the unfortunate ICTY case of Dražen Erdemović, a

---

and reasonable measures within his or her power to prevent or repress their commission or to submit the matter to the competent authorities for investigation and prosecution.

[83] At the ICC, Article 33 on "Superior orders and prescription of law" states that: 1. The fact that a crime within the jurisdiction of the Court has been committed by a person pursuant to an order of a Government or of a superior, whether military or civilian, shall not relieve that person of criminal responsibility unless: (a) The person was under a legal obligation to obey orders of the Government or the superior in question; (b) The person did not know that the order was unlawful; and (c) The order was not manifestly unlawful. 2. For the purposes of this article, orders to commit genocide or crimes against humanity are manifestly unlawful.

low-ranking soldier who participated in the genocidal massacre of Bosniak Muslims at Srebrenica in 1995. An ethnic Bosnian Croat, he joined the Bosnian Serb Army (VRS) which became an instrument of Bosnian Serb territorial aims and the persecution of non-Serbs.[84] A pacifist, he did not support the war, and joined to provide for his new family. Erdemović requested a noncombat desk position and was assigned to the 10th Sabotage Detachment of the Bosnian Serb Army. His unit was generally stationed away from the front lines. However, on 16 July 1995, the unit was suddenly swept into the worst crime of the war in Bosnia. That morning, Erdemović and seven members of his detachment were ordered to leave their base and go to the Pilica farm near Zvornik, where buses arrived carrying Bosnian Muslim men who had surrendered to, or been captured by, the VRS armed led by Ratko Mladić at Srebrenica.

Upon their arrival, hundreds of unarmed prisoners were led to a field and lined up with their backs to a firing squad. The commanding officer issued an order to shoot the prisoners. Dražan Erdemović balked at the order, imploring his peers and superior officer to desist, and asking, "Are you normal? Do you know what you are doing?" They replied, "If you are sorry for them, stand up, line up with them and we will kill you too."[85] He demurred, thinking of his wife and nine-month-old son and personally shot about seventy persons.[86] He claimed he tried to save one man's life, but his commanding officer insisted that there be no witnesses. Filled with remorse, he later confessed his actions to an ABC reporter and voluntarily surrendered to the ICTY.

Prosecutors did not dispute the accused's account of events. Erdemović assisted their investigations into the genocide at Srebrenica by informing them in detail about a site of mass murder. After two trials, the Trial Chamber sentenced him to five years' imprisonment, a clear recognition of his diminished capacity for autonomous agency and therefore individual criminal responsibility.[87] My central point about mental causation is illustrated in the Erdemović case. In a strong causal field where an order is issued by a superior officer in a military command and control structure, it is obvious where a subordinate's criminal intention originated from. Establishing that the order from his commanding officer to shoot prisoners directly influenced Erdemović's criminal intentions and actions was a relatively straightforward matter for the tribunal.

---

[84] Chiesa (2008) discusses the duress defense in *Erdemović* and international cirmina law.
[85] *Erdemović* TC §14. [86] *Erdemović* TC §15. [87] *Erdemović* TC §23.

8.6 FELICITOUS MODES OF LIABILITY FOR COMPLETED SPEECH CRIMES II: AIDING AND ABETTING

> Principals cause, accomplices encourage (or otherwise influence) or help.
> Glanville Williams (1989:398)

Complicity is one of the most complex and theoretically demanding forms of criminal responsibility and, according to James Stewart (2013:3), "poses a set of beautiful conceptual problems." I cannot do justice here to all the intricate debates on this subject, and refer the reader to recent literature on this vicarious theory of responsibility.[88] In the discussion that follows, my aim is more modest – to assess the applicability of accessorial liability to international speech crimes.

Complicity, or participation in a criminal act as an accomplice,[89] makes it possible to hold criminally liable those who help another person to commit an offence but are not the principal material perpetrator and whose acts may not directly cause the offence. Here, "help" can refer to actions, omissions, practical assistance or simply moral encouragement.[90] Since the essence of accomplice liability lies in the assistance and encouragement provided to others, this criminal law theory is the most relevant for propagandists, who are often supportive accomplices rather than direct instigators of crimes. Accomplice liability was the type of criminal responsibility favored by the prosecution and judges at Nuremberg in *Streicher*, and there are good reasons to follow it. Of all the modes of liability in international criminal law, complicity most closely approximates social science models of inciting speech that situate it within an array of multiple and concurrent causal factors. In sum, complicity is the goldilocks category of criminal responsibility for rogue politicians, media personalities and others who incite others to commit crimes, but who may not hold elected office or a position of command responsibility in the military.

Complicity is usually rendered in the statutes of international criminal tribunals as "aiding and abetting."[91] Aiding and abetting is included in the ICTR and ICTY Statutes,[92] and Article 25(3)(c) of

---

[88] See Aksenova (2016), Moore (2009) and Jackson (2015).

[89] *Black's Law Dictionary* (2009). Complicity in British law derives from the Accessories and Abettors Act of 1861 (24 & 25 Vict. c.94) of the United Kingdom of Great Britain and Northern Ireland (Turner 1958:106).

[90] Stewart (2013:11).

[91] *Akayesu* TC §485 states that "in many legal systems, aiding and abetting constitute acts of complicity." See also *Kvočka et al.* TC §253 on aiding and abetting as a form of complicity.

[92] ICTY Statute Article 7(1) and ICTR Statute Article 6(1).

the ICC Statute imposes individual criminal responsibility on a person who, "For the purpose of facilitating the commission of such a crime, aids, abets or otherwise assists in its commission or its attempted commission, including providing the means for its commission." Even though international criminal law generally understands aiding and abetting as entailing practical assistance[93] in the commission of the crime, the definition also includes providing "encouragement or moral support."[94] *Akayesu* clarified that aiding and abetting, "which may appear to be synonymous, are indeed different. Aiding means giving assistance to someone. Abetting, on the other hand, would involve facilitating the commission of an act by being sympathetic thereto."[95]

Abetting merits further attention because it is the completed crime equivalent of the inchoate crimes of incitement or hate speech, and Schabas (2009:324–5) understands abetting as the same as "incitement when the underlying crime occurs." Schabas cites the *Black's Law Dictionary* definition of "abet" – "to encourage, incite, or set another to commit a crime" – and he observes that it derives from the old French "*à beter*, meaning to bait or excite."[96] The view that incitement is a form of accessorial liability is not just confined to scholarly circles but is also entrenched in the criminal codes of many nation-states. The German Criminal Code (Section 26) provides for the prosecution of incitement upon the commission of the principle crime.[97] The complicity statute of the US Model Penal Code also includes a solicitation element: "A person is an accomplice of another person in the commission of an offence if with the purpose of promoting or facilitating the commission of the offence, he solicits such other person to commit it."[98]

In circumstances where ordering is not the appropriate mode of liability to hold an individual accountable for completed crimes because they do not occupy a position of superior or command responsibility, then aiding and abetting can be more fitting. Aiding and abetting implies relatively weak causation or no cause-and-effect relationship at all, in contrast to the exacting direct causation requirements of instigating and perpetrating/co-perpetrating. Furthermore, the low *mens rea* element of aiding and

---

[93] *Krstić* AC §137.

[94] *Šainović* AC §1626, §1649; *Furundžija* TC §§233–5; *Brđanin* TC §271.

[95] *Akayesu* TC §484. In the same paragraph, the judgment indicated that in order to make a finding of aiding and abetting, "either aiding or abetting alone is sufficient to render the perpetrator criminally liable."

[96] Schabas (2009:325).

[97] Attempted incitement that does not lead to commission of the crime is prosecuted under another provision of the German Criminal Code, Section 30.

[98] MPC §2.06(3)(a)(i).

abetting in ICTY and ICTR jurisprudence resolved the problems associated with mental causation by not requiring that the accomplice share the purpose of the perpetrator to commit an offence.

The elements of accessorial liability conform closely to how social research understands the chance-raising relationship between denigrating and inciting language and subsequent attacks on members of targeted groups. The social science of persuasion and political communication offers little support for the invariable sequence of direct causation demanded by instigating and inducing. In many instances, inciting speech or hate speech is only one element, and possibly not even a necessary or sufficient element in an ensemble of conditions that together are causally related to an outcome. In most instances, a certain speech act is one contributing factor in an assemblage of contributing factors that are jointly sufficient to cause mass atrocities.[99]

Speech acts are seldom a necessary and/or sufficient condition in and of themselves. The effects of persuasive speech are highly variable and dependent on a multiplicity of factors, including the authority and credibility of the speaker, the receptivity of the audience, the content and character of the message and the medium through which the message is delivered, and so on. Inciting and denigrating speech can have no effect at all, or a broad spectrum of effects, from influencing the general conditions of possibility to directly instigating and triggering specific violent acts. As Hart and Honoré (1985:45) attest, the more we know about the conditions culminating in an offence, the more conditions we discover, and the more we come to realize how they jointly contributed to the event in question.

In speech crimes trials at international tribunals, a full comprehension of the ensemble of conditions that were jointly sufficient is often lost as prosecutors and defense counsel seize upon opposite poles of the same continuum of causation. The prosecutors in Šešelj, for instance, sought to show how the accused's public performative utterances were directly causal and set in motion criminal actions. Prosecutors seized on the sliver of the continuum of causation that might prove criminal liability for instigation. Here, just one question matters – whether a specific speech act directly prompted specific crimes or not, an approach that often relies on a mechanistic

---

[99] By "contributing factor," I mean that contributing factor X is one that contributes to the occurrence of event Y by increasing its likelihood. The conventional usage of "contributing factor" is detailed further, and contrasted with "necessary and sufficient" causal factors in Monahan and Walker (2010:60).

model of speech that treats humans as automatons. This model may be more appropriate to the relationship between superior officers and their subordinates in the context of war, but is hardly salient in most other contexts.

In contrast, defense teams focus on the diffuse and generalized end of the continuum of causation to claim, as they did at the ICC in *Mbarushimana*, that propagandistic communications are inconsequential compared with other factors involved in the planning, coordination and execution of offences and are certainly not causal with respect to the crimes.[100] For defense counsel, speech acts should not really be considered acts at all; they are merely symbolic posturing, devoid of any tangible consequences. Furthermore, defense counsel is attentive to intervening causes that rupture the chain of causation between speaker and listener.

Of course, the characterizations of speech acts by prosecution and defense teams often have merit, but these views are highly partial, and they elide the fine gradations in between. In particular, they miss one of the most important findings of recent social research, that certain types of speech, while not attaining a *sine qua non* threshold, can elevate the probability conditions that a criminal harm or injury will ensue. Moreover, many of the effects of performative utterances operate at the level of unconscious psychology. They both draw from, and reshape the cultural domain. Such cultural and psychological effects are diffuse, indirect and hard to pin down in a criminal courtroom.

Yet in situations of war or genocide, denigrating speech and inciting speech may enhance a climate of intolerance that facilitates the persecution of protected groups, even if they fall short of constituting a *conditio sine qua non*. Such speech may convince an elite of the rightness of its strategy and raise the likelihood that a population will feel less empathy towards members of the out-group and be more willing to morally justify violence. Greater tolerance or willingness to condone violent actions is neither a necessary nor sufficient element for the persecution of a civilian population, since a government or non-state actor may act independently and of its own accord (e.g., through a state security apparatus). A greater sense of ideological unity and widespread approval and encouragement from the populace, however, smooths the

---

[100] *Mbarushimana*, ICC PTC I, 16 December 2011, §§9–10.

path of the criminal enterprise, and this is the essence of aiding and abetting.

Even though political speech seldom constitutes a necessary or sufficient cause of a harm in and of itself, it can have probability-enhancing effects, increasing the likelihood that discriminatory attacks will occur. Therefore the International Military Tribunal at Nuremberg accepted the prosecution's theory that Streicher's contribution was not causal in relation to specific crimes but the Tribunal nonetheless convicted Streicher as an accomplice to the Nazi plan to eradicate the Jews. Rather, Streicher's contribution to the Holocaust lay in how he helped to make the program of mass extermination a psychological possibility. Speech that advocates mass murder and genocide elevates risk. It conditions, creates an atmosphere and changes social cognition, but it seldom directly causes violent acts in concordance with judges' clichés of fire and weaponry. Incitement can also enhance and amplify violence that was overdetermined, and therefore is probably going to occur anyway, as Yanagizawa-Drott's (2014) study of RTLM in Rwanda suggests.

8.7 CAUSATION, INTENTION AND RISK IN ACCESSORY LIABILITY

Reviewing the *actus reus* and *mens rea* elements of aiding and abetting further substantiates these general comments regarding complicity. Regarding the *actus reus*, the ICC has not adjudicated a case involving aiding and abetting through to appeals yet, so the following discussion relies primarily on the jurisprudence of the two *ad hoc* international criminal tribunals, which states: "The *actus reus* of aiding and abetting consists of providing practical assistance, encouragement, or moral support that has a substantial effect on the perpetration of the crime."[101]

Aiding and abetting has the lowest causation standard of all modes of liability for completed international crimes. It is well established in

---

[101] *Kvočka* TC §253. In appeals chamber rulings, "practical assistance" is confirmed in *Tadić* AC §229 and substantial effect in *Vasiljević* AC §102. After a few controversial ICTY Trial Chamber judgments (e.g., *Perišić* and *Gotovina*), "specific direction" was an element of the *actus reus* of aiding and abetting. This caused confusion for a while, and many observers noted that the "specific direction" element introduced a *mens rea* element into the *actus reus* of the crime where it did not belong. The issue was finally resolved in the *Šainović* Appeals Chamber judgment which concluded that specific direction requirement was not a part of customary international law (§1650). Jackson (2015:80–5) skillfully reviews this debate.

ICTY jurisprudence that the accomplice's acts need not be causal with respect to the crime.[102] The ICTY Appeals Chamber in *Simić* states forthrightly: "It is not required that a cause–effect relationship between the conduct of the aider and abettor and the commission of the crime be shown, or that such conduct served as a condition precedent to the commission of the crime."[103] Jackson (2015:73) confirms that in international criminal law, "Any form of support, even tacit approval arising on the basis of mere presence, seems to fulfill the nexus requirement."[104] The absence of a causation provision for accomplice liability is not peculiar to international law, but is deeply embedded in the legal philosophy of accomplice liability, and Moore's (2009:299–323) magnum opus *Causation and Responsibility* includes an extended commentary on how complicity need not be causal with respect to the crime.

However, it is doubtful that causation can be entirely excised from the category of complicity, nor would this be desirable in instances where an accessory provides practical assistance. The absence of a causal contribution to the crime is primarily a feature of two types of aiding and abetting: complicity by omission and *ex post facto* complicity. International criminal law states that the aider and abettor may be liable for assistance provided before, during, or after the principal crime has been perpetrated.[105] The accessory after the fact engages in *ex post facto* acts of complicity[106] such as hiding evidence of a crime, and the ICTY has convicted individuals for aiding and abetting murder after the underlying crime was committed. For instance, Vidoje Blagojević, Commander of the Bratunac Brigade of the Bosnian Serb Army (VRS) and Dragan Jokić, chief of engineering, were found criminally responsible for reburying the bodies of victims from the genocide at Srebrenica.[107]

In another ICTY case, omission formed the basis for individual criminal responsibility under a theory of aiding and abetting that relied on the time-honored equation: *Omission + Duty = Act*. As commanding officer, Major Veselin Šljivančanin of the Yugoslav People's Army (JNA) was responsible for the Croatian prisoners in his care at Ovčara camp near Vukovar, and he possessed the duty, *inter alia*, to

---

[102] *Blaškić* AC §48. *Kvočka* TC §255 states that "There is no requirement that the aider or abettor have a causal effect on the act of the principal."
[103] *Simić* AC §85.   [104] Citing *Brđanin* AC §273.   [105] *Mrkšić* AC §81.
[106] *Simić* AC §85 "The actus reus of aiding and abetting a crime may occur before, during, or after the principal crime has been perpetrated."
[107] See *Blagojević* TC. The Trial Chamber indicated (at §314) that aiding and abetting after the fact required a prior agreement between the principal and accomplice.

provide adequate instructions to the military police guarding the prisoners.[108] The crimes were independently planned and executed by his subordinates, but because Major Šljivančanin did not issue orders to refrain from torturing prisoners of war, he was considered responsible as an aider and abettor of war crimes.

Logically, omissions and complicity after the fact are not causal to a crime. This principle could be applied to inciting speech acts that occur after an international offence. One of the more intriguing findings of Scott Straus's (2007:616–20, 622) study of the Rwandan genocide was that many of the overtly genocidal broadcasts from RTLM were transmitted after the actual killing of Tutsis had already taken place. For these broadcasts, abetting is a more fitting form of responsibility than instigating, which must occur before the underlying crime is committed.

This still leaves indeterminate those instances where the accomplice's actions take place prior to, or during, an offence. Stewart (2013:12) reminds us that in most jurisdictions the individual who shouts encouragement to a stranger while they are in the act of murdering a common enemy is customarily held responsible for the murder under a theory of accomplice liability. Tricky matters of causation then arise, such as whether it needs to be shown that the calls of encouragement had any material effect on the crime, or whether the perpetrator must have heard the accomplice's cries of approval. The *Tadić* Appeals Chamber judgment accepts that "indeed, the principal may not even know about the accomplice's contribution."[109] The person shouting their support and encouragement as their enemy is murdered may be considered an accomplice, even if the main perpetrator is not aware of their endorsement. If the perpetrator is not aware of the accomplice's expression of approval, then logically it cannot be causal to the crime.[110]

Evidently, complicity is a very broad type of liability that sweeps into its remit all manner of facilitating and assisting activities, some of which may be neither causal to the crime nor purposely undertaken to further the criminal objective. Many jurists are understandably

---

[108] *Mrkšić et al.*, AC §§131–5. [109] *Tadić* AC §229.
[110] However, one can also imagine a causal material contribution that assists the perpetrator without them knowing about it, for instance if a persuasive speaker recruits thousands of volunteers to a paramilitary organization, and those volunteers then participate, as part of a joint criminal enterprise, in the militia commander's plan to commit war crimes or crimes against humanity.

uncomfortable with this wide-ranging formulation, and both domestic courts and international criminal tribunals have imposed a causation element to circumscribe the boundary of complicity and limit its application. Without a threshold requirement, any person who engages in regular daily interactions (e.g., commerce) with a perpetrator may be liable for his or her subsequent crimes. Hence, case law at international criminal tribunals necessitates that the provision of material assistance or moral support have a "substantial effect"[111] on the perpetration of a crime.

Requiring that a contribution have a "substantial effect" on the commission of a crime displaces from the scope of complicity those innocent quotidian activities that ought not to be criminalized. In international law, the impulse to circumscribe the limits of complicity has created as much confusion as it has clarity. For starters, it is inconsistent to declare simultaneously that aiding and abetting may have no causal effect and yet stipulate that the accused's contribution has had a substantial effect. Sometimes both statements appear in the same paragraph of a judgment without any systematic explanation of how they might be harmonized.[112] My recommendation therefore is to recognize explicitly that the non-causal element of complicity only applies to omissions and assistance provided *ex post facto*. In all other instances of complicity, the contribution of the accomplice must have a substantial effect on the commission of the crime.

Omissions and *ex post facto* acts of accessorial liability notwithstanding, the "substantial effect" requirement for aiding and abetting is now a settled matter in international law, and it implies a degree of causation in cases where the actions in question transpire before or during the offence. The question then becomes the level of causation that qualifies as a substantial effect. The immediate answer is that the lowest level of contribution usually suffices, and the ICTY has included under this rubric any assistance that is more than *de minimis*.[113] The Appeals Chamber in *Brđanin* upheld the view that the accused may be convicted for acts that had a substantial effect on the commission of crimes, even if the principal perpetrators are unknown.[114] In this formulation,

---

[111] *Tadić* AC §229(iii); *Vasiljević* AC §102(i), *Simić* AC §85. The term "substantial effect" has also been used alongside "substantial contribution" (e.g., in *Mrkšić et al.*, AC §81). Jackson (2015:72) does not see a meaningful distinction between the two terms.

[112] *Simić* AC §85.

[113] Cryer (2014:371). See Stewart (2013:19) for a discussion of *de minimis* contributions in aiding and abetting.

[114] *Brđanin* AC §355.

the aider and abettor may be relatively peripheral to the planning, coordinating and executing of crimes, and there is no burden to show that the accused had a proximate and significant connection to the principal perpetrators.

Thus described, the causation element of aiding and abetting fits the fact patterns of inciting speech acts of the kind brought before international tribunals. First, speech acts that aid and abet can transpire before, during and after the commission of the underlying crime. Secondly, the level of causation required is either nonexistent, as in the case of *ex post facto* utterances, or minimal, as with some utterances that precede or are concurrent with the offence. Thirdly, as was suggested in Yanagizawa-Drott's (2014) study of RTLM radio broadcasts in the Rwandan genocide, hate speech can often have an "amplifier effect" that extends the range of mass atrocities, and this could potentially qualify as the "significant effect" sought by international courts. Finally, and perhaps most importantly, the *actus reus* of aiding and abetting permits a more diffuse and minimal set of effects. This could conceivably encompass denigrating or inciting speech that precedes or occurs in the context of widespread or systematic attacks on a civilian population, and that raises the relative risk of mass atrocities.

In discussing complicity, Moore (2009:307) identifies a subcategory of accomplices that he terms "chance raising accomplices," who he contrasts with "truly causal" or "necessary" accomplices. The contribution of chance raising accomplices is conditional rather than causal in that it heightens the probability that a crime will be committed. For Moore (p. 307), chance-raising is not equivalent to causation in itself, but it is a reasonable test of causation and he observes that in law, an increase in the probability of effectuating a result is part of the definition of cause: "a cause is the raising of the probability of its effect."[115] Moore (p. 308–9) notes that "risk-based" liability for raising the probability of a harm or crime is widely recognized in both criminal and civil[116] responsibility doctrines, and he references the doctrines of attempt and reckless endangerment in criminal law. He cites numerous domestic cases that pinpoint the accomplice's assistance in the increased likelihood of success of the principal's criminal

---

[115] Hart and Honoré (1985:469) note that a "cause" in adequate cause theory must satisfy two conditions: it must be a *sine qua non* of the harm and also increase the objective probability of the harm by a significant degree. Therefore, elevating relative risk in itself is not sufficient for there to be causation.

[116] See the *Restatement (Third) of Torts* §30 which requires that a cause must generally raise the probability of a harm: "[a]n actor is not liable for harm when the tortious aspect of the actor's conduct was of a type that does not generally increase the risk of that harm."

objectives. Relative risk, understood as the likelihood of occurrence of a harmful effect, is a guiding principle in toxic torts cases, and it is considered that causality is established if the relative risk is greater than 2.0 (i.e., the factor doubles the risk).[117] Relative risk is also a lynchpin of adequate cause theory that has been influential in German criminal law and was brought into Anglo-American legal philosophy by Hart and Honoré (1985:465).

Assessing the probability-raising properties of a speech act is another juncture where social science expertise can assist a criminal court. Social research of the type presented in the last chapter indicates that certain types of speech, including revenge speech and speech that dehumanizes or recalls past atrocities, can have a variety of effects on an audience. These include lowering their empathy for members of another group, reducing the degree to which they see others as possessing intentionality and increasing their willingness to morally justify violence. We should exercise care at this point, since a robust causal connection between these psychological states and a propensity to act violently is not clearly established. Nevertheless, reducing empathy and generating greater tolerance for violence increases the relative risk that violence will follow.[118] An inciting speaker does not have to convince the entire audience, or a majority: radicalizing even a few members of the audience can have lethal consequences for members of the target group.

Conceiving of demagogues as potential "chance-raising accomplices" (rather than direct instigators) allows social science experts to be called into the courtroom to testify on more favorable terms than expert witness Anthony Oberschall in the ICTY trial of Vojislav Šešelj. Defining complicity in terms of the relative risk implications of the speech of chance-raising accomplices would release social science experts from the inappropriate (and often inaccurate) position of asserting a direct causal relationship between a specific speech act and certain crimes, or even a type of speech and a class of crimes. Instead, expert reports and courtroom testimony would deal with the range of multiple and concurrent causal factors, and assess the degree to which a type of speech uttered in certain conditions elevated the probability of the offence being committed.[119]

---

[117] National Research Council (2002:20). [118] By how much exactly, we do not yet know.

[119] See Jasanoff (1995:29–31, 116–31) for an enlightening discussion of multiple factors and causation in toxic torts cases.

Having reviewed the causation elements of aiding and abetting, we need to consider the mental dimension, and here we can begin by noting that complicity entails a relatively low level of intent. The *mens rea* standard for aiding and abetting is markedly lower than that for instigating in international law. With complicity, the accomplice need not share the intent of the principal perpetrator, only be aware of it. Crucially, the aider and abettor is not the source of the orchestrated program of genocide or persecution, nor need they be privy to the nature of the criminal enterprise. The aider and abettor plays an accompaniment role with respect to the criminal plan of the principals. As Timmermann and Schabas (2013:171) confirm, "The instigator is therefore the intellectual author of the crime: unlike the mere aider and abettor, the instigator sets in motion a chain of events that eventually leads to the commission of the crime." I asked one ICTY judge to reflect on the difference between the two forms of responsibility and he replied:

> What is the difference between instigating and aiding and abetting? In instigating, I plant in the mind the not-yet-existing intention that the crime be committed. In aiding and abetting there is already a shared intent in place and I give support such as encouraging, providing materials etc. That is, I support an already existing intention or plan to commit a crime.[120]

At the ICTY and ICTR, the *mens rea* standard for aiding and abetting is knowledge, not purpose, in relation to the commission of the crime: "In the case of aiding and abetting, the requisite mental element is knowledge that the acts performed by the aider and abettor assist the commission of a specific crime by the principal."[121] In international criminal tribunal judgments, "knowledge" for complicity implies only that the accomplice was aware that a crime would be committed in the ordinary course of events by the direct perpetrators; that is, that a crime was a possible and foreseeable consequence of his or her conduct.[122] In the hierarchy of mental states, awareness is lower than knowledge, and furthermore, international tribunal judgments have determined that the accomplice's awareness of the exact nature of the crime may be only partial:

---

[120] Author interview, 2013.
[121] *Tadić* AC §229. The same language is repeated in *Vasiljević* AC §102(ii), *Blaškić* AC §49; and *Kvocka* TC §253.
[122] *Kvocka* TC §255.

It is not necessary that the aider or abettor know the precise crime that was intended or which was actually committed. If he is aware that one of a number of crimes will probably be committed, and one of those crimes is in fact committed, he has intended to assist or facilitate the commission of that crime, and is guilty as an aider or abettor.[123]

The *mens rea* element of aiding and abetting stands in stark contrast to the more elevated "common plan, design or purpose"[124] of joint criminal enterprise – the enhanced form of accessorial liability. Aiding and abetting has a less demanding *mens rea* test, and proof of a shared intent between the accomplice and the direct perpetrators is not stipulated:[125] "In the case of aiding and abetting no proof is required of the existence of a common concerted plan, let alone of the pre-existence of such a plan. No plan or agreement is required."[126] This merits attention because, with the closure of the ICTY and ICTR, aiding and abetting replaces joint criminal enterprise as the prevailing mode of accessorial liability. Both are forms of complicity, but JCE is technically more complex and specialized compared with aiding and abetting.[127] As JCE recedes into the shadows of international law, prosecutors are advised to charge inciters and propagandists with aiding and abetting in future trials at the ICC and other international tribunals.[128]

If a common plan or collective intentionality is not a mental element of aiding and abetting, then it is not necessary for the prosecution to demonstrate the transmission of criminal intentionality from speaker to direct perpetrator (as is required for instigating). In instigation cases, prosecutors have struggled to provide sufficient evidence of a shared intent between speaker and material perpetrator and to demonstrate that that intent arose because of specific speech acts. The transmission of a criminal intentionality is especially demanding when the accused does not hold an official position of superior responsibility, as was the

---

[123] *Simić* AC §86, citing the authority of *Blaškić* AC §50, which opined, "It is not necessary that the aider and abettor has knowledge of the precise crime that was intended or that was actually committed, as long as he was aware that one of a number of crimes would probably be committed, including the one actually perpetrated." This language is repeated in *Kvočka* TC §255.

[124] In establishing the mental elements for JCE, *Tadić* AC §227 refers to: "The existence of a common plan, design or purpose to commit a crime."

[125] *Blagojević & Jokić* AC §221; *Simić* AC §86.   [126] *Tadić* AC §229.

[127] Jackson (2015:60) on JCE and aiding and abetting as forms of complicity and as "kindred forms of responsibility in international criminal law," especially the extended, third form of JCE.

[128] The similarities and differences between aiding and abetting and JCE are discussed in *Tadić* AC §229 and *Kvočka* AC §90.

case in *Šešelj, Mbarushimana, Nahimana* and *Ruto and Sang*, to mention four trials where the accused were acquitted of instigating. With ordering, the strong causal field of military command and control structures mostly resolves the agent causation problem because of the presumption that the issuing of an order successfully ensures the uptake of the officer's speech act by the subordinate. The utility, nay the beauty, of aiding and abetting is that it circumvents the hurdle of mental causation entirely by not requiring shared intent in the first place.

Given the minimal quality of the knowledge element for aiding and abetting, some scholars have doubted whether "knowledge" is indeed the proper mental state, and Stewart (2012b:38) writes that "Clearly, awareness of a probability is constitutive of culpable risk-taking, not knowledge." That is, because no one truly knows what will happen in the future with any certainty, the requisite mental state for complicity is more a question of prediction and foreseeability than exact knowledge or purpose. Accomplices are aware of the likelihood that their actions could contribute to a harm, and their decision to proceed anyway is based on their willingness to tolerate a risk that can only be vaguely surmised. This means their likely mental state is a notch lower than "knowledge." For instance, when an individual provides guns, ammunitions or explosives to an extremist group, he may not be aware of their full intentions but he has undertaken an act that is intrinsically risky, and an international court is likely to apply a standard of recklessness to his actions.

Citing legal theorist Andrew Ashworth, Stewart (2013:28, 38) has pursued this line of argumentation, maintaining that even though criminal law requires knowledge for accessorial liability, in practice international tribunals apply a standard of recklessness, "As a matter of pure doctrine, recklessness is the mental element for complicity most frequently applied by international criminal courts."[129] Recklessness in the common law corresponds approximately to a notion of *mens rea* commonly used in civil law jurisdictions known as *dolus eventualis*,[130] which refers to a course of conduct that carries an unreasonable risk to cause harm, but the actor accepts that risk and proceeds anyway. One authority on individual criminal responsibility in international criminal law, Van Sliedregt (2012:114), seems ready to accept the implication that in fact, recklessness is the requisite *mens rea* for aiding and abetting.

---

[129] Ashworth (2009:416). There is a certain amount of controversy on this question, which Van Sliedregt (2012:122, fn. 231) addresses capably.

[130] *Dolus eventualis* in international criminal law is defined and discussed in Cassese and Gaeta (2013:41).

Given the imperfections in humans' ability to predict events and the status of recklessness as the *de facto* standard for complicity, then a trial for accessorial liability ought to focus on what Stewart (2013:7) calls "the risk-enhancing character of the accomplice's act." The recklessness standard is consistent with what transpires when political demagogues publicly denigrate a target group. This is what one instinctively feels when listening to a demagogue; that they are reckless in their disregard for the safety of other persons, who are frequently members of already disadvantaged minority groups. It is not always the case that the speaker directly causes violent crimes, although that can occur under certain conditions, but their reckless speech acts can elevate the risk on aggregate that there will be discriminatory attacks on members of target groups. Again, it is the ensemble of conditions that produces the deleterious result in a context of multiple causal factors.

Just when it seems that we are making progress, the ICC Statute has dramatically elevated the *mens rea* element for aiding and abetting. Article 25(3)(c) holds a person criminally responsible for a crime if that person, "for the purpose of facilitating the commission of such a crime, aids, abets or otherwise assists in its commission or its attempted commission, including providing the means for its commission." By adding the language "for the purpose," the Statute introduces a heightened mental element that verges on motive and markedly raises the *mens rea* requirement. Comparatively, the "purpose" of the ICC Statute is sharply divergent from the knowledge standard used for complicity in most criminal jurisdictions.[131]

Aiding and abetting has yet to be fully adjudicated at the ICC, so there is still a degree of uncertainty as to its interpretation, but Van Sliedregt (2012:129) is pessimistic that the purpose language in Article 25(3)(c) will be reconciled with existing case law on the topic, because of the ICC's "misguided black-letter approach." Her pessimism is probably justified, given the explicit commentary of the ICC's Pre-Trial Chamber in *Mbarushimana* that "the jurisprudence of the ad hoc tribunals does not require the aider and abettor to share the intent of the perpetrator to commit the crime, whereas under Article 25(3)(c) of the Statute, the aider and abettor must act with the purpose of facilitating the commission of that crime."[132] The purpose standard was a central justification for the Pre-Trial Chamber's refusal in *Mbarushimana* to

---

[131] However, it is consistent with the US Model Penal Code at §2.06(4).

[132] *Mbarushimana*, ICC PTC I, 16 December 2011, §281.

confirm the charges against the defendant, a spokesman and unscrupulous propagandist for the Forces Démocratiques pour la Libération du Rwanda (FDLR).[133] Callixte Mbarushimana issued communiqués stating that "the price of a country is blood not water"[134] at a time when the FDLR was systematically murdering civilians and creating a humanitarian catastrophe in the eastern Democratic Republic of the Congo.

If applied strictly, the ICC's purpose test is likely to hinder the prosecution of professional propagandists such as Mr. Mbarushimana. My recommendation is to adhere to the long-standing knowledge standard of *mens rea* that is the settled law of aiding and abetting at international criminal tribunals. Stewart (2013:24) is also critical of the "purpose" doctrine of aiding and abetting at the ICC, because it "gives an almost unattainable height to the subjective element of complicity, misapplying desert and miscommunicating responsibility." While a reasonable *mens rea* element is surely needed, "purpose" is an overcorrection, and there is a consensus in the literature (a literature, mind, where consensus seldom abounds) that international criminal law must retain knowledge as the intent requirement of aiding and abetting.[135] Stated plainly, the accomplice need not share the purpose to commit an international crime, but he or she must have knowledge of the material perpetrators intention to commit the crime.[136]

My proposal that aiding and abetting is the most pertinent charge against propagandists and politicians who incite is supported by the prosecutorial strategy eventually adopted in the ICC's *Ruto and Sang* case. This trial dealt with a radio DJ (Joshua arap Sang) who broadcast support for presidential candidate William Ruto as he campaigned during the 2007 Kenyan elections. Towards the end of the trial in 2015, the prosecution petitioned the Court to consider changing the legal characterization of the charges and it identified the possibility of convictions based on Article 25(3)(b) which prohibits ordering, soliciting or inducing the commission of the offence, and Article 25(3)(c) which refers to aiding and abetting. The prosecution indicated that Joshua Sang could be held liable for aiding and abetting crimes against humanity when he broadcast live calls from Mr. Ruto's supporters while

---

[133] *Mbarushimana*, ICC PTC I, 16 December 2011, §274, §291.
[134] *Mbarushimana*, ICC PTC I, 16 December 2011, §321.
[135] Cryer et al. (2014:374), Jackson (2015:80), Stewart (2013:24–7), Van Sliedregt (2012:129).
[136] An approach adopted in *Krstić* AC §142, that Schabas (2009:351) summarizes but criticizes in favor of a lesser *mens rea* standard.

they were physically attacking civilians of other ethnic groups during the elections.[137] Sang allegedly requested updates from the perpetrators, vocally encouraged their attacks and coordinated the movement of material resources to facilitate the attacks.[138] This prosecutorial gambit, while procedurally correct and strategically intelligible, did not save the crumbling prosecution case, which would have benefitted from introducing charges of aiding and abetting earlier at the indictment stage.

There are at least two possible objections to my claim that aiding and abetting represents the most appropriate form of responsibility for completed speech crimes; one from social science and the other from law.[139] The first is that, despite the vibrant differences of opinion in social science, speech acts do shape behavior in a way that could fulfill the direct causation element in international criminal law, thus rendering accomplice liability inappropriate and impelling us towards more direct modes of liability such as instigating and inducing. I am sympathetic to this objection. There is still much about incitement that social science does not know, including the interactions of different types of speech, the effects of pitch and volume of the speaker's voice, and whether the sequence of distinct types of speech affects the outcome. The social and cultural context of speech acts remains outside many social psychology studies. Additionally, many of the effects of speech are unconscious, but new research methods and theories may render

---

[137] Prosecution's Request for notice under regulation 55(2) of possibility of variation with respect to individual criminal responsibility of Mr. Joshua Arap Sang, *Ruto and Sang* (ICC-01/09–01/11–1951), Trial Chamber, 8 September 2015 at §18.

[138] *Ibid.*

[139] There are, of course, potentially many more objections that I cannot adequately address here. One deserving of mention pertains to the general concern that the minimal *mens rea* requirement for complicity dilutes the special intent requirement for genocide, a debate summarized in Cryer et al. (2014:374). If the aider and abettor does not need to know the exact crime being committed, then complicity is a general intent crime with respect to the underlying offence, but this clashes with the statutory definition of genocide as a specific intent crime. Van Sliedregt (2012:123) replies that it is now a matter of settled law that the aider and abettor does not need to share the special intent of the principal perpetrator of genocide. An accomplice only needs to have knowledge of the principal perpetrator's intent and to have aided the perpetrator or provided the means by which the perpetrator may realize his intention to commit genocide. This conundrum is resolved in the Appeals Chamber judgment in *Simić*, which addresses aiding and abetting for the special intent crime of persecution thus: "In relation to the crime of persecutions, an offence with a specific intent, he must thus be aware not only of the crime whose perpetration he is facilitating but also of the discriminatory intent of the perpetrators of that crime. He need not share the intent but he must be aware of the discriminatory context in which the crime is to be committed and know that his support or encouragement has a substantial effect on its perpetration" (§86).

such effects more visible and measurable. I would happily revise my view if this type of evidence, which is not to my knowledge presently available, were to surface.

Another objection, this time from the perspectives of prosecutors and victims, is that complicity is a truncated form of criminal responsibility that results in lower sentences that do not fully reflect the gravity of the offence. Certainly, this is the case in many domestic settings, and under StGB§26 of the German Criminal Code, instigators and inducers incur the same liability for a crime as the principal perpetrator, whereas aiders and abettors are sentenced to no more than three-quarters of the maximum sentence for full commission of the underlying crime.[140] Yet there is an obvious rejoinder to this objection. At international criminal tribunals, sentencing for aiding and abetting is not markedly lower than for the full commission of a crime, mostly because the underlying crime (e.g., genocide) has more effect on the sentence than the mode of liability. At the ICTY, General Radislav Krstić was sentenced to forty-six years' imprisonment for full commission of genocide, and this was reduced to thirty-five years for aiding and abetting genocide, murders (violations of the laws or customs of war), extermination and persecutions (crimes against humanity). This represents a drop in sentence to three-quarters of the original, certainly, but the eventual outcome is likely the same: General Krstić dies in prison. Furthermore, General Krstić's sentence is commensurate with that of former Bosnian President Radovan Karadžić, who was sentenced by the ICTY Trial Chamber to forty years for full commission of genocide.

We do not have to rely solely on anecdotal comparisons. Hola et al. (2011) and Hola (2012) have conducted systematic empirical studies of sentencing at the ICTR and ICTY, and their figures do not show a great variance in sentencing for aiding and abetting when compared to other modes of liability. Aiders and abettors at the ICTY have been sentenced on average to sixteen years, with a median sentence of fifteen years, as compared with an average of seventeen years and median of thirteen for principal perpetrators and an average of twenty years and a median of twenty-five years for instigators.[141] At the ICTR, the median sentences are higher overall for defendants convicted of aiding and abetting, who have received a median sentence of forty-five years

[140] German Criminal Code (2015, Bohlander trans.). Sections §27, §49(1)(2) refer to liability and sentencing for aiding and abetting.
[141] Hola (2012:98).

compared with a median of fifty years for perpetrators and fifty years for instigators.[142]

A statistical analysis of sentencing reveals that a conviction for aiding and abetting does not result in a drastically lower sentence than for other modes of liability charged at international criminal tribunals. It is true that instigators receive a higher sentence, but it is debatable whether the higher sentence justifies the additional resources required to secure a conviction. According to Hola's analysis, the mode of liability is but one independent variable among others that include the rank of the offender, any aggravating and mitigating factors and the underlying crime itself. Intriguingly, Hola (2012:159) includes the sentences of propagandists in her study, and she finds that propagandists at the ICTR received a median sentence of fifteen years (with a range of six to thirty-five years), compared with twelve years (range of seven to twenty-five years) for all types of perpetrators involved in a single isolated incident and thirty-five years (range of six years to life) for those involved in recurrent incidents. Again, the variance is not especially pronounced.

In sum, charging propagandists as aiders and abettors is justified not only because the charge is most appropriate to the offence based on the potential chance-raising effects of inciting speech, but also because the potential sentence for complicity passes a proportionality test. The recommendation of this book is that international criminal tribunals return to the approach to incitement developed at Nuremberg that held Julius Streicher liable as an accomplice to wider crimes planned and perpetrated by the Nazi High Command. By charging demagogues and media figures who call for acts of public violence under theories of direct causation, prosecutors are compelled to advocate an inaccurate account of the consequences of speech, and they are also less likely to persuade the court and secure a conviction. In most criminal law settings, it is better to be on secure ground, and to defend a moderate position effectively and successfully, rather than to grasp for a level of causation and responsibility that is out of reach.

8.8 TOWARDS A CONTEXTUAL JURISPRUDENCE

Reflecting on causation questions as they pertain to international speech crimes opens a window on causation more generally in international

---

[142] Hola (2012:160).

criminal law. Until wider uncertainties related to causation are addressed explicitly, and basic concepts such as the reasonable doubt standard are defined, it is hard to remedy the array of causation issues that arise with respect to criminal speech acts.

In short, international criminal law needs to get its house in order. I have three hopefully constructive recommendations to make in this regard. Firstly, international criminal law ought to distinguish in a clear manner between material causation and legal causation, as many domestic criminal jurisdictions commonly do. International criminal tribunals could expressly demarcate material (or factual) causes from legal causes; i.e., those that are relevant for attributing criminal liability. Bifurcating causation in this way would allow the trial chamber, in the first instance, to consider the entire constellation of conditions jointly sufficient to result in a harm or injury, using a broad formulation of cause and effect. This would promote a more "contextual jurisprudence," what McDougal and Lasswell (1967:500) defined as a "contextually oriented jurisprudence [that] is deliberately designed to bring the whole tangled web of causes and consequences into view."[143]

At the outset, an international court's primary task is to understand as definitely and comprehensively as possible who did what to whom, before it attributes criminal liability. In many instances, cause-in-fact cannot be fully grasped using mere "common sense," which is little more than an unsystematic patchwork of, inter alia, yesterday's science, personal intuitions, cultural dispositions and cognitive biases. Social research can be incorporated at the fact-finding stage without hazard, as the bench of professional judges (i.e., there is no jury to sway) in an international criminal trial is aware that a social science expert conveys knowledge about general patterns of behavior, not the specific contribution of the accused to the crime, or the state of mind of the accused.

Here, the social science expert in a speech crimes trial would answer general causation questions of the type: has X type of speech been associated with a pattern of Y harms in Z type of conditions? What is the relative frequency of XYZ classes of events? The court could benefit from new knowledge about human behavior that is produced by methods, be they scientific or humanistic, that are often far removed from (but accessible to) ordinary reasoning. Social research could assist

---

[143] Each generation of historically and culturally minded legal scholars seems to discover the virtues of contextualism anew, and recent advocates include (Gerken 2017:12–14) and McKinley (2016:1141).

international tribunals in distinguishing more meticulously between types of speech that may be repugnant but minimal in their effects, and types of speech that are known to elevate the risk of criminal acts in a statistically significant manner.

Social research pertains to the factual, not the normative and guilt-attribution stage of the legal process. With respect to legal causation, international courts need to be explicit that the attribution of responsibility is determined by the "scope of liability,"[144] that is, the conduct that the defendant should have taken reasonable steps to avoid since an offence was a foreseeable consequence of their act or omission, acknowledging that the scope of liability is a policy decision derived from the statutes and the case law. Foreseeability is a central concept here that in both criminal law and torts law typically does the work of linking the general frequency conditions to the specific scope of liability in the case.

The arc of the trial could then more closely resemble a "decision tree" on causation questions, which proceeds from general/material causation (where social research is relevant) to specific causation elements and the facts of the case, which only international tribunal judges can determine. Crucially, if international courts were to unequivocally distinguish general (or material) causes from specific (or proximate) causes, then this would compel the parties to explain exactly how social science research applies to the specific facts of the case, instead of relying on oblique references and innuendo, as is often the case at present.

Secondly, international criminal law has created many meaningless tests for the threshold of causation and the requisite level of contribution of the accused. Requiring a "significant contribution" for one mode of liability, a "substantial contribution" for another and a "substantial effect" for yet another gives the false appearance of a rigorous and technically specific framework for evaluating causation. Legal scholars have written more about modes of liability than any other issue in international criminal law, either excoriating them for their unintelligibility, or performing intellectual somersaults to render order out of the chaos, to no avail.[145]

As many participants in this study acknowledged, the tests often break down in practice, and this partially explains why judges

---

[144] *Restatement (Third)* §6 introduces scope of liability to replace "proximate cause." Criminal law contemplates causes differently than tort law, but the principle of delimiting causation as a matter of policy is the same and I have amended the definition here for the purposes of international criminal law.

[145] See Stewart (2012b).

adjudicating speech crimes frequently reach for metaphors and clichés to describe the causal nexus. Even experienced international judges, prosecutors and defense attorneys may not fully understand the *actus reus* elements of the crimes they are adjudicating, and this becomes obvious when reading judgments and encountering variations and inconsistencies in the stated level of contribution within the same mode of liability.[146] The majority of international judges and attorneys interviewed for this book admitted privately that the classifications of essential, substantial and significant contribution often represent distinctions without a difference. Partly this confusion results from the fact that international criminal law is a hybrid of the civil and common law systems, without either an overarching system of judicial review or the customary centuries of trial and error in actual criminal courtrooms to iron out the irregularities. Furthermore, a byzantine framework of specialized language appears to be one of the occupational hazards of the civil law system from whence legal innovations, such as the "essential contribution" standard and the "control of the crime" theory that informs it, emanated.[147] Lacking juries who must be instructed in a non-technical language, the civil law tradition is more susceptible than the common law to theoretically intricate formulations that are ultimately more obfuscating than elucidating.[148]

My suggestion is to abandon the ornate framework of levels of causal contribution and utilize a single test of causation across all forms of criminal responsibility. Then the mode of liability – truly the most indicative part of the equation when compared with the causation threshold – can do the rest of the work. The question of how to set the limits of liability is resolved by the imposition of a legal rule about the scope of liability, not some vague test of the threshold of causation. This may seem like a radical solution, and indeed it is, yet the status quo is radical also in its inconsistency and disorder. Some international jurists have acknowledged the prevailing confusion in the law, and they have also taken a substantial step down this path. This is what the trial chamber did in *Kvočka*, when it indicated that the element of causation for instigating "is satisfied if it is shown that the conduct of the accused was *a clear contributing factor* to the conduct of the other person(s). It is

---

[146] E.g., for instigating, see Van Sliedregt (2012:104).

[147] *Lubanga* TC, Separate Opinion of Judge Adrian Fulford, §§10–12.

[148] No system of human justice is perfect, and each has its strengths and weaknesses. The common law has its frailties too, and its rules of evidence are wholly inappropriate to the prosecution of crimes in an international armed conflict.

not necessary to demonstrate that the crime would not have occurred without the accused's involvement"[149] (my emphasis). A "clear contributing factor," construed outside the *sine qua non* paradigm of causation, seems a promising criterion for evaluating whether the accused's contribution qualifies for inclusion into the scope of liability.

For a while, there was hope that the ICC would resolve these conceptual problems in causation, but instead it has muddied the waters further. Unfortunately, the *Lubanga* Trial Chamber introduced yet another threshold of "essential causation" for the commission of crimes under Article 25(3)(a) of the Statute. This controversial innovation, derived from the German legal system as a way of distinguishing between principals and accomplices, immediately caused alarm in international legal circles.[150] Advocating plain language and a lesser test, Judge Adrian Fulford in *Lubanga* recommended simply requiring "a contribution to the crime, which may be direct or indirect, provided either way there is a causal link between the individual's contribution and the crime."[151] As in *Kvočka*, a single test for causation, plainly stated by a widely respected common law judge. A contributing factor is one which is neither necessary nor sufficient but contributes to the crime by increasing the likelihood of its occurrence.

The third and final recommendation refers to how international criminal tribunals are not fully benefitting from certain types of expertise. In particular, judges seem reticent to admit quantitative social science testimony on questions of social behavior that they feel they can resolve using common sense and ordinary reasoning. Whilst recognizing the uniqueness of the law, judicial pronouncements on human behavior are greatly weakened when they contradict the mainstream of social science opinion on a subject. Greater openness and flexibility on the part of international judges is therefore warranted, but here it is important to recognize that moral exhortations are not enough, and judges probably need some help getting to this point. International judges would profit from an ongoing program of continuing legal education, of the kind that is customary and uncontroversial in the domestic setting, to equip them with the tools they need to evaluate social science expert testimony.[152]

---

[149] *Kvočka* TC §252. This language is also present in *Blaškić* TC §270.

[150] The control of crime theory, developed by German legal theorist Claus Roxin in the 1960s in response to the Eichmann trial, is contentious even in Germany.

[151] *Lubanga* TC, Separate Opinion of Judge Adrian Fulford, §16.c.

[152] See the National Research Council (2002:13–14).

International criminal law desperately needs to replace the piece-meal case law on expert evidence with a *Daubert*,[153] that is, an unam-biguous and authoritative statement on the principles guiding the admissibility of experts. Domestic criminal justice systems regularly wrestle with complex evidential questions about the use of statistics and social science expertise,[154] but international criminal law has hardly begun its process of reflection, even though it relies on social science evidence much more than most domestic criminal jurisdictions. Such a document would detail what kind of expert knowledge is valued and what bases of understanding (e.g., science, experience, or another) are acceptable. It would provide guidance on how courts might profit-ably handle statistical evidence that includes indications of risk and probability. It is presently hazy how statistical probability and chance-raising acts relate to the "beyond reasonable doubt" standard ostensibly applied by international criminal tribunals, and a precise analysis of how probability maps onto the reasonable doubt standard would be beneficial.

Social science expertise is often incapable of showing direct and specific causation in a particular case, but it can illuminate the patterns of general causation; that is, the conditioning effects of certain acts that can alter psychological dispositions and prepare the groundwork of a widespread or systematic campaign against a civilian population.

---

[153] Three US Supreme Court cases beginning with *Daubert v. Merrell Dow Pharmaceuticals* (1993) identified the tests for evaluating the admissibility of expert evidence.
[154] See Friedland et al. (2012: Chapter 9).

APPENDIX 1: FOCUS GROUP DISCUSSIONS WITH PROSECUTORS AND DEFENSE ATTORNEYS (TWO SEPARATE GROUPS)

It is 2020. An armed conflict in the country of Colonia has just ended after widespread and systematic violations of international law by both sides in the conflict. You have been appointed as a trial judge at the newly established *ad hoc* international criminal tribunal, the International Criminal Tribunal for Colonia (ICTC). The ICTC statute indicates that cases are to be adjudicated on the basis of the body of international criminal law existing when the conflict occurred between 2018–20. The case you are to hear has the following fact pattern:

The country of Colonia is made up of two equal-sized national groups, Locrians and Dorians, who have a history of peaceful co-existence, as well as periodic violence. During the period of the indictment, there was heightened political tension around national elections. In the east of the country, Locrian nationalists seized public buildings and airports and clashed with Dorian police and civilians. The Accused is Locrian political leader, Mr. Mixo Lydian, who founded his own parliamentary party made up of local branches with their own armed local security groups. On 4 June 2018, Mr. Lydian arrived in the town of Fugue, which is made up equally of the two national groups. He was accompanied by an entourage of twenty armed men in Locrian nationalist uniforms who assumed prominent positions in the center of the town. At 6PM, he gave a public speech in the town square to a crowd of 400. Lydian's speech was recorded by several onlookers and it included this passage:

> We don't want Dorians in Fugue, and they must clear out of Colonia altogether. They collaborated with the imperialists and ruled over us brutally in the past. When we Locrians sought to defend our rights, they burned our villages and slaughtered our women and children and even

our animals. Now Dorian soldiers are coming again to murder our families in their beds. We will not let them do that to us this time. They'll pay for the Locrian bloodshed in the past. The only way to be free is to pull up the invasive weeds that blew in with the imperialists. Locrians be strong, be patriotic and go to work pulling up weeds for Colonia. If Dorians do not leave of their own accord, then we can provide buses to drive them to the border and they can walk on from there. When we win the elections, those who stay will regret it. They'll wish they had left when we gave them the chance.

After the speech, Mr. Lydian left the town and returned to the capital. The mixed crowd of Dorians and Locrians dispersed peacefully. The next night, a 54-year-old Dorian man was killed by a hit-and-run driver on a backstreet of the town. Many Dorian homes were burned down in the following week and four members of Mr. Lydian's political party were charged by the authorities of Colonia. Over the next three weeks, ninety percent of Dorians in the town left their homes and traveled to a nearby country where Dorians form a majority. Locrians who had themselves been attacked in neighboring towns moved into the abandoned homes. Mr. Lydian gave fifty election speeches overall and, of these, thirty-five towns were marked by subsequent violence and fifteen towns remained peaceful. He publicly called for calm on radio and television numerous times.

INITIAL QUESTIONS FOR DISCUSSION

1. What charges against Mr. Lydian do you anticipate reviewing in the indictment and pretrial stage?
2. What in the fact pattern is incriminating and what is exculpatory?
3. What further evidence will be needed to prove the charges at trial?
4. To what degree would a social science expert assist the court in determining the charges?

APPENDIX 2: CATEGORIES OF EXPERTISE AND TITLES

Categories of Expertise and Titles		
Medicine	Clinical Psychologist Court Medical Expert Medical Expert Military Medical Expert Neurologist Neuropsychiatrist	Psychiatrist Psychotherapist Sexual Assault Expert Sexual Violence Expert Socio-Psychological Expert

Military, Police and
    Intelligence
	Confidential
	Crisis Staff Analyst
	Intelligence Expert
	Internal Affairs
	    Investigator
	Military Expert
	Operational Logistics
	    Expert
		Police Expert
		RS MUP Analyst
		Scene of Crime Officer
		Security and Police
		    Expert
		Terrorism Expert
		US Navy

Forensics	DNA Expert
	Exhumation and
	    Identification
	Forensic Anthropologist
	Forensic Biologist
	Forensic Genetics
	Forensic Medicine
	Forensic Pathologist
	Forensic Scientist
		Forensic Textile Analyst
		Orthopaedic and
		    Trauma Specialist
		Palaeontologist [sic]
		Palynologist
		Physical Anthropologist
		Radiologist
		Serology

Engineering	Communication Devices Electronic Engineer Mechanical Engineer	Radio Relay Communications Seiko Watch Analyst Traffic Engineer

(Cont.)

Categories of Expertise and Titles

Document Verification and Authentication	Document Analyst Handwriting Expert	Photographic and Video Expert Signature Expert
	Quantitative	**Qualitative**
Social Research	Demographer Demographics Expert Economic Expert Economist Political Science Expert Statistics Expert	Anthropologist Balkans Specialist Communicability Expert Cultural Heritage Expert Eastern Europe Specialist Historian Journalism Expert Linguist Media Expert Phonetics Expert Political Expert Sociologist
Law and Human Rights	Constitutional Expert Criminal Procedure	Legal Expert Statistics and Human Rights
Weapons and Ballistics	Artillery Expert Ballistics Expert Explosives Expert Firearms Expert	Gunpowder Expert Mortar Expert Sniper Expert
Finance	Financial Expert	

APPENDIX 3: COMPOSITE SPEECHES BY VOJISLAV ŠEŠELJ

REVENGE

"When it comes to revenge, you know, revenge is blind . . . if the West Margolians try to massacre us, the East Margolians will not forgive nor forget. Our revenge will be horrific . . . Let them just continue attacking our lives – and then we shall not only present them with the bill for current victims, but we shall collect the fee for the victims . . . Those who survived have no right to forgive in the name of the slaughtered."

PAST ATROCITIES

"Who started ethnic cleansing first? The West Margolians. They first started to pacify East Margolian territories with the sword and fire! Remember our history, West Margolia expelled over 300,000 East Margolians from their territory. When the West Margolians were arming themselves en masse, when they were importing huge quantities of arms, what was supposed to be done? A repetition of previous violence they committed against us? . . . They marked their borders with East Margolian graves."

DIRECT THREAT

"The West Margolians will split up East Margolia. The West Margolians intend a horrible fate for us, and now we understand what kind of fate they intend. There's nothing to lose – we have to fight, decidedly, till the end . . . The East Margolian people are endangered . . . The West Margolians are planning our deaths; we only want to stop the genocide they envision."

VICTIMIZATION

"There is a horrific propaganda war being led against the East Margolian people, in which all means are allowed. The West Margolians make us out to be Satan, so that the public opinion would justify all measures against the East Margolian people. These kinds of crimes, which the West Margolians have committed towards others, East Margolians have not committed ... And the media only accuse us."

NATIONALISM

"In all East Margolian chests, there is a heroic heart beating. If we remain in concord and unity, there will be no war; there will be no bloodshed. It's enough for us for our enemies to look at us, in concord and unity as we are, and hide ... This is the last lesson to the West Margolian people. We are less well armed than they are, but we have got a heart of a knight and an unbreakable will"

NEGATIVE OUT-GROUP STEREOTYPES

"The West Margolians are not a nation, but the dregs of society ... It's easy to recognize them. They are very primitive people. And you may find one literate guy among 100 West Margolians, and they do not even know they are not. They are a genocidal people although we know they are cowards on the battlefield and capable of nothing."

DEHUMANIZATION

"We, East Margolians, as a people, let a poisonous snake bite our heart three times after holding it in our arms. That poisonous snake, that's the West Margolians. This is the third time that poisonous snake has headed for us, and for the third time bit us in the heart. Now we need to smash its head so it never bites anyone again."

JUSTICE

"If one state treats a particular national minority a certain way that is non-civilized, outside of the legal norms, then international public law justifies a similar treatment of the neighbor state to the national minority of the previous state ... If the West Margolians expelled

300,000 East Margolians from the Western Margolian land, what is more natural than to demand that they leave East Margolia as well?"

POLITICS

"We, the East Margolians, will not enter into any compromises with anyone at the price of sacrificing certain national interests . . . We fight with all means of peace-loving political action . . . The West Margolians cannot push us from the political stage; and they cannot turn us away from our faithful service to the East Margolian people."

CONTROL SPEECH

"The climate of East Margolia is greatly influenced by its closeness to the sea. In the north, the climate is more continental, with cold winters, and hot, humid summers along with well-distributed rainfall patterns . . . Most of West Margolia has a moderately warm and rainy climate. The coldest parts of West Margolia have a snowy-forested climate and are found at high elevations."

APPENDIX 4

4.1 Personality Correlations for the United States Study

	Moral Justification	Empathy for In-group	Empathy for Out-group	Perception of Intent for In-group	Perception of Intent for Out-group	Overall In-group Positive Attitudes	Overall Out-group Negative Attitudes
Authoritarian	-.087	.163**	.010	-.094	-.043	.046	.024
System justification	.020	.128*	.144*	.074	.085	.128*	-.165**
Belief in a just world	-.111*	.121*	.117*	-.001	.045	.079	-.117*
Disgust sensitivity	-.086	.170**	-.005	.057	.066	.145**	-.042
Religiosity	-.026	.096	.039	.103*	.052	.129*	-.066
Politics Conservative	.122*	-.040	.016	.037	.068	-.002	-.056
Violent media	.293**	.082	.226**	.067	.074	.093	-.208**
Gender (Male)	.319**	.050	.114*	.030	-.011	.050	-.069
Socio-economic status (SES)	-.004	.081	-.024	.041	.024	.080	.000
Age	-.095	-.044	-.031	.046	.083	-.001	-.037

* $p < .05$
** $p < .01$

4.2 Personality Correlations for the Serbian Study

	Moral Justification	Empathy for In-Group	Empathy for Out-Group	Perception of Intent for In-Group	Perception of Intent for Out-Group	Overall In-Group Positive Attitudes	Overall Out-Group Negative Attitudes
Authoritarian	.082	.170**	.054	.135**	.031	.213**	.058
Belief in a just world	.090	.105*	.010	-.072	.070	.015	-.148**
Nationalism	.025	.464**	.012	-.147**	.079	.222**	.067
Self-esteem	-.001	.085	-.067	.068	.187**	.107*	.095
Religiosity	-.048	.238**	.003	-.164**	-.107*	.053	-.077
Politics Conservative	.058	.092	-.060	-.109*	-.139**	-.012	-.142**
Violent Media	.290**	-.012	.069	.122*	-.149**	.077	-.065
Gender (Male)	-.151**	-.086	.028	.134***	.128*	.034	.113*
Socio-economic status (SES)	.102*	-.068	.028	.149***	.153**	.056	.131**
Age	-.197**	.073	-.026	-.115*	.071	-.029	.036
Region	.042	-.016	-.089	-.065	-.099*	-.057	-.131**

* p <.05
** p <.01

BIBLIOGRAPHY

Cases

Abrams v. United States, 250 US 616 (1919).

Application of the Convention on the Prevention and Punishment of the Crime of Genocide. (Bosnia and Herzegovina v. Serbia and Montenegro.) International Court of Justice. Judgment of 26 February 2007.

Atlantic Coast Line Railway Company v. Daniels (1911) 8 Ga. App. 775, 70 SE 203.

Berkey v. Third Ave. Ry. Co. 244 N.Y. 84, 94, 155 N.E. 58, 61 (1926).

Brandenburg v. Ohio, 395 US 444 (1969).

Burrage v. United States, 571 US___ (2014).

Chaplinsky v. State of New Hampshire, 315 US 568 (1942).

Clark v. Commonwealth, 676 S.E.2d 332 (2009).

Commonwealth v. Berggren, 398 Mass. 338, 496 N.E.2d 660 (1986).

Daubert v. Merrell Dow Pharmaceuticals, Inc., 113 S. Ct. 2786 (1993).

Elonis v. United States, 13–983 US (2015).

Folkes v. Chadd, 3 Dougl. 157, 99 Eng. Rep. 589 (K.B. 1782).

Hess v. Indiana, 414 US 105 (1973).

In re Winship, 397 US 358, 90 S.Ct. 1068, 25 L.Ed. 2d 368 (1970), 9.

M'Naghten's Case, 8 Eng.Rep. 718 (1843).

McCullough v. State, 99 Nev. 72, 657 P.2d 1157 (Nev. 1983).

Oxendine v. State 528 A.2d 870 (Del. 1987).

Palsgraf v. Long Island R.R. Co. (1928) 248 NY 339, 162 NE 99.

People v. Acosta, 284 Cal. Rptr. 117 (1991).

Prosecutor v. Jean Paul Akayesu
Trial Chamber Judgment, ICTR-96-4-T, 2 September 1998.
Judgment on Appeal, ICTR-96-4-A, 1 June 2001.

Prosecutor v. Ignace Bagilishema
Trial Chamber Judgment, ICTR-95-1A-T, 7 June 2001.

Prosecutor v. Predrag Banović
Trial Chamber Judgment, IT-02-65/1-S, 28 October 2003.

Prosecutor v. Simon Bikindi
Trial Chamber Judgment, ICTR-01-72-T, 2 December 2008.
Judgment on Appeal, ICTR-01-72-A, 18 March 2010.

Prosecutor v. Vidoje Blagojević & Dragan Jokić
Trial Chamber Judgment, IT-02-60-T, 17 January 2005.
Appeals Chamber Judgment, IT-02-60-A, 9 May 2007.
Prosecutor v. Tihomir Blaškić
Trial Chamber Judgment, IT-95-14-T, 3 March 2000.
Appeals Chamber Judgment, IT-95-14-A, 29 July 2004.
Prosecutor v. Charles Blé Goudé
Decision on the Confirmation of Charges Against Charles Blé Goudé, ICC-02/11-02/11-186, 11 December 2014.
Prosecutor v. Ljube Boškoski and Johan Tarčulovski
Appeals Chamber Judgment, IT-04-82-A, 19 May 2010.
Prosecutor v. Radoslav Brđanin
Trial Chamber Judgment, IT-99-36-T, 1 September 2004.
*Prosecutor v. Zejnil Delalić, Zdravko Mucić, Hazim Delić and Esad Landžo*Appeals Chamber Judgment, IT-96-21-A, 20 February 2001.
Prosecutor v. Dražen Erdemović
Trial Chamber Judgment, IT-96-22-Tbis, 5 March 1998.
Prosecutor v. Anto Furundžija
Trial Chamber Judgment, IT-95-17/1-T, 10 December 1998.
Prosecutor v. Sylvestre Gacumbtsi
Appeals Chamber Judgment, ICTR-2001-64-A, 7 July 2006.
Prosecutor v. Sefer Halilović
Trial Chamber Judgment, IT-01-48-T, 16 November 2005.
Prosecutor v. Ahmad Muhammad Harun & Ali Muhammad Al Abd-Al-Rahman
Warrant of Arrest, ICC-02/05-01/07, 27 April 2007.
Prosecutor v. Goran Jelisić
Appeals Chamber Judgment, IT-95-10-A, 5 July 2001.
In the Case Against Petar Jojić, Jovo Ostojić and Vjerica Radeta
Trial Chamber Decision, Order Lifting Confidentiality of Order in Lieu of Indictment and Arrest Warrants, IT-03-67-R77.5, 1 December 2015.
Prosecutor v. Juvénal Kajelijeli
Trial Chamber Judgment, ICTR-98-44A-T, 1 December 2003.
Appeals Chamber Judgment, ICTR-98-44A-A, 23 May 2005.
Prosecutor v. Callixte Kalimanzira
Trial Chamber Judgment, ICTR 05-88-T, 22 June 2009.
Prosecutor v. Jean Kambanda
Trial Chamber Judgment, ICTR 97-23-T, 4 September 1998.
Prosecutor v. Radovan Karadžić
Third Amended Indictment, IT-95-5/18-PT, 27 February 2009.
Trial Chamber Judgment, IT-95-5/18-T, 24 March 2016.
Prosecutor v. François Karera
Trial Chamber Judgment, ICTR-01-74-T, 7 December 2007.
Prosecutor v. Clément Kayishema & Obed Ruzindana

Trial Chamber Judgment, ICTR-95-1-T, 21 May 1999.
Prosecutor v. Dario Kordić and Mario Čerkez
Trial Chamber Judgment, IT-95-14/2-T, 26 February 2001.
Appeals Chamber Judgment, IT-95-14/2-A, 17 December 2004.
Prosecutor v. Momcilo Krajišnik
Appeals Chamber Judgment, IT-00-39-A, 17 March 2009.
Prosecutor v. Radislav Krstić
Trial Chamber Judgment, IT-98-33-T, 2 August 2001.
Appeals Chamber Judgment, IT-98-33-A, 19 April 2004.
Prosecutor v. Miroslav Kvočka et al.
Trial Chamber Judgment, IT-98-30/1-T, 2 November 2001.
Prosecutor v. Thomas Lubanga Dyilo
Pre-Trial Chamber Decision on Confirmation of Charges, 29 January 2007.
Trial Chamber Judgment, ICC-01/04-01/06, 14 March 2012.
Prosecutor v. Milan Lukić and Sredoje Lukić
Decision on Second Prosecution Motion for the Admission of Evidence
    Pursuant to Rule 92 *bis* (Two Expert Witnesses), IT-98-32/1-T, 23 July
    2008.
Prosecutor v. Callixte Mbarushimana
Decision on the Confirmation of Charges, ICC-01/04-01/10, 16 December
    2011, Section VII.3.b.
Prosecutor v. Milan Milutinović et al.
Trial Chamber Judgment, IT-05-87-T, 26 February 2009.
Prosecutor v. Mile Mrkšić, Miroslav Radić & Veselin Šljivančanin
Appeals Chamber Judgment, IT-95-13/1-A, 5 May 2009.
Prosecutor v. Justin Mugenzi and Prosper Mugiraneza
Appeals Chamber Judgment, ICTR-99-50-A, 4 February 2013.
Prosecutor v. Alfred Musema
Trial Chamber Judgment, ICTR-96-13-T, 27 January 2000.
Prosecutor v. Tharcisse Muvunyi
Appeals Chamber Judgment, ICTR-2000-55-A-A, 29 August 2008.
Prosecutor v. Ferdinand Nahimana, Jean-Bosco Barayagwisa, Hassan Ngeze
Trial Chamber Judgment, ICTR-99-52-T, 3 December 2003.
Appeals Chamber Judgment, ICTR-99-52-A, 28 November 2007.
Prosecutor v. Augustin Ngirabatware
Trial Chamber Judgment, ICTR-99-54-T, 20 December 2012.
Prosecutor v. Mathieu Ngudjolo Chui
Trial Chamber Judgment, ICC-01/04-02/12 52, 18 December 2012.
Appeals Chamber, Second Public Redacted Version of "Prosecution's
    Document in Support of Appeal Against the 'Jugement rendu en applica-
    tion de l'article 74 du Statut'," ICC-01/04-02/12, 15 October 2014.
Prosecutor v. Eliézer Niyitegeka
Trial Chamber Judgment, ICTR-96-14-T, 16 May 2003.

Prosecutor v. Bosco Ntaganda
Decision on the Confirmation of Charges, ICC-01/04-02/06, 9 June 2014.
Prosecutor v. Momčilo Perišić
Trial Chamber Judgment, IT-05-88-T, 6 September 2011.
Appeals Chamber Judgment, IT-05-88-A, 28 February 2013.
Prosecutor v. Vujadin Popović et al.
Trial Chamber Judgment, IT-05-88-T, 10 June 2010.
Prosecutor v. Jadranko Prlić et al.
Trial Chamber Judgment, T-04-74-T, Separate and Partially Dissenting
   Opinion of Presiding Judge Jean-Claude Antonetti, Vol. 6 of 6, 29 May
   2013.
Prosecutor v. Georges Ruggiu
Trial Chamber Judgment, ICTR-97-32-I, 1 June 2000.
Prosecutor v. William Samoei Ruto, Henry Kiprono Kosgey & Joshua Arap Sang
Decision on the Confirmation of Charges Pursuant to Article 61(7)(a) and (b)
   of the Rome Statute (ICC-01/09-01/11), 23 January 2012.
Prosecutor v. William Samoei Ruto and Joshua Arap Sang
Decision No. 5 on the Conduct of Trial Proceedings (Principles and Procedure
   on 'No Case to Answer' Motions), 3 June 2014.
Prosecution's Request for notice under regulation 55(2) of possibility of var-
   iation with respect to individual criminal responsibility of Mr. Joshua Arap
   Sang (ICC-01/09-01/11-1951), 8 September 2015.
Decision on Defence Applications for Judgments of Acquittal (ICC-01/09-
   01/11), 5 April 2016.
Prosecutor v. Georges Anderson Rutaganda
Trial Chamber Judgment, ICTR-96-3-T, 6 December 1999.
Appeals Chamber Judgment, ICTR-69-3-A, 26 May 2003.
Prosecutor v. Nikola Šainović et al.
Appeals Chamber Judgment, IT-05-87-A, 23 January 2014.
Prosecutor v. Issa Hassan Sesay, Morris Kallon and Augustine Gbao
Appeals Chamber Judgment, SCSL-04-15-A, 26 October 2009.
Prosecutor v. Vojislav Šešelj
Decision on Anthony Oberschall's Status as an Expert, IT-03-67-T, 30
   November 2007.
Third Amended Indictment, IT-03-67-T, 7 December 2007.
Prosecution's Closing Brief, IT-03-67-T, 5 February 2012.
Trial Chamber Judgment, IT-03-67-T, 31 March 2016.
Partially Dissenting Opinion of Judge Flavia Lattanzi-Amended Version,
   Vol. 3, IT-03-67-T, 31 March 2016.
Prosecutor v. Milan Simić
Appeals Chamber Judgment, IT-95-9-A, 28 November 2006.
Prosecutor v. Milomir Stakić
Appeals Chamber Judgment, IT-97-24-A, 22 March 2006.

Prosecutor v. Pavle Strugar
Decision on the Defence Motions to Oppose Admission of Prosecution Expert Reports Pursuant to Rule 94*bis*, IT-01-42-PT, 1 April 2004.
Prosecutor v. Zdravko Tolomir
Appeals Chamber Judgment, IT-05-88/2-A, Separate and Partially Dissenting Opinion of Judge Antonetti, 14 July 2015.
Prosecutor v. Mitar Vasiljević
Appeals Chamber Judgment, IT-98-32-A, February 2004.
R. v. Derek William Bentley (Deceased). Judgement of England and Wales Court of Appeal (Criminal Division) [1998] EWCA Crim 2516, 1998.
R. v. Towers (1987) 12 Cox 530 (T.A.C.).
Robert Faurisson v. France, Communication No. 550/1993, UN Doc. CCPR/C/58/D/550/1993 (1996).
Schenck v. United States, 250 US 616 (1919).
State v. Griffin, 251 Conn. 671, 712–13 n. 17 (1999).
State v. Henderson, 27 A.3d 872 (N.J. 2011).
State v. Petersen, 270 Or. 166, 526 P.2d 1008 (1974).
State v. Portillo, 182 Ariz.592, 898 P.2d 970 (Ariz. 1995).
Tauza v. Susquehanna Coal Company, 220 N.Y. 259, 115 N.E. 915 (1917).
Trial of the Major War Criminals Before the International Military Tribunal, Nuremberg, 14 November 1945 – 1 October 1946. (Section on Julius Streicher; Part 22, p182, p501).
United States v. Frye, 293 F. 1013 (1923).
Velazquez v. State. District Court of Appeal of Florida, 1990. 561 So.2d 347.

Books and Articles
Agbor, Avitus A. (2013) *Instigation to Crimes Against Humanity: The Flawed Jurisprudence of the Trial and Appeal Chambers of the International Criminal Tribunal for Rwanda (ICTR)*. Leiden: Martinus Nijhoff.
Ahmetasević, Nidzara (2010) "Hague Recognizes Propaganda's Role in Srebrenica Genocide." *Balkan Insight*, 7 July 2010. www.balkaninsight.com/en/article/hague-recognises-propaganda-s-role-in-srebrenica-genocide/ Accessed 11 June 2016.
Akhavan, Payam (2001) "Beyond Impunity: Can International Criminal Justice Prevent Future Atrocities?" *American Journal of International Law*, 95(1): 7–31.
Aksenova, Marina (2016) *Complicity in International Criminal Law*. Oxford: Hart.
Alexander, Larry and Kimberly Kessler (1997) "Mens Rea and Inchoate Crimes." *Journal of Criminal Law and Criminology*. 87: 1138–93.
American Law Institute (2010) *Restatement (Third) of Torts: Liability for Physical & Emotional Harm*. St. Paul, MN: American Law Institute Publishers, 2010–2012.

Anders, Gerhard (2011) "Testifying About 'Uncivilized Events': Problematic Representations of Africa in the Trial Against Charles Taylor." *Leiden Journal of International Law*. 24(4): 937–59. DOI: 10.1017/S0922156511000446

Anderson, Elizabeth S. and Richard H. Pildes (2000) "Expressive Theories of Law: A General Restatement." *Pennsylvania Law Review*. 148: 1503–75.

(2001/1941) *The Basic Works of Aristotle*. Trans. Richard McKeon. New York: Random House.

Aristotle (2004) *Rhetoric*. Trans. W. Rhys Roberts. Dover: New York.

Ashworth, Andrew (2009) *Principles of Criminal Law*. Oxford: Oxford University Press.

Ashworth, Andrew and Lucia Zedner (2014) *Preventative Justice*. Oxford: Oxford University Press.

Austin, J. L. (1962) *How to Do Things with Words. The William James Lectures Delivered at Harvard University in 1955*. 1st Edn. Cambridge: Harvard University Press.

Axelrod, Robert (1984) *The Evolution of Cooperation*. New York: Basic Books.

Belavusau, Uladzislau (2014) "Experts in Hate Speech Cases. Towards a Higher Standard of Proof in Strasbourg?" In Wouter Werner and Łukasz Gruszczyński (eds.), *Deference in International Courts and Tribunals: Standard of Review and Margin of Appreciation*. Oxford: Oxford University Press, pp. 254–71.

Benesch, Susan (2004) "Inciting Genocide, Pleading Free Speech." *World Policy Journal*, V21(2): 62–9.

(2008) "Vile Crime or Inalienable Right: Defining Incitement to Genocide." *Virginia Journal of International Law*, 48(3): 486–528.

(2012) "The Ghost of Causation in International Speech Crime Cases." In P. Dojčinović (ed.), *Propaganda, War Crimes and International Law: From Speakers' Corner to War Crimes*. Abingdon, NY: Routledge, pp. 254–68.

Berger, Linda L. (2013) "Metaphor and Analogy: The Sun and Moon of Legal Persuasion." *Journal of Law and Policy*, 22(1): 147–95.

Berger, Sebastian and Wolfram Elsner (2007) "European Contributions to Evolutionary Institutional Economics: The Cases of Cumulative Circular Causation (CCC) and Open System Approach (OSA). Some Methodological and Policy Implications." *Journal of Economic Issues*, 41 (2): 529–37.

Bernays, Edward (1928/2005) *Propaganda*. New York: Ig Publishing.

Black, Henry Campbell (2009) *Black's Law Dictionary*. 9th Edn. Bryan A. Garner (ed.). St. Paul, MN: West.

Boas, Gideon (2007) *The Milosevic Trial: Lessons for the Conduct of Complex International Criminal Proceedings*. Cambridge: Cambridge University Press.

Bosmajian, Haig A. (1992) *Metaphor and Reason in Judicial Opinions*. Carbondale: Southern Illinois University Press.

Bourdieu, Pierre (1984) *Distinction. A Social Critique of the Judgement of Taste*. Cambridge: Harvard University Press.

(2000) *Pascalian Meditations*. Palo Alto: Stanford University Press.

Brass, Marcel and Patrick Haggard (2007) "To Do or Not to Do: The Neural Signature of Self-Control." *Journal of Neuroscience*. 27(34): 9141–5.

Browning, Christopher (1998) *Ordinary Men: Reserve Police Battalion 101 and the Final Solution in Poland*. New York: Harper Collins. First published 1992.

Burger, J. M. (2009) "Replicating Milgram: Would People Still Obey Today?" *American Psychologist*. 64: 1–11.

Cahill, Michael T. (2012) "Defining Inchoate Crimes: An Incomplete Attempt." *Ohio State Journal of Criminal Law*. 9: 751–9.

Camp, Elizabeth (2006) "Metaphor in the Mind: The Cognition of Metaphor." *Philosophy Compass*. 1/2: 154–70.

Campbell, Duncan (1998) "Justice at Last, 45 Years Too Late." *The Guardian*. 31 July 1998.

Caplan, Gerald (2007) "Rwanda: Walking the Road to Genocide." In Allan Thompson (ed.), *The Media and the Rwanda Genocide*. London: Pluto Press, pp. 20–37.

Cardozo, Benjamin (1931) *Law and Literature and Other Essays and Addresses*. New York: Harcourt Brace and Co.

Carruthers, Susan (2000) *The Media Wars*. New York: St. Martin's Press.

Carver, Richard (2000) "Broadcasting and Political Transition: Rwanda and Beyond." In R. Fardon and G. Furniss (eds.), *African Broadcast Cultures: Radio in Transition*. Oxford: James Currey, pp. 188–97.

Cassese, Antonio (2008) *International Criminal Law*. 2nd Edn. Oxford: Oxford University Press.

Cassese, Antonio and Paola Gaeta (2013) *Cassese's International Criminal Law*. Revised by A. Cassese, P. Gaeta, L. Baig, M. Fan, C. Gosnell and A. Whiting. 3rd Edn. Oxford: Oxford University Press.

Cavell, Stanley (1979) *The Claim of Reason: Wittgenstein, Skepticism, Morality and Tragedy*. New York: Oxford University Press.

(2005) "Passionate and Performative Utterances." In R. B. Gordon (ed.), *Contending with Stanley Cavell*. New York: Oxford University Press, pp. 178–98.

Chiesa, Luis (2008) "Duress, Demanding Heroism and Proportionality: The Erdemovic Case and Beyond." *Vanderbilt Journal of Transnational Law*, (41): 741–73.

Chrétien, J. P., J. F. Dupaquier, M. Kabanda and J. Ngarambe (1995) *Rwanda: Les Medias du Genocide*. Paris: Karthala.

Clarke, Kamari (2009) *Fictions of Justice: The International Criminal Court and the Challenge of Legal Pluralism in Sub-Saharan Africa*. New York: Cambridge University Press.

(2010) "Rethinking Africa Through Its Exclusions: The Politics of Naming Criminal Responsibility." *Anthropological Quarterly* 83(3): 625–52.

Clermont, Kevin and Emily Sherwin (2002) "A Comparative View of Standards of Proof." *American Journal of Comparative Law*. 50(2): 243–76.

Cohen, Felix (1935) "Transcendental Nonsense and the Functional Approach." *Columbia Law Review*. 35(6): 809–49.

Collins, Barry E. (1974) "Four Components of the Rotter Internal-External Scale: Belief in a Difficult World, a Just World, a Predictable World, and a Politically Responsive World." *Journal of Personality and Social Psychology*, 29(3): 381–91. http://dx.doi.org/10.1037/h0036015.

Combs, Nancy A. (2010) *Fact-Finding Without Facts. The Uncertain Evidentiary Foundations of International Criminal Convictions*. Cambridge: Cambridge University Press.

Constable, Marianne (2014) *Our Word Is Our Bond: How Legal Speech Acts*. Stanford: Stanford University Press.

Corcoran, Hannah, Deborah Lader and Kevin Smith (2015) *Hate Crime, England and Wales, 2014/15*, Statistical Bulletin 05/15, London: UK Home Office.

Cryer, Robert, Håkan Friman, Darryl Robinson and Elizabeth Wilmshurst (2014) *An Introduction to International Criminal Law and Procedure*. 3rd Edn. Cambridge: Cambridge University Press.

Dale, A. C. (2001) "Countering Hate Messages That Lead to Violence: The United Nations' Chapter VII Authority to Use Radio Jamming to Halt Incendiary Broadcasts." *Duke Journal of Comparative & International Law*, 11: 109–451.

Davidson, Donald (2001) "What Metaphors Mean." In *Inquiries into Truth and Interpretation*. 2nd Edn. Oxford: Clarendon Press, pp. 245–64.

Davidson, H. Ron (2004) "The International Criminal Tribunal for Rwanda's Decision in *The Prosecutor v. Ferdinand Nahimana et al.*: The Past, Present, and Future of International Incitement Law." *Leiden Journal of International Law*, 17(3): 505–19.

Davies, Thomas (2009) "How the Rome Statute Weakens the International Prohibition on Incitement to Genocide." *Harvard Human Rights Journal*. (22): 245–70.

Davis, G. Scott (1996) *Religion and Justice in the War over Bosnia*. London: Routledge.

De le Brosse, Renaud (2003) *Political Propaganda and a Plan to Create a "State for All Serbs": Consequences of Using the Media for Ultra-Nationalist Ends*. Report Compiled at the request of the Office of the Prosecutor of the

International Criminal Tribunal for the Former Yugoslavia (ICTY). 4 February 2003. Case Slobodan Milošević, Case No. IT-02–54.

De Quervain, D. J. F., U. Fischbacher, V. Treyer, M. Schellhammer, U. Schnyder, A. Buck and E. Fehr (2004) "The Neural Basis of Altruistic Punishment." *Science.* 27 August 2004; 305(5688): 1254–8. DOI: 10.1126/science.1100735

DeCoux, Elizabeth L. (2007) "The Admission of Unreliable Expert Testimony Offered by the Prosecution: What's Wrong with Daubert and How to Make It Right." *Utah Law Review.* pp 131–166.

Del Ponte, Carla (2008) *Madam Prosecutor: Confrontations with Humanity's Worst Criminals and the Culture of Impunity: A Memoir.* With Chuck Sudetic. New York: Other Press.

Dembour, Marie-Bénédicte and Tobias Kelly (2007) *Paths to International Justice: Social and Legal Perspectives.* Cambridge: Cambridge University Press.

Des Forges, Alison (1999) "Propaganda and Practice." *Leave None to Tell the Story: Genocide in Rwanda.* New York: Human Rights Watch. March 1999.

Dharmapala, Dhammika and Richard H. McAdams (2005) "Words That Kill? An Economic Model of the Influence of Speech on Behavior (with Particular Reference to Hate Speech)." *Journal of Legal Studies,* 34(1): 93–136.

Dion, Karen, Ellen Berscheid and Elaine Walster (1972) "What Is Beautiful Is Good." *Journal of Personality and Social Psychology,* 24(3): 285–290.

Dodd, Thomas J. *Defense of Streicher,* University of Connecticut: Archives & Special Collections at the Thomas J. Dodd Research Center, http://arc hives.lib.uconn.edu/islandora/object/20002%3A1953#page/1/mode/2up.

Individual Responsibility of the Defendant Julius Streicher, University of Connecticut: Archives & Special Collections at the Thomas J. Dodd Research Center, http://archives.lib.uconn.edu/islandora/object/20002% 3A1942#page/1/mode/2up.

Office of US Chief of Counsel Memorandum for Mr. Dodd, Harriet Zetterberg Margolies, 29 May 1946, at http://archives.lib.uconn.edu/islandora/objec t/20002%3A1953#page/1/mode/2up.

Prosecution oral Presentation against Fritzsche, University of Connecticut: Archives & Special Collections at the Thomas J. Dodd Research Center, http://archives.lib.uconn.edu/islandora/object/20002:1536#pag e/1/mode/2up.

Dojčinović, Predrag (ed.) (2012) *Propaganda, War Crimes and International Law: From Speakers' Corner to War Crimes.* Abingdon, NY: Routledge.

(2014) "The Chameleon of Mens Rea and the Shifting Guises of Genocidal Intent in International Criminal Proceedings," Visiting Gladstein Professor Lecture in Human Rights, University of Connecticut, 3 April 2014.

Donia, Robert J. (2015) *Radovan Karadžić: Architect of the Bosnian Genocide.* Cambridge: Cambridge University Press.

Douglas, Lawrence (1995) "Film as Witness: Screening 'Nazi Concentration Camps' Before the Nuremberg Tribunal." *The Yale Law Journal,* 105(2): 449–81.

(2001) *The Memory of Judgment: Making Law and History in the Trials of the Holocaust.* New Haven: Yale University Press.

Dower, John (1986) *War without Mercy: Race and Power in the Pacific War.* New York: Pantheon.

Dressler, Joshua (2009) *Understanding Criminal Law.* 5th Edn. Newark: Matthew Bender.

Dressler, Joshua and Stephen P. Garvey (2012) *Cases and Materials in Criminal Law.* 6th Edn. St. Paul, MN: West Academic.

Drumbl, Mark (2007) "The Expressive Value of Prosecuting and Punishing Terrorists: Hamdan, the Geneva Conventions, and International Criminal Law." *George Washington Law Review,* 75(5–6): 1165–99.

Eastwood, Margaret (2012) "Hitler's Notorious Jew-Baiter: The Prosecution of Julius Streicher." In Predrag Dojčinović (ed.), *Propaganda, War Crimes and International Law: From Speakers' Corner to War Crimes.* Abingdon, NY: Routledge.

Enoch, David, Levi Spectre and Talia Fisher (2012) "Statistical Evidence, Sensitivity, and the Legal Value of Knowledge." *Philosophy and Public Affairs,* 40(3): 197–224.

Eltringham, Nigel (2004) *Accounting for Horror: Post-Genocide Debates in Rwanda.* London: Pluto Press.

(2006) "'Invaders Who Have Stolen the Country': The Hamitic Hypothesis, Race and the Rwandan Genocide." *Social Identities,* 12(4): 425–46.

(2012) "Spectators to the Spectacle of Law: The Formation of a 'Validating Public' at the International Criminal Tribunal for Rwanda." *Ethnos: Journal of Anthropology,* 773: 425–45.

(2013) "'Illuminating the Broader Context': Anthropological and Historical Knowledge at the International Criminal Tribunal for Rwanda." *Journal of the Royal Anthropological Institute,* 19(2): 338–55.

Fazio, R. H. (1990) "Multiple Processes by Which Attitudes Guide Behavior: The MODE Model as an Integrative Framework." *Advances in Experimental Social Psychology,* 23: 75–110.

Fehr, E. and S. Gächter (2002) "Altruistic Punishment in Humans." *Nature,* 415(6868): 137–40.

Feingold, A. (1992) "Good-Looking People Are Not What We Think." *Psychological Bulletin,* 111: 304–41.

Feldman, Robin (2009) *The Role of Science in Law.* Oxford: Oxford University Press.

Fišer, Nenad (2012) "The Indictable Propaganda: A Bottom Up Perspective." In Predrag Dojčinović (ed.) *Propaganda, War Crimes and International Law: From Speakers' Corner to War Crimes.* Abingdon, NY: Routledge, pp. 33–70.

Fish, Stanley (1994) *There's No Such Thing as Free Speech and It's a Good Thing, Too.* Oxford: Oxford University Press.

Fishbein, M. (1967) "Attitude and the Prediction of Behaviour." In Fishbein, M. (ed.), *Readings in Attitude Theory and Measurement.* New York: Wiley.

Fishbein, M and I. Ajzen (1974). "Attitudes Towards Objects as Predictors of Single and Multiple Behavioural Criteria." *Psychological Review*, 81(1): 29–74.

Fiske, S. T. and C. Dupree (2014). "Gaining Trust as Well as Respect in Communicating to Motivated Audiences About Science Topics." *PNAS: Proceedings of the National Academy of Sciences of the United States of America*, 111(4): 13593–7.

Fiske, S. T. and F. Durante (2014) "Never Trust a Politician? Collective Distrust, Relational Accountability, and Voter Response." In J.-W. van Prooijen and P. van Lange (eds.), *Power, Politics & Paranoia.* Cambridge University Press.

Fiske, S. T., A. J. Cuddy, P. Glick and J. Xu (2002) "A Model of (Often Mixed) Stereotype Content: Competence and Warmth Respectively Follow from Perceived Status and Competition." *Journal of Personality and Social Psychology*, 82(6): 878–902.

Friedland, Steven I., Paul Bergman and Andrew E. Taslitz (2012) *Evidence Law and Practice.* 5th Edn. New Providence: LexisNexis.

Garland, Brent (ed.) (2004) *Neuroscience and the Law: Brain, Mind and the Scales of Justice.* New York: Dana Press.

Gatowski, S. I., Dobbin S. A., Richardson J. T., Ginsburg G. P., Merlino M. L. and Dahir V. (2001) "Asking the Gatekeepers: A National Survey of Judges and Judging Expert Evidence in a Post-*Daubert* World." *Law and Human Behavior*, 25(5): 433–58.

Gaudreault-DesBiens, J. (2000) "From Sisyphus's Dilemma to Sisyphus's Duty? A Meditation on the Regulation of Hate Propaganda in Relation to Hate Crimes and Genocide." *McGill Law Journal*, 46: 121–38.

Gazzaniga, Michael S. and Megan S. Steven (2004) "Free Will in the Twenty-First Century: A Discussion of Neuroscience and the Law." In Brent Garland (ed.), *Neuroscience and the Law: Brain, Mind and the Scales of Justice.* Dana Press: New York.

Geertz, Clifford (1983) "Common Sense as a Cultural System." *Local Knowledge: Further Essays in Interpretive Anthropology.* New York: Basic Books.

Gerken, Heather (2017) "Federalism 3.0." New York University Law School: 2017 Thomas M. Jorde Symposium, 1 March 2017.

Gey, Steven (2010) "The Brandenburg Paradigm and Other First Amendments." *University of Pennsylvania Journal of Constitutional Law*, 12: 971–1052.

German Criminal Code (Übersetzung des Strafgesetzbuches) (2015), Trans. Michael Bohlander. Saarbrücken: Juris GmbH. www.gesetze-im-inter net.de/englisch_stgb/englisch_stgb.html

Goff, Phillip Atiba et al. (2008) "Not Yet Human: Implicit Knowledge, Historical Dehumanization, and Contemporary Consequences." *Journal of Personality and Social Psychology*, 94(2): 292–306.

Goodale, Mark (2017) *Anthropology and Law: A Critical Introduction*. New York: NYU Press.

Goodman, Russell (ed.) (2005) *Contending with Stanley Cavell*. Oxford: Oxford University Press.

Gordon, Gregory S. (2005) "A War of Media, Words, Newspapers, and Radio Stations: The ICTR Media Trial Verdict and a New Chapter in the International Law of Hate Speech." *Virginia Journal International Law*, 45(139): 1–60.

(2008) "From Incitement to Indictment? Prosecuting Iran's President for Advocating Israel's Destruction and Piecing Together Incitement Law's Emerging Analytical Framework." *Journal of Criminal Law & Criminology*, 98(3): 853–920.

(2010) "Music and Genocide: Harmonizing Coherence, Freedom and Nonviolence in Incitement Law." *Santa Clara Law Review*, 50: 607–46.

(2012) "Formulating a New Atrocity Speech Offense: Incitement to Commit War Crimes." *Loyola University Chicago Law Journal*, 43(2): 281–316.

Gray, Kurt and Daniel M. Wegner (2012) "The Social Psychology of Morality: Exploring the Causes of Good and Evil." In Mario Mikulincer and Phillip R. Shaver (eds.), *Morality Takes Two: Dyadic Morality and Mind Perception*. Washington, DC: American Psychological Association pp. 109–27, http://dx.doi.org/10.1037/13091–006

Green, Leon (1927) *Rationale of Proximate Cause*. Kansas City: Vernon Law Book Company.

Green, Michael Steven (2005) "Legal Realism as Theory of Law." *William & Mary Law Review*, (46): 1915–2000. http://ssrn.com/abstract=761007

Greenawalt, Kent (1989) *Speech, Crime, and the Uses of Language*. New York: Oxford University Press.

Grice, Paul (1986) *Studies in the Ways of Words*. Cambridge, MA: Harvard University Press.

Groscup, Jennifer L. et. al. (2002) "The Effects of Daubert on the Admissibility of Expert Testimony in State and Federal Criminal Cases." *Psychology, Public Policy, and Law*, 8(4): 339–72.

Gustafsson, Martin and Richard Sorli (2012) *The Philosophy of J. L. Austin*. Oxford: Oxford University Press.

Haidt, J., C. McCauley and P. Rozin (1994) "Individual Differences in Sensitivity to Disgust: A Scale Sampling Seven Domains of Disgust Elicitors." *Personality and Individual Differences*, 16: 701–13.

Haiman, Franklyn S. (1992) *"Speech Acts" and the First Amendment*. Carbondale, IL; Southern Illinois University Press.

Hare, Ivan and James Weinstein (eds.) (2010) *Extreme Speech and Democracy*. Oxford: Oxford University Press.

Harris, Lasana T. and Susan T. Fiske (2006) "Dehumanizing the Lowest of the Low: Neuroimaging Responses to Extreme Out-Groups." *Journal of Psychological Science*, 17(10): 847–53.

(2011) "Dehumanized Perception: A Psychological Means to Facilitate Atrocities, Torture and Genocide?" *Journal of Psychology*, 219(3): 175–81.

Hart, H. L. A. (1961) *The Concept of Law*. Oxford: Clarendon Press.

Hart, H. L. A. and Tony Honoré (1985) *Causation in the Law*. 2nd Edn. Oxford: Clarendon Press.

Harvard Law Review (2012) "Evidence – Eyewitness Identifications – New Jersey Supreme Court Uses Psychological Research to Update Admissibility Standards for Out-of-Court Identifications. – State v. Henderson, 27 A.3d 872 (N.J. 2011)." 125(6): 1514–21.

Haslam, N. (2006) "Dehumanization: An Integrative Review." *Personality and Social Psychology Review*, 10(3): 252–64.

Haslam, N., P. Bain, L. Douge, M. Lee and B. Bastian (2005) "More Human than You: Attributing Humanness to Self and Others." *Journal of Personality and Social Psychology*, 89(6): 937–50.

Healy, Thomas (2009) "Brandenburg in a Time of Terror." *Notre Dame Law Review*, 84(2): 655–731.

Hola, Barbora (2012) *International Sentencing: A Game of Russian Roulette or Consistent Practice?* Amsterdam: VU Universiteit/Uitgeverij BOXPress.

Hola, Barbora, A. Smeulers and C. Bijleveld (2011) "International Sentencing Facts and Figures: Sentencing Practice at the ICTY." and ICTR, *Journal of International Criminal Justice*, 9(2): 411–39.

International Commission on Intervention and State Sovereignty (2002) *The Responsibility to Protect: The Report of the International Commission on Intervention and State Sovereignty*. Ottawa: IDRC.

Independent International Commission on Kosovo (2000) *Kosovo Report: Conflict, International Response, Lessons Learned.* Oxford: Oxford University Press.

International Criminal Court Rules of Procedure and Evidence. Adopted by the Assembly of States Parties. First session. New York, 3–10 September 2002. Official Records ICC-ASP/1/3. Legal citation: ICC-ASP/1/3, at 10, and Corr. 1 (2002), UN Doc. PCNICC/2000/1/Add.1 (2000).

International Criminal Court (2011) *Elements of Crimes.* The Hague: International Criminal Court. Legal Citation: ICC-PIDS-LT-03–002/ 11_Eng

International Criminal Tribunal for the Former Yugoslavia (2015) *Rules of Procedure and Evidence.* IT/32/Rev.50. 8 July 2015. Hague: ICTY.

International Law Commission (1996) *Draft Code of Crimes Against the Peace and Security of Mankind.* Report of the International Law Commission on the work of its forty-eighth session, 6 May–26 July 1996, Official Records of the General Assembly, Fifty-first session, Supplement No. 10, Extract from the *Yearbook of the International Law Commission 1996.* UN Doc. A/ CN.4/L.532, corr. 1, corr. 3 (1996).

Irwin, Rachel (2012) "Prosecutors Seek 28-Year Jail Term for Šešelj." *Institute for War and Peace Reporting.* http://iwpr.net/report-news/prosecutors-seek-28-year-jail-term-seselj. Accessed 9 March 2017.

Jacoby, Susan (1983). *Wild Justice: The Evolution of Revenge.* HarperCollins Publishers.

Jackson, Miles (2015) *Complicity in International Law.* Oxford: Oxford University Press.

Janis, Mark W., Richard S. Kay and Anthony W. Bradley (2008) *European Human Rights Law.* 3rd Edn. Oxford: Oxford University Press.

Jasanoff, Sheila (1995) *Science at the Bar.* Cambridge: Harvard University Press.

Jenkins, Pamela J. and Steve Kroll-Smith (eds.) (1996) *Witnessing for Sociology: Sociologists in Court.* Westport: Praeger.

Jordan, Constance (ed.) (2013) *Reason and Imagination: The Selected Correspondence of Learned Hand.* Oxford: Oxford University Press.

Jost, J. T. and E. P. Thompson (2000) "Group-Based Dominance and Opposition to Equality as Independent Predictors of Self-Esteem, Ethnocentrism, and Social Policy Attitudes Among African Americans and European Americans." *Journal of Experimental Social Psychology,* 36(3): 209–232. DOI: 10.1006/jesp.1999.1403

Jowett, Garth S. and Victoria O'Donnell (2006) *Propaganda and Persuasion.* 4th Edn. London: SAGE.

(2012) *Propaganda and Persuasion.* 5th Edn. London: SAGE.

Kahan, Dan M., David A. Hoffman and Donald Braman (2009) "Whose Eyes are You Going to Believe? Scott v. Harris and the Perils of Cognitive Illiberalism." *Harvard Law Review,* 122(3): 838–903.

Kahan, Dan M., David Hoffman, Danieli Evans, Neal Devins, Eugene Lucci and Katherine Cheng (2016) "'Ideology' or 'Situation Sense'? An Experimental Investigation of Motivated Reasoning and Professional Judgment." *University of Pennsylvania Law Review*, 64: 349–439.

Kaid, Linda Lee (2004) *Handbook of Political Communication Research*. Mahwah, NJ: Lawrence Erlbaum Publishers.

Kalyvas, Stathis (2006) *The Logic of Violence in Civil War*. New York: Cambridge University Press.

Kao, Justine T., Leon Bergen and Noah D. Goodman (2014) "Formalizing the Pragmatics of Metaphor Understanding." Unpublished paper. http://coco lab.stanford.edu/papers/KaoEtAl2014.pdf

Kearney, M. G. (2007) *The Prohibition of Propaganda for War in International Law*. Oxford: Oxford University Press.

Kearney, Joseph D. and Thomas W. Merrill (2000) "The Influence of Amicus Briefs on the Supreme Court." *University of Pennsylvania Law Review*. 148(3): 743–855.

Kelly, Tobias (2011) *This Side of Silence: Human Rights, Torture, and the Recognition of Cruelty*. Philadelphia: University of Pennsylvania Press.

Kelman, Herbert G. (1973) "Violence Without Moral Restraint: Reflections on the Dehumanization of Victims and Victimizers." *Journal of Social Issues*, 29(4): 25–61.

Kelsall, Tim (2009) *Culture Under Cross-Examination: International Justice and the Special Court for Sierra Leone*. Cambridge: Cambridge University Press.

Kiper, Jordan (2015) "War Propaganda, War Crimes and Post-Conflict Justice in Serbia: An Ethnographic Account." *The International Journal of Human Rights*, 19(2): 1–20.

Klinkner, Melanie (2008) "Proving Genocide? Forensic Expertise and the ICTY." *Journal of International Criminal Justice*, 6(3): 447–466.

Klug, Heinz and Sally Merry (eds.) (2016) *The New Legal Realism: Studying Law Globally*. Vol. II. Cambridge: Cambridge University Press.

Krauss, Robert M. and Chi-Yue Chiu (1997) In D. Gilbert, S. Fiske and G. Lindsey (eds.), *Handbook of Social Psychology*. Vol. 2. Oxford: Oxford University Press, pp. 41–88.

Kruger, J. and Gilovich, T. (2004) "Actions, Intentions, and Self-Assessment: The Road to Self-Enhancement Is Paved with Good Intentions." *Personality and Social Psychology Bulletin*, 30(3): 328–39.

Kuper, Leo (1985) *The Prevention of Genocide*. New Haven: Yale University Press.

La Mort, Justin (2009) "The Soundtrack to Genocide in the Bikindi Trial to Protect Free Speech and Uphold the Promise of Never Again." *Interdisciplinary Journal of Human Rights Law*, 4(1): 43–60.

La Tour, Bruno (2010) *The Making of Law: An Ethnography of the Conseil D'État*. London: Polity Press.

Lacey, Nicola (2004) *A Life of HLA Hart: The Nightmare and the Noble Dream*. Oxford: Oxford University Press.

Lakoff, George (2009) "The Neural Theory of Metaphor." 2 January 2009. http://papers.ssrn.com/sol3/papers.cfm?abstract_id=1437794

Lakoff, George and Mark Johnson (1980) *Metaphors We Live By*. Chicago: University of Chicago Press.

Lamoine, George, ed. (1992) *Charges to the Grand Jury 1689–1803*. Camden Fourth Series. Vol. 43. London: Royal Historical Society.

Langer, Máximo (2005) "The Rise of Managerial Judging in International Criminal Law." *American Journal of Comparative Law*, 53(4): 835–909.

Langton, Rae (1993) "Speech Acts and Unspeakable Acts." *Philosophy and Public Affairs*, 22(4): 293–330.

Lasswell, Harold (1927) *Propaganda Technique in the World War*. New York: Knopf.

Lewis, David (1973) "Causation." *Journal of Philosophy*, 70(17): 556–67.

Li, Darryl (2004) "Echoes of Violence: Considerations on Radio and Genocide in Rwanda." *Journal of Genocide Research*. 6(1): 9–28.

Libet, Benjamin W. (1999) "Do We Have Free Will?" *Journal of Consciousness Studies*, 6 (8–9): 47–57.

Lillie, Christine M., Brock Knapp, Lasana T. Harris and Richard Ashby Wilson (2015) "This Is the Hour of Revenge: The Psychology of Propaganda and Mass Atrocities." 18 March 2015. http://ssrn.com/abstract=2580521 or http://dx.doi.org/10.2139/ssrn.2580521

Loxley, James (2007) *Performativity*. London: Routledge.

Mackie, J. L. (1965) "Causes and Conditions." *American Philosophical Quarterly*, 2(4): 245–64.

MacKinnon, Catherine A. (1993) *Only Words*. Cambridge, MA: Harvard University Press.

(2009) Prosecutor v. Nahimana, Barayagwiza, & Ngeze. Case No. ICTR 99-52-T. *American Journal of International Law*, 98(2): 325–30.

Maine, Henry Sumner (1982/1861) *Ancient Law*. London: John Murray. Original reprinted by The Legal Classics Library, Birmingham, Alabama.

Maravilla, Christopher Scott (2008) "Hate Speech as a War Crime: Public and Direct Incitement to Genocide in International Law." *Tulane Journal of International and Comparative Law*, 17(1): 113–44.

Mayson, Sandra G. (2016) "Dangerous Defendants." University of Pennsylvania Law School, Public Law Research Paper No. 16–30. https://ssrn.com/abstract=2826600

McCullough, M. E., R. Kurzban and B. A. Tabak (2010) "Evolved Mechanisms for Revenge and Forgiveness." In P. R. Shaver and M. Mikulincer (eds.), *Understanding and Reducing Aggression, Violence, and Their Consequences*. Washington, DC: American Psychological Association, pp. 221–39.

McDougal, Myres S. and Harold D. Lasswell (1967) "Jurisprudence in Policy-Oriented Perspective." Yale University Faculty Scholarship Series, Paper 2582 (New Haven, CT: Yale). http://digitalcommons.law.yale.edu/fss_papers/2582

McKinley, Maggie (2016) "Lobbying and the Petition Clause." *Stanford Law Review.* 68(5): 1131–1205.

Meijers, Tim and Marlies Glashuis (2013) "Expression of Justice or Political Trial? Discursive Battles in the Karadžić Case." *Human Rights Quarterly* 35(3): 720–52.

Melzer, Nils (2009) *Interpretive Guidance on the Notion of Direct Participation in Hostilities Under Humanitarian Law.* Geneva: ICRC.

Mendel, Toby (2006) *Study on International Standards Relating to Incitement to Genocide or Racial Hatred.* United Nations: UN Special Advisor on the Prevention of Genocide.

Merry, Sally Engle, Kevin Davis and Benedict Kingsbury (eds.) (2015) *The Quiet Power of Indicators: Measuring Governance, Corruption, and Rule of Law.* Cambridge: Cambridge University Press.

Mertz, Elizabeth (ed.) (2008) *The Role of Social Science in Law.* Farnham: Ashgate.

Mertz, Elizabeth, Stewart Macaulay and Thomas W. Mitchell (eds.) (2016) *The New Legal Realism: Translating Law-and-Society for Today's Legal Practice.* Vol. 1. Cambridge: Cambridge University Press.

Metzl, J. F. (1997) "Rwandan Genocide and the International Law of Radio Jamming." *American Journal of International Law,* 91(4): 628–51.

Miles, Thomas J. and Cass R. Sunstein (2007) "The New Legal Realism." *University of Chicago Law Review,* 75: 831–51.

Milgram, Stanley (1974) *Obedience to Authority: An Experimental View.* New York: Harper and Row.

Mill, John Stuart (1989/1859) *On Liberty and Other Writings.* Edited by Stefan Collini. Cambridge: Cambridge University Press.

Mironko, Charles (2007) "The Effect of RTLM's Rhetoric of Ethnic Hatred in Rural Rwanda." In Allan Thompson (ed.), *The Media and the Rwanda Genocide.* London: Pluto Press, pp. 125–35.

Misser, Francois and Yves Jaumain (1994) "Death by Radio," *Index on Censorship,* 23:72.

Mitchell, Neil J. (2004) *Agents of Atrocity: Leaders, Followers and the Violation of Human Rights in Civil War.* New York, NY: Palgrave Macmillan

Moenssens, Andre A., Ronald J. Bacigal, Gerald G. Ashdown and Virginia E. Hench (2003) *Criminal Law.* 7th Edn. New York: Foundation Press.

Monahan, John and Jennifer L. Skeem (2016) "Risk Assessment in Criminal Sentencing." *Annual Review of Clinical Psychology,* 12: 489–513. DOI: 10.1146/annurev-clinpsy-021815-092945

Monahan, John and W. Laurens Walker (2010) *Social Science in Law: Cases and Materials*, 7th Edn. New York: Thomson Reuters/Foundation Press.

Moore, Michael S. (2009) *Causation and Responsibility: An Essay in Law, Morals, and Metaphysics*. Oxford: Oxford University Press.

Moran, Rachel (2010) "What Counts as Knowledge? A Reflection on Race, Social Science, and the Law." *Law and Society Review*, 44(3/4): 515–51.

Morse, Stephen J. (2004) "Inevitable Mens Rea." *Harvard Journal of Law and Public Policy*, (27): 51–64.

(2008) "Determinism and the Death of Folk Psychology: Two Challenges to Responsibility from Neuroscience." *Minnesota Journal of Law, Science and Technology*, (9): 1–36.

Morse, Stephen J. and Adina L. Roskies (2013) *A Primer on Criminal Law and Neuroscience*. Oxford: Oxford University Press.

Moyn, Samuel (2013) "Judith Shklar Versus the International Criminal Court." *Humanity: An International Journal of Human Rights, Humanitarianism and Development*, 4(3): 473–500.

Mundis, Daryl (2001) "From 'Common Law' Towards 'Civil Law': The Evolution of the ICTY Rules of Procedure and Evidence." *Leiden Journal of International Law*, 14: 367–82.

Myrdal, Gunnar (1944) *An American Dilemma, Volume 2: The Negro Problem and Modern Democracy*. Vol. 2. Edison, NJ: Transaction Publishers.

(1957) *Economic Theory and Underdeveloped Regions*. London: Methuen.

(1978) "Institutional Economics." *Journal of Economic Issues*, 12(4): 771–83.

Nahmias, Eddy (2015) "Why We Have Free Will." *Scientific American*. January, pp. 77–9.

National Research Council (2002) *The Age of Expert Testimony: Science in the Courtroom, Report of a Workshop*. Washington, DC: National Academy Press.

O'Keefe, Daniel J. (2002) "Guilt as a Mechanism of Persuasion." In J. P. Dillard and M. Pfau (eds.), *The Persuasion Handbook: Developments in Theory and Practice*. Thousand Oaks, CA: Sage, pp. 329–44.

Oberschall, Anthony (2006) "Vojislav Šešelj's Nationalist Propaganda: Contents, Techniques, Aims and Impacts, 1990–1994." Expert report for the United Nations International Criminal Tribunal for the Former Yugoslavia, Case No. IT-03–67, MFI P5.

(2012) "Propaganda, Hate Speech and Mass Killings." In Predrag Dojčinović (ed.), *Propaganda, War Crimes and International Law: From Speakers' Corner to War Crimes*. Abingdon, UK: Routledge, pp. 171–200.

Ohlin, Jens David (2009) "Incitement and Conspiracy to Commit Genocide." In Paola Gaeta (ed.), *The UN Genocide Convention – A Commentary*. New York, NY: Oxford University Press.

Olatunji, B. O., Williams, N. L., Tolin, D. F., Sawchuck, C. N., Abramowitz, J. S. and Lohr, J. M. et al. (2007) "The Disgust Scale: Item Analysis, Factor Structure, and Suggestions for Refinement." *Psychological Assessment*, 19: 281–97.

Orentlicher, Diane (2005) "Criminalizing Hate Speech in the Crucible of Trial: Prosecutor v. Nahimana." *New England Journal of International and Comparative Law*, 12(17): 1–34.

Osiel, Mark (2009) *Making Sense of Mass Atrocity*. Cambridge: Cambridge University Press.

Ostrom, E. (1990) *Governing the Commons: The Evolution of Institutions for Collective Action*. Cambridge University Press.

Paul, L. A. and Ned Hall (2013) *Causation: A User's Guide*. Oxford: Oxford University Press.

Perloff, Richard M. (2010) *The Dynamics of Persuasion: Communication and Attitudes in the 21st Century*. New York and London: Routledge.

Petty, R. E. and D. T. Wegener (1998) "Matching Versus Mismatching Attitude Functions: Implications For Scrutiny of Persuasive Messages." *Personality and Social Psychology Bulletin*, 24: 227–40.

Pildes, Richard H. (2014) "Institutional Formalism and Realism in Constitutional and Public Law." 2013 *Supreme Court Review*, 1; NYU School of Law, Public Law Research Paper No. 14–09. http://ssrn.com/abstract=2411141

Pirie, Fernanda (2013) *The Anthropology of Law*. Oxford: Oxford University Press.

Plato (1993) *Republic*. Trans. Robin Waterfield. Oxford: Oxford University Press.

Power, Samantha (2002) *A Problem from Hell: America and the Age of Genocide*. New York: Basic Books.

Prewitt, Kenneth, Thomas A. Schwandt and Miron L. Straf (eds.) (2012) *Using Science as Evidence in Public Policy*. Washington, DC: National Academies Press. DOI: 10.17226/13460

Pricewaterhouse Coopers, LLP (2011) "Daubert Challenges to Financial Experts: A Yearly Study of Trends and Outcomes." www.pwc.com/en_US/us/forensic-services/publications/assets/daubert-study-2011.pdf

Prosser, William and W. Page Keeton (1984) *Prosser and Keeton on the Law of Torts*. 5th Edn. St. Paul: West.

Rhodes N. and W. Wood (1992) "Self-Esteem and Intelligence Affect Influenceability: The Mediating Role of Message Reception." *Psychological Bulletin*, 111: 156–71.

Rikhof, Joseph (2005) "Hate Speech and International Criminal Law: The Mugesera Decision by the Supreme Court of Canada." *Journal of International Criminal Justice*, 3(5): 1121–33.

Risinger, D. Michael (2000) "Navigating Expert Reliability: Are Criminal Standards of Certainty Being Left on the Dock?" *Albany Law Review*, 64(1): 99–149.

Robinson, John Paul, Phillip R. Shaver and Lawrence S. Wrightsman (eds.) (1991) *Measures of Personality and Social Psychological Attitudes, Volume 1 (Measures of Social Psychological Attitudes)*. London: Academic Press.

Robinson, Paul H. and Michael T. Cahill (2012) "Causation: The Requirements for Holding an Actor Accountable for a Result." In Michael T. Cahill, Paul H. Robinson and Shima Baradaran Baughman (eds.), *Criminal Law: Cases and Controversies*. Alphen aan den Rijn: Wolters Kluwer.

Rosenfeld, Michael (2001) "Hate Speech in Constitutional Jurisprudence: A Comparative Analysis." Public Law Research Paper No. 41. Cardozo Law School: Yeshiva University, New York.

Rosenfeld, Sophia (2011) *Common Sense: A Political History*. Cambridge: Harvard University Press.

Rossini, Andrea Oskari (2016) "Šešelj Verdict: The Dissenting Judge." *Osservatorio Balcani e Caucaso*, 8 April 2016. www.balcanicaucaso.org/en g/Areas/Serbia/Seselj-verdict-the-dissenting-judge-169740. Accessed 9 March 2017.

Russell, Bertrand (1965) *On the Philosophy of Science*. New York: Bobbs-Merrill.

Ruzindana, Mathias (2012) "The Challenges of Understanding Kinyarwanda Key Terms Used to Instigate the 1994 Genocide in Rwanda." In Predrag Dojčinović (ed.), *Propaganda, War Crimes and International Law: From Speakers' Corner to War Crimes*. Abingdon, NY: Routledge, pp. 145–70.

Ruzindana, Mathias, Balinda Rwigamba and Laurent Nkusi (1998) *The Kinyarwanda Language: Its Use and Impact in the Various Media During the Period 1990–1994: A Sociolinguistic Study*. March. Prosecution Exhibit P110A in ICTR-99–52-T (Nahimana et al.).

Rwandan Patriotic Front, www.rpfinkotanyi.org/en/index.php. Accessed 21 November 2014.

Saks, Michael J. and David L. Faigman (2005) "Expert Evidence After Daubert". *Annual Review of Law and Social Science*, 1: 105–130.

Sarat, Austin, Lawrence Douglas and Martha Merrill Umphrey (2007) *How Law Knows*. Stanford: Stanford University Press.

Schabas, William A. (1999) "International Decision: Mugesera v. Minister of Citizenship and Immigration. *American Journal of International Law*. 93(2): 529–33. DOI: 10.2307/2998009.

(2000) "Hate Speech in Rwanda: The Road to Genocide." *McGill Law Journal*, 46: 141–71.

(2007) *An Introduction to the International Criminal Court*. 3rd Edn. Cambridge: Cambridge University Press.

(2009) *Genocide in International Law: The Crime of Crimes*. 2nd Edn. Cambridge: Cambridge University Press.

Scheffer, David and Anthony Dinh (2010) "The Pre-Trial Chamber's Significant Decision on Joint Criminal Enterprise for Individual Responsibility." 3 June 2010. www.cambodiatribunal.org/sites/default/files/resources/ctm_scheffer_dinh_jce_commentary_3_june_2010.pdf. Accessed 9 March 2017.

Seaman, Julie (2008) "Triangulating Testimonial Hearsay: The Constitutional Boundaries of Expert Opinion Testimony." *Georgetown Law Journal*, 96: 827–84.

Searle, John R. (1969) *Speech Acts: An Essay on the Philosophy of Language.* Cambridge: Cambridge University Press.

(1983) *Intentionality: An Essay on the Philosophy of Mind.* Cambridge: Cambridge University Press.

(1994) "Metaphor." In Andrew Ortony (ed.), *Metaphor and Thought.* 2nd Edn. Cambridge: Cambridge University Press.

(1995) *Freedom and Neurobiology: Reflections on Free Will, Language and Political Power.* New York: Columbia University Press.

(1998) *Mind, Language and Society: Philosophy in the Real World.* New York: Basic Books.

(2001) *Rationality in Action.* Cambridge: MIT Press.

(2010) *Making the Social World: The Structure of Human Civilization.* Oxford: Oxford University Press.

Shklar, Judith (1986) *Legalism: Law, Morals, and Political Trials.* Cambridge: Harvard University Press.

Shuy, Roger (1993) *Language Crimes: The Use and Abuse of Language Evidence in the Courtroom.* Oxford: Blackwell.

(2003) "Response to the March 1998 Report and Testimony of Dr. Mathias Ruzindana." 20 January 2003. Report with Author.

(2005) *Creating Language Games: How Law Enforcement Uses (and Misuses) Language.* Oxford: Oxford University Press.

Sluiter, Göran (2007) "Compromising the Authority of International Criminal Justice–How Vojislav Šešelj Runs His Trial." *Journal of International Criminal Justice*, 5(2): 529–36.

Smith S. M. and D. R. Shaffer (1995) "Speed of Speech and Persuasion: Evidence for Multiple Effects." *Personality and Social Psychology Bulletin.* 21: 1051–60.

Sopory, Pradeep and James P. Dillard (2002) "Figurative Language and Persuasion." In J. P. Dillard and M. Pfau (eds.), *The Persuasion Handbook: Developments in Theory and Practice,* pp. 407–426.

Sproule, J. M. (1994) *Channels of Propaganda.* Bloomington, IN: Edinfo.

Stapleton, Jane (1988) "Law, Causation and Common Sense." *Oxford Journal of Legal Studies,* 8(1): 111–31.

(2001) "Legal Cause: Cause-in-Fact and the Scope of Liability for Consequences." *Vanderbilt Law Review,* 54(3): 941–1009.

(2008) "Choosing What We Mean by 'Causation' in the Law." *Missouri Law Review.* 73(2): 433–80.

Sontag, Susan (1978) "*Illness as Metaphor.*" New York: Farrar, Straus and Giroux.

(1989) "*Aids and Its Metaphors.*" New York: Farrar, Straus and Giroux.

(1991) *Illness as Metaphor. AIDS and Its Metaphors.* London: Penguin.

Stewart, James G. (2012a) "Overdetermined Atrocities." *Journal of International Criminal Justice,* 10(5): 1189–1218.

(2012b) "The End of 'Modes of Liability' for International Crimes." *Leiden Journal of International Law,* 25(1): 165–219.

(2014) "Complicity." In Markus Dubber and Tatjana Hörnle (eds.), *Oxford Criminal Law Handbook.* Oxford: Oxford University Press.

Straus, Scott (2006) *The Order of Genocide: Race, Power, and War in Rwanda.* Ithaca, NY: Cornell University Press.

(2007) "What Is the Relationship Between Hate Radio and Violence? Rethinking Rwanda's 'Radio Machete.'" *Politics & Society,* 35(4): 609–37.

Sumner, L.W. (2011) "Criminalizing Expression: Hate Speech and Obscenity." In Deigh, John and David Dolinko (eds.), *The Oxford Handbook of Philosophy of Criminal Law.* Oxford: Oxford University Press, pp. 17–36.

Sunstein, Cass (1995) "The Expressive Function of the Law." *Pennsylvania Law Review,* 144: 2021–53.

Surdukowski, Jay (2005) "Is Poetry a War Crime-Reckoning for Radovan Karadzic the Poet-Warrior." *Michigan Journal of International Law,* 26(2): 673–99.

Swigart, Leigh (2015) "African Languages in International Criminal Justice: the International Criminal Tribunal for Rwanda and Beyond." In Charles Chernor Jalloh and Alhagi B. M. Marong (eds.), *Promoting Accountability Under International Law for Gross Human Rights Violations in Africa: Essays in Honor of Prosecutor Hassan Bubacar Jallow.* The Hague: Brill Nijhoff, pp. 578–611.

Tabeau, Ewa and Jakub Bijak (2005) "War-Related Deaths in the 1992–1995 Armed Conflicts in Bosnia and Herzegovina: A Critique of Previous Estimates and Recent Results." *European Journal of Population,* 21: 187–215.

Tamanaha, Brian Z. (2008) "Understanding Legal Realism," St. John's Legal Studies Research Paper No. 08–0133. http://ssrn.com/abstract=1127178

Taylor, Christopher (1999) *Sacrifice as Terror: the Rwandan Genocide of 1994.* Oxford: Berg Press.

Taylor, Telford (1992) *The Anatomy of the Nuremberg Trials: A Personal Memoir.* Boston: Little, Brown and Co.

Timmermann, Wibke K. (2005) "The Relationship Between Hate Propaganda and Incitement to Genocide: A New Trend in International Law

Towards Criminalization of Hate Propaganda?" *Leiden Journal of International Law*, 18(2): 257–82.

(2006) "Incitement in International Law." *International Review of the Red Cross*, 88: 823–52.

(2015) *Incitement in International Law*. New York: Routledge.

Timmermann, Wibke and William A. Schabas (2013) "Incitement to Genocide." In Paul Behrens and Ralph Henham (eds.), *Elements of Genocide*. London: Routledge.

Turner, J. W. Cecil (1958) *Kenny's Outlines of Criminal Law*. 17th Edn. Cambridge University Press: Cambridge.

Twining, William L. (1943) *Karl Llewellyn and the Realist Movement*. London: Weidenfeld & Nicolson.

United Nations. *Convention on the Prevention and Punishment of the Crime of Genocide*. 9 December 1948, 78 U.N.T.S. 227 (entered into force 12 January 1951).

United Nations. Report of the International Law Commission on the Work of its Forty-Eighth Session, 6 May–26 July 1996. Official Records of the General Assembly, Fifty-first session, Supplement No. 10. Extract from the Yearbook of the International Law Commission: 1996. Vol. II(2). UN Document A/51/10.

United Nations. *Rome Statute of the International Criminal Court*. Adopted by the United Nations Diplomatic Conference of Plenipotentiaries in the Establishment of the International Criminal Court on 17 July 1998. UN Doc. A/CONF. 183/9; 37 ILM 1002 (1998); 2187 UNTS 90.

United Nations Human Rights Council. *Prevention of Genocide*. A/HRC/RES/28/34, adopted 59th meeting, 27 March 2015.

United Nations International Law Commission, *Draft Code of Crimes Against the Peace and Security of Mankind*, 48th Session., 17 July 1996, UN Doc. A/CN.4/L.532; UN GAOR 51st Session., Supp. No. 10, art. 2.3(f), *reprinted in* [1996] 2 Y.B. Int'l L. Comm'n 17.

United Nations Interregional Crime and Justice Research Institute (UNICRI) (2011) *Manual on International Criminal Defence ADC-ICTY Developed Practices*. Turin: UNICRI.

United Nations Secretary General (2009) *Implementing the Responsibility to Protect*. Official Records of the General Assembly, Sixty-third session. UN Document A/63/677.

United Nations Security Council. *Statute of the International Criminal Tribunal for the Former Yugoslavia*. 1993. S.C. Res. 827, UN SCOR, 3217th mtg., Adopted 25 May 1993, UN Doc. S/RES/827 (1993).

United Nations Security Council. *Statute of the International Criminal Tribunal for Rwanda*. 1994. S.C. Res. 955, UN SCOR, 3453d mtg., Annex, art. 6, UN Doc. S/RES/955 (1994).

Van Schaack, Beth and Ronald Slye (2010) *International Criminal Law and Its Enforcement: Cases and Materials*. 2nd Edn. New York: Thomson Reuters/ Foundation Press.

(2014) *International Criminal Law and its Enforcement: Cases and Materials*. 3rd Edn. St. Paul: West Academic.

Van Sliedregt, Elies (2012) *Individual Criminal Responsibility in International Law*. Oxford: Oxford University Press.

Vinen, Richard (2003) "Servant Problems", *Historically Speaking* (2): 2–5. www.bu.edu/historic/hs/november03.html#vinen. Accessed 9 March 2017.

Wald, Patricia (2001) "To 'Establish Incredible Events by Credible Evidence' The Use of Affidavit Testimony in Yugoslav War Crimes Tribunal Proceedings." *Harvard International Law Journal*, 42(2): 535–53.

(2004) "ICTY Judicial Proceedings-An Appraisal from Within." *Journal of International Criminal Justice*, 2(2): 466–73.

Waldron, Jeremy (2012) *The Harm in Hate Speech*. Cambridge: Harvard University Press.

Warburton, Nigel (2009) *Free Speech: A Very Short Introduction*. Oxford: Oxford University Press.

Wegner, Daniel M. (2002) *The Illusion of Conscious Will*. Cambridge: MIT Press.

Werle, Gerhard (2007) "Individual Criminal Responsibility in Article 25 ICC Statute," *International Criminal Justice*, 5(4): 953–75. DOI: 10.1093/jicj/ mqm059.

White House (2013) "The Obama Administration's Comprehensive Efforts to Prevent Mass Atrocities Over the Past Year." 1 May 2013. www.white house.gov/sites/default/files/docs/fact_sheet_-_administration_efforts_to_ prevent_mass_atrocities5.pdf

Wigfield, Allan and Jacquelynne S. Eccles (2000) "Expectancy–Value Theory of Achievement Motivation." *Contemporary Educational Psychology*, 25: 68–81. DOI: 10.1006/ceps.1999.1015.

Williams, Glanville (1989) "Finis for *Novus Actus?*" *The Cambridge Law Journal*, 48(3): 391–416.

Wilson, Richard Ashby (2011) *Writing History in International Criminal Trials*. Cambridge: Cambridge University Press.

(2015) "Inciting Genocide with Words." *Michigan Journal of International Law*, 36(2): 100–46.

Winter, Steven L. (1989) "Transcendental Nonsense, Metaphoric Reasoning, and the Cognitive Stakes for Law." *University of Pennsylvania Law Review*, 137(4): 1105–1237.

Workman, Lance and Will Reader (2014) *Evolutionary Psychology*. 3rd Edn. Cambridge: Cambridge University Press.

Wright, Richard W. (1985) "Causation in Tort Law." *California Law Review*, 73(6): 1737–1828.

(1988) "Causation, Responsibility, Risk, Probability, Naked Statistics, and Proof: Pruning the Bramble Bush by Clarifying the Concepts." *Iowa Law Review*, 73: 1001–77.

(2011) "Proving Causation: Probability Versus Belief." In R. Goldberg (ed.), *Perspectives on Causation*. Ch. 10, Oxford: Hart Publishing. http://ssrn.com/abstract=1918474

Yanagizawa-Drott, David (2014) "Propaganda and Conflict: Evidence from the Rwandan Genocide." *The Quarterly Journal of Economics*, 129(4): 1947–94. DOI: 10.1093/qje/qju020

Yeager, Daniel (2006) *J. L. Austin and the Law*. Lewisburg, PA: Bucknell University Press.

Zahar, Alexander (2005) "The ICTR's 'Media" Judgment and the Reinvention of 'Direct' and Public Incitement to Commit Genocide." *Criminal Law Forum*. 16(1): 33–48.

(2008) "Legal Aid, Self-Representation and the Crisis at The Hague Tribunal." *Criminal Law Forum*, 19(2): 241–63.

INDEX

Accessories. *See* Aiding and abetting
Accomplice liability. *See* Aiding and abetting
Actus reus. See also Causation; Physical
    causation
  aiding and abetting and, 286–91
  causation and, 15–16, 71–2, 74, 80,
    88–9, 223
  in *Šešelj* case, 101, 104–5, 107, 132
Agency. *See also* New intervening acts
  in criminal law, 173–4
  defined, 162, 169
  illocutionary aspects of speech and, 169–70,
    173–4
  instigation and, 275–6
  as intervening act, 9
  legally responsible agents, 165
  locutionary aspects of speech and, 169–70,
    173–4
  ordering and, 278–80
  perlocutionary aspects of speech and,
    169–70
  persuasion and, 172–4
  as problem in prosecution, 9
  in psychology, 169
Agius, Carmel, 218
Aiding and abetting
  actus reus and, 286–91
  in *Akayesu* case, 283
  appropriateness of, 296–9
  causation and, 82, 284–5, 286–91
  "chance raising accomplices," 290–1
  in completed speech crimes, 282–6
  culture and, 285–6
  defined, 283
  de minimis contributions, 289
  direct and public incitement to commit
    genocide compared, 67–70
  direct causation and, 15–16, 283
  ex post facto acts and, 287, 289
  in Germany, 283
  in ICC, 282–3, 286, 293, 295–7
  in ICTR, 282–4, 292–3
  in ICTY, 282–4, 286–8, 292–3
  intention and, 292–6
  joint criminal enterprise compared, 293

  knowledge as requisite mental state for, 294
  mens rea and, 283–4, 292–6
  mental causation and, 167–8
  in Nuremberg Tribunal, 282, 286
  objections to, 297–8
  omission and, 287–8
  practical assistance as element of, 286
  recklessness as requisite mental state for,
    294–5
  risk assessment and, 290–1
  sentencing for, 298–9
  in *Šešelj* case, 139, 284
  social science and, 284, 297–8
  substantial contribution and, 288–90
  in United Kingdom, 282
  in United States, 283
AIDS and its Metaphors (Sontag), 156
Akayesu, Jean-Paul, 32, 35–6, 189–93, 250.
    See also Akayesu case (ICTR 2001)
Akayesu case (ICTR 2001)
  generally, 47, 138, 188
  aiding and abetting in, 283
  causation in, 35–6, 39, 44, 55, 234
  direct causation in, 234
  direct incitement in, 48
  language experts in, 142, 189–93, 198
  specific intent requirement in, 45–6, 160
Allen, Woody, 155
American Dilemma (Myrdal), 177
American Law Institute, 68, 74, 78–9
Amnesty International, 52
Analogia legis, 152–3, 160
Anti-Semitism, 9, 31, 150, 175, 245–6
Antonetti, Jean-Claude, 112–15, 122–5, 132,
    140, 202, 204, 205
Aristotle, 2, 107, 149, 164, 214, 225–8, 229
Ashworth, Andrew, 262, 264, 294
Association of Defense Counsel of the
    ICTY, 183
Attempt
  in ICC, 168, 257–9
  in ICTR, 168
  in ICTY, 168
  as inchoate crime, 257–9
  underlying crime of genocide, 259

340

Winter, Steven, 156
Witnesses
  fact witnesses, 117, 142–4, 202, 220,
    222, 235
  hostile witnesses, 119
  insider witnesses, 117, 273
  recanting of testimony, 119–20
Wright, Richard W., 78, 91

Yanagizawa-Drott, David, 17, 53, 141,
    286, 290
Yebei, Meshak, 119–20
Yugoslavia. See Bosnia and Hercegovina;
    Croatia; Serbia

Zahar, Alexander, 43, 46
Zedner, Lucia, 262, 264

CAMBRIDGE STUDIES IN LAW AND SOCIETY

Law's Fragile State: Colonial, Authoritarian, and Humanitarian Legacies in Sudan
Mark Fathi Massoud

Rights for Others: The Slow Home-Coming of Human Rights in the Netherlands
Barbara Oomen

European States and Their Muslim Citizens: The Impact of Institutions on Perceptions and Boundaries
Edited by John R. Bowen, Christophe Bertossi, Jan Willem Duyvendak and Mona Lena Krook

Environmental Litigation in China
Rachel E. Stern

Indigeneity and Legal Pluralism in India: Claims, Histories, Meanings
Pooja Parmar

Paper Tiger: Law, Bureaucracy and the Developmental State in Himalayan India
Nayanika Mathur

Religion, Law and Society
Russell Sandberg

The Experiences of Face Veil Wearers in Europe and the Law
Edited by Eva Brems

The Contentious History of the International Bill of Human Rights
Christopher N. J. Roberts

Transnational Legal Orders
Edited by Terence C. Halliday and Gregory Shaffer

Lost in China?, Law, Culture and Society in Post-1997 Hong Kong
Carol A. G. Jones

Security Theology, Surveillance and the Politics of Fear
Nadera Shalhoub-Kevorkian

Opposing the Rule of Law: How Myanmar's Courts Make Law and Order
Nick Cheesman

The Ironies of Colonial Governance: Law, Custom and Justice in Colonial India
James Jaffe

The Clinic and the Court: Law, Medicine and Anthropology
Edited by Tobias Kelly, Ian Harper and Akshay Khanna